Leen Lambers

Certifying Rule-Based Models using Graph Transformation

Leen Lambers

Certifying Rule-Based Models using Graph Transformation

Extended, Improved and New Graph Transformation Analysis Techniques: Clearing the Way for a General Road Map to Certification

Südwestdeutscher Verlag für Hochschulschriften

Impressum/Imprint (nur für Deutschland/ only for Germany)
Bibliografische Information der Deutschen Nationalbibliothek: Die Deutsche Nationalbibliothek
verzeichnet diese Publikation in der Deutschen Nationalbibliografie; detaillierte bibliografische
Daten sind im Internet über http://dnb.d-nb.de abrufbar.

Alle in diesem Buch genannten Marken und Produktnamen unterliegen warenzeichen-, marken- oder patentrechtlichem Schutz bzw. sind Warenzeichen oder eingetragene Warenzeichen der jeweiligen Inhaber. Die Wiedergabe von Marken, Produktnamen, Gebrauchsnamen, Handelsnamen, Warenbezeichnungen u.s.w. in diesem Werk berechtigt auch ohne besondere Kennzeichnung nicht zu der Annahme, dass solche Namen im Sinne der Warenzeichen- und Markenschutzgesetzgebung als frei zu betrachten wären und daher von jedermann benutzt werden dürften.

Verlag: Südwestdeutscher Verlag für Hochschulschriften Aktiengesellschaft & Co. KG
Dudweiler Landstr. 99, 66123 Saarbrücken, Deutschland
Telefon +49 681 37 20 271-1, Telefax +49 681 37 20 271-0
Email: info@svh-verlag.de
Zugl.: Berlin, Technische Universität, Dissertation, 2009

Herstellung in Deutschland:
Schaltungsdienst Lange o.H.G., Berlin
Books on Demand GmbH, Norderstedt
Reha GmbH, Saarbrücken
Amazon Distribution GmbH, Leipzig
ISBN: 978-3-8381-1650-1

Imprint (only for USA, GB)
Bibliographic information published by the Deutsche Nationalbibliothek: The Deutsche
Nationalbibliothek lists this publication in the Deutsche Nationalbibliografie; detailed
bibliographic data are available in the Internet at http://dnb.d-nb.de.

Any brand names and product names mentioned in this book are subject to trademark, brand or patent protection and are trademarks or registered trademarks of their respective holders. The use of brand names, product names, common names, trade names, product descriptions etc. even without a particular marking in this works is in no way to be construed to mean that such names may be regarded as unrestricted in respect of trademark and brand protection legislation and could thus be used by anyone.

Publisher: Südwestdeutscher Verlag für Hochschulschriften Aktiengesellschaft & Co. KG
Dudweiler Landstr. 99, 66123 Saarbrücken, Germany
Phone +49 681 37 20 271-1, Fax +49 681 37 20 271-0
Email: info@svh-verlag.de

Printed in the U.S.A.
Printed in the U.K. by (see last page)
ISBN: 978-3-8381-1650-1

Copyright © 2010 by the author and Südwestdeutscher Verlag für Hochschulschriften
Aktiengesellschaft & Co. KG and licensors
All rights reserved. Saarbrücken 2010

Preface

The contents of this book are conform to the dissertation with title "Certifying Rule-Based Models using Graph Transformation" published at the digital repository of the Technische Universität Berlin — http://opus.kobv.de/tuberlin/volltexte/2010/2522/ — submitted at the Faculty of Electrical Engineering and Computer Science (Fakultät IV Elektrotechnik und Informatik) of the TU Berlin to attain the degree of Doktor der Naturwissenschaften (Dr. rer. nat.). The PhD defense (Tag der wissenschaftlichen Aussprache) took place on October 30th, 2009 at the TU Berlin with Prof. Dr. Hartmut Ehrig as my supervisor, Prof. Dr. Fernando Orejas and Prof. Dr. Gabriele Taentzer as external examiners (Berichter) and Prof. Dr. Sabine Glesner as chair of the examining comittee (Vorsitzende des Promotionsausschusses).

Berlin, 2010   Leen Lambers

Abstract

Many systems exhibit rule-based behavior that can be modeled very well by means of graph transformation. In this thesis, a new graph transformation theory is introduced for a more expressive kind of graph transformation than the usual one. This kind of graph transformation not only allows positive pre- and post-conditions to be expressed in rules, but also allows so-called negative application conditions. Present analysis techniques are extended for this more expressive kind of graph transformation. These techniques allow, amongst other things, the static detection of potential conflicts and causal dependencies between transformations, and the detection of local confluence in cases of conflicts. For this purpose, the theory of critical pairs is extended. Moreover, new kinds of analysis techniques are introduced and present techniques are improved. One new technique enables, for example, the static analysis of applicability (resp. non-applicability) of rule sequences. The main part of the newly developed theory in this thesis does not only apply to graph transformation. In addition, it is formulated in the more abstract adhesive high-level-transformation framework. Consequently, the analysis techniques can be applied not only to graphs, but also to other complex structures such as, for example, Petri nets and attributed graphs. Finally, a general road map is presented leading to the certification of a selection of properties in rule-based models. The certification, based on graph transformation analysis techniques, is illustrated by a case study of an elevator control system. Moreover, the current tool support for certification of rule-based models using graph transformation provided by AGG is outlined.

Acknowledgements

Writing this thesis was a challenge that I was able to accept, by and by, thanks to the encouragement of several people accompanying me during the last few years.
In particular, I would like to thank . . .

Hartmut Ehrig, for the continuous monitoring of this thesis and for giving me the opportunity to work in your group, benefit from your wealth of experience, and learn from the accuracy and intensity that you apply when doing research.

Fernando Orejas, for enabling my research stays at the UPC in Barcelona where we had several inspiring discussions, providing a solid basis for joint work and encouraging me to keep working on many subjects elaborated in this thesis.

Gabriele Taentzer, for your valuable comments with regard to this thesis, for believing in my skills, and for being such an animating counterpart. I hope to be able to continue our close cooperation in the near future. In this regard, many thanks also to Stefan Jurack and Katharina Mehner for our productive Berlin-Marburg-Munich collaboration during the past two years.

Mauro Pezzè, for facilitating my research stay in your group at the university of Milano, Bicocca, where you gave me the opportunity to report on my research and to learn about inventive applications developed in your lab. In this regard, special thanks also to Leonardo Mariani, for the fruitful cross-border cooperation beyond my stay and to all members of the lab, for being such welcoming interim colleagues.

Annegret Habel, for our recently started cooperation – in the middle of writing up this thesis. I look forward to continuing our joint work.

The many friendly and inspiring colleague researchers of the graph transformation community that I met during conferences, workshops, and research stays, making these gatherings to memorable and motivating experiences.

My colleagues in Berlin, with whom I share – or shared – daily working life, for your companionship during seminars, co-authoring papers, teaching, TFS breakfasts, coffee breaks, floor chats, ... Special thanks to Claudia Ermel, Ulrike Prange, and Alexander Rein for carefully proofreading parts of this thesis, and to Olga Runge, for being so hard-working when implementing new features in AGG. Thank you to Käte Schlicht, for your support concerning all kinds of administrative matters. Moreover, many thanks to Maria Oswald and Margit Russ, for the enjoyable joint time as office mates.

My friends, for having fun with me and encouraging me, and giving me timely distractions from graph transformation and all that kind of stuff. Special thanks to Mieke, for your professional advice with regard to the musical example in the introduction.

My family, and in particular, my parents, for presenting me with an always welcoming home, helping me to hang in there: "bedankt".

Daniel, for giving me the special kind of energy needed to bring this thesis to an end.

Contents

1	**Introduction**	**9**
2	**Rule-Based Modeling using Graph Transformation**	**19**
	2.1 Introduction	19
	2.2 Modeling with Graphs	22
	2.3 Rule-Based Modeling using Graph Transformation	27
	2.4 Independence and Parallelism	41
	2.5 Concurrency	45
	2.6 Conflicts and Causal Dependencies for Transformations	51
	2.7 Critical Pairs and Critical Sequences	60
	2.8 Independence, Conflicts and Causal Dependencies for Rules	69
	2.9 Applicability and Non-Applicability of Rule Sequences	75
	2.10 Embedding and Confluence	88
	2.11 Efficient Conflict and Causal Dependency Detection	97
3	**Rule-Based Modeling using High-Level Transformation**	**107**
	3.1 Introduction	107
	3.2 Modeling with High-Level Structures	109
	3.3 Rule-Based Modeling using High-Level Transformation	114
	3.4 Independence and Parallelism	119
	3.5 Concurrency	124
	3.6 Conflicts and Causal Dependencies for Transformations	130
	3.7 Critical Pairs and Critical Sequences	138
	3.8 Independence, Conflicts and Causal Dependencies for Rules	143
	3.9 Applicability and Non-Applicability of Rule Sequences	150
	3.10 Embedding and Confluence	160
	3.11 Efficient Conflict and Causal Dependency Detection	169
4	**Certifying Rule-Based Models**	**171**
	4.1 Introduction	171
	4.2 Road to Certification	172
	4.3 Certifying a Selection of Properties	180
	4.4 Application Areas	212
	4.5 Tool Support	215

5 Comparing, Concluding, and Continuing 219
5.1 Related Work 219
5.2 Summary 222
5.3 Future Work 224

Chapter 1

Introduction

When people in a concert hall are listening, for example, to a Beethoven piano sonata, then they are probably simply enjoying a wonderful evening of music. Only a minority of the audience might be aware of the fact that some *modeling* was conducted in order to realize such a concert evening. If there were no scores, for example, it would be very difficult for the musicians to play the piano sonata that Beethoven had in mind about two hundred years ago. Instead, Beethoven wrote down the notes for his piece of music into scores, and that is why people today can still enjoy his music. Precisely these scores can be understood as a model for his music.

By means of the musical example, I would like to point out to the reader, in an introductory way, the characteristics of modeling that play an important role in this thesis. In particular, I concentrate on the way models abstract from contextual data, the communication of models by formulating them in a specific language, and how models provide an advantage for the analysis of the modeling subject.

A fundamental property of models is that they *abstract* from the reality that they describe. For example, the scores for the piano sonata usually do not give any information about which pianist should interpret them – or even on which kind of piano the music should be played. As long as the pianist masters the techniques required for playing the music, expressed by the scores, the concert evening can take place. Moreover, the model does not give complete information about the temperament of the artist when playing the music. Therefore, although the notes are the same, and annotations on the scores about tempo, temperament, and sound volume might be given, concerts will be similar, but not identical. There is still freedom for the artist when interpreting the scores.

Another important property of models is that they are expressed in a proper *modeling language*, which can be understood or should be learnt by the model interpreter. For example, musicians understand the language of scores after learning how to read them. Thanks to this common language, composers can communicate their music – the subject that they are modeling. Moreover, as already mentioned, the existence of such a modeling language for music enables us to listen to music that was composed a couple of centuries earlier. The scores keep hold of the music in their own language.

A third property of models, which I would like to highlight, is that their *analysis* is useful for finding out more about the modeling subject. For example, music theoreticians listen to live or recorded music of a certain composition in order to understand better what the composer is trying to express with it. However, in addition, they examine the scores to find out more about the character of the music. When examining the scores, it is easy to find out the timbre in which a piece of music is written. If someone does not have an absolute pitch, however, it becomes difficult to find out the timbre just by listening to the music. In particular, when analyzing contemporary music, specific kinds of mathematical techniques might be used to examine the scores. Such type of analysis leads to a better understanding of the music. It would be very tedious – or sometimes nearly impossible – to arrive at the same level of understanding by just listening to the music. Even in the case that merely scores, and no recordings, for some musical piece are available, it is possible to obtain a good impression of the music through examining the scores.

The *kind of models* that I concentrate on in this thesis are *rule-based*. Rules are able to reflect dynamics in the system being modeled in the following way: they express what condition holds before (resp. after) a certain system change occurs. A rule, therefore, encloses a so-called precondition and postcondition. The *modeling language* I concentrate on in this thesis is *graph transformation* [109]. It is a visual and formal language enabling us to describe rule-based models in a very concise way. In addition, it enables us to apply *analysis* techniques on these models. If we expect that specific properties hold in our system, then they can be verified on the rule-based model of our system. If the verification of the property by means of graph transformation theory is successful, then a corresponding *certification* may be added to the rule-based model.

The *use of graph transformation* as a modeling language for systems showing rule-based behavior has been successful in the last few decades in many application fields [30, 108], for example, the modeling of distributed systems, visual language definition, object-oriented modeling, and model transformation. The advantage of graph transformation is that, on the one hand graphs visualize in a natural way the inner structure of complex system data and on the other hand, we have graph rules expressing modifications of these structures in an easily understandable and schematic way. Another important advantage is the formal foundation of graph transformation, enabling concise modeling and formal analysis. The expressiveness of graph transformation has been increased significantly since its emergence in the 70s as generalization of Chomsky grammars and term rewriting in the context of formal languages. In the mean time, graph transformation is able to support the precise modeling of a wide range of applications. However, the development of corresponding *graph transformation theory has not always kept up* with this evolution. Therefore, the formal analysis of these more expressive models becomes at least inaccurate or impossible. In order to verify specific properties of rule-based models, graph transformation theory is indispensable though. Moreover, it is important for the increasing success of this modeling technique. In particular, if safety-critical systems are modeled using graph transformation, then powerful analysis techniques are essential. Furthermore, in view of the commercialization of specific applications, formal analysis of the corresponding models can be of particular importance in order to avoid expensive development cycle iterations.

Negative application conditions (NACs) [44] make graph transformation more expressive as a modeling technique. However, the development of theory has not completely kept up with the introduction of these conditions. NACs forbid specific structures before or after applying a rule, and are already used extensively in modeling praxis using graph transformation (see, for example, [19, 59, 84, 116]). Therefore, as the first main topic in this thesis, we concentrate on the *generalization of analysis techniques* for graph transformation with so-called negative application conditions (NACs). In addition, the efficiency of already existing analysis techniques is improved, and new kinds of analysis techniques are proposed. As a second topic in this thesis, we propose a *generic way to apply analysis techniques*, rooted in graph transformation theory, to verify specific properties of rule-based models. If the verification of the property is successful, then a corresponding certificate can be awarded. Moreover, for a selection of properties the road to certification is outlined, using graph transformation analysis techniques. This allows for documenting and developing concise tool support with regard to these properties, enabling the automation of the *certification* process.

This thesis starts off with an *informal* description of the *main contents* of this work at the end of this chapter. It should enable the reader to decide if the contents of this thesis might be interesting to study more in detail. First, we introduce the *running example*, the *control of an elevator*, and use it to illustrate the characteristics of rule-based modeling. Moreover, we explain how graph transformation comes into play for the purpose of rule-based modeling. Finally, we sketch the main properties, dealt with in this thesis, that can be certified using graph transformation, and illustrate it on the example of the elevator control.

Chapter 2 is concerned with presenting the *graph transformation theory* that can be used for rule-based modeling. One of the main achievements of this thesis is that existing graph transformation theory in the algebraic approach is extended to graph transformation with so-called *negative application conditions*. These conditions express that specific structures are forbidden before or after applying a rule. Another achievement of this thesis, with regard to the extension of graph transformation theory, is the introduction of a new analysis technique, called applicability analysis of rule sequences. Moreover, this thesis improves the efficiency of existing analysis techniques detecting statically potential conflicts and causal dependencies between rules. The theory introduced in this chapter is explained continuously using the running example of the elevator control. Note that most results in this chapter are instantiated from the corresponding results in the abstract framework of adhesive HLR systems with NACs, as presented in the next chapter.

Chapter 3 presents the main results of Chapter 2 in the more abstract framework of *adhesive HLR systems with NACs*, another important achievement of this work. This abstract framework is based on a special kind of category, called the NAC-adhesive HLR category. Formulating all results on this more abstract level has the following main advantages: the proof reasoning for all results is performed on the basis of *category theory*, mostly allowing for more elegant and compact proofs than for the set-theoretical case. Moreover, the obtained results can be instantiated for the transformation theory of all kinds of high-level structures. Not only graph transformation is a valid instantiation, but also, for example, typed attributed graph transformation, hypergraph transformation, algebraic signature or specification transformation, and Petri net transformation. Readers who are not interested in the categorical background of rule-based modeling, as presented in this chapter, might also skip it.

After these two theoretical chapters, Chapter 4 explains how this theory can be applied for the purpose of *certifying rule-based models* using graph transformation. It presents a general road map towards certification supported by analysis techniques based on graph transformation theory. In this thesis, thereby, we concentrate on static analysis techniques. They run on components of the rule-based model without actually applying the rules (cf. compile time). In contrast, dynamic techniques might have to run through the whole state space generated by the rule-based model, which in many cases is infinitely big (cf. run time). A selection of properties, significant for rule-based models, is presented, for which the road to certification is described. On the running example of the elevator control it is illustrated how each of these properties can be certified. Moreover, typical application areas are described for certifying rule-based models using graph transformation, as presented in this thesis. Finally, in this chapter, tool support for certifying rule-based models is discussed. In particular, a survey is given on tool support

CHAPTER 1. INTRODUCTION

for the certification process in the tool environment AGG [115, 114, 13, 1]. It supports the algebraic approach to graph transformation, and consists of a graph transformation engine, analysis tools and a graphical user interface for convenient user interaction.

Chapter 5 starts with an overview of related work. It points out why the certification approach of rule-based models as presented in this thesis can be a good alternative to other verification techniques for graph transformation. In the second section of this chapter, we summarize the main results of this thesis, and outline the relationship with own work published already. Finally, in the last section, the most important lines of future work arising from this thesis are discussed.

What's in a Name?

*"What's in a name? That which we call a rose
By any other name would smell as sweet.
So Romeo would, were he not Romeo call'd,
Retain that dear perfection which he owes
Without that title. Romeo, doff thy name;
And for that name, which is no part of thee,
Take all myself."*

William Shakespeare. Romeo and Juliet (1597).

"Certifying Rule-Based Models using Graph Transformation" is the title of this thesis. The reader might just quickly gain an understanding of the topic. Therefore, in this section, we point out the terminology used in this thesis in a compact and informal way. In particular, we start by clarifying what is meant by *rule-based modeling using graph transformation* in this thesis. Afterwards, we explain how specific properties of rule-based models using graph transformation can be *certified*. We introduce the *running example* of this thesis first, and illustrate all concepts with this example.

We model an elevator control system *with the following requirements as a running example. The type of control that we consider is meant to be used in buildings where the elevator should transport people from or to one main stop, for example, in apartment buildings or multi-story car parks [11]. Each floor in the building is equipped with one button in order to call the elevator. The elevator car stops at a floor for which an internal stop request is given. External call requests are served by the elevator only if it is in downward mode in order to transport people to the main stop. The direction of the elevator car is not changed as long as there are remaining requests in the running direction. External call requests as well as internal stop requests are not deleted until the elevator car has arrived.*

Graphs are a well-suited means to describe in a natural way all kind of systems, where nodes describe system entities and edges describe relations between them. The manipulation, evolution, or reconfiguration of systems can often be described in a *rule-based* manner. Thereby, rules specify in a local way the pre- and post-condition of such system modifications, expressing which graph structure should be present before (resp. after) applying the rule to a graph, expressing some *system state*. Note that the rule's pre-condition (or post-condition) may hold some special conditions, so-called *negative application conditions* (NACs) [44]. In particular, they express what structure may *not* be present before (resp. after) applying the rule. In this thesis, these conditions play an important role since graph transformation theory is extended from rules without NACs to rules with NACs. In the end, the application of a graph transformation rule leads to a *graph transformation step*, modeling some concrete rule-based system modification. For a tutorial introduction to graph transformation from a software-engineering perspective, see [8]. Moreover, for a presentation of the graph transformation approach used in this thesis for rule-based modeling (based on [32, 28, 23, 29]), see Chapter 2.

The different types of entities and relations that we can recognize in the above presented elevator control system are captured by the graph below on the left, where nodes represent entity types and edges represent relation types.

CHAPTER 1. INTRODUCTION

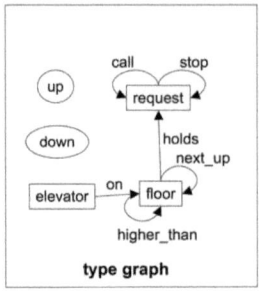
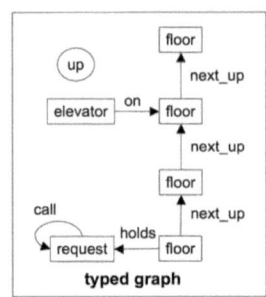

This so-called type *graph expresses that an elevator car of type* elevator *exists, which can be on a specific* floor. *Moreover, the elevator can be in* up*ward or* down*ward mode. Floors are connected by* next_up *edges expressing which floor is directly above another floor. Moreover,* higher_than *edges express that a floor is arranged higher in the building than another floor. Each floor can* hold request*s of two different types. The first type is a* call *request expressing that an external call for the elevator car on this floor is given. The second type is a* stop *request expressing that a call in the elevator car is given for stopping it on this floor.*

Having modeled by the type graph, which type of system entities and relations occur, we can now consider single system states. They are modeled by a typed *graph, consisting of a concrete node and edge configuration respecting the node and edge types defined by the type graph. In particular, the above typed graph on the right expresses that the elevator is in upward mode on the second floor in a four-storey building with a call request pending on the ground floor. Now, for the elevator control rules may describe the pre- and post-condition of its operations. For example, the rule* set_direction_down, *as depicted on the next page, describes the pre- and post-condition of changing the elevator's direction mode from upward to downward*[1]. *In particular, this rule expresses that before switching the direction mode, there must be some request on a floor that is lower than the elevator floor for the elevator being in upward mode. After applying this operation, the elevator must have changed its direction mode from upward to downward. Moreover, according to the requirements of the elevator control, as introduced in the beginning of this section, we need to consider the following constraint: "The direction of the elevator car is not changed as long as there are remaining requests in the running direction." In order to meet this requirement, in addition, the rule's pre-condition holds two* NACs *that need to be fulfilled before applying the rule.*

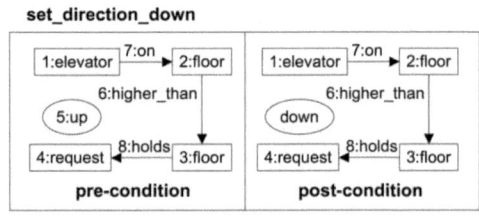

In particular, the first NAC of rule set_direction_down, *as depicted below on the left, expresses that the rule may only be applied if no stop request is still pending on the elevator floor. This*

---

[1]Thereby, note that nodes and edges in pre- and post-condition should be interpreted as identical ones according to the numbering.

is because in upward direction stop requests on the elevator floor need to be processed first. Moreover, the second NAC, as depicted below on the right, expresses that the rule may only be applied if no request at all is still pending on a higher floor than the elevator floor. This is because in upward direction remaining requests need to be processed first.

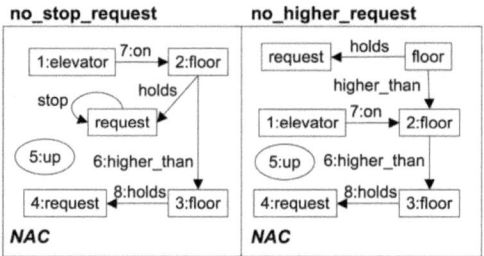

Note that it would be very tedious to express these NACs, by formulating them somehow in a positive way. This illustrates the usefulness of NACs. Finally, the rule set_direction_down can be applied to the typed graph presented earlier, since it fulfills the pre-condition for this rule[2]. The application of rule set_direction_down then leads to a graph transformation step such that in the resulting graph, the elevator is in downward direction mode.

Rules occurring in a rule-based model can be characterized according to the type of modification they are describing. Roughly speaking, we can distinguish three kinds of modifications: *syntactical*, *operational*, or *transformational*. In the first case, rules define how to generate – and afterwards edit – the *syntactical structure of a system*. Thereby, these rules are applied to graphs, modeling some state of the system structure. In the second case, rules define the *operational semantics of a system*. Thereby, these rules are applied to graphs, modeling some operational state of the system. In the third case, rules define some *model transformation*. Thereby, these rules are applied to graphs, modeling some state of the model transformation. Such model transformations can have as an objective to structurally improve the model of the system one is modeling. Moreover, model transformations may lead to refined models, describing the system one is modeling in a more detailed way. Model transformations may also lead to adapted models, describing the system one is modeling, fulfilling some revised requirements.

In this thesis, for example, we model the control of an elevator system. We develop rules describing the generation of the elevator system structure, and rules describing its operational semantics (see Example 2.3.16). The generating rules, for example, add additional floors to a building, or generate edges of type higher_than, by building the transitive closure of the opposite edges for type next_up. The operational rules, describe – other than switching the direction mode of the elevator – how requests are made and processed, and how the elevator car can move upward or downward. In this thesis, we do not describe any rules transforming the model of the elevator system. However, one could imagine rules structurally improving the model of the elevator system, as presented in this thesis. For example, attributes or inheritance could be introduced to describe more appropriately the direction mode of the elevator, resp. the inner stop or outer call requests. One could also consider a model transformation, refining the model such that in addition an elevator door control is described by the model. Finally, one could,

---

[2]Thereby, note that in this graph, the edges of type *higher_than* have been omitted since they would overload the picture.

CHAPTER 1. INTRODUCTION

for example, consider a model transformation, such that outer call requests are served with the same priority as inner stop requests also in upward direction.

We can distinguish the following main components of a *rule-based model using graph transformation*: primarily, it consists of graph transformation *rules*, possibly constrained by means of a *type graph*. Moreover, some distinguished *start graphs*, representing initial system states, may be present. Optionally, additional constraints – not captured by the type graph yet – may be imposed on the rule-based model, describing which kind of system states are valid ones. We refer to Example 2.2.11 in Chapter 2 for more details on this kind of constraints. It is possible to consider particular parts of the rule-based model, zooming in on interesting aspects with regard to *verification*. For example, one can consider particular graph transformation steps via rules of the rule-based model, specific rule sequences – with or without a distinguished start graph, or also particular control structures over its rules, expressing more precisely in which order to apply which rule, ... As soon as dedicated start graphs are available for the rule-based model, it is also possible to consider its so-called *state space*. It consists of all graphs, respecting the type graph and possible additional constraints, that are reachable from these start graphs by modifying them using rules of the rule-based model.

Now, having built a rule-based model for a system under consideration, we can analyze it in order to find out if specific properties hold in this model. Therefore, in this thesis, an overview is given of *how to certify a selection of properties for rule-based models* using graph transformation. If it is possible to verify that a property holds for the corresponding rule-based model, then a so-called certificate can be awarded[3]. The properties investigated in this thesis describe, for example, how rules of the model may conflict with each other, or also causally dependent on other rules. Moreover, we consider safety properties, expressing that rules preserve specific constraints, or expressing that in a terminal state specific constraints are guaranteed. Concerning liveness, for example, it is investigated if specific rule sequences are applicable. Moreover, due to the non-deterministic nature of rule-based models, properties like local confluence and termination – leading to functional behavior – are investigated. Each of these properties is illustrated on the running example of the elevator control system. See Section 4.2.2 for a short overview and see Section 4.3 for more detailed explanations. Exemplarily, we will show here the *certification of one of these properties*, being local confluence, in an introductory way. Thereby, the characteristics of using static analysis techniques for graph transformation – as presented in this thesis – is illustrated. Static analysis techniques run on components of the rule-based model without actually applying the rules (cf. compile time). In contrast, dynamic techniques might have to run through the whole state space of the rule-based model (cf. run time), which may become very large or even infinitely large. Note that in Section 4.5 of this thesis, explanations on tool support, implementing static analysis techniques for graph transformation, are given.

Suppose that two rules are applicable to the same state in a rule-based model. *Then, it is important to know if no matter which rule I choose, it is possible to* reach the same state again *by applying other available rules of the rule-based model. If this is the case, then we say that the transformations via these two rules fulfill the property* local confluence. *Now, the running example of the elevator control holds different rules that may process requests if the elevator is in downward direction:* process_stop_down, process_call_down, *and* process_stop_and_call *(see Fig.*

---

[3]A general certification procedure for rule-based models using graph transformation is explained in Section 4.2 of this thesis.

2.18 and 2.17). *If two rules compete for processing the same request in downward direction mode, then it should be possible to reach a common state afterwards anyway. In this case, this will be the state in which all requests on the elevator floor are processed.*

We can certify the property local confluence for these rules as follows. Roughly speaking, a set of rules is locally confluent if all conflicts in a minimal context via these rules can be resolved in a specific way (see local confluence theory in Section 2.10 of Chapter 2). We explain this on the figure depicted on the next page in an informal way. On the left, it depicts the competition of rules process_call_down and process_stop_and_call for the same request – surrounded by a thick black dashed line – in a minimal context[4]. These are conflicting transformations in a minimal context – also called critical pairs. Now, the picture describes on the right, how this minimal conflict can be resolved *since after processing a call request in downward direction, the elevator can process also a single stop request, reaching the same state again.* If this minimal solution, in addition, respects some additional condition, called strict NAC-confluence (see Def. 2.10.7 and explanations in Chapter 2), then it can be repeated as a solution in each possible context. Thereby, strictness means that the solution may not delete graph structures that are preserved by both conflicting transformations. NAC-confluence means that the NACs occurring in the solution are satisfied in each bigger context, if they are satisfied for the conflicting transformations in this bigger context as well. Summarizing, whenever the same conflicting minimal situation occurs in a bigger context – no matter how many other floors and requests are present – it is possible to repeat an analog rule application as in the minimal solution, leading to a common system state again. This certification procedure can be repeated for all rules, being able to process requests in downward direction. It is explained more in detail in Section 4.3.18 of Chapter 4, where we award the above-mentioned processing rules of the elevator example with a local confluence certificate. Finally, note that in order to find out if it is possible to reach a common state in all possible situations after competitive processing of requests, it was not necessary to explore the whole state space *of the rule-based model of our elevator example.*

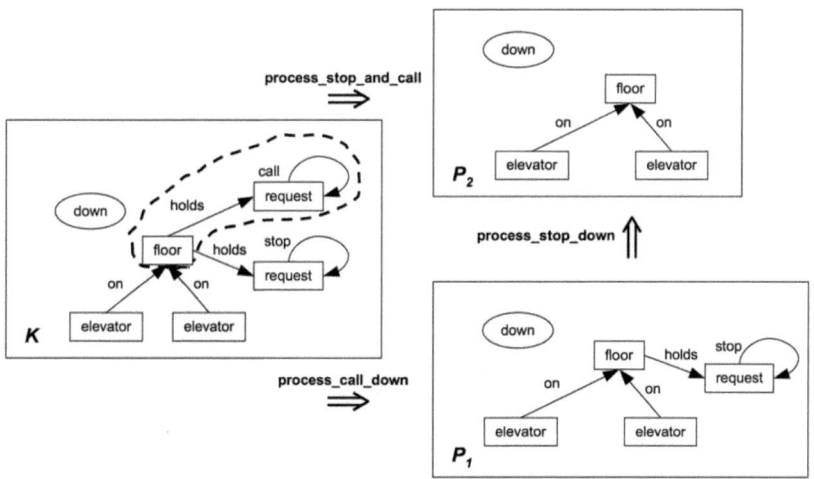

---
[4]Thereby, imagine that the *elevator* nodes are glued in our model since we describe the operations of *one* elevator car.

CHAPTER 1. INTRODUCTION

These were the main concepts elaborated in this thesis, presented in a compact and informal way, and the reader is now invited to commence reading through the main body of this work. We conclude this section with the following remarks. The running example in this thesis is concerned with modeling an elevator control system. In Section 4.4.1 and Section 5.1, also other kinds of *application areas for rule-based modeling* are presented. Moreover, Section 4.4.2 describes which kind of properties may be worthwhile certifying for rule-based models, depending on the kind of modifications described by the rules. Finally, note that systems do not necessarily have to be modeled by typed graphs; for example, *Petri nets* [102] or *typed attributed graphs* (see several examples described in Section 4.4.1) can also be used for rule-based modeling. Thereby, the rules do not describe modifications of typed graphs, but modifications of Petri nets or typed attributed graphs, correspondingly. The analysis techniques as presented in this thesis can be applied to the reconfiguration of these structures as well, as explained in more detail in Chapter 3.

Chapter 2

Rule-Based Modeling using Graph Transformation

2.1 Introduction

As described in the previous chapter, graphs are a well-suited means to describe all kinds of systems in a natural way. The manipulation, evolution, or reconfiguration of systems can often be described in a rule-based manner. Thereby, rules specify in a local way the pre- and post-condition of such system modifications. The application of rules then leads to *graph transformation*, modeling concrete rule-based system modifications. See [8] for a tutorial introduction to graph transformation from a software-engineering perspective.

In the *algebraic approach* to graph transformation as initiated in [32, 28], two gluing constructions are used to describe a graph transformation step. For this reason, this approach is known as the double-pushout (DPO) [23] approach, in contrast to the single-pushout (SPO) [100, 81] approach. In this thesis, we concentrate on the former approach. This approach is recapitulated with all main theoretical results in [29]. In particular, it is explained how to define application conditions for rules to restrict their application. However, most of the theoretical results in [29] have been formulated for graph transformation systems based on rules without application conditions. These results should be generalized to graph transformation systems based on rules holding application conditions. The most frequently used (see, for example, [19, 59, 84, 116]) kind of application condition is the so-called *negative application condition* (NAC), as introduced in [44]. It forbids a certain structure to be present before or after applying a rule. One of the main achievements of this thesis is generalizing the theoretical results formulated for graph transformation rules without application conditions to rules holding NACs.

Note that in [29], the algebraic theory on transformation systems has been presented in the categorical framework of *adhesive High-Level Replacement (HLR) systems*. As a consequence, more high-level structures such as, for example, typed attributed graphs can be handled by the algebraic approach. In Chapter 3, it is proven that the most important extensions introduced in this thesis to DPO graph transformation hold as well for adhesive High-Level Replacement systems with NACs. As a consequence, the theory introduced in this thesis also holds for the instantiation of typed, attributed graph transformation with NACs. However, in this chapter we restrict ourselves to *typed graph transformation with NACs* without attribution, such that the reader does not have to be familiar with the attribution concept as presented in [29]. Note

CHAPTER 2. RULE-BASED MODELING USING GRAPH TRANSFORMATION

that most results in this chapter are instantiated from the corresponding results in the abstract framework of adhesive HLR systems with NACs, as presented in the next chapter.

The algebraic approach to graph transformation is supported by AGG [115, 114, 13], a tool environment consisting of a graph transformation engine, analysis tools, and a graphical user interface for convenient user interaction. How the algebraic graph transformation approach can be used for rule-based modeling is explained in a *running example, modeling the control of an elevator*. All results introduced in this chapter are illustrated on the rule-based model of the elevator control. AGG is used as a tool environment to support the modeling of this running example. The use of the analysis tools of AGG is illustrated in Chapter 4.

The structure of this chapter is as follows: in Section 2.2, we present a way to specify graphs formally. Moreover, the notion of graph constraints, as presented already in [29], is reintroduced. In Section 2.3, it is explained how graph rules are captured formally and how they can be applied to graphs leading to *graph transformation*. Thereby, we follow the algebraic approach as presented in [29]. After having reintroduced typed graph transformation with NACs, we start presenting a new theory for this kind of graph transformation. In Section 2.4, we introduce the *local Church-Rosser property* for graph transformation with NACs [69]. Therefore, a new notion of parallel independence, and thus, also sequential independence is defined between transformations with NACs. This is because the NACs can be responsible for new kinds of dependencies between the transformations. Based on the definition of sequential and parallel independence for transformations with NACs, it is possible to formulate a *Parallelism Theorem* for transformations with NACs. It expresses how to summarize a sequence of two sequentially independent transformations into one parallel transformation step with the same effect. The analysis part of the Parallelism Theorem, on the other hand, expresses under which condition it is possible to analyze a direct parallel transformation step into two sequentially independent transformation steps. Note that the Parallelism Theorem in this thesis is an enhanced version of the one presented in [72].

Not every sequence of two direct transformations consists of sequentially independent transformations. Therefore, it is not possible to summarize this sequence into one transformation step via the Parallelism Theorem. In this more general case, the notion of concurrency comes into play, which we present in Section 2.5. For the *Concurrency Theorem*, it is explained how to construct a concurrent rule holding NACs from a sequence of rules holding NACs. The Concurrency Theorem with NACs states that the concurrent rule with NACs is applicable with the same result if and only if the rule sequence with NACs is applicable. The construction of the concurrent rule itself is analogous to the case without NACs. In addition though, it is necessary to shift all NACs occurring in the rule sequence to equivalent NACs on the concurrent rule. To this end, we use a construction translating application conditions over rules as described in [29] and a construction translating NACs over a morphism. Note that in [46], similar shifting results are presented for the more general nested conditions. Moreover, in [31], based on these results, a Parallelism Theorem and Concurrency Theorem are presented for rules with nested application conditions.

If a pair of transformations is not parallel independent, we say that they are in conflict. If a sequence of two transformations is not sequentially independent, we say that they are causally dependent. For these pairs of transformations (resp. sequences of transformations) the Local Church-Rosser property does not hold, and we investigate them further. Therefore, in Section 2.6, we characterize different kinds of conflicts and causal dependencies. In particular, two transformations with NACs are in *conflict* if one of the following situations occur: one transformation deletes a graph part that is used by the other transformation. One transformation produces a graph part that is forbidden by the other one. A sequence of two transformations with NACs is *causally dependent* if one of the following situations occur: the first transformation produces a graph part that is used by the second one. The first transformation deletes a graph part forbidden by the second one. The first transformation has forbidden a graph part that is produced by the second one. The second transformation deletes a graph part delivered by the first one. Moreover, as presented already in [68], yet another characterization is shown accentuating the reason for the arising conflict or dependency between transformations.

In order to come up with techniques for static conflict (resp. dependency) detection and analysis, it is central to describe the theory for so-called *critical pairs* (resp. *critical sequences*). We concentrate on this theory in Section 2.7. The notion of critical pairs was introduced in the area of term rewriting systems [53], and later, introduced in the area of graph transformation for hypergraph rewriting [95, 94], and then, for all kinds of transformation systems fitting into the framework of adhesive HLR categories [29]. Critical pairs (resp. sequences) describe conflicts (resp. causal dependencies) in a minimal context. By means of the conflict (resp. causal dependency) characterization for transformations with NACs it is possible to define a generalized critical pair (resp. sequence) notion for graph transformation systems with NACs. Critical pairs (resp. sequences) should fulfill two important properties that were fulfilled in the case of graph transformation systems without NACs as well. It should be possible to formulate a Completeness Theorem [69] and a so-called Local Confluence Theorem [73]. The Completeness Theorem describes that for every pair of transformations in conflict (resp. sequences of causally dependent transformations), there exists a critical pair (resp. sequence) expressing the same conflict (resp. causal dependency) in a minimal context. We prove that the critical pair (resp. sequence) definition for graph transformations with NACs is complete in this sense. Local confluence theory is dealt with in Section 2.10 of this chapter. In the next sections, we first deal with another topic.

We can not only formulate the notion of *conflicts and causal dependencies* on the level of transformations, but also *on the level of rules*. We address this topic in Section 2.8. If transformations along a pair of rules exist that are in conflict, then we say that the rules are in conflict. Analogously, if a sequence of transformations along a sequence of rules is causally dependent, then we say that the rules are causally dependent. Critical pairs (resp. sequence) help out in detecting rules in conflict or causally dependent rules in rule sequences. Moreover, conflict and causal dependency characterizations can be transferred to the level of rule conflicts and causal dependencies. This notion transfer to rules is important, amongst other things, to enforce static analysis techniques such as investigating *applicability (resp. non-applicability) of rule sequences* [74] as we do in Section 2.9. Sufficient criteria are given that infer applicability (resp. non-applicability), and in addition reduction techniques for rule sequences are presented that deduce applicability (resp. non-applicability) from its original rule sequences. Some basic reduction techniques of this kind have been shown already in [54, 76]. Moreover, in the beginning of this section we relate the notion of constraints to applicability (resp. non-applicability) of a single rule.

In Section 2.10, we address local confluence. In order to formulate and prove the *Local Confluence Theorem* for graph transformation systems with NACs, we need to generalize the *Embedding and Extension* Theorem to transformations with NACs [73]. Using the Concurrency Theorem with NACs, it is not too difficult to find an extended condition on the extension morphism in order to also generalize the Embedding and Extension Theorem to graph trans-

CHAPTER 2. RULE-BASED MODELING USING GRAPH TRANSFORMATION

formation systems with NACs. After that, we are finally able to handle critical pairs and local confluence with NACs. The Local Confluence Theorem [73] for graph transformation systems with NACs is not yet fully satisfactory since the sufficient condition on the set of critical pairs (resp. sequences) is difficult to check. Therefore, an extra theorem is formulated expressing a stronger sufficient condition, which is easier to check, and seems to be useful for showing local confluence in many practical cases. Moreover, a necessary and sufficient condition for local confluence is introduced by means of the notion of extended critical pairs. This condition is, in general, difficult to check, but it is helpful to decide on the running example of the elevator control that specific rules, which do not fulfill the sufficient condition of the Local Confluence Theorem with NACs, lead to local confluence anyway.

In the last sections of this chapter, two improved notions of critical pairs (resp. sequences), called critical pairs (resp. sequences) satisfying negative constraints and essential critical pairs [71] (resp. sequences), are presented. They promise a more *efficient static conflict (resp. causal dependency) detection* since these new sets of critical pairs (resp. sequences) are smaller than the usual set of critical pairs (resp. sequences), but still complete. Note that the notion of essential critical pairs (resp. sequences) does not yet consider conflicts and causal dependencies caused by negative application conditions in rules.

2.2 Modeling with Graphs

In this section, we introduce the running example of this chapter. It models an elevator control system. We illustrate in this example system how graphs can be used to model system states, and how graph constraints can be used to describe properties that may be satisfied by specific – or even all – system states. Graph rules and transformations are reintroduced in the next section, and they are used in the remaining part of this chapter to model dynamic aspects of this example system. We reintroduce in this section the formal notion of typed graphs and typed graph morphisms first.

2.2.1 Example (running example *Elevator*). As a running example throughout this chapter we will deal with the modeling of the control of an elevator. The type of control that we consider is meant to be used in buildings where the elevator should transport people from or to one main stop, for example, in apartment buildings or multi-story car parks [11]. Each floor in the building is equipped with one button in order to call the elevator. The elevator car stops at a floor for which an internal stop request is given. External call requests are served by the elevator only if it is in downward mode in order to transport people to the main stop. The direction of the elevator car is not changed as long as there are remaining requests in the running direction. External call requests as well as internal stop requests are not deleted until the elevator car has arrived.

2.2.2 Definition (graph and graph morphism). A *graph* $G = (G_V, G_E, s, t)$ consists of a set G_V of vertices, a set G_E of edges and two mappings $s, t : G_E \to G_V$, assigning to each edge $e \in G_E$ a source $s(e) \in G_V$ and target $t(e) \in G_V$. A *graph morphism* $f : G_1 \to G_2$ between two graphs $G_i = (G_{i,V}, G_{i,E}, s_i, t_i)$, $(i = 1, 2)$ is a pair $f = (f_V : G_{V,1} \to G_{V,2}, f_E : G_{E,1} \to G_{E,2})$ of mappings, such that $f_V \circ s_1 = s_2 \circ f_E$ and $f_V \circ t_1 = t_2 \circ f_E$. The category having graphs as objects and graph morphisms as arrows is called **Graphs**.

2.2. MODELING WITH GRAPHS

2.2.3 Definition (typed graph and typed graph morphism). A *type graph* is a distinguished graph $TG = (V_{TG}, E_{TG}, s_{TG}, t_{TG})$. V_{TG} and E_{TG} are called the vertex and the edge type alphabets, respectively. A tuple $(G, type)$ of a graph G together with a graph morphism $type : G \to TG$ is then called a *typed graph*. Consider typed graphs $G_1^T = (G_1, type_1)$ and $G_2^T = (G_2, type_2)$, a *typed graph morphism* $f : G_1^T \to G_2^T$ is a graph morphisms $f : G_1 \to G_2$ such that $type_2 \circ f = type_1$.

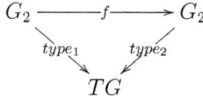

The category having typed graphs as objects and typed graph morphisms as arrows is called **Graphs**$_{TG}$.

2.2.4 Assumption (typed graphs and morphism). For the rest of this chapter we work within the category **Graphs**$_{TG}$. Each graph is typed, although not explicitly mentioned. Analogously, a morphism between typed graphs is automatically typed, although we do not explicitly mention it. Note that the category **Graphs** can be interpreted as a special case of **Graphs**$_{TG}$ with $TG = F$ the graph consisting of one node and a loop on this node. In category theory graph F is called the final object of **Graphs**. Each graph in **Graphs**$_F$ consists then of nodes and edges of the same type.

2.2.5 Definition (injective, (jointly) surjective morphisms, overlapping). A graph morphism $f : G_1 \to G_2$ is *injective (resp. surjective)* if f_V and f_E are injective (resp. surjective) mappings. Two graph morphisms $m_1 : L_1 \to G$ and $m_2 : L_2 \to G$ are *jointly surjective* if $m_{1,V}(L_{1,V}) \cup m_{2,V}(L_{2,V}) = G_V$ and $m_{1,E}(L_{1,E}) \cup m_{2,E}(L_{2,E}) = G_E$. A pair of jointly surjective morphisms (m_1, m_2) is also called an *overlapping* of L_1 and L_2.

2.2.6 Example (initial system state of *Elevator* as typed graph). In Fig. 2.1, a type graph for *Elevator* is depicted. This type graph expresses that an elevator car of type *elevator* must exist, which can be *on* a specific *floor*. Moreover, the elevator can be in *up*ward or *down*ward mode. Floors are connected by *next_up* edges expressing which floor is directly above another floor. Moreover, *higher_than* edges express that a floor is arranged higher in the building than another floor. Each floor can *hold requests* of two different types. The first type is a *call* request expressing that an external call for the elevator car on this floor is given. The second type is a *stop* request expressing that a call in the elevator car is given for stopping it on this floor. Note that in addition maximal and minimal multiplicities for nodes and edges are shown. They can be formalized by constraints (see Def. 2.2.7 and 2.2.9) as mentioned in Remark 2.2.10. In Fig. 2.2, an initial system state of *Elevator* as a graph typed over the type graph as shown in Fig. 2.1 is depicted. It models a building with four floors, where the elevator is on the ground floor, and the direction mode is set upward. Note that each node and edge is labeled with some type occurring in the type graph indicating how to map this graph by a graph morphism to the type graph in Fig. 2.1.

In this thesis, negative application conditions (see Def. 2.3.3) for rules play an important role, but we also consider so-called constraints, expressing properties that may be valid for specific – or even all – system states. The difference between constraints and application conditions is that a constraint can be checked against each graph representing a system state, where application conditions are attached to a rule, and thus, checked locally with respect to

CHAPTER 2. RULE-BASED MODELING USING GRAPH TRANSFORMATION

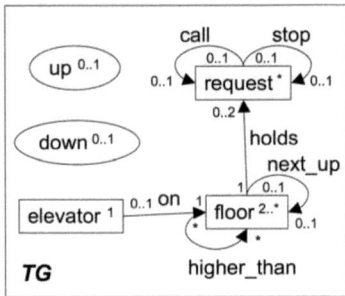

Figure 2.1: type graph of *Elevator*

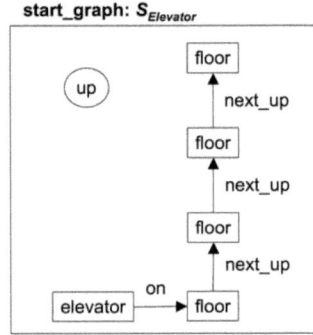

Figure 2.2: system state of *Elevator* as typed graph

a match (resp. comatch) to a graph, representing the system state before – in the case of left application conditions – or after – in the case of right application conditions – applying this rule (see Def. 2.3.6).

Note that in Section 2.9, we investigate the interrelationship of rule applicability and constraints. In Section 2.11.1, we use them to make conflict and causal dependency detection more efficient. Moreover, in Chapter 4 we propose a way to verify the fact that rules preserve specific constraints. The expensive checking of constraints imposed on the rule-based model can be made superfluous if it is possible to prove in such a static way that they hold at any time anyway. Imposed constraints must hold in each graph, representing a potential system state of the rule-based model. In a model with imposed constraints, a graph transformation step from a graph, representing a system state fulfilling the imposed constraints, is valid only if the resulting graph still fulfills these constraints.

The following definition reintroduces constraints as presented in [29]. Note that in [46], more general kinds of constraints and application conditions are considered, but they are beyond the scope of this thesis[1].

---

[1] In this regard, note that nested application conditions would make some of the rules of *Elevator* more compact and elegant. Moreover, the running example would benefit from concepts like attribution and inheritance. It is beyond the scope of this thesis, however, to treat the corresponding theory for these concepts in all details.

2.2. MODELING WITH GRAPHS

2.2.7 Definition (positive atomic constraint). A *positive atomic graph constraint* is of the form $PC(a)$, where $a : P \to C$ is a graph morphism. A graph G *satisfies* a positive atomic graph constraint $PC(a)$ if for every injective graph morphism $p : P \to G$, there exists an injective graph morphism $q : C \to G$ such that $q \circ a = p$. A graph G satisfies a set of positive graph constraints $\mathcal{PC}$ if it satisfies each positive graph constraint belonging to this set.

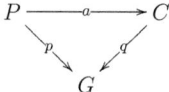

A positive graph constraint of the form $PC(a)$ with $a : \emptyset \to C$ is also notated as $PC(C)$. A graph G satisfies this constraint if an injective graph morphism $q : C \to G$ exists.

2.2.8 Example (positive atomic constraint for *Elevator*). Consider the positive atomic constraint $PC(U)$, where U is a graph, consisting of a single node of type *up*. This constraint is fulfilled in each system state in which the elevator is operating in upward mode. Moreover, consider the positive atomic constraint that consists of the inclusion from a graph, containing one *request* node, to a graph, containing in addition a *stop* loop to this node as depicted in Fig. 2.3. This constraint expresses that each graph fulfilling this constraint should possess only requests holding a stop loop.

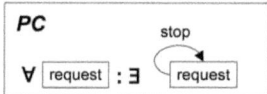

Figure 2.3: positive atomic constraint for *Elevator*

2.2.9 Definition (negative atomic constraint). A *negative atomic graph constraint* is of the form $NC(a)$, where $a : P \to C$ is a graph morphism. A graph G satisfies a negative atomic constraint $NC(a)$ if for every injective graph morphism $p : P \to G$, there exists no injective graph morphism $q : C \to G$ such that $q \circ a = p$. A graph G satisfies a set of negative constraints $\mathcal{NC}$ if it satisfies each negative constraint belonging to this set.

A negative graph constraint of the form $NC(a)$ with $a : \emptyset \to C$ is also notated as $NC(C)$. A graph G satisfies this constraint if no injective graph morphism $q : C \to G$ exists.

2.2.10 Remark (multiplicities and constraints). Note that maximal multiplicities as depicted for *Elevator* in the type graph in Fig. 2.1 can be formalized by negative atomic constraints. The fact that at most one elevator exists in the system is formalized by a negative atomic constraint $NC(C)$, where C consists of two elevator nodes. As soon as more than one elevator is present in some graph G, the negative atomic constraint $NC(C)$ is not satisfied. Maximal edge multiplicities, expressing, for example, that a *request* node is connected with an incoming *holds* edge from at most one *floor* node, can be formalized as follows: Consider the negative atomic constraint $NC(floors\_no\_same\_req)$ where $floors\_no\_same\_req$ is a graph, consisting of a *request* node connected with two incoming *holds* edges from two different *floor* nodes as depicted in Fig. 2.4. Analogously, minimal multiplicities can be formalized by positive atomic constraints, expressing that at least a specific number of nodes (resp. edges) should be present.

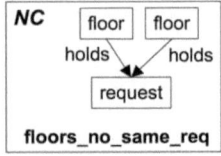

Figure 2.4: maximal edge multiplicity as negative atomic constraint for *Elevator*

Note that multiplicities are constraints imposed on the rule-based model, expressing that only graphs satisfying them represent valid system states.

2.2.11 Example (negative atomic constraints for *Elevator*). Consider in addition to the maximal multiplicities as given in the type graph depicted in Fig. 2.1 the following negative atomic constraints as depicted in Fig. 2.5. We explain more in detail two of these constraints: the negative constraint *NC(no_up_and_down)* describes that the elevator car cannot simultaneously be in upward and downward mode. Moreover, the negative constraint *NC(higher_is_not_next)* describes that some floor f that is higher than another floor f' cannot be the next lower floor of floor f'. Note that these constraints can be imposed on the rule-based model of *Elevator*. However, it is possible to verify that the set of these negative atomic constraints is satisfied in each system state of *Elevator* anyway. This avoids checking after each graph transformation step to ascertain whether the resulting graph still fulfills the imposed constraints. How it is possible to verify that a constraint is preserved, is explained in more detail in Section 4.3.9 in Chapter 4. Since these negative atomic constraints hold in each potential system state of *Elevator*, it is possible to use them in order to restrict the number of critical pairs, representing potential conflicts between rules in a minimal context. This is explained in more detail in Section 2.11.1.

2.2.12 Remark (critical pairs (resp. sequences) satisfying negative constraints). Note that in Section 2.11.1, a more efficient way of static conflict (resp. causality) detection is proposed, considering only critical pairs (resp. sequences) satisfying negative constraints of the form $NC(C)$. If each potential system state under consideration of the rule-based model satisfies these negative constraints, then it is sufficient to compute this reduced set of critical pairs.

2.2.13 Definition (constraint). A *graph constraint* is a boolean formula over positive atomic graph constraints. A graph G *satisfies* a graph constraint c, if $c = true$, $c = PC(a)$ and G satisfies $PC(a)$, $c = \neg c'$ and G does not satisfy c', $c = c_1 \wedge c_2$ and G satisfies c_1 and c_2, $c = c_1 \vee c_2$ and G satisfies c_1 or c_2.

As remarked in [29], a negative atomic graph constraint does not give more expressive power. For every negative atomic graph constraint, there is an equivalent constraint: if $a : P \to C$ is injective, then $NC(a)$ is equivalent to $\neg PC(C)$; otherwise $NC(a)$ is equivalent to *true*.

2.2.14 Example (constraint for *Elevator*). Consider graph U (resp. graph D), consisting of one node of type *up* (resp. *down*). Each system state of *Elevator* should fulfill the constraint $(PC(U) \wedge \neg PC(D)) \vee (\neg PC(U) \wedge PC(D))$. This is because the elevator operates either in upward or in downward mode, but not in both of these modes contemporarily.

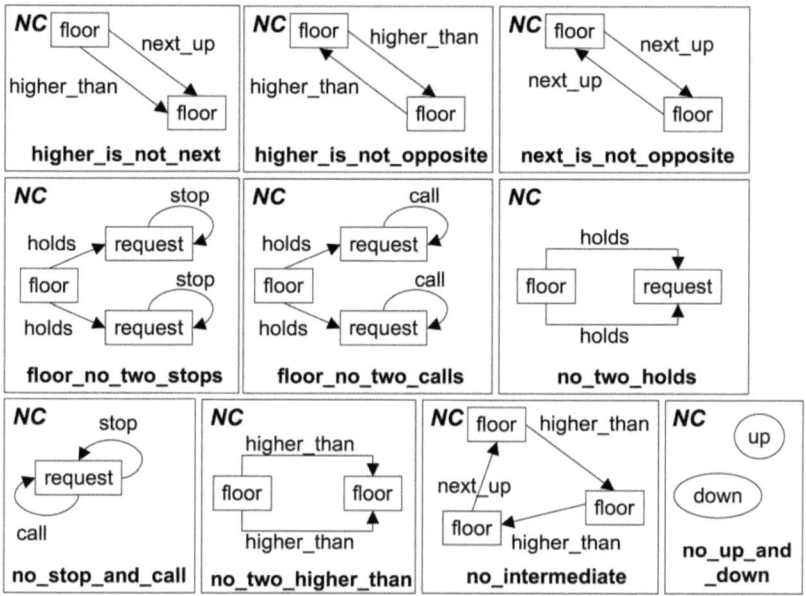

Figure 2.5: negative atomic constraints for *Elevator*

2.3 Rule-Based Modeling using Graph Transformation

Now that we have introduced graphs as a formal means to model systems, we can model their modification by introducing graph transformation. The way in which a system can potentially be modified is described by some graph transformation rules. A rule application corresponds to a graph transformation step, modeling a system modification step. In this chapter, we reintroduce graph transformation rules with NACs, and describe how these rules can be applied to graphs in order to obtain graph transformations. Thereby, we follow the double-pushout approach as presented in [29]. We illustrate each concept on our running example *Elevator* as introduced in the previous chapter.

We start with defining the notion of graph rules. A rule $p : L \leftarrow K \rightarrow R$ consists of a span of total graph morphisms, where its left-hand side describes the pre-condition, and its right-hand side describes the post-condition of the rule. Therefore, before applying the rule to a graph, at least L should be present, which is replaced by R through the rule's application. In particular, the graph part in L that does not belong to the image of its left-hand-side morphism describes which graph nodes and edges are to be deleted, when applying the rule. On the other hand, the graph part in R that does not belong to the image of its right-hand-side morphism describes which graph nodes and edges are to be added, when applying the rule. Finally, the domain K of both morphisms describes which part is to be preserved, when applying the rule.

2.3.1 Definition (rule). A graph transformation *rule* $p : L \xleftarrow{l} K \xrightarrow{r} R$ consists of a rule name p and a pair of injective graph morphisms $l : K \rightarrow L$ and $r : K \rightarrow R$. The graphs L, K and R are called the left-hand side (LHS), the interface, and the right-hand side (RHS) of p, respectively.

CHAPTER 2. RULE-BASED MODELING USING GRAPH TRANSFORMATION

2.3.2 Definition (match). Given a rule $p : L \xleftarrow{l} K \xrightarrow{r} R$ and a graph G, one can try to apply p to G if there is an occurrence of L in G i.e. a graph morphism, called *match* $m : L \to G$.

A negative application condition or NAC as introduced in [44] forbids a certain graph part to be present before or after applying the rule. A NAC is a morphism with as codomain the LHS or RHS of the rule. The part of the codomain that is not in the image of this morphism describes the forbidden part.

2.3.3 Definition (negative application condition, rule with NACs).

- A *negative application condition* or $NAC(n)$ on L is an arbitrary graph morphism $n : L \to N$. A graph morphism $g : L \to G$ satisfies $NAC(n)$ on L, written $g \models NAC(n)$, if and only if $\nexists\, q : N \to G$ such that q is injective and $q \circ n = g$.

$$L \xrightarrow{n} N$$
$$\downarrow g \quad \swarrow q$$
$$G$$

A set of NACs on L is denoted by $NAC_L = \{NAC(n_i) | i \in I\}$. A graph morphism $g : L \to G$ satisfies NAC_L if and only if g satisfies all single NACs on L i.e. $g \models NAC(n_i)\ \forall i \in I$.

- Similarly, a *negative application condition* or $NAC(n)$ on R is an arbitrary graph morphism $n : R \to N$. A graph morphism $h : R \to H$ satisfies $NAC(n)$ on R, written $h \models NAC(n)$, if and only if $\nexists\, q : N \to H$ such that q is injective and $q \circ n = h$.

- A set of NACs NAC_L (resp. NAC_R) on L (resp. R) for a rule $p : L \xleftarrow{l} K \xrightarrow{r} R$ is called *left* (resp. *right*) NAC on p. $NAC_p = (NAC_L, NAC_R)$, consisting of a set of left and a set of right NACs on p is called a *set of NACs on p*. A *rule (p, NAC_p) with NACs* is a rule $p : L \xleftarrow{l} K \xrightarrow{r} R$ with a set of NACs on p.

2.3.4 Remark (different NAC satisfaction). Note that Def. 2.3.3 demands the non-existing morphism $q : N \to G$ to be injective. Another interpretation of the satisfaction of NACs demands the morphism $q : N \to G$ to be non-injective only on $N \setminus n(L)$. This has as a consequence that q may glue the same graph parts as the match is gluing. The translation of this approach, as implemented in the tool environment AGG [1], to the one in Def. 2.3.3 is described in [52]. Basically, for each kind of potential gluing of the LHS, a corresponding NAC needs to be added. For example, see NAC *no_stop_request_glue* of rule *move_up* as described in the following example.

2.3.5 Example (rules *stop_request* and *move_up* for *Elevator*). In Fig. 2.6, the rule *stop_request* is shown expressing that an internal stop request is recorded for a certain floor. This rule holds a NAC *no_stop_yet* expressing that there is no stop request already recorded for this floor. In Fig. 2.7, the rule *move_up* is shown expressing that the elevator car moves upward to the next floor if the upward mode is set and a request is present on one of the upper floors. NAC *no_stop_request* disallows the rule to be applied if a stop request is present on the elevator floor. This is because stop requests in upward mode need to be served, and thus, processed first (see rules *process_stop_up* and *process_stop_and_call*) in Example 2.3.16. NAC *no_stop_request_glue* is analogous to NAC *no_stop_request* with the difference that it takes hold of matches that map in a non-injective way the floors with labels 3 and 5. This is necessary

2.3. RULE-BASED MODELING USING GRAPH TRANSFORMATION

for the case that a request is present on the floor to which the elevator moves to. Finally, note that a possible external call request is ignored in upward direction since rule *move_up* could be applied in this case anyway. This corresponds to the requirements for *Elevator* as described in Example 2.2.1.

Note that only the LHS L and RHS R of the rules are depicted in Fig. 2.6 and 2.7. Rules in this chapter are always depicted in this way. Thereby, the intermediate graph K and morphisms l and r can be derived as follows. Graph K consists of all nodes and edges occurring in L and R that are labeled by the same number. Morphism l and r then map nodes and edges according to the numbering. Analogously, the morphism n from L into some NAC consists of mappings according to the numbering of nodes and edges. Finally, note that also in [44] the control of an elevator was modeled using graph transformation rules with NACs, illustrating their usefulness.

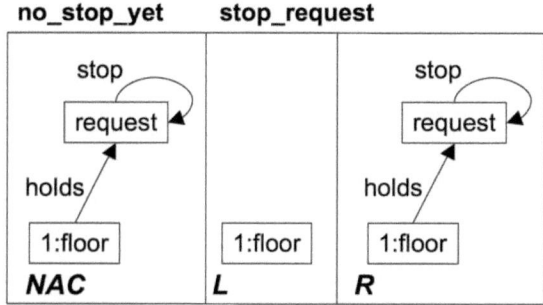

Figure 2.6: rule *stop_request*

In the following definition, we introduce the notion of graph transformation (GT) based on the double-pushout (DPO) approach. Thereby, the left pushout of a direct graph transformation describes the deletion of graph parts, and the right pushout describes the addition of graph parts, marked accordingly by the corresponding rule. A pushout is constructed over a span of morphisms. Intuitively speaking, it describes how the codomain graphs of this span can be glued together along the common domain graph. We refer to [29] for a definition and construction of pushouts (POs).

2.3.6 Definition (GT system, grammar, transformation, language with NACs).

- A *graph transformation system with NACs* $GTS = (P, TG)$ consists of a set of rules with NACs P typed over a type graph TG. A *graph transformation grammar with NACs* $GR = (GTS, S)$ consists of a graph transformation system with NACs GTS and a start graph S.

- A *direct graph transformation* $G \overset{p,g}{\Rightarrow} H$ from G to H via a rule $p : L \leftarrow K \rightarrow R$ with $NAC_p = (NAC_L, NAC_R)$ and a match $g : L \rightarrow G$ (resp. comatch $h : R \rightarrow G$) consists of the double pushout (DPO) [23] in **Graphs**$_{TG}$

$$\begin{array}{ccccc} L & \leftarrow & K & \rightarrow & R \\ {\scriptstyle g}\downarrow & & \downarrow & & \downarrow{\scriptstyle h} \\ G & \leftarrow & D & \rightarrow & H \end{array}$$

CHAPTER 2. RULE-BASED MODELING USING GRAPH TRANSFORMATION

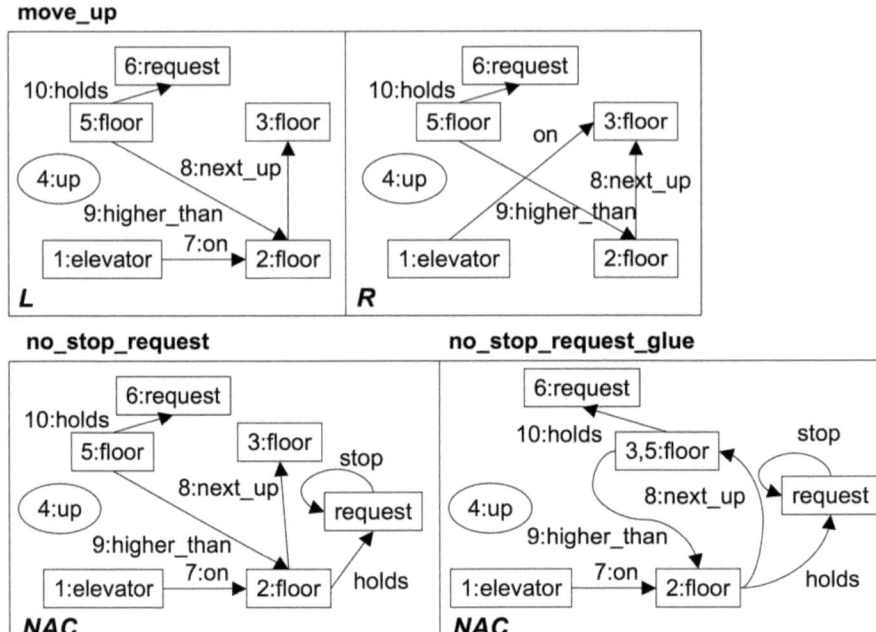

Figure 2.7: rule *move_up*

where g satisfies NAC_L, written $g \models NAC_L$ and $h : R \to H$ satisfies NAC_R, written $h \models NAC_R$. Since pushouts along injective morphisms in the category $\mathbf{Graphs}_{TG}$ always exist, the DPO can be constructed if the pushout complement of $K \to L \to G$ exists. If so, we say that the match g satisfies the *gluing condition* of rule p. A *graph transformation*, denoted as $G_0 \stackrel{*}{\Rightarrow} G_n$, is a sequence $G_0 \Rightarrow G_1 \Rightarrow \cdots \Rightarrow G_n$ of direct transformations. For $n = 0$, we have the identical graph transformation $G_0 \Rightarrow G_0$. Moreover, for $n = 0$ we also allow graph isomorphisms $G_0 \cong G'_0$, because pushouts, and hence also direct graph transformations, are only unique up to isomorphism.

- A *graph language* $\mathcal{L}(GR)$ consists of S and all graphs G such that there exists a graph transformation from S to G via rules in P.

2.3.7 Remark (gluing condition). Note that a match fulfills the gluing condition if and only if it fulfills the dangling edge condition – expressing that nodes to be deleted are matched such that all incident edges are to be deleted as well such that no dangling edges arise – and the identification condition – expressing that graph elements glued by the match are not to be deleted. For a more detailed explanation of this topic see [29].

2.3.8 Remark (GTS with NACs is adhesive HLR system with NACs). As mentioned in Chapter 3 in Fact 3.2.15 and Remark 3.3.3, (typed) graph transformation systems with injective rule morphisms and NACs are adhesive HLR systems with NACs. This means that all results proven in Chapter 3 for adhesive HLR systems with NACs hold for (typed) graph transformation systems with NACs. Thus, in this chapter we repeat each relevant result for the instantiation

2.3. RULE-BASED MODELING USING GRAPH TRANSFORMATION

of graph transformation systems with NACs, and refer for the proofs of these results to Chapter 3.

2.3.9 Assumption (left NACs). From now on we consider only graph transformation systems with rules having an empty set of right negative application conditions.

This is without loss of generality, because each right NAC can be shifted to an equivalent left NAC as explained in [34] and [29], where Def. 7.16 and Theorem 7.17 can be specialized to NACs as shown in the following construction and lemma. Note that [46] presents this result for more general nested application conditions.

2.3.10 Definition (construction of left from right NACs). For each $NAC(n_i)$ on R with $n_i : R \to N_i$ of a rule $p = (L \leftarrow K \to R)$, the equivalent left application condition $L_p(NAC(n_i))$ is defined in the following way:

$$\begin{array}{ccc} L & \leftarrow K \rightarrow & R \\ n'_i \downarrow & (2) \quad \downarrow \quad (1) & \downarrow n_i \\ N'_i & \leftarrow Z \rightarrow & N_i \end{array}$$

- If the pair $(K \to R, R \to N_i)$ has a pushout complement, we construct $(K \to Z, Z \to N_i)$ as the pushout complement (1). Then we construct pushout (2) with the morphism $n'_i : L \to N'_i$. Now we define $L_p(NAC(n_i)) = NAC(n'_i)$.

- If the pair $(K \to R, R \to N_i)$ does not have a pushout complement, we define $L_p(NAC(n_i)) = true$.

For each set of NACs on R, $NAC_R = \cup_{i \in I} NAC(n_i)$ we define the following set of left NACs:

$$L_p(NAC_R) = \cup_{i \in I'} L_p(NAC(n'_i))$$

with $i \in I'$ if and only if the pair $(K \to R, R \to N_i)$ has a pushout complement.

2.3.11 Remark. Note that Z is unique since pushout complements along injective graph morphisms are unique up to isomorphism in the category **Graphs**$_{TG}$ [29].

2.3.12 Lemma (equivalence of left and right NACs). *For every rule p with NAC_R a set of right NACs on p, $L_p(NAC_R)$ as defined in Def. 2.3.10 is a set of left NACs on p such that for all direct transformations $G \overset{p,g}{\Rightarrow} H$ with comatch h,*

$$g \models L_p(NAC_R) \Leftrightarrow h \models NAC_R$$

Proof. Follows from Fact 3.2.15 and Lemma 3.3.7 in Chapter 3. □

2.3.13 Example (construction of left from right NACs for *Elevator*). Consider the rule *stop_request* as depicted in Fig. 2.6. Suppose that it holds a right NAC *no_call* as depicted in the right bottom of Fig. 2.8. Then the pushout complement Z exists, and consists of a floor with a call request. The construction of the pushout no longer adds anything new to Z. The left NAC, therefore, consists of a floor with a call request. If a call request is not there before applying the rule, then it will not be there afterwards either. Vice versa: if a call request is not there after applying the rule, then it was not there before either.

CHAPTER 2. RULE-BASED MODELING USING GRAPH TRANSFORMATION

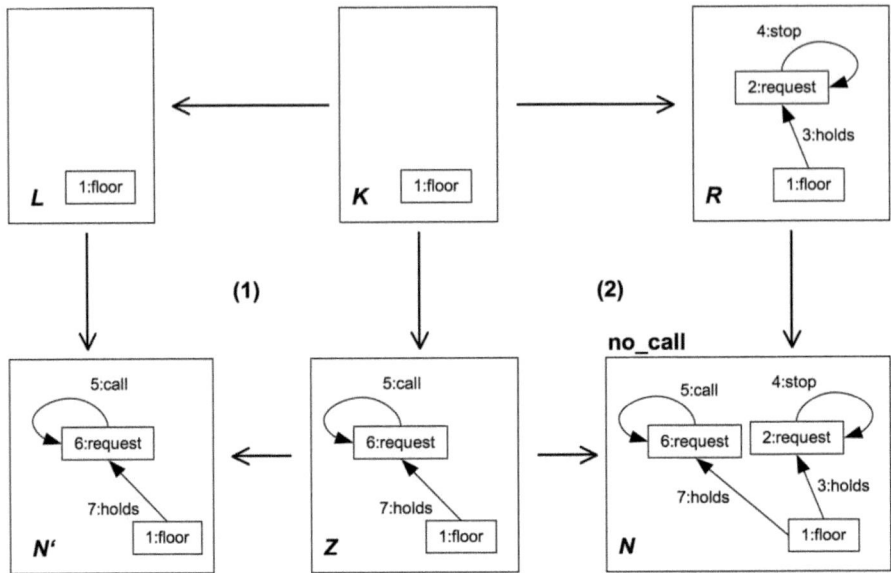

Figure 2.8: shifting right NAC into left NAC for *Elevator*

Since we have assumed without loss of generality that NAC_p consists of only a set of NACs on its left-hand side, we can define applicability of a rule with NACs as follows. The construction of a direct transformation remains the same as for transformations without NACs [29].

2.3.14 Definition (applicability of rule). *Let $p : L \xleftarrow{l} K \xrightarrow{r} R$ be a rule with NAC_p. For a graph G and a match $m : L \to G$, p is applicable via m if the pushout complement for $K \xrightarrow{l} L \xrightarrow{m} G$ exists (i.e. m fulfills the gluing condition), and in addition m satisfies NAC_p.*

2.3.15 Fact (construction of direct transformations). *Given rule p and match $m : L \to G$ such that p is applicable to G via m as given in Def. 2.3.14, then a direct transformation can be constructed in two steps:*

1. *Construct the pushout complement $K \xrightarrow{k} D \xrightarrow{f} G$ of $K \xrightarrow{l} L \xrightarrow{m} G$ in diagram (1) below.*

2. *Construct the pushout $D \xrightarrow{g} H \xleftarrow{n} R$ of $D \xleftarrow{k} K \xrightarrow{r} R$ in diagram (2).*

This construction is unique up to isomorphism.

$$L \xleftarrow{l} K \xrightarrow{r} R$$
$$\downarrow m \quad (1) \quad \downarrow k \quad (2) \quad \downarrow n$$
$$G \xleftarrow{f} D \xrightarrow{g} H$$

Proof. Follows from Fact 3.2.15 and Fact 3.3.9 in Chapter 3. □

2.3.16 Example (generating and operating *Elevator* using graph transformation). Consider rule *add_floor* together with the start graph as depicted in Fig. 2.9. This rule adds with

2.3. RULE-BASED MODELING USING GRAPH TRANSFORMATION

each application a floor to the elevator building. Thereby, we start with a model of a two-storey building and an elevator in upward mode. Rule *add_floor*, rule *initial_higher*, and rule

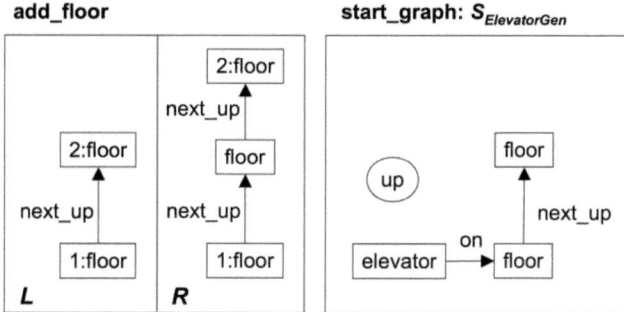

Figure 2.9: rule *add_floor* and start graph of grammar $GG_{ElevatorGen}$

transitive_higher constitute a graph transformation system $GTS_{ElevatorGen}$. Together with the start graph as depicted in Fig. 2.9, we have a generating graph grammar $GG_{ElevatorGen} = (GTS_{ElevatorGen}, S_{ElevatorGen})$. The corresponding graph language consists of graphs, modeling different kinds of multi-story buildings in which the elevator can operate. Rule *initial_higher* (see Fig. 2.10) adds for each edge of type *next_up* between two floors an edge of type *higher_than* in the other direction. Rule *transitive_higher* (see Fig. 2.11) adds the transitive closure of all *higher_than* edges if it is applied as long as possible. The NAC *not_yet* of both rules takes care that there is only one edge of type *higher_than* between each pair of floors. Thus, these rules generate for each pair of floors in the building an edge of type *higher_than*, expressing which one of both floors is the highest.

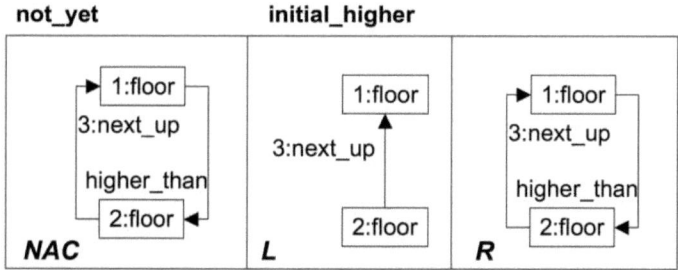

Figure 2.10: rule *initial_higher*

In Figs. 2.12 - 2.19, additional rules of *Elevator* are depicted. They constitute together with rule *stop_request* (see Fig. 2.6) and *move_up* (see Fig. 2.7) a graph transformation system $GTS_{Elevator}$ describing the operational semantics of our elevator system. Together with the initial system state $S_{Elevator}$ as depicted in Fig. 2.2, we have a graph grammar $GG_{Elevator} = (GTS_{Elevator}, S_{Elevator})$. The graph $S_{Elevator}$ models a building with four different floors and an elevator with in its initial system state being on the ground floor in upward mode[2]. The

---
[2]Note that $S_{Elevator}$ can be generated with the above introduced grammar $GG_{ElevatorGen}$.

CHAPTER 2. RULE-BASED MODELING USING GRAPH TRANSFORMATION

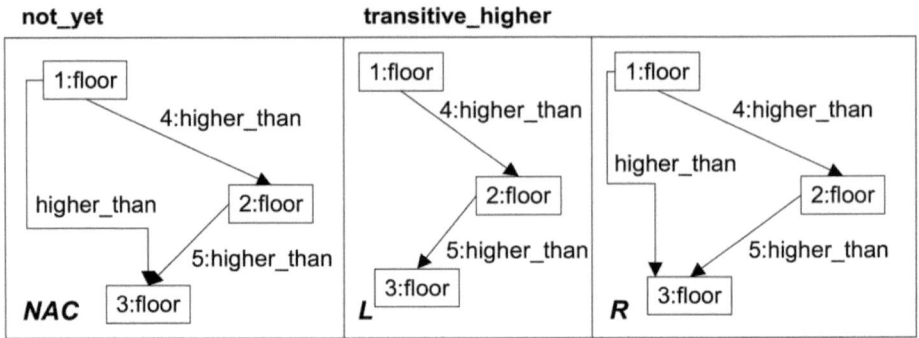

Figure 2.11: rule *transitive_higher*

corresponding graph language consists of graphs modeling system states in which the elevator can get into, starting from the initial system state $S_{Elevator}$, and operating according to the rules in $GTS_{Elevator}$. We briefly describe each additional rule belonging to $GTS_{Elevator}$. Rule *call_request* (see Fig. 2.12) is analogous to rule *stop_request* (see Fig. 2.6) with the only difference that an external call request is recorded instead of an internal stop request. Rule

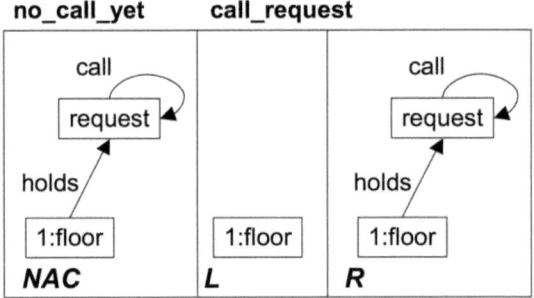

Figure 2.12: rule *call_request*

move_down (see Fig. 2.13) moves the elevator car in downward direction. Therefore, it requires that a request is present for one of the lower floors. Moreover, NAC *no_request* makes sure that the elevator car starts moving only if a possible request still present for the given floor is processed first. NAC *no_request_glue* takes hold of matches in which floors 4 and 5 are mapped in a non-injective way. This is the case if the elevator moves down to a floor on which a request is present. Note that in contrast to rule *move_up*, rule *move_down* is not applied if a request is still present regardless of its type. This is because only in upward direction internal stop requests do have priority over external call requests. This corresponds to the requirements for *Elevator* as explained in Example 2.2.1. In addition to rules moving the elevator car and rules producing requests, we need rules allowing the elevator car to change its direction. Rule *set_direction_down* changes the direction mode of the elevator from upward to downward. Therefore, it requires the presence of some request on a lower floor. NAC *no_stop_request* takes care that no internal stop request is still present on the elevator floor. Moreover, NAC *no_higher_request* allows to change

2.3. RULE-BASED MODELING USING GRAPH TRANSFORMATION

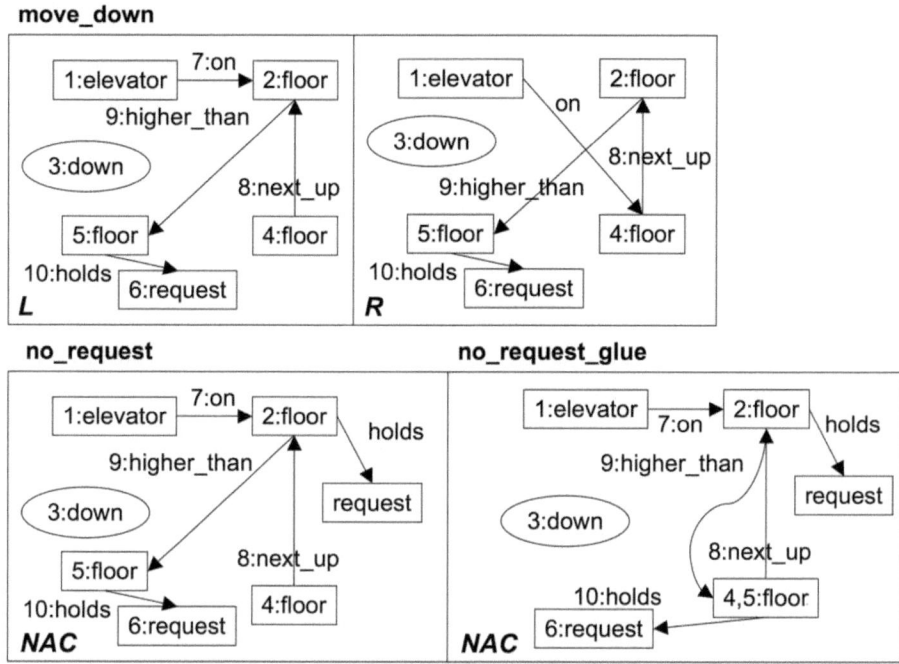

Figure 2.13: rule *move_down*

direction only if no request still has to be processed on an upper floor. Rule *set_direction_up* is depicted in Fig. 2.15. It changes the direction mode for the elevator from downward to upward. NAC *no_request* allows to change direction only if no request is still left on the elevator floor itself. Moreover, NAC *no_lower_request* takes care that no request still has to be processed on some lower floor. Note that this corresponds to the requirements for *Elevator* as explained in Example 2.2.1. Finally, we present rules that can process a request if the elevator has arrived on the corresponding floor. Note that, when extending *Elevator* with the modeling of a door control, these processing rules should be connected with the door-controlling rules. Rule *process_stop_up* (see Fig. 2.16) describes that an internal stop request can be deleted in upward direction mode if there is no external call request on this floor (see NAC *no_call*). If there was a call request on this floor as well, then it should be deleted together with the stop request by rule *process_stop_and_call* (see Fig. 2.17). Regardless of the elevator's direction mode, this rule deletes a stop request and a call request. This rule as well as the processing rules *process_call_down* and *process_stop_down* have no NACs. Rule *process_stop_down* (resp. *process_call_down*) deletes a stop (resp. call) request in downward mode as shown in Fig. 2.18. Rule *process_call_down* is not depicted, but analogous to rule *process_stop_down* with the only difference that no stop request, but rather a call request is deleted. Finally, we have a rule *process_call_up_highest* (resp. *process_call_up_lowest*), describing that a call request on the elevator floor is processed exceptionally in upward mode if the call request is the highest request in the building. Rule *process_call_up_highest* is depicted in Fig. 2.19 with a single NAC

35

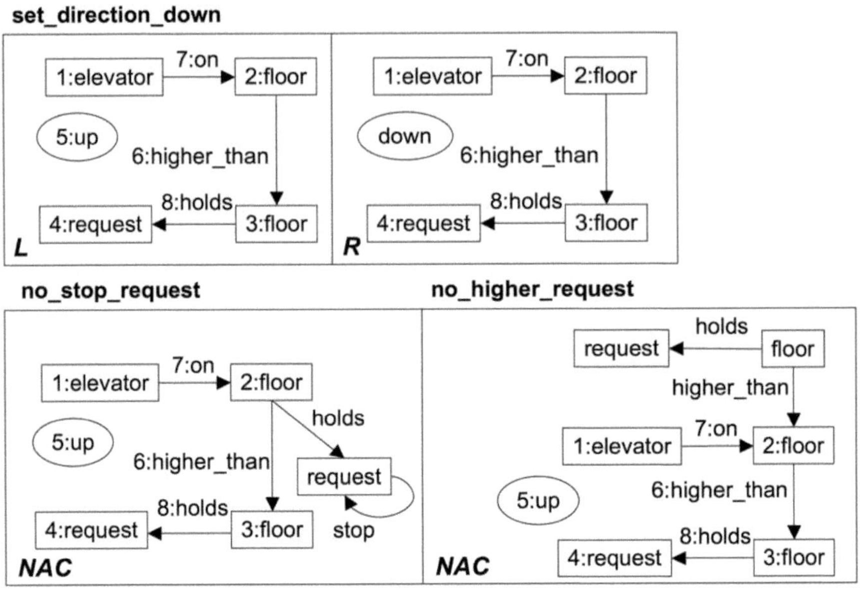

CHAPTER 2. RULE-BASED MODELING USING GRAPH TRANSFORMATION

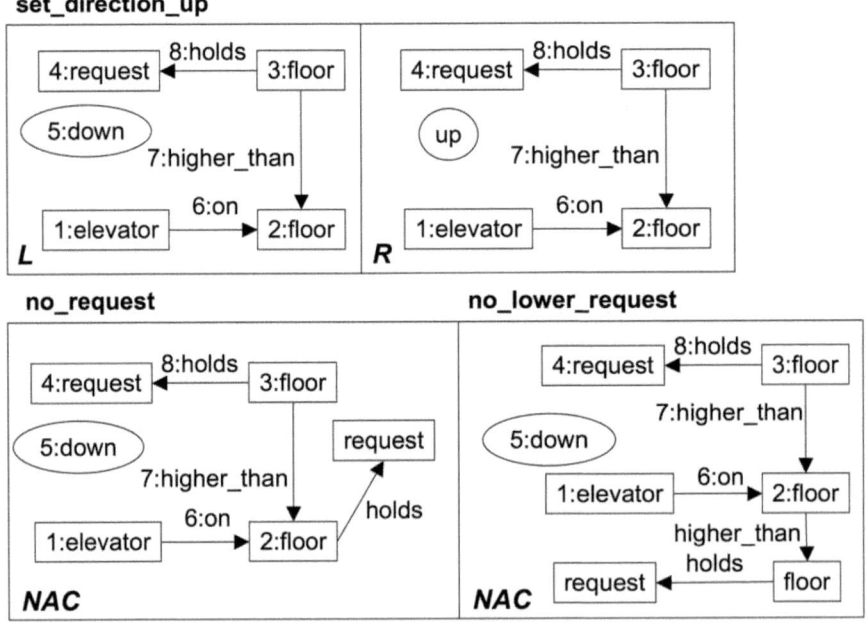

Figure 2.14: rule *set_direction_down*

Figure 2.15: rule *set_direction_up*

highest_request forbidding a higher request than the call request on the elevator floor. Rule *process_call_up_lowest*, on the other hand, is not depicted, but is analogous to this rule with a different NAC *lowest_floor* expressing that the elevator does not serve any lower floor, and therefore, the call request can exceptionally processed in upward mode.

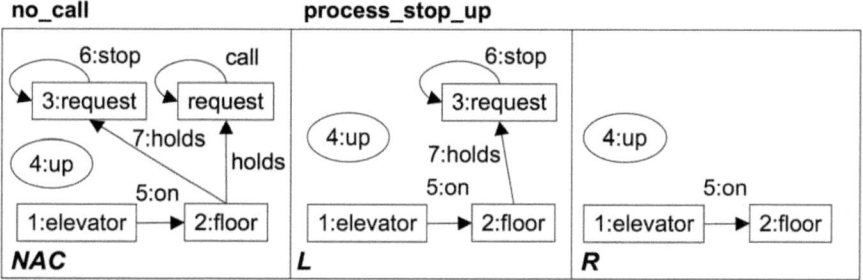

Figure 2.16: rule *process_stop_up*

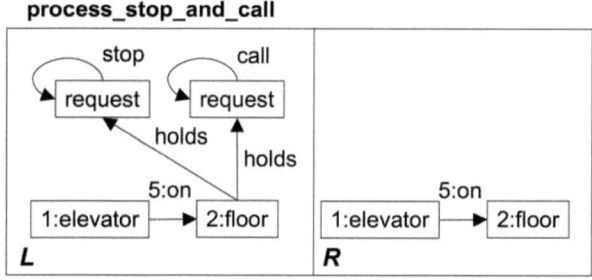

Figure 2.17: rule *process_stop_and_call*

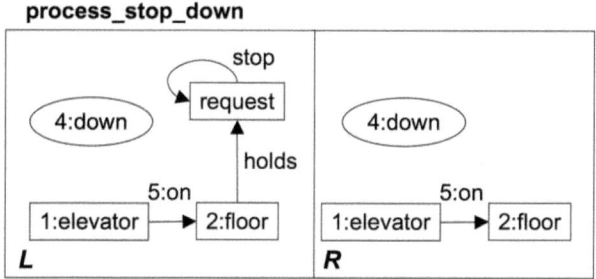

Figure 2.18: rule *process_stop_down*

In Fig. 2.20, an exemplary graph transformation sequence starting with the initial system state $S_{Elevator}$ is depicted. It models the recording of a stop request for the 3rd floor and a call request for the 2nd floor; consequently the elevator car moves upward to the next floor because

CHAPTER 2. RULE-BASED MODELING USING GRAPH TRANSFORMATION

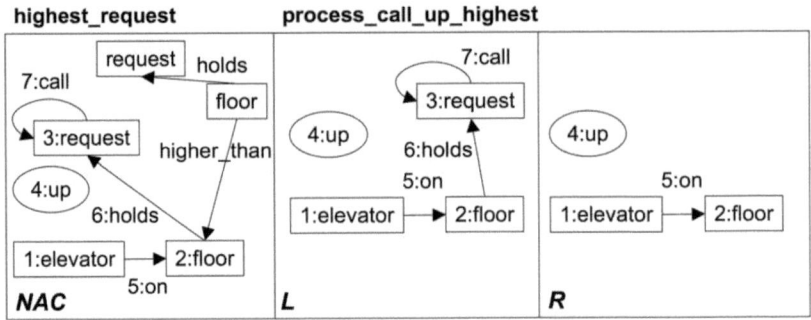

Figure 2.19: rule *process_call_up_highest*

of the triggering stop request on the 3rd floor. This transformation can be continued by moving the elevator car such that it serves first the stop request, and afterwards in downward mode the call request. The graph, modeling the final state of $S_{Elevator}$ after serving and processing both requests, is depicted in Fig. 2.20. Note that the way of serving the requests corresponds to the requirements for *Elevator* as described in Example 2.2.1.

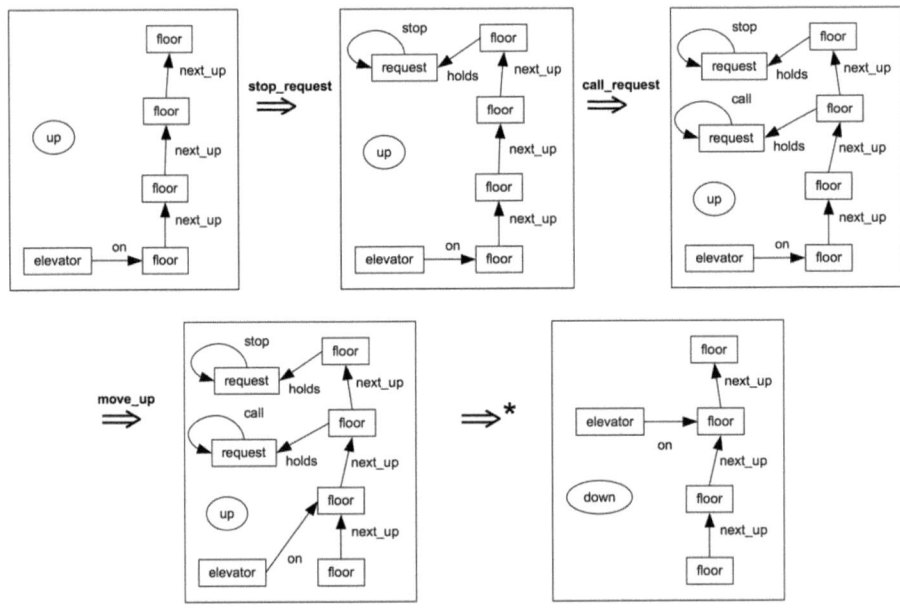

Figure 2.20: transformation sequence for *Elevator*

By means of the following definition and theorem, we show that it is possible to apply a rule inversely. It is based on the shifting of NACs over a rule as presented in Def. 2.3.10. Inverse transformations will be used, for example, in Section 2.6 to define causal dependencies (see Def.

2.3. RULE-BASED MODELING USING GRAPH TRANSFORMATION

2.6.2) between transformations. In particular, it is shown that a transformation can become irreversible, after applying an intermediate transformation.

2.3.17 Definition (inverse rule with NACs). For a rule $p : L \leftarrow K \rightarrow R$ with $NAC_p = (NAC_L, \emptyset)$, the inverse rule is defined by $p^{-1} = R \leftarrow K \rightarrow L$ with $NAC_{p^{-1}} = (L_{p^{-1}}(NAC_L), \emptyset)$.

2.3.18 Theorem (inverse direct transformation with NACs). *For each direct transformation with NACs $G \Rightarrow H$ via a rule $p : L \leftarrow K \rightarrow R$ with NAC_p a set of left NACs on p, there exists an inverse direct transformation with NACs $H \Rightarrow G$ via the inverse rule p^{-1} with $NAC_{p^{-1}}$.*

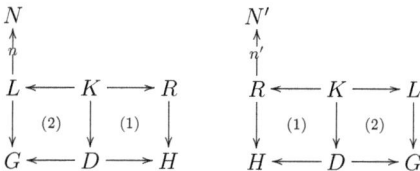

Proof. Follows from Fact 3.2.15 and Theorem 3.3.11 in Chapter 3. □

In Def. 2.3.10, we have shown how to shift NACs over a rule. The following definition introduces how to shift NACs over a morphism. Consider a graph A with NACs, and some graph morphism $m : A \rightarrow B$. In order to obtain the set of equivalent NACs on B, it is not enough to consider the PO of m and the single NACs on A. In addition, all overlaps have to be considered, where in addition graph elements not stemming from A may be glued. Thereby, note that elements in the NAC of A may not be glued. In Section 2.5, we use this construction to define concurrent rules with NACs. Note that [46] presents the following result for more general nested application conditions.

2.3.19 Definition (construction of NACs on B from NACs on A with $m : A \rightarrow B$). Consider the following diagram:

$$\begin{array}{ccc} N'_j & \xrightarrow{e_{ji}} & N_i \\ {\scriptstyle n'_j}\uparrow & (1) & \uparrow{\scriptstyle n_i} \\ A & \xrightarrow{m} & B \end{array}$$

For each $NAC(n'_j)$ on A with $n'_j : A \rightarrow N'_j$ and $m : A \rightarrow B$, let

$$D_m(NAC(n'_j)) = \{NAC(n_i) | i \in I, n_i : B \rightarrow N_i\}$$

where I and n_i are constructed as follows: $i \in I$ if and only if (e_{ji}, n_i) with $e_{ji} : N'_j \rightarrow N_i$ jointly surjective, $e_{ji} \circ n'_j = n_i \circ m$ and e_{ji} injective.
For each set of NACs $NAC_A = \{NAC(n_j) | j \in J\}$ on A the downward shift of NAC_A is then defined as:

$$D_m(NAC_A) = \cup_{j \in J} D_m(NAC(n'_j))$$

2.3.20 Lemma (equivalence of set of NACs on A and set of NACs on B with $m : A \rightarrow B$).

Given $g : A \to G_0$, $m : A \to B$ with NAC_A and $g' = g \circ m$ as in the following diagram:

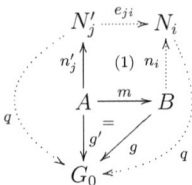

then the following holds :

$$g' \models NAC_A \Leftrightarrow g \models D_m(NAC_A).$$

Proof. Follows from Fact 3.2.15 and Lemma 3.3.13 in Chapter 3. □

The following corollary reduces the set of NACs obtained by the above shifting operation over a morphism for the case that we have injective matching only. In this case, it is sufficient to keep all NACs consisting of an injective morphism. In order to obtain the restricted set of injective NACs shifted over a morphism $m : A \to B$, it is again not enough to consider the PO of m and the single NACs on A. In addition, all overlaps have to be considered, where graph elements not stemming from A may be glued. Thereby, note that neither elements from the NAC of A may be glued, nor may elements from B be glued. Thus, additional overlaps arise only if forbidden graph elements from a NAC on A can be glued with graph elements in B not stemming from A.

2.3.21 Corollary. *Assuming in the previous lemma that g is injective, then the construction of NACs on B from NACs on A with $m : A \to B$ as given in Def. 2.3.19 can be restricted to a subset*

$$D_m^{inj}(NAC_A) = \cup_{j \in J} D_m^{inj}(NAC(n'_j))$$

with

$$D_m^{inj}(NAC(n'_j)) = \{NAC(n_i) | i \in I, n_i : B \to N_i \text{ injective}\}.$$

Proof. We need to prove that

$$g' \models NAC_A \Leftrightarrow g \models D_m^{inj}(NAC_A).$$

We show that $g \models D_m^{inj}(NAC_A) \Leftrightarrow g \models D_m(NAC_A)$, and then, this follows trivially from Lemma 2.3.20. Consider $NAC(n_i)$ with $i \in I$, $n_i : B \to N_i$ and n_i non-injective, then $g \models NAC(n_i)$. Otherwise there would exist some injective morphism $q : N_i \to G_0$ such that $q \circ n_i = g$. This is a contradiction since by decomposition of injective graph morphisms, it holds that n_i is injective if g and q are. □

2.3.22 Example (shift NAC over a morphism for *Elevator*). Consider the morphism as depicted in Fig. 2.21 and a NAC *no_call* on its domain graph. Fig. 2.21 shows how to shift the NAC *no_call* over a morphism embedding the floor with label 2 into a graph with an extra floor with label 1 holding a stop request. Note that not all NACs of $D_m(NAC_A)$ are shown. In principle, there still exist some more NACs gluing not only floor 1 and 2, but moreover, gluing the *request* nodes, and possibly also the corresponding *holds* edges. However, in *Elevator* such

2.4. INDEPENDENCE AND PARALLELISM

graphs never occur, because of the multiplicities given in the type graph as shown in Fig. 2.1. Therefore, we can omit these kinds of NACs.

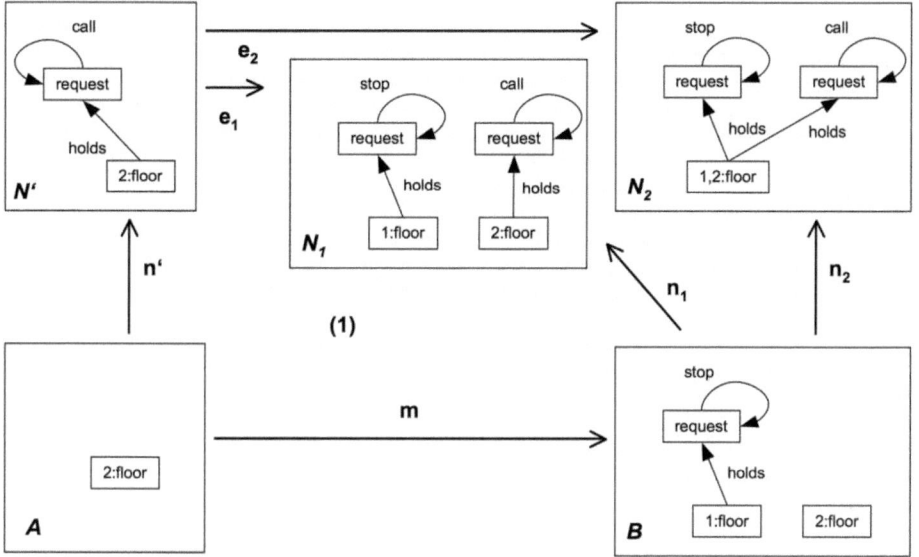

Figure 2.21: shift NAC over a morphism for *Elevator*

2.4 Independence and Parallelism

In order to generalize the notion of parallelism to graph transformation systems with NACs, it is first necessary to define when two direct transformations with NACs are parallel and sequentially independent. For a pair of transformations with NACs it is not only possible that one transformation deletes a structure that is needed by the other one, but also that one transformation produces a structure that is forbidden by the other one. Moreover, for a sequence of two direct transformations with NACs it is not only possible that the first transformation produces a structure that is needed by the second one, but also that the first transformation deletes a structure that is forbidden by the second one. For this new notion of parallel and sequential independence we formulate the local Church-Rosser property with NACs and also a Parallelism Theorem with NACs.

2.4.1 Definition (parallel and sequential independence). Two direct transformations $G \overset{p_1,m_1}{\Longrightarrow} H_1$ with NAC_{p_1} and $G \overset{p_2,m_2}{\Longrightarrow} H_2$ with NAC_{p_2} are *parallel independent* if

$$\exists h_{12} : L_1 \to D_2 \text{ s.t. } (d_2 \circ h_{12} = m_1 \text{ and } e_2 \circ h_{12} \models NAC_{p_1})$$

and

$$\exists h_{21} : L_2 \to D_1 \text{ s.t. } (d_1 \circ h_{21} = m_2 \text{ and } e_1 \circ h_{21} \models NAC_{p_2})$$

CHAPTER 2. RULE-BASED MODELING USING GRAPH TRANSFORMATION

as in the following diagram:

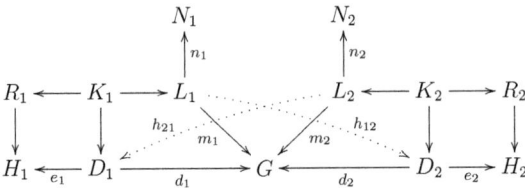

Two direct transformations $G \overset{p_1,m_1}{\Longrightarrow} H_1$ with NAC_{p_1} and $H_1 \overset{p_2,m_2}{\Longrightarrow} H_2$ with NAC_{p_2} are *sequentially independent* if

$$\exists h_{12} : R_1 \to D_2 \text{ s.t. } (d_2 \circ h_{12} = m'_1 \text{ and } e_2 \circ h_{12} \models NAC_{p_1^{-1}})$$

and

$$\exists h_{21} : L_2 \to D_1 \text{ s.t. } (e_1 \circ h_{21} = m_2 \text{ and } d_1 \circ h_{21} \models NAC_{p_2})$$

as in the following diagram:

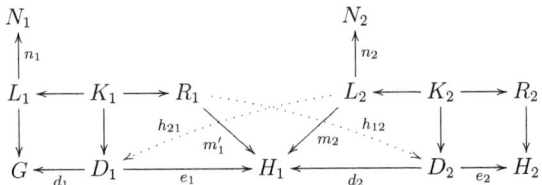

2.4.2 Remark. Note that as for the case without NACs we have the following relationship between parallel and sequential independence: $G \overset{p_1}{\Rightarrow} H_1 \overset{p_2}{\Rightarrow} H_2$ are sequentially independent iff $G \overset{p_1^{-1}}{\Leftarrow} H_1 \overset{p_2}{\Rightarrow} H_2$ are parallel independent.

2.4.3 Theorem (local Church-Rosser theorem with NACs). *Given a graph transformation system with NACs GTS and two parallel independent direct transformations with NACs $H_1 \overset{p_1,m_1}{\Longleftarrow} G \overset{p_2,m_2}{\Longrightarrow} H_2$, there are a graph G' and direct transformations $H_1 \overset{p_2,m'_2}{\Longrightarrow} G'$ and $H_2 \overset{p_1,m'_1}{\Longrightarrow} G'$ such that $G \overset{p_1,m_1}{\Longrightarrow} H_1 \overset{p_2,m'_2}{\Longrightarrow} G'$ and $G \overset{p_2,m_2}{\Longrightarrow} H_2 \overset{p_1,m'_1}{\Longrightarrow} G'$ are sequentially independent. Vice versa, given two sequentially independent direct transformations with NACs $G \overset{p_1,m_1}{\Longrightarrow} H_1 \overset{p_2,m'_2}{\Longrightarrow} G'$ there are a graph H_2 and sequentially independent direct transformations $G \overset{p_2,m_2}{\Longrightarrow} H_2 \overset{p_1,m'_1}{\Longrightarrow} G'$ such that $H_1 \overset{p_1,m_1}{\Longleftarrow} G \overset{p_2,m_2}{\Longrightarrow} H_2$ are parallel independent:*

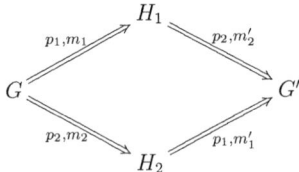

Proof. Follows from Fact 3.2.15 and Theorem 3.4.3 in Chapter 3. □

2.4. INDEPENDENCE AND PARALLELISM

2.4.4 Example (independent transformations for *Elevator*). Consider the graph $S_{Elevator}$ modeling the initial system state of *Elevator*. Rule *stop_request* (see Fig. 2.6) and rule *call_request* (see Fig. 2.12) can be applied to $S_{Elevator}$ resulting in the upper graph (resp. lower graph) as depicted in Fig. 2.22. These transformations are parallel independent since induced matches exist such that *call_request* is applicable to the upper graph and *stop_request* is applicable to the lower graph leading to the same resulting graph. Theorem 2.4.3 also implies that $S_{Elevator} \Rightarrow H_1 \Rightarrow G'$ and $S_{Elevator} \Rightarrow H_2 \Rightarrow G'$ are sequentially independent.

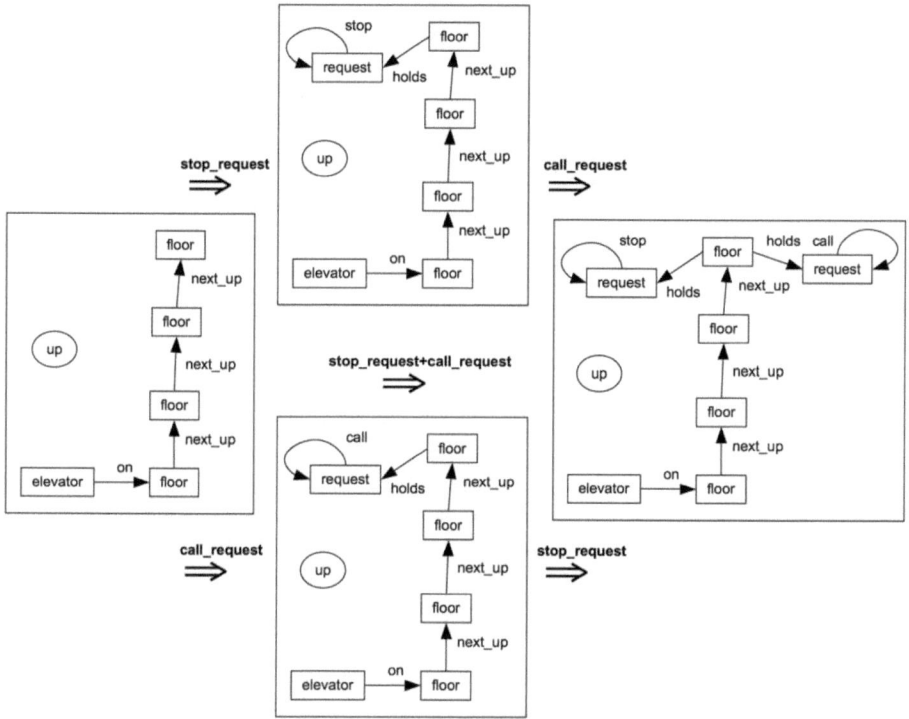

Figure 2.22: parallel and sequentially independent transformations for *Elevator*

Now we can generalize the notion of parallelism to graph transformation systems with NACs. Recall that in Def. 2.3.19, a construction is given to shift NACs on some graph A to a set of equivalent NACs on some graph B via some morphism $m : A \to B$. Moreover, recall that in Def. 2.3.10, it is explained how to construct an equivalent set of left NACs from a set of right NACs on a rule. In the following definition, we use these constructions to define a set of NACs on the parallel rule $p_1 + p_2$.

2.4.5 Definition (parallel rule and transformation with NAC). Given two rules $p_1 = (L_1 \xleftarrow{l_1} K_1 \xrightarrow{r_1} R_1)$ with NAC_{p_1} and $p_2 = (L_2 \xleftarrow{l_2} K_2 \xrightarrow{r_2} R_2)$ with NAC_{p_2}, the *parallel rule* $p_1 + p_2$ with $NAC_{p_1+p_2}$ is defined by the disjoint union of the corresponding graphs and morphisms: $p_1 + p_2 = (L_1 + L_2 \xleftarrow{l_1+l_2} K_1 + K_2 \xrightarrow{r_1+r_2} R_1 + R_2)$ and $NAC_{p_1+p_2} = D_{i_1}(NAC_{p_1}) \cup D_{i_2}(NAC_{p_2}) \cup$

$L_{p_{1,2fix}}(D_{i'_2}(NAC_{p_2})) \cup L_{p_{1fix,2}}(D_{i'_1}(NAC_{p_1}))$ with $p_{1,2fix} = L_1 + L_2 \leftarrow K_1 + L_2 \rightarrow R_1 + L_2$ and $p_{1fix,2} = L_1 + L_2 \leftarrow L_1 + K_2 \rightarrow L_1 + R_2$.

$$\begin{array}{ccccccc}
L_1 & \xleftarrow{l_1} & K_1 & \xrightarrow{r_1} & R_1 & & L_2 \\
{\scriptstyle i_1}\downarrow & (1) & \downarrow & (2) & \searrow^{i'_2} & & \\
L_1+L_2 & \xleftarrow{l_1+id_{L_2}} & K_1+L_2 & \xrightarrow{r_1+id_{L_2}} & R_1+L_2 & & \\
\end{array}$$

$$\begin{array}{ccccccc}
L_2 & \xleftarrow{l_2} & K_2 & \xrightarrow{r_2} & R_2 & & L_1 \\
{\scriptstyle i_2}\downarrow & (3) & \downarrow & (4) & \searrow^{i'_1} & & \\
L_1+L_2 & \xleftarrow{id_{L_1}+l_2} & L_1+K_2 & \xrightarrow{id_{L_1}+r_2} & L_1+R_2 & & \\
\end{array}$$

A direct transformation $G \Rightarrow G'$ via $p_1 + p_2$ with $NAC_{p_1+p_2}$ and a match $m : L_1 + L_2 \rightarrow G$ satisfying $NAC_{p_1+p_2}$ is a *direct parallel transformation with NAC* or *parallel transformation with NAC* for short.

The following theorem describes that two sequentially independent transformations with NACs can be synthesized to a parallel transformation with NACs, and – the other way around – that a parallel transformation with NACs can be analyzed to two sequentially independent transformations with NACs.

2.4.6 Theorem (parallelism theorem with NACs). **Synthesis.** *Given a sequentially independent direct transformation sequence with NACs $G \Rightarrow H_1 \Rightarrow G'$ via p_1, m_1 (resp. p_2, m'_2) with NAC_{p_1} (resp. NAC_{p_2}), there is a construction leading to a parallel transformation with NACs $G \Rightarrow G'$ via $[m_1, m_2]$ and the parallel rule $p_1 + p_2$ with $NAC_{p_1+p_2}$, called a* synthesis construction.

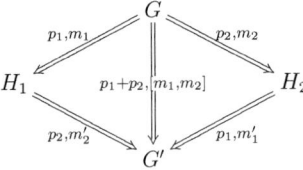

Analysis. *Given a direct parallel transformation with NACs $G \Rightarrow G'$ via $m : L_1 + L_2 \rightarrow G$ and the parallel rule $p_1 + p_2$ with $NAC_{p_1+p_2}$, then there is a construction leading to two sequentially independent transformation sequences with NACs $G \Rightarrow H_1 \Rightarrow G'$ via p_1, m_1 and p_2, m'_2 and $G \Rightarrow H_2 \Rightarrow G'$ via p_2, m_2 and p_1, m'_1, called an* analysis construction.

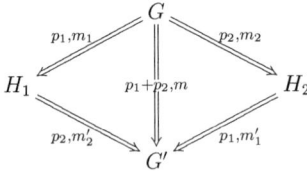

Bijective Correspondence. *The synthesis and analysis construction are inverse to each other up to isomorphism.*

Proof. Follows from Fact 3.2.15 and Theorem 3.4.7 in Chapter 3. □

2.4.7 Remark. Note that in [72], $NAC_{p_1+p_2}$ is defined differently. It contains fewer single NACs as contained in $NAC_{p_1+p_2}$ in Def. 2.4.5. Therefore, the analysis part of the Parallelism Theorem with NACs in [72] needs an extra compatibility condition.

2.4.8 Example (parallel transformation for *Elevator*). Consider the graph $S_{Elevator}$ modeling the initial system state of *Elevator*. Rule *stop_request* (see Fig. 2.6) and rule *call_request* (see Fig. 2.12) can be applied in parallel with non-injective matching to $S_{Elevator}$ resulting in the right graph in Fig. 2.22. The parallel rule *stop_request + call_request* is depicted in the upper row in Fig. 2.23 together with its parallel NAC consisting of four single NACs. The two first (resp. last) NACs in the second row stem from the two single NACs on *stop_request* (resp. *call_request*). Recall that the construction of $D_{i'_2}(NAC_{call\_request})$ is explained in detail in Example 2.3.22.

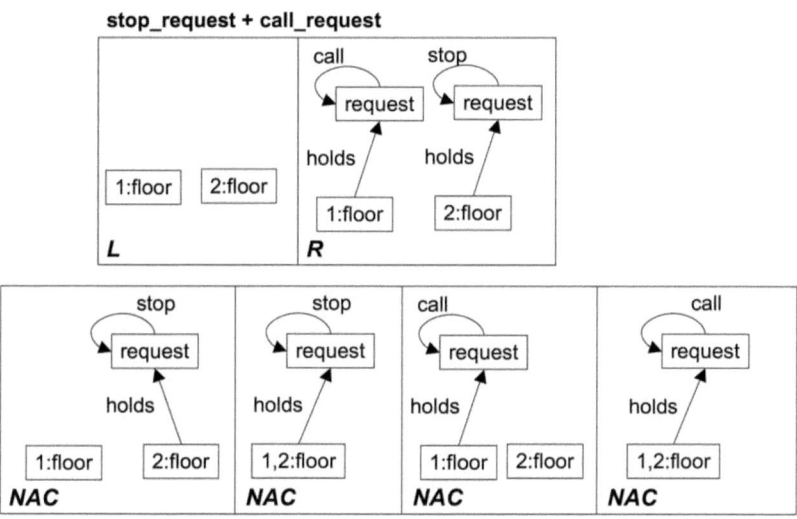

Figure 2.23: parallel rule for *Elevator*

2.5 Concurrency

Let t be a transformation via some rule sequence $p_0, \ldots, p_{n-1}, p_n$ with NACs and matches $g_0, \ldots, g_{n-1}, g_n$. In general, there will be causal dependencies between several direct transformations in this transformation sequence. Therefore, it is not possible to apply the Parallelism Theorem in order to summarize the transformation sequence successively into one equivalent transformation step. It is possible however, to formulate a Concurrency Theorem expressing how to summarize such a sequence into one equivalent transformation step anyway via some induced concurrent rule. The other way around: it is possible to split up a transformation via such a concurrent rule into a sequence via single rules. In order to develop the corresponding theory, we build on the notion of concurrent rules without NACs as introduced in [29]. Moreover, we have to shift all the NACs occurring in the rule sequence $p_0, \ldots, p_{n-1}, p_n$ backward into an equivalent set of NACs on the concurrent rule p_c of this rule sequence. This means that we are looking for a set NAC_{p_c} for the concurrent rule p_c such that NAC_{p_c} is equivalent to $NAC_{p_0}, \ldots, NAC_{p_{n-1}}, NAC_{p_n}$ for the transformation rules in t. This section describes gradually how to obtain this concurrent NAC, and then generalizes the Concurrency Theorem to transformations with NACs.

At first, we define how concurrent rules for rule sequences without NACs can be constructed. This definition corresponds to the definition of concurrent rules in [29]. We generalize this definition however, to rule sequences containing more than two rules. Then we reintroduce the Concurrency Theorem for transformations without NACs, and thereby, define what a concurrent rule *induced by* a transformation t is[3]. After that, we also introduce concurrent rules with NACs for rule sequences with NACs. This definition is based on a shifting operation of all NACs on the rules in a rule sequence to an equivalent set of NACs on its concurrent rule. Finally, a Concurrency Theorem for transformations with NACs is formulated.

First we reintroduce how to construct a pair factorization of morphisms with the same codomain into a pair of jointly surjective morphisms and an injective morphism (see also Remark 5.26 in [29]).

2.5.1 Construction (pair factorization). Given a pair of morphisms $f_1 : A_1 \to C$ and $f_2 : A_2 \to C$ with the same codomain, then a pair factorization of (f_1, f_2) consists of a pair of jointly surjective morphisms $e_1 : A_1 \to K$ and $e_2 : A_2 \to K$ and an injective morphism $m : K \to C$ constructed as follows: Consider the disjoint union $A_1 + A_2$ of A_1 and A_2 and the induced morphism $f : A_1 + A_2$ into C. Construct an epi-mono factorization of f with $m \circ e = f$, $m : K \to C$ and $e : A_1 + A_2 \to K$. Now $e_1 = e \circ \tau_1$ and $e_2 = e \circ \tau_2$ with τ_1 and τ_2 the injections of A_1 (resp. A_2) into $A_1 + A_2$.

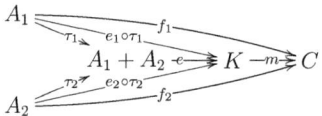

2.5.2 Definition (concurrent rule for a rule sequence).

$n = 0$ The *concurrent rule* p_c for rule p_0 is p_c itself.

$n \geq 1$ A *concurrent rule* p_c for the rule sequence $p_0, \ldots p_n$ is defined by $p_c = (L_c \overset{l \circ k'_c}{\leftarrow} K \overset{r \circ k_n}{\to} R)$ as shown in the following diagram, where $p'_c : L'_c \leftarrow K'_c \to R'_c$ is a concurrent rule for the rule sequence $p_0, \ldots p_{n-1}$, (e'_c, e_n) jointly surjective, (1),(2), (3) and (4) are pushouts and

---

[3]Note that in comparison to [29] we do not demand explicitly for a transformation to be E-related. Each transformation t for some graph transformation system with NACs is automatically E-related since in the category **Graphs**$_{TG}$ a unique pair factorization into jointly surjective and injective morphisms exists, and the $\mathcal{M} - \mathcal{M}'$ PO-PB decomposition property ($\mathcal{M} = \mathcal{M}'$ =injective graph morphisms) holds (this follows directly from Fact 5.29 in [29]).

(5) is a pullback. We denote the concurrent rule p_c also as $p'_c *_E p_n$.

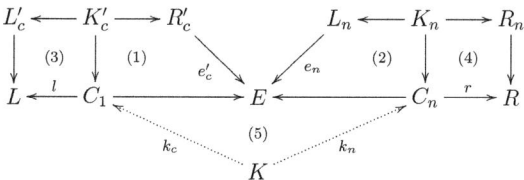

2.5.3 Remark. Since pullbacks, pushouts and pushout complements are unique in the category **Graphs**$_{TG}$ [29], a concurrent rule for $n \geq 1$ is uniquely determined by its E-dependency relations (e'_c, e_n) as defined in [29].

2.5.4 Definition (concurrent rule, concurrent (co-, lhs-)match *induced by* $G_0 \stackrel{n+1}{\Longrightarrow} G_{n+1}$).

$n = 0$ For a direct transformation $G_0 \Rightarrow G_1$ via match $g_0 : L_0 \to G_0$, comatch $g_1 : R_1 \to G_1$, and rule $p_0 : L_0 \leftarrow K_0 \to R_0$, the *concurrent rule* p_c for p_0 induced by $G_0 \Rightarrow G_1$ is defined by $p_c = p_0$, the *concurrent comatch* h_c is defined by $h_c = g_1$, the *concurrent lhs-match* by $id : L_0 \to L_0$, and the *concurrent match* g_c by $g_c = g_0 : L_0 \to G_0$.

$n \geq 1$ Consider $p'_c : L'_c \leftarrow K'_c \to R'_c$ (resp. $g'_c : L'_c \to G_0$, $h'_c : R'_c \to G_n$, $m'_c : L_0 \to L'_c$), the concurrent rule (resp. concurrent match, comatch, lhs-match) for $p_0, \ldots, p_{n-1}$ induced by $G_0 \stackrel{n}{\Rightarrow} G_n$. Let $((e'_c, e_n), h)$ be the pair factorization of the comatch h'_c and match g_n of $G_n \Rightarrow G_{n+1}$. Then the following diagram can be constructed (see explanation in Remark 2.5.5), where (1) is a pullback and all other squares are pushouts:

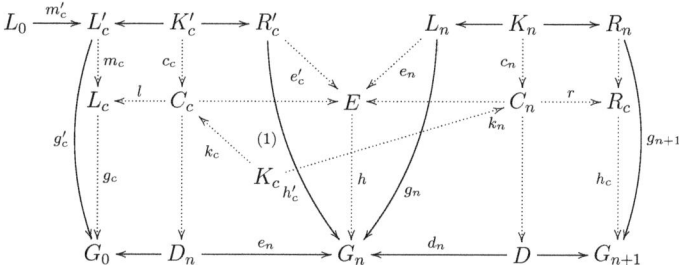

For a transformation sequence $G_0 \stackrel{n+1}{\Longrightarrow} G_{n+1}$, the *concurrent rule* p_c (resp. concurrent match, comatch, lhs-match) for $p_0, \ldots, p_n$ induced by $G_0 \stackrel{n+1}{\Longrightarrow} G_{n+1}$ is defined by $p_c = L_c \stackrel{l \circ k_c}{\leftarrow} K_c \stackrel{r \circ k_n}{\to} R_c$ ($g_c : L_c \to G_0$, $h_c : R_c \to G_{n+1}$, $m_c \circ m'_c : L_0 \to L_c$).

2.5.5 Remark. The second and third square in the lower row of the above diagram can be constructed as PBs via h and e_n (resp. h and d_n). Because of the universal property of PBs, the morphisms c_c and c_n can be constructed such that the second and third square in the upper row commute. Because of PO-PB decomposition, it follows that the second and third square in the upper and lower row are POs. Now the first square and last square in the upper row can be constructed as POs. Because of the universal property of POs, then also the first and last square of the second row can be constructed such that they commute. Because of PO decomposition, then also the first and last square of the lower row are POs. Finally, (1)

CHAPTER 2. RULE-BASED MODELING USING GRAPH TRANSFORMATION

can be constructed as a PB. Note that the concurrent rule induced by some transformation t is uniquely determined because of the uniqueness of the pair factorization as presented in Construction 2.5.1, PBs, and POs, and the universal property of PBs and POs.

2.5.6 Theorem (concurrency theorem without NACs).

1. *Synthesis. Given a transformation sequence* $t : G_0 \overset{*}{\Rightarrow} G_{n+1}$ *via a sequence of rules* $p_0, p_1, \ldots, p_n$, *then there is a* synthesis construction *leading to a direct transformation* $G_0 \Rightarrow G_{n+1}$ *via the induced concurrent rule* $p_c : L_c \leftarrow K_c \to R_c$, *match* $g_c : L_c \to G_0$ *and comatch* $h_c : R_c \to G_{n+1}$ *induced by* $t : G_0 \overset{*}{\Rightarrow} G_{n+1}$.

2. *Analysis. Given a direct transformation* $G_0 \Rightarrow G_{n+1}$ *via some concurrent rule* $p_c : L_c \leftarrow K_c \to R_c$ *of rules* $p_0, p_1, \ldots, p_n$, *then there is an* analysis construction *leading to a transformation sequence* $t : G_0 \overset{*}{\Rightarrow} G_{n+1}$ *via* $p_0, p_1, \ldots, p_n$.

Proof. Follows from Fact 3.2.15 and Theorem 3.5.5 in Chapter 3. □

Now we present a construction that we use to shift a set of NACs on some rule occurring in a transformation t to a set of equivalent NACs on the concurrent rule induced by t. Recall that in Def. 2.3.19, a construction is already given to shift NACs on some graph A into a set of equivalent NACs on some graph B over some morphism $m : A \to B$. Moreover, recall that in Def. 2.3.10, it is explained how to construct an equivalent set of left NACs from a set of right NACs on a rule. A combination of these constructions leads to a construction of a set of equivalent NACs on the LHS of a concurrent rule for a rule sequence from the set of NACs on each rule in this sequence.

2.5.7 Definition (concurrent rule with NACs for a rule sequence).

$n = 0$ The *concurrent rule* p_c *with NACs* for rule p_0 with NACs is p_0 with NACs itself.

$n \geq 1$ A *concurrent rule* $p_c = p'_c *_E p_n$ *with NACs* for the rule sequence $p_0, \ldots p_n$ with NACs is defined recursively as in Def. 2.5.2 and equals $p_c = (L_c \overset{lok_c}{\leftarrow} K \overset{rok_n}{\to} R)$ as shown in the following diagram in which (1)-(4) are POs and (5) is a PB

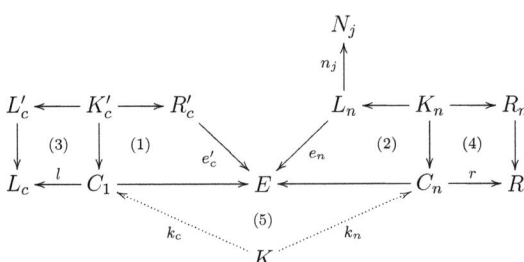

with $NAC_{p_c} = DL_{p_c}(NAC_{L_n}) \cup D_{m_c}(NAC_{L'_c})$ with D_{m_c} according to Def. 2.3.19 and $DL_{p_c}(NAC_{L_n})$ with $NAC_{L_n} = \{NAC(n_j) | j \in J\}$ constructed as follows:

$$DL_{p_c}(NAC_{L_n}) = \cup_{j \in J} DL_{p_c}(NAC(n_j)) = \cup_{j \in J} L_p(D_{e_n}(NAC(n_j)))$$

with $p : L_c \leftarrow C_1 \to E$ and D_{e_n} (resp. L_p) according to Def. 2.3.19 (resp. Def. 2.3.10).

2.5. CONCURRENCY

2.5.8 Definition (concurrent rule with NAC induced by $G_0 \overset{n+1}{\Longrightarrow} G_{n+1}$).

$n = 0$ For a direct transformation $G_0 \Rightarrow G_1$ via match $g_0 : L_0 \to G_0$, comatch $g_1 : R_1 \to G_1$, and rule $p_0 : L_0 \leftarrow K_0 \to R_0$ with NAC_{p_0} the *concurrent rule p_c with NAC induced by* $G_0 \Rightarrow G_1$ is defined by $p_c = p_0$ with $NAC_{p_c} = NAC_{p_0}$, the *concurrent comatch h_c* is defined by $h_c = g_1$, the *concurrent lhs-match* by $id : L_0 \to L_0$, and the *concurrent match g_c* by $g_c = g_0 : L_0 \to G_0$.

$n \geq 1$ Consider $p'_c : L'_c \leftarrow K'_c \to R'_c$ (resp. $g'_c : L'_c \to G_0$, $h'_c : R'_c \to G_n, m'_c : L_0 \to L'_c$), the concurrent rule with NACs (resp. concurrent match, comatch, lhs-match) induced by $G_0 \overset{n}{\Rightarrow} G_n$. For a transformation sequence $G_0 \overset{n+1}{\Longrightarrow} G_{n+1}$ the *concurrent rule p_c with NACs* (resp. concurrent match, comatch, lhs-match) induced by $G_0 \overset{n+1}{\Longrightarrow} G_{n+1}$ is defined by $p_c = L_c \leftarrow K_c \to R_c$ ($g_c : L_c \to G_0$, $h_c : R_c \to G_{n+1}$, $m_c \circ m'_c : L_0 \to L_c$) the induced concurrent rule p_c (resp. concurrent match, comatch, lhs-match) as defined in Def. 2.5.4 for transformations without NACs. Thereby, NAC_{p_c} is defined by $NAC_{p_c} = DL_{p_c}(NAC_{L_n}) \cup D_{m_c}(NAC_{L'_c})$.

2.5.9 Theorem (concurrency theorem with NACs).

1. *Synthesis.* Given a transformation sequence $t : G_0 \overset{*}{\Longrightarrow} G_{n+1}$ via a sequence of rules $p_0, p_1, \ldots, p_n$, then there is a synthesis construction leading to a direct transformation $G_0 \Rightarrow G_{n+1}$ via the concurrent rule $p_c : L_c \leftarrow K_c \to R_c$ with NAC_{p_c}, match $g_c : L_c \to G_0$ and comatch $h_c : R_c \to G_{n+1}$ induced by $t : G_0 \overset{*}{\Longrightarrow} G_{n+1}$.

2. *Analysis.* Given a direct transformation $G_0 \Rightarrow G_{n+1}$ via some concurrent rule $p_c : L_c \leftarrow K_c \to R_c$ with NAC_{p_c} for a sequence of rules $p_0, p_1, \ldots, p_n$, then there is an analysis construction leading to a transformation sequence $t : G_0 \overset{*}{\Longrightarrow} G_{n+1}$ with NACs via $p_0, p_1, \ldots, p_n$.

Proof. Follows from Fact 3.2.15 and Theorem 3.5.8 in Chapter 3. □

2.5.10 Example (concurrent transformation for *Elevator*). In Fig. 2.24, the concurrent rule is shown induced by the first three direct steps starting from $S_{Elevator}$ of the transformation in Fig. 2.20 as described in Example 2.3.16. In this transformation a stop request is recorded on the upper floor, then a call request is recorded on the third floor, and afterwards the elevator car moves one floor upward. On the first row in Fig. 2.24, the concurrent rule induced by this transformation is shown, summarizing into one rule the pre- and postcondition of what happened during this transformation. The first NAC on the second row in Fig. 2.24 stems from rule *stop_request*, as presented in Fig. 2.6. Analogously, the second NAC stems from rule *call_request*, as presented in Fig. 2.12. The first NAC on the third row, forbidding a stop request on the ground floor, stems from rule *move_up*, as presented in Fig. 2.7. The second NAC on the third row corresponds to the shifted NAC *no_stop_request_glue* leading to a non-injective NAC. Note that not all NACs of the concurrent rule are shown. Shifting NACs over a morphism leads to more NACs gluing in all possible ways the floors in the NACs depicted in Fig. 2.24. This procedure was explained already in Example 2.3.22. Note that for the construction of the complete set of NACs only the gluing of floors $(1,3), (2,4), (3,4), (2,3)$, and $(3,2,4)$ should be considered. Other kinds of gluing can be omitted since they would lead to graph structures that never occur anyway in *Elevator* (for example, floor 1 and 2 cannot be mapped to the same floor since there is an edge of type *next_up* in between). Because of similar reasons, it is

CHAPTER 2. RULE-BASED MODELING USING GRAPH TRANSFORMATION

possible to omit NACs in which in addition a call request is glued with a stop request. This has already been explained in more detail in Example 2.3.22. Finally, note that assuming rules operating with *injective matching* only the construction of concurrent NACs becomes more straightforward since each non-injective NAC can be omitted as stated in Corollary 2.3.21.

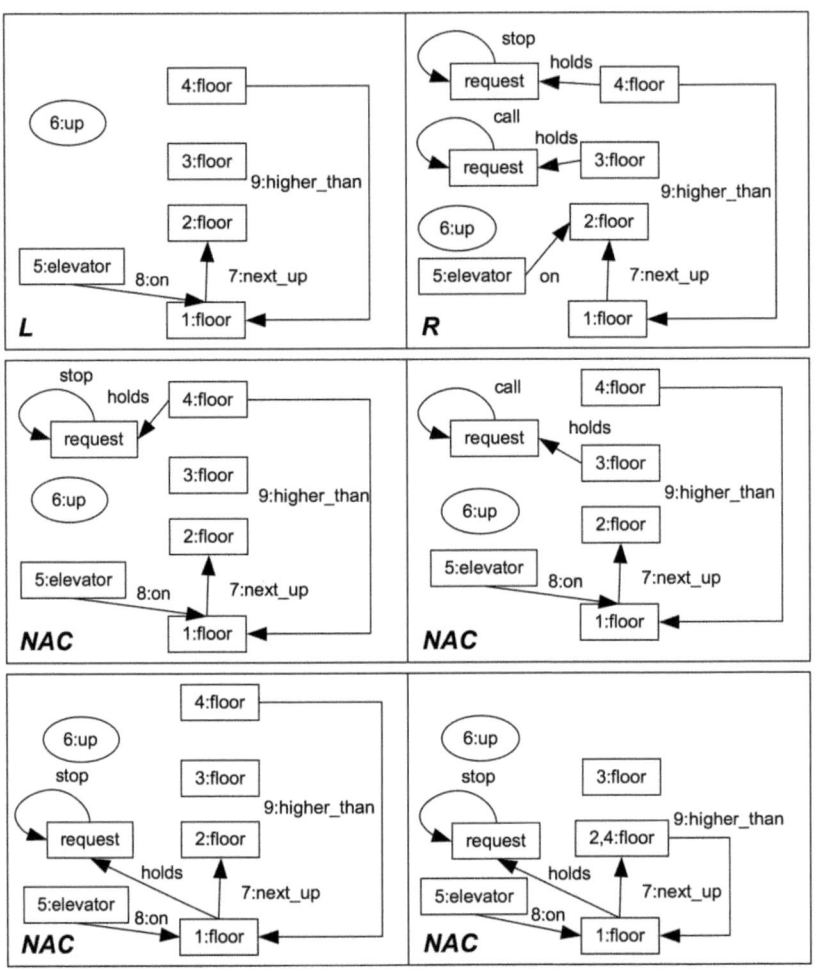

Figure 2.24: concurrent rule *stop_request* ∗ *call_request* ∗ *move_up* induced by the first three direct steps starting from $S_{Elevator}$ of the transformation in Fig. 2.20 for *Elevator*

Finally, we can characterize the notion of parallelism for rules and transformations, as given in Def. 2.4.5, by describing it by means of concurrency as in the following theorem.

2.5.11 Theorem (characterization of parallelism via concurrency). *A direct parallel transformation with NACs $G \Rightarrow G'$ via $m : L_1 + L_2 \to G$ and the parallel rule $p_1 + p_2$ with $NAC_{p_1+p_2}$ exist if and only if $G \Rightarrow G'$ is a direct transformation with NACs via $m : L_1 + L_2 \to G$ and the*

2.6. CONFLICTS AND CAUSAL DEPENDENCIES FOR TRANSFORMATIONS

concurrent rule $p_1 *_{R_1+L_2} p_2$ with $NAC_{p_1*_{R_1+L_2}p_2}$ and $G \Rightarrow G'$ is a direct transformation with NACs via $m : L_1 + L_2 \to G$ and the concurrent rule $p_2 *_{R_2+L_1} p_1$ with $NAC_{p_2*_{R_2+L_1}p_1}$.

Proof. Follows from Fact 3.2.15 and Theorem 3.5.9 in Chapter 3. □

2.6 Conflicts and Causal Dependencies for Transformations

Two graph transformations are not always parallel or sequentially independent. In this section, we explain what it means for two direct transformations to be in conflict (resp. to depend on each other), i.e. not being parallel independent (resp. not being sequentially independent).

2.6.1 Definition (conflict). Two direct transformations $G \overset{p_1,m_1}{\Longrightarrow} H_1$ with NAC_{p_1} and $G \overset{p_2,m_2}{\Longrightarrow} H_2$ with NAC_{p_2} are *in conflict* if they are not parallel independent, i.e. if

$$\nexists h_{12} : L_1 \to D_2 \text{ s.t. } (d_2 \circ h_{12} = m_1 \text{ and } e_2 \circ h_{12} \models NAC_{p_1})$$

or

$$\nexists h_{21} : L_2 \to D_1 \text{ s.t. } (d_1 \circ h_{21} = m_2 \text{ and } e_1 \circ h_{21} \models NAC_{p_2}).$$

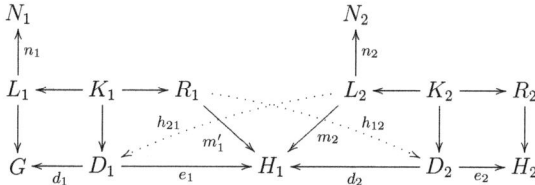

2.6.2 Definition (causal dependency). Consider a sequence of two direct transformations $G \overset{p_1,m_1}{\Longrightarrow} H_1 \overset{p_2,m_2}{\Longrightarrow} H_2$ with NAC_{p_1} and NAC_{p_2}. These transformations are *causally dependent* if they are not sequentially independent, i.e. if

$$\nexists h_{12} : R_1 \to D_2 \text{ s.t. } (d_2 \circ h_{12} = m'_1 \text{ and } e_2 \circ h_{12} \models NAC_{p_1^{-1}})$$

or

$$\nexists h_{21} : L_2 \to D_1 \text{ s.t. } (e_1 \circ h_{21} = m_2 \text{ and } d_1 \circ h_{21} \models NAC_{p_2}).$$

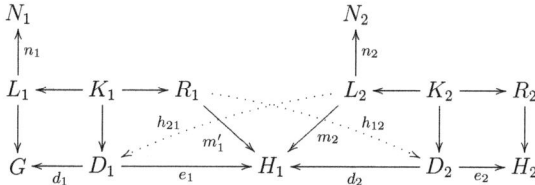

The following lemmata allow an elegant characterization of conflicts and causal dependencies in Theorem 2.6.5 and Theorem 2.6.7. They state that if a morphism exists that potentially leads to parallel or sequential independence of two direct transformations, then it is unique.

2.6.3 Lemma. *Given two direct transformations $G \overset{p_1,m_1}{\Longrightarrow} H_1$ with NAC_{p_1} and $G \overset{p_2,m_2}{\Longrightarrow} H_2$ with NAC_{p_2}, then the following holds:*

CHAPTER 2. RULE-BASED MODELING USING GRAPH TRANSFORMATION

- if $\exists h_{12} : L_1 \to D_2$ s.t. $d_2 \circ h_{12} = m_1$ then h_{12} is unique,

- if $\exists h_{21} : L_2 \to D_1$ s.t. $d_1 \circ h_{21} = m_2$ then h_{21} is unique.

Moreover, if the match morphism m_1 (resp. m_2) is injective, then also h_{12} (resp. h_{21}) is injective.

Proof. Follows from Fact 3.2.15 and Lemma 3.6.3 in Chapter 3. □

2.6.4 Lemma. *Given a sequence of two direct transformations $G \overset{p_1,m_1}{\Longrightarrow} H_1$ with NAC_{p_1} and $H_1 \overset{p_2,m_2}{\Longrightarrow} H_2$ with NAC_{p_2}, then the following holds:*

- if $\exists h_{12} : R_1 \to D_2$ s.t. $d_2 \circ h_{12} = m'_1$ then h_{12} is unique,

- if $\exists h_{21} : L_2 \to D_1$ s.t. $e_1 \circ h_{21} = m_2$ then h_{21} is unique.

Proof. Follows from Fact 3.2.15 and Lemma 3.6.4 in Chapter 3. □

The following conflict characterization describes which types of conflicts may arise between a pair of direct transformations $G \overset{p_1,m_1}{\Longrightarrow} H_1$ and $G \overset{p_2,m_2}{\Longrightarrow} H_2$. In particular, $G \overset{p_1,m_1}{\Longrightarrow} H_1$ causes a so-called delete-use conflict with $G \overset{p_2,m_2}{\Longrightarrow} H_2$ if rule p_1 deletes something that is used by p_2. $G \overset{p_1,m_1}{\Longrightarrow} H_1$ causes a so-called produce-forbid conflict with $G \overset{p_2,m_2}{\Longrightarrow} H_2$ if rule p_1 produces something forbidden by NAC_{p_2} of p_2. Analogously, $G \overset{p_2,m_2}{\Longrightarrow} H_2$ can cause a delete-use conflict (resp. produce-forbid conflict) with $G \overset{p_1,m_1}{\Longrightarrow} H_1$.

2.6.5 Theorem (conflict characterization). *Two direct transformations $G \overset{p_1,m_1}{\Longrightarrow} H_1$ with NAC_{p_1} and $G \overset{p_2,m_2}{\Longrightarrow} H_2$ with NAC_{p_2} are in conflict if and only if at least one of the following assumptions holds:*

1. $\nexists h_{12} : L_1 \to D_2 : d_2 \circ h_{12} = m_1$,

2. *there exists a unique $h_{12} : L_1 \to D_2 : d_2 \circ h_{12} = m_1$, but $e_2 \circ h_{12} \not\models NAC_{p_1}$,*

3. $\nexists h_{21} : L_2 \to D_1 : d_1 \circ h_{21} = m_2$,

4. *there exists a unique $h_{21} : L_2 \to D_1 : d_1 \circ h_{21} = m_2$, but $e_1 \circ h_{21} \not\models NAC_{p_2}$.*

Proof. Follows from Fact 3.2.15 and Theorem 3.6.5 in Chapter 3. □

2.6.6 Definition (conflict characterization). Consider two direct transformations $G \overset{p_1,m_1}{\Longrightarrow} H_1$ with NAC_{p_1} and $G \overset{p_2,m_2}{\Longrightarrow} H_2$ with NAC_{p_2} that are in conflict. If case (1) in Theorem 2.6.5 occurs, we say that $G \overset{p_2,m_2}{\Longrightarrow} H_2$ causes a delete-use conflict with $G \overset{p_1,m_1}{\Longrightarrow} H_1$. If case (2) occurs, we say that $G \overset{p_2,m_2}{\Longrightarrow} H_2$ causes a produce-forbid conflict with $G \overset{p_1,m_1}{\Longrightarrow} H_1$. If cases (1) or (2) occur, we say in general that $G \overset{p_2,m_2}{\Longrightarrow} H_2$ causes a conflict with $G \overset{p_1,m_1}{\Longrightarrow} H_1$. If case (3) occurs, we say that $G \overset{p_1,m_1}{\Longrightarrow} H_1$ causes a delete-use conflict with $G \overset{p_2,m_2}{\Longrightarrow} H_2$. If case (4) occurs, we say that $G \overset{p_1,m_1}{\Longrightarrow} H_1$ causes a produce-forbid conflict with $G \overset{p_2,m_2}{\Longrightarrow} H_2$. If cases (3) or (4) occur, we say in general that $G \overset{p_1,m_1}{\Longrightarrow} H_1$ causes a conflict with $G \overset{p_2,m_2}{\Longrightarrow} H_2$.

Note that case (1) (resp. case (3)) cannot occur simultaneously to case (2) (resp. case (4)) in Theorem 2.6.5, since $1 \Rightarrow \neg 2$ (resp. $3 \Rightarrow \neg 4$). This means that $G \overset{p_2,m_2}{\Longrightarrow} H_2$ (resp. $G \overset{p_1,m_1}{\Longrightarrow} H_1$) can only cause a produce-forbid conflict with $G \overset{p_1,m_1}{\Longrightarrow} H_1$ (resp. $G \overset{p_2,m_2}{\Longrightarrow} H_2$) if it does not cause a delete-use conflict. All other cases can occur simultaneously. This means that $G \overset{p_2,m_2}{\Longrightarrow} H_2$

2.6. CONFLICTS AND CAUSAL DEPENDENCIES FOR TRANSFORMATIONS

can cause a delete-use conflict or produce-forbid conflict with $G \overset{p_1,m_1}{\Longrightarrow} H_1$, and simultaneously $G \overset{p_1,m_1}{\Longrightarrow} H_1$ can cause a delete-use conflict or produce-forbid conflict with $G \overset{p_2,m_2}{\Longrightarrow} H_2$.

The following causal dependency characterization describes which types of causal dependencies may arise between $G \overset{p_1,m_1}{\Longrightarrow} H_1$ and $H_1 \overset{p_2,m_2}{\Longrightarrow} H_2$ in a sequence of two direct transformations. In particular, $G \overset{p_1,m_1}{\Longrightarrow} H_1$ is in a produce-use dependency with $H_1 \overset{p_2,m_2}{\Longrightarrow} H_2$ if rule p_1 produces something that is used by p_2. $G \overset{p_1,m_1}{\Longrightarrow} H_1$ is in a delete-forbid dependency with $H_1 \overset{p_2,m_2}{\Longrightarrow} H_2$ if rule p_1 deletes something forbidden by NAC_{p_2} of p_2. These causal dependencies express that the application of rule p_2 is triggered by the application of rule p_1. Moreover, $G \overset{p_1,m_1}{\Longrightarrow} H_1$ is in a deliver-delete dependency with $H_1 \overset{p_2,m_2}{\Longrightarrow} H_2$ if rule p_1 preserves or produces something that is thereafter deleted by p_2. $G \overset{p_1,m_1}{\Longrightarrow} H_1$ is in a forbid-produce dependency with $H_1 \overset{p_2,m_2}{\Longrightarrow} H_2$ if rule p_2 produces something forbidden by $NAC_{p_1^{-1}}$. These causal dependencies express that the application of p_1 cannot be made irreversible anymore after applying p_2 by applying thereafter p_1^{-1}.

2.6.7 Theorem (dependency characterization). *Given a sequence of two direct transformations $G \overset{p_1,m_1}{\Longrightarrow} H_1 \overset{p_2,m_2}{\Longrightarrow} H_2$ with NAC_{p_1} and NAC_{p_2}, then they are causally dependent if and only if at least one of the following assumptions holds:*

1. $\nexists h_{12} : R_1 \to D_2 : d_2 \circ h_{12} = m_1'$,

2. *there exists a unique $h_{12} : R_1 \to D_2 : d_2 \circ h_{12} = m_1'$, but $e_2 \circ h_{12} \not\models NAC_{p_1^{-1}}$,*

3. $\nexists h_{21} : L_2 \to D_1 : e_1 \circ h_{21} = m_2$,

4. *there exists a unique $h_{21} : L_2 \to D_1 : e_1 \circ h_{21} = m_2$, but $d_1 \circ h_{21} \not\models NAC_{p_2}$.*

Proof. Follows from Fact 3.2.15 and Theorem 3.6.7 in Chapter 3. □

2.6.8 Definition (causal dependency characterization). Consider a sequence of two direct transformations $G \overset{p_1,m_1}{\Longrightarrow} H_1 \overset{p_2,m_2}{\Longrightarrow} H_2$ with NAC_{p_1} and NAC_{p_2} such that $G \overset{p_1,m_1}{\Longrightarrow} H_1$ and $H_1 \overset{p_2,m_2}{\Longrightarrow} H_2$ are causally dependent. If case (1) in Theorem 2.6.7 occurs, we say that $G \overset{p_1,m_1}{\Longrightarrow} H_1$ is in a *deliver-delete dependency* with $H_1 \overset{p_2,m_2}{\Longrightarrow} H_2$. If case (2) occurs, we say that $G \overset{p_1,m_1}{\Longrightarrow} H_1$ is in *forbid-produce dependency* with $H_1 \overset{p_2,m_2}{\Longrightarrow} H_2$. If cases (1) or (2) occur, we say in general that $G \overset{p_1,m_1}{\Longrightarrow} H_1$ is *irreversible after* $H_1 \overset{p_2,m_2}{\Longrightarrow} H_2$. If case (3) occurs, we say that $H_1 \overset{p_2,m_2}{\Longrightarrow} H_2$ is in *produce-use dependency* with $G \overset{p_1,m_1}{\Longrightarrow} H_1$. If case (4) occurs, we say that $H_1 \overset{p_2,m_2}{\Longrightarrow} H_2$ is in *delete-forbid dependency* with $G \overset{p_1,m_1}{\Longrightarrow} H_1$. If cases (3) or (4) occur, we say in general that $H_1 \overset{p_2,m_2}{\Longrightarrow} H_2$ *is triggered by* $G \overset{p_1,m_1}{\Longrightarrow} H_1$.

Note that analogous to the conflict cases, case (1) (resp. case (3)) cannot occur simultaneously to case (2) (resp. case (4)) in Theorem 2.6.7. This means that $G \overset{p_1,m_1}{\Longrightarrow} H_1$ can only be in forbid-produce dependency (resp. delete-forbid dependency) with $H_1 \overset{p_2,m_2}{\Longrightarrow} H_2$ if it is not in deliver-delete dependency (resp. produce-use dependency). All other cases can occur simultaneously. This means that $G \overset{p_1,m_1}{\Longrightarrow} H_1$ can be irreversible after $H_1 \overset{p_2,m_2}{\Longrightarrow} H_2$ and simultaneously $H_1 \overset{p_2,m_2}{\Longrightarrow} H_2$ can be triggered by $G \overset{p_1,m_1}{\Longrightarrow} H_1$.

2.6.9 Example (conflicts and causal dependencies for *Elevator*). Consider Fig. 2.25 depicting a conflict for *Elevator*. Note that we omit showing edges of type *higher_than* since they would blow up the figure. A graph G is given, modeling the situation that the elevator is on the first floor, set in downward direction, and with a request on the upper floor. On the one hand, the elevator can be set in upward mode by applying rule *set_direction_up*. On the other hand, an external call request can be recorded for the ground floor by applying rule *call_request*. In this case, $G \Rightarrow H_2$ via rule *call_request* causes a produce-forbid conflict with $G \Rightarrow H_1$ via *set_direction_up*. This is because rule *call_request* has generated a request that is forbidden by NAC *no_lower_request* of rule *set_direction_up*. Consider Fig. 2.26 depicting another conflict

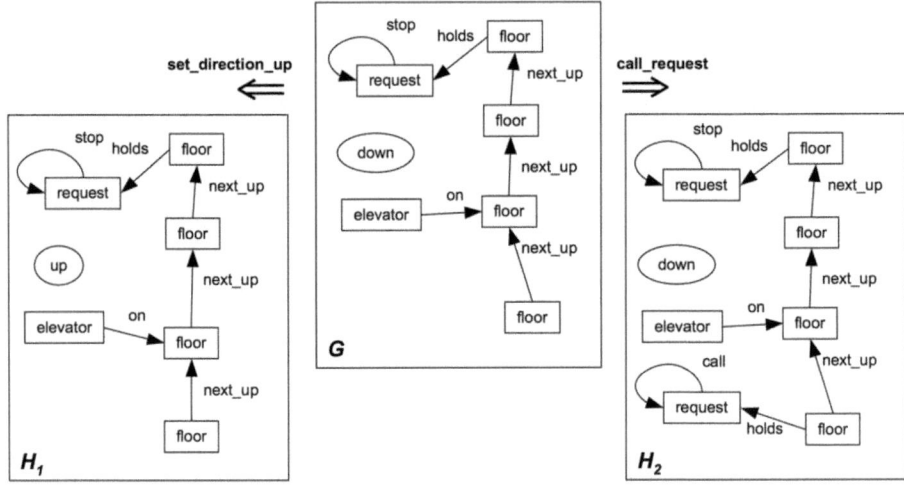

Figure 2.25: produce-forbid conflict for *Elevator*

for *Elevator*. Here, a graph G is given, modeling that the elevator is on the second floor in downward mode with a stop request and a call request on the second floor and a call request on the first floor. On the one hand, the call request on the second floor can be processed by applying rule *process_call_down*. On the other hand, both the call and stop request on the second floor can be processed by applying rule *process_stop_and_call*. In this case, $G \Rightarrow H_1$ via rule *process_call_down* causes a delete-use conflict with $G \Rightarrow H_2$ via *process_stop_and_call* and the other way round. This is because rule *process_call_down* deletes a call request that is still used (in order to delete) by *process_stop_and_call*. The other way round, rule *process_stop_and_call* deletes a call and stop request from which the call request is still used (in order to delete) by *process_call*.

Consider Fig. 2.27 depicting a causal dependency for *Elevator*. A graph G is given, modeling the initial state of *Elevator*. After a stop request is recorded for the upper floor by applying rule *stop_request*, the elevator starts moving upward by applying rule *move_up*. In this case, $G \Rightarrow H_1$ is in produce-use dependency with $H_1 \Rightarrow H_2$. This is because rule *stop_request* generates a request on an upper floor that is used by rule *move_up*. We also say that $H_1 \Rightarrow H_2$ is triggered by $G \Rightarrow H_1$. Consider Fig. 2.28 depicting another causal dependency for *Elevator*. Here, a graph G is given, modeling that the elevator is on the first floor in upward direction holding a stop request, and in addition the upper floor is holding a stop request. After the stop request is processed for the first floor by applying rule *process_stop_up*, the elevator continues moving upward by applying rule *move_up*. In this case, $G \Rightarrow H_1$ is in delete-forbid dependency with $H_1 \Rightarrow H_2$. This is because rule *process_stop_up* deletes the stop request that

2.6. CONFLICTS AND CAUSAL DEPENDENCIES FOR TRANSFORMATIONS

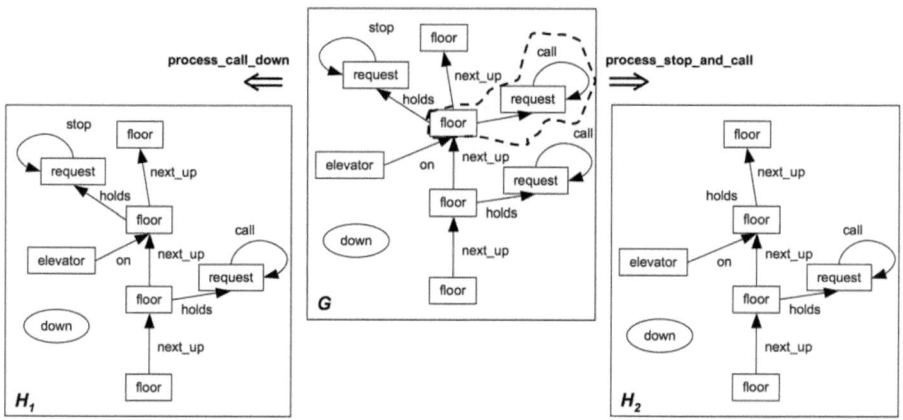

Figure 2.26: delete-use conflict for *Elevator*

is forbidden by rule *move_up*. We also say that $H_1 \Rightarrow H_2$ is triggered by $G \Rightarrow H_1$. Consider Fig. 2.29 depicting another causal dependency for *Elevator*. A graph G is given, modeling that the elevator is on the first floor in downward mode. After a call request is recorded for the first floor by applying rule *call_request*, the request is immediately processed by applying rule *process_call_down*. In this case $G \Rightarrow H_1$ is in deliver-delete dependency with $H_1 \Rightarrow H_2$. This is because rule *process_call_down* deletes on the first floor the call request that is delivered by rule *call_request*. We also say that $G \Rightarrow H_1$ is irreversible after $H_1 \Rightarrow H_2$. In this example the application of *call_request* can no longer be made irreversible because the generated request has already been processed by *process_call_down*. Consider Fig. 2.30 depicting another causal dependency for *Elevator*. A graph G is given, modeling that the elevator is in upward direction on the first floor holding a stop request, and in addition the upper floor is also holding a stop request. After the stop request is processed for the first floor by applying rule *process_stop_up*, a call request is recorded for the first floor by applying rule *call_request*. In this case, $G \Rightarrow H_1$ is in forbid-produce dependency with $H_1 \Rightarrow H_2$. This is because rule *process_stop_up* forbids a call request that is produced by rule *call_request*. We also say that $G \Rightarrow H_1$ is irreversible after $H_1 \Rightarrow H_2$. In this example, the application of *process_stop_up* can no longer be made anymore because rule *call_request* has produced a call request that is forbidden by *process_stop_up*.

In the last part of this section, we give yet another characterization of conflicts and causal dependencies. The following definitions emphasize in a more constructive way the reasons for conflicts and causal dependencies. By means of specific pullback constructions, graphs are distinguished that may constitute the reason for a conflict or causal dependency between transformations. For example, if there exist two transformations on G, then a graph S_1 can be constructed that contains deleted parts of the first transformation and used parts of the second transformation. We restrict ourselves here to characterizing delete-use conflicts, produce-use dependencies and deliver-delete dependencies. It is part of future work to characterize in an analogous way conflicts and causal dependencies caused by NACs in the transformations.

The construction of conflict and causal dependency reasons is based on the construction of initial pushouts over morphisms. Therefore, here we reintroduce their construction (see

CHAPTER 2. RULE-BASED MODELING USING GRAPH TRANSFORMATION

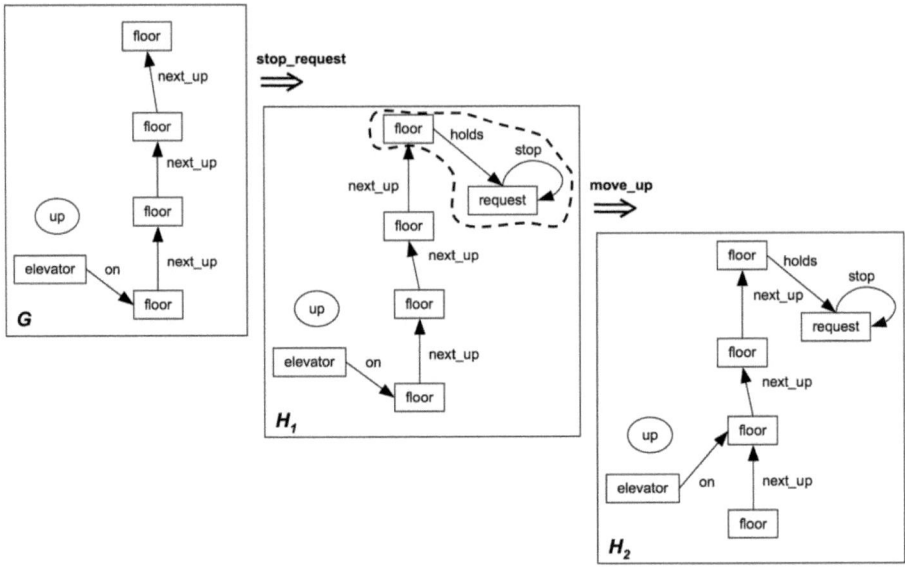

Figure 2.27: produce-use dependency for *Elevator*

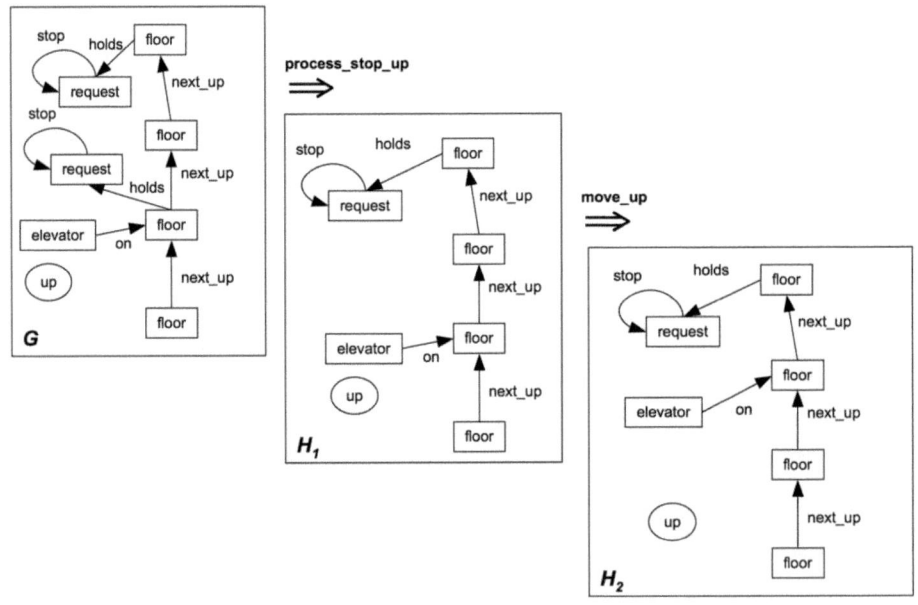

Figure 2.28: delete-forbid dependency for *Elevator*

2.6. CONFLICTS AND CAUSAL DEPENDENCIES FOR TRANSFORMATIONS

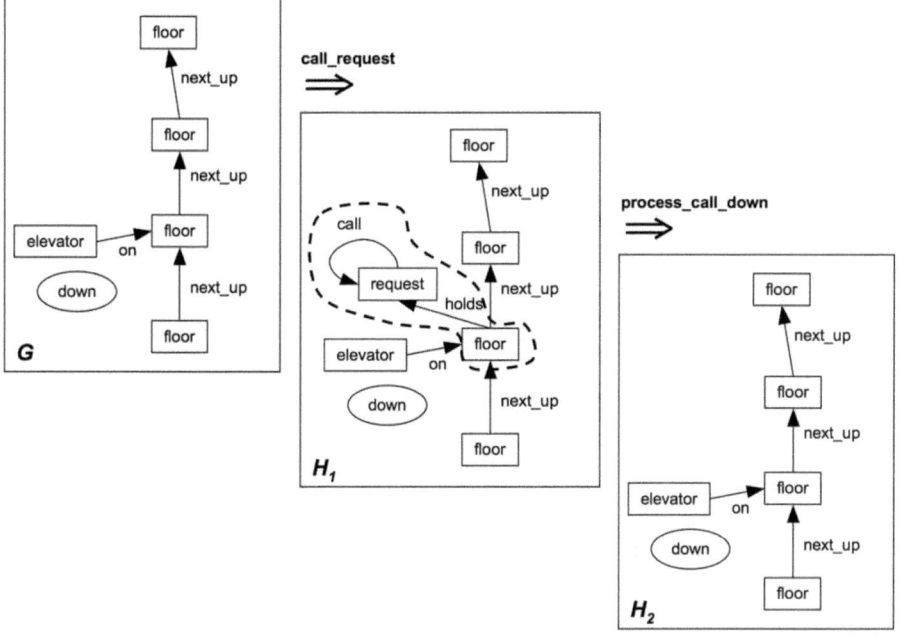

Figure 2.29: deliver-delete dependency for *Elevator*

Example 6.2 in [29]). Initial pushouts over morphisms are constructed by means of boundary and context graphs. The boundary graph of a morphism f contains all nodes and edges that are glued by f, and all nodes to which edges are added by f. Roughly speaking, the initial pushout expresses that the codomain of f is the gluing of the domain of f and some context graph of f along the boundary graph.

2.6.10 Construction (initial pushout, boundary, context). Consider an injective graph morphism $f : A \to A'$. The boundary graph B of f consists of all nodes $a \in A$ such that $f(a)$ is adjacent to an edge in $A' \setminus f(A)$. The context graph C of f is equal to $A' \setminus f(A) \cup f(b(B))$. Then A' is a gluing of A and C via B such that (1) is an initial pushout over f. If the given graph morphism f is not injective, we have to add to the boundary object B all nodes and edges $x, y \in A$ with $f(x) = f(y)$, and those nodes that are the source or target of two edges that are equally mapped by f.

$$\begin{array}{ccc} B & \xrightarrow{b} & A \\ \downarrow & (1) & \downarrow \\ C & \xrightarrow{c} & A' \end{array}$$

In addition, we need pullbacks of graph morphisms that are constructed componentwise in **Sets**. The construction idea of a conflict (resp. dependency) reason is the following: By means of the initial pushout of the LHS-morphism of a rule (resp. RHS-morphism of a rule) we concentrate on the parts that are actually deleted (resp. produced) by a rule. Then the conflict

CHAPTER 2. RULE-BASED MODELING USING GRAPH TRANSFORMATION

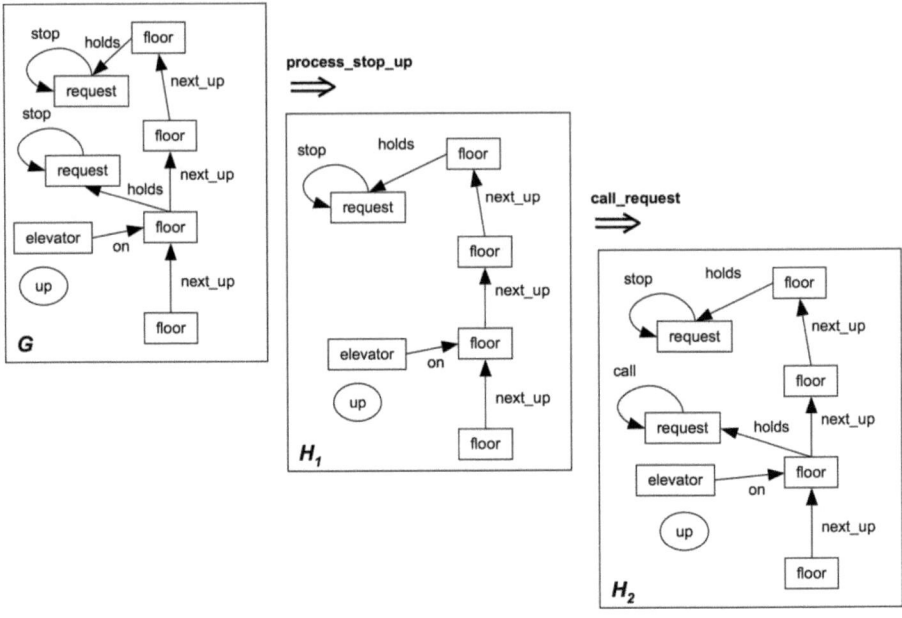

Figure 2.30: forbid-produce dependency for *Elevator*

reason can be constructed by building a specific pullback zooming in on the deleted parts of one rule and used parts of the other rule. Analogous to causal dependencies, the reason can be constructed by building a specific pullback zooming in on produced (resp. delivered) parts of one rule and used (resp. deleted) parts of the other rule.

2.6.11 Definition (conflict reason). Given a pair of direct transformations $H_1 \overset{p_1,m_1}{\Leftarrow} G \overset{p_2,m_2}{\Rightarrow} H_2$ with $p_1 : L_1 \overset{l_1}{\leftarrow} K_1 \overset{r_1}{\rightarrow} R_1$ (resp. $p_2 : L_2 \overset{l_2}{\leftarrow} K_2 \overset{r_2}{\rightarrow} R_2$) and (2_1) (resp. (2_2)) the initial pushout over l_1 (resp. l_2), then

- if $(S_1, o_1 : S_1 \to C_1, q_{12} : S_1 \to L_2)$ is the pullback of $(m_1 \circ g_1, m_2)$, and if $\not\exists s_1 : S_1 \to B_1$ injective such that $c_1 \circ s_1 = o_1$, then $(S_1, g_1 \circ o_1, q_{12})$ is called a *conflict reason* for $H_1 \overset{p_1,m_1}{\Leftarrow} G \overset{p_2,m_2}{\Rightarrow} H_2$.

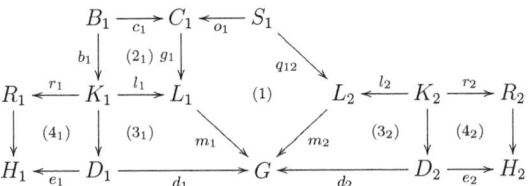

- if $(S_2, q_{21} : S_2 \to L_1, o_2 : S_2 \to C_2)$ is the pullback of $(m_1, m_2 \circ g_2)$, and if $\not\exists s_2 : S_2 \to B_2$ injective such that $c_2 \circ s_2 = o_2$, then $(S_2, q_{21}, g_2 \circ o_2)$ is called a *conflict reason* for $H_1 \overset{p_1,m_1}{\Leftarrow}$

2.6. CONFLICTS AND CAUSAL DEPENDENCIES FOR TRANSFORMATIONS

$G \overset{p_2,m_2}{\Rightarrow} H_2$.

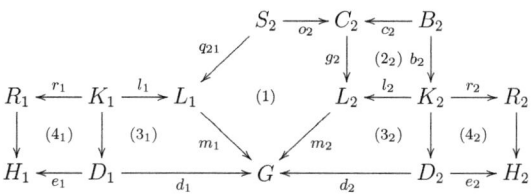

2.6.12 Definition (causal dependency reason). Given a sequence of two direct transformations $G \overset{p_1,m_1}{\Rightarrow} H_1 \overset{p_2,m_2}{\Rightarrow} H_2$ with $p_1 : L_1 \overset{l_1}{\leftarrow} K_1 \overset{r_1}{\rightarrow} R_1$ (resp. $p_2 : L_2 \overset{l_2}{\leftarrow} K_2 \overset{r_2}{\rightarrow} R_2$) and (2_1) (resp. (2_2)) the initial pushout over r_1 (resp. l_2), then

- if $(S_1, o_1 : S_1 \to C_1, q_{12} : S_1 \to L_2)$ is the pullback of $(m'_1 \circ g_1, m_2)$, and if: $\nexists s_1 : S_1 \to B_1$ injective such that $c_1 \circ s_1 = o_1$, then $(S_1, g_1 \circ o_1, q_{12})$ is called a *causal dependency reason* for $G \overset{p_1,m_1}{\Rightarrow} H_1 \overset{p_2,m_2}{\Rightarrow} H_2$.

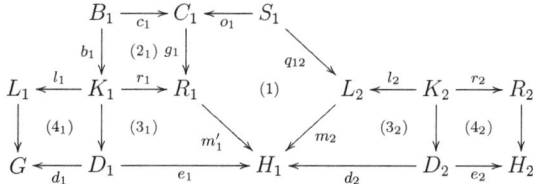

- if $(S_2, q_{21} : S_2 \to L_1, o_2 : S_2 \to C_2)$ is the pullback of $(m'_1, m_2 \circ g_2)$, and if $\nexists s_2 : S_2 \to B_2$ injective such that $c_2 \circ s_2 = o_2$, then $(S_2, q_{21}, g_2 \circ o_2)$ is called a *causal dependency reason* for $G \overset{p_1,m_1}{\Rightarrow} H_1 \overset{p_2,m_2}{\Rightarrow} H_2$.

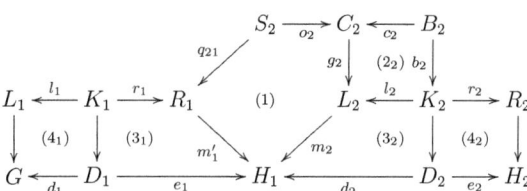

The following theorems now state that a conflict (resp. causal dependency) occurs between transformations if and only if a corresponding conflict reason (resp. causal dependency reason) exists.

2.6.13 Theorem (conflict characterization with reason). *Given a pair of direct transformations $H_1 \overset{p_1,m_1}{\Leftarrow} G \overset{p_2,m_2}{\Rightarrow} H_2$, then the following equivalences hold:*

- $G \overset{p_1,m_1}{\Rightarrow} H_1$ *causes a delete-use conflict with* $G \overset{p_2,m_2}{\Rightarrow} H_2$

$$\Leftrightarrow$$

$(S_1, g_1 \circ o_1, q_{12})$ *as given in Def. 2.6.11 is a conflict reason for* $H_1 \overset{p_1,m_1}{\Leftarrow} G \overset{p_2,m_2}{\Rightarrow} H_2$.

- $G \stackrel{p_2,m_2}{\Longrightarrow} H_2$ causes a delete-use conflict with $G \stackrel{p_1,m_1}{\Longrightarrow} H_1$

$$\Leftrightarrow$$

$(S_2, q_{21}, g_2 \circ o_2)$ as given in Def. 2.6.11 is a conflict reason for $H_1 \stackrel{p_1,m_1}{\Longleftarrow} G \stackrel{p_2,m_2}{\Longrightarrow} H_2$.

Proof. Follows from Fact 3.2.15 and Lemma 3.6.12 in Chapter 3. □

Note that in the first case S_1 represents what is deleted by rule p_1, and used by rule p_2. Thus, S_1 represents the reason for the conflict with $G \stackrel{p_2,m_2}{\Longrightarrow} H_2$ caused by $G \stackrel{p_1,m_1}{\Longrightarrow} H_1$. Analogously, in the second case S_2 represents what is deleted by rule p_2, and used by p_1. Thus, S_2 represents the reason for the conflict with $G \stackrel{p_1,m_1}{\Longrightarrow} H_1$ caused by $G \stackrel{p_2,m_2}{\Longrightarrow} H_2$.

2.6.14 Theorem (causal dependency characterization with reason). *Given a sequence of two direct transformations $G \stackrel{p_1,m_1}{\Longrightarrow} H_1 \stackrel{p_2,m_2}{\Longrightarrow} H_2$, then the following equivalences hold:*

- $G \stackrel{p_1,m_1}{\Longrightarrow} H_1$ is in produce-use dependency with $H_1 \stackrel{p_2,m_2}{\Longrightarrow} H_2$

$$\Leftrightarrow$$

$(S_1, g_1 \circ o_1, q_{12})$ as given in Def. 2.6.12 is a causal dependency reason.

- $G \stackrel{p_1,m_1}{\Longrightarrow} H_1$ is in deliver-delete dependency with $H_1 \stackrel{p_2,m_2}{\Longrightarrow} H_2$

$$\Leftrightarrow$$

$(S_2, q_{21}, g_2 \circ o_2)$ as given in Def. 2.6.12 is a causal dependency reason.

Proof. Follows from Fact 3.2.15 and Lemma 3.6.13 in Chapter 3. □

Note that S_1 represents in case 1 what is produced by rule p_1, and used by rule p_2. Thus, S_1 represents the reason for the triggering of $H_1 \stackrel{p_2,m_2}{\Longrightarrow} H_2$ by $G \stackrel{p_1,m_1}{\Longrightarrow} H_1$. Analogously, S_2 represents in case 2 what is preserved or produced by rule p_1 and deleted by p_2. Thus, S_2 represents the reason for the irreversibility of $G \stackrel{p_1,m_1}{\Longrightarrow} H_1$ after $H_1 \stackrel{p_2,m_2}{\Longrightarrow} H_2$.

2.6.15 Example (conflicts and causal dependency reasons for *Elevator*). Consider Fig. 2.26, where the reason for the delete-use conflict for *Elevator* – as explained in Example 2.6.9 – is surrounded by a thick black dashed line. A call request is deleted and used by both rules. Consider Fig. 2.27, where the reason for the produce-use dependency for *Elevator* – as explained in Example 2.6.9 – is surrounded by a thick black dashed line. The elevator can start moving upward, because a stop request is generated on the highest floor. Consider Fig. 2.29, where the reason for the deliver-delete dependency for *Elevator* – as explained in Example 2.6.9 – is surrounded by a thick black dashed line. A call request is delivered that is deleted immediately afterwards.

2.7 Critical Pairs and Critical Sequences

The conflict (resp. causal dependency) characterization formulated in Theorem 2.6.5 (resp. Theorem 2.6.7) leads to a new critical pair (resp. so-called critical sequence) notion for transformations with NACs. A critical pair (resp. critical sequence) definition is given in this section

2.7. CRITICAL PAIRS AND CRITICAL SEQUENCES

describing a conflict (resp. causal dependency) between two rules in a minimal context. Moreover, it is proven in this section that the new critical pair (resp. sequence) definition satisfies completeness. This means that for each conflict (resp. causal dependency) occurring between two direct transformations with NACs there is a critical pair (resp. sequence) expressing the same conflict (resp. causal dependency) in a minimal context. At the end of this section, it is shown that if there are no critical pairs (resp. sequences) for a given transformation system, then all direct transformations are parallel (resp. sequentially) independent. Such kinds of systems is called conflict-free (resp. dependency-free).

2.7.1 Definition (critical pair). A *critical pair* is a pair of direct transformations $K \overset{p_1,m_1}{\Rightarrow} P_1$ with NAC_{p_1} and $K \overset{p_2,m_2}{\Rightarrow} P_2$ with NAC_{p_2} such that:

1. (a) $\nexists h_{12} : L_1 \to D_2 : d_2 \circ h_{12} = m_1$ and (m_1, m_2) jointly surjective
   (delete-use conflict)
   or
   (b) there exists $h_{12} : L_1 \to D_2$ s.t. $d_2 \circ h_{12} = m_1$, but for one of the NACs $n_1 : L_1 \to N_1$ of p_1 there exists a morphism $q_{12} : N_1 \to P_2$ injective s.t. $q_{12} \circ n_1 = e_2 \circ h_{12}$ and thus, $e_2 \circ h_{12} \not\models NAC_{n_1}$, and (q_{12}, m'_2) jointly surjective (produce-forbid conflict)

or

2. (a) $\nexists h_{21} : L_2 \to D_1 : d_1 \circ h_{21} = m_2$ and (m_1, m_2) jointly surjective
   (delete-use conflict)
   or
   (b) there exists $h_{21} : L_2 \to D_1$ s.t. $d_1 \circ h_{21} = m_2$, but for one of the NACs $n_2 : L_2 \to N_2$ of p_2 there exists an injective morphism $q_{21} : N_2 \to P_1$ s.t. $q_{21} \circ n_2 = e_1 \circ h_{21}$ and thus, $e_1 \circ h_{21} \not\models NAC_{n_2}$, and (q_{21}, m'_1) jointly surjective (produce-forbid conflict)

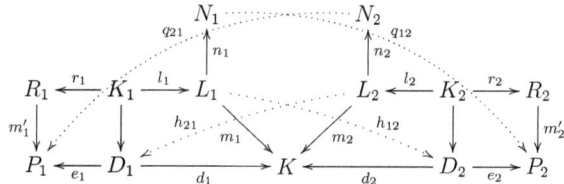

2.7.2 Example (critical pairs for *Elevator*). Consider Fig. 2.31 depicting a critical pair for *Elevator*. $K \overset{call\_request}{\Rightarrow} P_2$ causes a produce-forbid conflict with $K \overset{set\_direction\_up}{\Rightarrow} P_1$ since a call request is produced by rule *call_request* on a lower floor as the elevator floor. Such a request is forbidden by rule *set_direction_up*. Note that P_2 is an overlapping of the negative application condition *no_lower_request* of *set_direction_up* and the right-hand side of rule *call_request*. Consider Fig. 2.32 depicting another critical pair for *Elevator*. $K \overset{process\_call\_down}{\Rightarrow} P_1$ causes a delete-use conflict with $K \overset{process\_stop\_and\_call}{\Rightarrow} P_2$ since the first transformation deletes a call request still used (in order to delete) by the other transformation. Note that K is an overlapping of the left-hand sides of rules *process_call_down* and *process_stop_and_call*.

2.7.3 Definition (critical sequence). A *critical sequence* is a sequence of direct transformations $K \overset{p_1,m_1}{\Rightarrow} P_1$ with NAC_{p_1} and $P_1 \overset{p_2,m_2}{\Rightarrow} P_2$ with NAC_{p_2} such that at least one of the following four assumptions holds:

CHAPTER 2. RULE-BASED MODELING USING GRAPH TRANSFORMATION

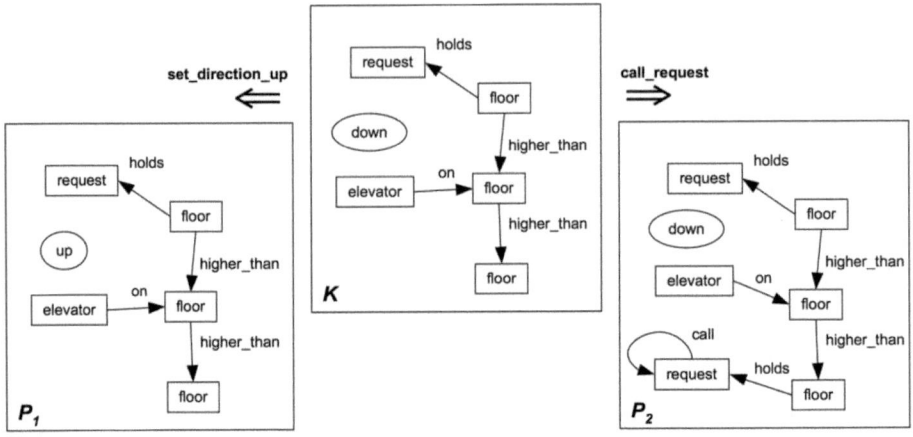

Figure 2.31: critical pair for *Elevator*

1. $\nexists h_{12} : R_1 \to D_2 : d_2 \circ h_{12} = m_1'$ and (m_1', m_2) jointly surjective (deliver-delete dependency),

2. there exists $h_{12} : R_1 \to D_2$ s.t. $d_2 \circ h_{12} = m_1'$, but for one of the NACs $n_1 : R_1 \to N_1$ of $NAC_{p_1^{-1}}$ there exists an injective morphism $q_{12} : N_1 \to P_2$ s.t. $q_{12} \circ n_1 = e_2 \circ h_{12}$ and (q_{12}, m_2') jointly surjective (forbid-produce dependency),

3. $\nexists h_{21} : L_2 \to D_1 : e_1 \circ h_{21} = m_2$ and (m_1', m_2) jointly surjective (produce-use dependency)

4. there exists $h_{21} : L_2 \to D_1$ s.t. $e_1 \circ h_{21} = m_2$, but for one of the NACs $n_2 : L_2 \to N_2$ of p_2 there exists an injective morphism $q_{21} : N_2 \to P_1$ s.t. $q_{21} \circ n_2 = d_1 \circ h_{21}$ and (q_{21}, m_1) jointly surjective (deliver-delete dependency)

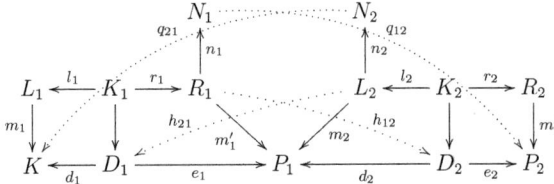

2.7.4 Remark. As noted already in Remark, 2.4.2 $K \stackrel{p_1}{\Rightarrow} P_1 \stackrel{p_2}{\Rightarrow} P_2$ are sequentially independent if and only if $K \stackrel{p_1^{-1}}{\Leftarrow} P_1 \stackrel{p_2}{\Rightarrow} P_2$ are parallel independent. Thus, the above critical sequence definition is obtained by Def. 2.7.1 for the pair $K \stackrel{p_1^{-1}}{\Leftarrow} P_1 \stackrel{p_2}{\Rightarrow} P_2$.

2.7.5 Example (critical sequences for *Elevator*). Consider Fig. 2.33 depicting a critical sequence for *Elevator*. $K \stackrel{stop\_request}{\Rightarrow} P_1 \stackrel{move\_up}{\Rightarrow} P_2$ is in produce-use dependency since a stop request is generated on a higher floor than the elevator floor by rule *stop_request*. This request is then used by rule *move_up*, and triggers a movement of the elevator in upward direction. Note that P_1 is the overlapping of the right-hand side of rule *stop_request* and the left-hand side of *move_up*. Consider Fig. 2.34 depicting another critical sequence for *Elevator*. $K \stackrel{process\_stop\_up}{\Rightarrow} P_1 \stackrel{move\_up}{\Rightarrow} P_2$

2.7. CRITICAL PAIRS AND CRITICAL SEQUENCES

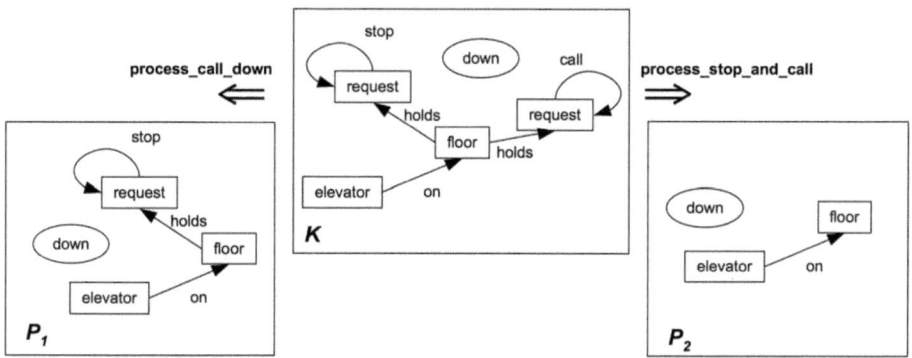

Figure 2.32: critical pair for *Elevator*

is in delete-forbid dependency since a stop request is processed by rule *process_stop_up* such that the elevator can afterwards move one floor upwards. This is because the NAC *no_stop_request* is then fulfilled. Note that K is an overlapping of the NAC *no_stop_request* of rule *move_up* with the left-hand side of rule *process_stop_up*. Consider Fig. 2.35, depicting another critical sequence for *Elevator*. $K \overset{call\_request}{\Rightarrow} P_1 \overset{process\_call\_down}{\Rightarrow} P_2$ is in deliver-delete dependency since rule *call_request* delivers a call request that afterwards is deleted by rule *process_call_down*. Note that P_1 is an overlapping of the right-hand side of rule *call_request* and the left-hand side of rule *process_call_down*. Consider Fig. 2.36, depicting another critical sequence for *Elevator*. $K \overset{process\_stop\_up}{\Rightarrow} P_1 \overset{call\_request}{\Rightarrow} P_2$ is in forbid-produce dependency since rule *call_request* produces a call request that is forbidden by rule *process_stop_up*. Note that P_2 is an overlapping of the shifted NAC *no_call* of rule *process_stop_up* to its right-hand side (consisting of a *floor* node holding a *call request*) and the right-hand side of rule *call_request*.

By means of the following definition and theorem, it is possible to prove that Def. 2.7.1 (resp. 2.7.3) of critical pairs (resp. sequences) leads to completeness. In particular, an extension diagram with NACs describes how a transformation $t : G_0 \Rightarrow^* G_n$ with NACs can be extended to a transformation $t' : G'_0 \Rightarrow^* G'_n$ with NACs via an extension morphism $k_0 : G_0 \to G'_0$. On the other hand, the restriction theorem with NACs states that a direct transformation with NACs can be restricted to a direct transformation with NACs, starting with a smaller context. For showing completeness of critical pairs (resp. sequence), it can then be shown that each pair of conflicting transformations (resp. sequence of causally dependent transformations) can be restricted to some critical pair (resp. critical sequence).

2.7.6 Definition (extension diagram with NACs). An *extension diagram* is a diagram (1),

$$\begin{array}{ccc} G_0 & \overset{t}{\Rightarrow^*} & G_n \\ {\scriptstyle k_0}\downarrow & (1) & \downarrow{\scriptstyle k_n} \\ G'_0 & \overset{t'}{\Rightarrow^*} & G'_n \end{array}$$

where, $k_0 : G_0 \to G'_0$ is a morphism, called extension morphism, and $t : G_0 \overset{*}{\Rightarrow} G_n$ and $t' : G'_0 \overset{*}{\Rightarrow} G'_n$ are transformations with NACs via the same rules $(p_0, \cdots, p_{n-1})$, and matches

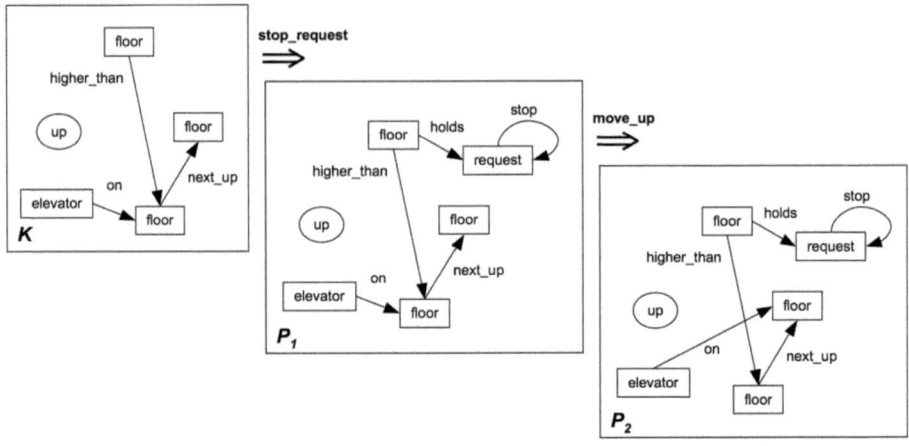

Figure 2.33: critical sequence for *Elevator*

$(m_0, \cdots, m_{n-1})$ and extended matches $(k_0 \circ m_0, \cdots, k_{n-1} \circ m_{n-1})$, respectively, defined by the following DPO diagrams :

$$p_i : \begin{array}{ccc} L_i & \xleftarrow{l_i} K_i \xrightarrow{r_i} & R_i \\ m_i \downarrow & j_i \downarrow & n_i \downarrow \\ G_i & \xleftarrow{f_i} D_i \xrightarrow{g_i} & G_{i+1} \\ k_i \downarrow & d_i \downarrow & k_{i+1} \downarrow \\ G'_i & \xleftarrow{f'_i} D'_i \xrightarrow{g'_i} & G'_{i+1} \end{array}$$

2.7.7 Theorem (restriction theorem with NACs). *Given a direct transformation* $G' \overset{p,m'}{\Rightarrow} H'$ *with NACs, an injective morphism* $s : G \to G'$, *and a match* $m : L \to G$ *such that* $s \circ m = m'$, *then there is a direct transformation* $G \overset{p,m}{\Rightarrow} H$ *with NACs leading to the following extension diagram:*

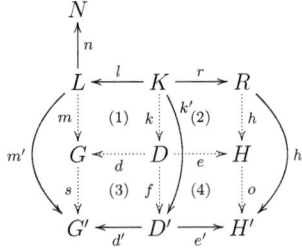

Proof. Follows from Fact 3.2.15 and Theorem 3.7.5 in Chapter 3. □

Now, we are ready to formulate the completeness theorem for critical pairs with NACs, stating that each potential conflict is represented in a minimal context by some critical pair.

2.7. CRITICAL PAIRS AND CRITICAL SEQUENCES

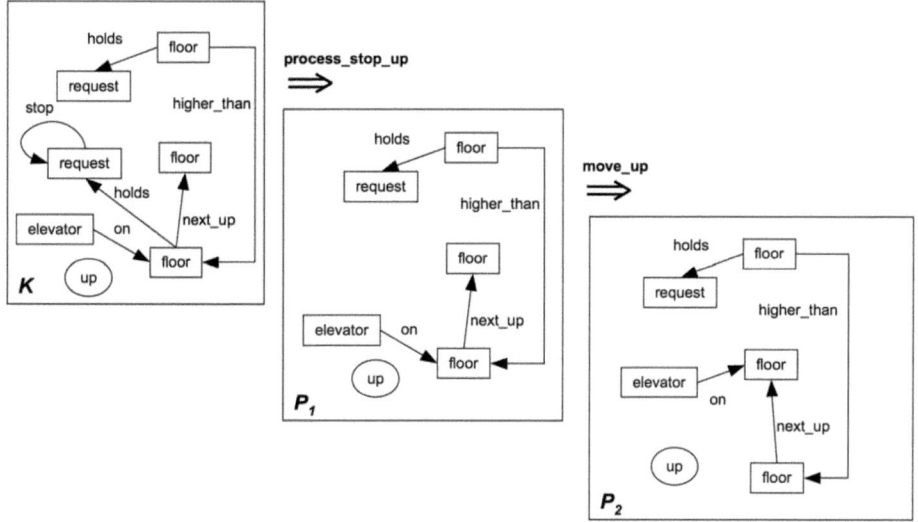

Figure 2.34: critical sequence for *Elevator*

2.7.8 Theorem (completeness of critical pairs with NACs). *For each pair of direct transformations* $H_1 \stackrel{p_1,m_1'}{\Longleftarrow} G \stackrel{p_2,m_2'}{\Longrightarrow} H_2$ *in conflict, there is a critical pair* $P_1 \stackrel{p_1}{\Longleftarrow} K \stackrel{p_2}{\Longrightarrow} P_2$ *with extension diagrams (1) and (2) and m injective.*

$$\begin{array}{ccccc} P_1 & \Longleftarrow & K & \Longrightarrow & P_2 \\ \downarrow & (1) & \downarrow m & (2) & \downarrow \\ H_1 & \Longleftarrow & G & \Longrightarrow & H_2 \end{array}$$

Proof. Follows from Fact 3.2.15 and Theorem 3.7.6 in Chapter 3. □

2.7.9 Remark. Note that the critical pair that can be found exhibits the same type of conflict (see Def. 2.6.6) as the pair of conflicting direct transformations.

Critical pairs allow for static conflict detection. Each conflict, which may occur at some moment in the graph transformation, is represented by a critical pair. Thus, it is possible to foresee each potential conflict by computing the set of all critical pairs before running the graph transformation system (GTS). A conflict detection algorithm is implemented in the graph transformation tool AGG. In Chapter 3, with regard to the certification of Property *Conflicts as Expected*, a more detailed explanation is given about the visualization of the critical pairs in AGG. Each pair of rules of the GTS induces a set of critical pairs. Computing this set for each pair of rules delivers us in the end the complete set of critical pairs. Here, a straightforward construction is given to compute a set of critical pairs for a given pair of rules.

CHAPTER 2. RULE-BASED MODELING USING GRAPH TRANSFORMATION

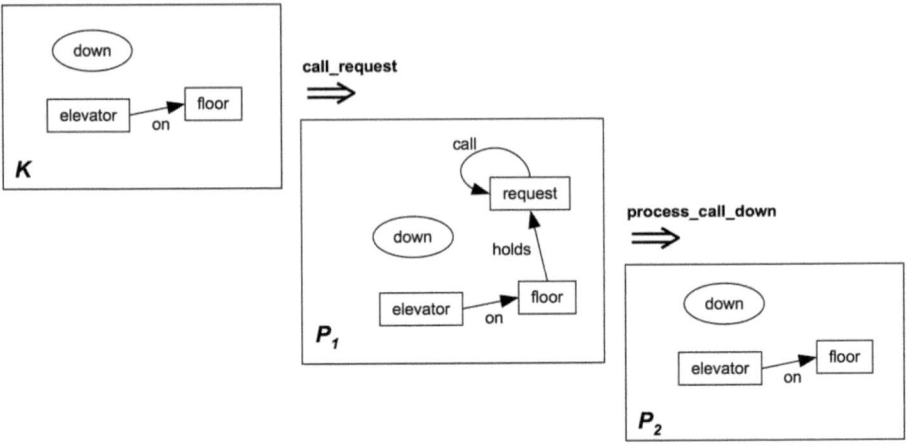

Figure 2.35: critical sequence for *Elevator*

2.7.10 Construction. Consider a pair of rules $p_1 : L_1 \leftarrow K_1 \to R_1, p_2 : L_2 \leftarrow K_2 \to R_2$ with NACs:

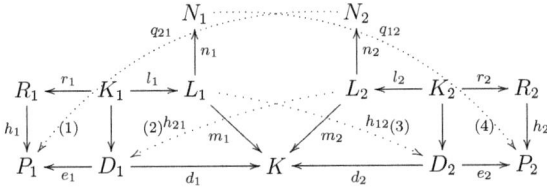

1. Consider any jointly surjective pair $(m_1 : L_1 \to K, m_2 : L_2 \to K)$.

    (a) Check the gluing condition for (l_1, m_1) and (l_2, m_2). If it is satisfied for both cases, then construct PO-complements D_1, D_2 in (2),(3) and POs P_1, P_2 in (1) and (4).

    (b) Check if the pair of direct transformations $P_1 \Leftarrow K \Rightarrow P_2$ is in delete-use conflict, leading to the critical pair $P_1 \Leftarrow K \Rightarrow P_2$.

2. Consider for each NAC $n_1 : L_1 \to N_1$ of p_1 any jointly surjective pair of morphisms $(h_2 : R_2 \to P_2, q_{12} : N_1 \to P_2)$ with q_{12} injective.

    (a) Check the gluing condition for (h_2, r_2). If it is satisfied, then construct the PO-complement D_2 in (4).

    (b) Construct PO K in (3) and abort if $m_2 \not\models NAC_{p_2}$.

    (c) Check existence of $h_{12} : L_1 \to D_2$ s.t. $e_2 \circ h_{12} = q_{12} \circ n_1$. If not existent, then abort.

    (d) Define $m_1 = d_2 \circ h_{12} : L_1 \to K$ and abort if $m_1 \not\models NAC_{p_1}$.

    (e) Check the gluing condition for (m_1, l_1). If it is satisfied, then construct the PO-complement D_1 in (2).

    (f) Construct P_1 as PO in (1) leading to the critical pair $P_1 \Leftarrow K \Rightarrow P_2$.

2.7. CRITICAL PAIRS AND CRITICAL SEQUENCES

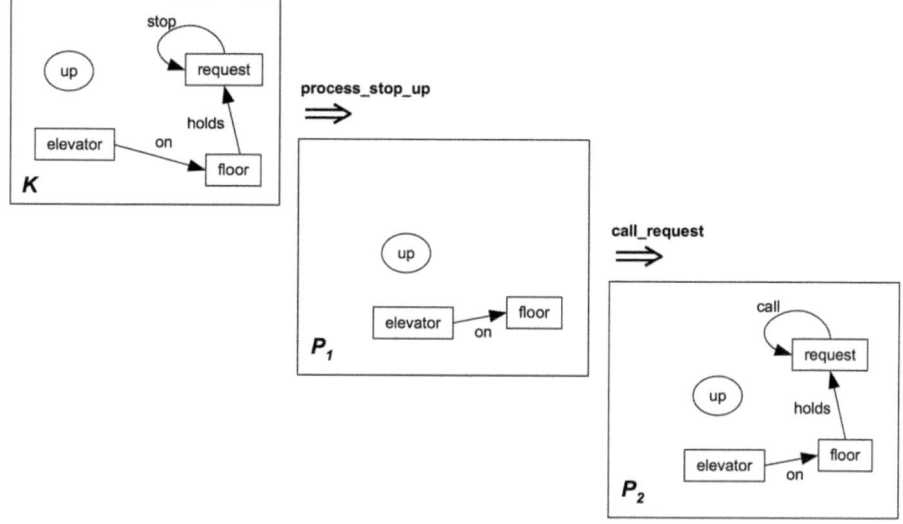

Figure 2.36: critical sequence for *Elevator*

3. Consider for each NAC $n_2 : L_2 \to N_2$ of p_2 any jointly surjective pair of morphisms $(h_1 : R_1 \to P_1, q_{21} : N_2 \to P_1)$ with q_{21} injective and continue analogously to step 2.

This construction is derived quite straightforwardly from Definition 2.7.1. We are able to show that it yields all critical pairs of a pair of rules of the GTS with NACs[4].

2.7.11 Theorem (correctness of critical pair construction). *The critical pair construction in 2.7.10 yields the set of all critical pairs for a pair of rules (p_1, p_2) of a GTS with NACs.*

Proof. • First we prove that the pair of direct transformations constructed in steps 1, 2 and 3 is indeed a critical pair. Step 1: Since the matches (m_1, m_2) of $P_1 \Leftarrow K \Rightarrow P_2$ are jointly surjective and this pair is in delete-use conflict, it is a critical pair. Step 2: Since there exists a morphism $h_{12} : L_1 \to D_2$ with $m_1 = d_2 \circ h_{12}$ and an injective morphism $q_{12} : N_1 \to P_2$ with $e_2 \circ h_{12} = q_{12} \circ n_1$ and (h_2, q_{12}) jointly surjective, it is a critical pair in produce-forbid conflict. Step 3: Analogous to Step 2.

• Secondly, we prove that each critical pair is constructed by step 1, 2 or 3. Looking at Definition 2.7.1 there are four different types of critical pairs. Given a critical pair $P_1 \Leftarrow K \Rightarrow P_2$ of type 1a or 2a (delete-use conflict), then it is constructed by step 1. This is because the matches (m_1, m_2) are jointly surjective, (l_1, m_1) and (l_2, m_2) satisfy the gluing condition since (2) and (3) are pushouts, (1) and (4) are also pushouts, pushouts are unique up to isomorphisms, and $P_1 \Leftarrow K \Rightarrow P_2$ are in delete-use conflict. Given a critical pair $P_1 \Leftarrow K \Rightarrow P_2$ of type (1b) (produce-forbid conflict), then it is constructed by step 2. This is because (h_2, q_{12}) are jointly surjective, the gluing condition for (h_2, r_2)

---

[4]Note that this construction and theorem are analogous for any other instantiation of adhesive HLR systems with NACs.

is satisfied because (4) is a pushout, (3) is a pushout, $m_2 \models NAC_{p_2}$, $h_{12} : L_1 \to D_2$ exists s.t. $e_2 \circ h_{12} = q_{12} \circ n_1$, $m_1 \models NAC_{p_1}$, the gluing condition for (m_1, l_1) holds since (2) is a pushout, (1) is a pushout and pushouts are unique up to isomorphisms. Given a critical pair $P_1 \Leftarrow K \Rightarrow P_2$ of type (2b) (produce-forbid conflict), then it is constructed by step 3, analogous to a critical pair of type (1b). □

As for the conflict case, we can now formulate the completeness theorem for critical sequences with NACs, stating that each potential causal dependency is represented in a minimal context by some critical sequence.

2.7.12 Theorem (completeness of critical sequences with NACs). *For each sequence of causally dependent direct transformations $G \overset{p_1, m_1'}{\Longrightarrow} H_1 \overset{p_2, m_2'}{\Longrightarrow} H_2$, there is a critical sequence $K \overset{p_1}{\Longrightarrow} P_1 \overset{p_2}{\Longrightarrow} P_2$ with extension diagrams (1) and (2) and m injective.*

$$\begin{array}{ccccc} K & \Longrightarrow & P_1 & \Longrightarrow & P_2 \\ \downarrow & (1) & m \downarrow & (2) & \downarrow \\ G & \Longrightarrow & H_1 & \Longrightarrow & H_2 \end{array}$$

Proof. Follows from Fact 3.2.15 and Theorem 3.7.8 in Chapter 3. □

2.7.13 Remark. Note that, analogous to Remark 2.7.9, the critical sequence that can be constructed exhibits the same type of dependency (see Def. 2.6.8) as the sequence of causally dependent direct transformations.

Critical sequences allow for static causal dependency detection. Each causal dependency, which may occur at some moment in the graph transformation, is represented by a critical sequence. Thus, it is possible to foresee each potential causal dependency by computing the set of all critical sequences before running the GTS. A causal dependency detection algorithm is implemented in the graph transformation tool AGG. In Chapter 3, with regard to the certification of property *Causalities as Expected*, a more detailed explanation is given about the visualization of the critical sequences in AGG. Each sequence of two rules of the GTS induces a set of critical sequences. Computing this set for each sequence of two rules delivers us in the end the complete set of critical sequences. Because of Remark 2.7.4, the construction of such a set of critical sequences can be derived from the one for critical pairs (see Construction 2.7.10).

2.7.14 Construction. Consider a sequence of rules $(p_1 : L_1 \leftarrow K_1 \to R_1, p_2 : L_2 \leftarrow K_2 \to R_2)$ with NACs:

1. compute p_1^{-1} according to Def. 2.3.17

2. compute the set of critical pairs for p_1^{-1} and p_2 according to Construction 2.7.10

3. interpret each critical pair $P_1 \overset{p_1^{-1}}{\Leftarrow} K \overset{p_2}{\Rightarrow} P_2$ in this set as a critical sequence $K' \overset{p_1}{\Rightarrow} P_1' \overset{p_2}{\Rightarrow} P_2$ with $K' = P_1$ and $P_1' = K$ according to Theorem 2.3.18.

2.7.15 Example (completeness for *Elevator*). Consider again the conflicts and causal dependencies described in Example 2.6.9. The conflicts shown in Fig. 2.25 (resp. Fig. 2.26) are represented by the critical pairs described in Example 2.7.2 and depicted in Fig. 2.31 (resp.

Fig. 2.32). Analogously, the causal dependencies shown in Fig. 2.27 (resp. Fig. 2.28,2.29, and 2.30) are represented by the critical sequences described in Example 2.7.5 and depicted in Fig. 2.33 (resp. Fig. 2.34,2.35, and 2.36).

The following fact characterizes that each pair of direct graph transformations is not in conflict if the corresponding graph transformation system has an empty set of critical pairs. Such a system is called conflict-free. Thereby, note that a pair of direct transformations via the same rule must be non-conflicting as well.

2.7.16 Fact (a necessary and sufficient condition for parallel independence). *Each pair of direct transformations $H_1 \Leftarrow G \Rightarrow H_2$ in a graph transformation system with NACs is parallel independent if and only if there are no critical pairs for this graph transformation system with NACs.*

Proof. Follows from Fact 3.2.15 and Fact 3.7.10 in Chapter 3. □

2.7.17 Definition (conflict-free system). A graph transformation system with NACs in which each pair of direct transformations $H_1 \Leftarrow G \Rightarrow H_2$ is parallel independent is called *conflict-free*.

Analogously, we have a fact characterizing that a sequence of two direct graph transformations is not causally dependent if the corresponding graph transformation system has an empty set of critical sequences. Such a system is called dependency-free. Thereby, note that a sequence of two direct transformations via the same rule must be independent as well.

2.7.18 Fact (a necessary and sufficient condition for sequential independence). *Each sequence of direct transformations $G \Rightarrow H_1 \Rightarrow H_2$ in a graph transformation system with NACs is sequentially independent if and only if there are no critical sequences for this graph transformation system with NACs.*

Proof. Follows from Fact 3.2.15 and Fact 3.7.12 in Chapter 3. □

2.7.19 Definition (dependency-free system). A graph transformation system with NACs in which each sequence of direct transformations $G \Rightarrow H_1 \Rightarrow H_2$ is sequentially independent is called *dependency-free*.

2.7.20 Example (dependency-free subsystem of *Elevator*). Consider the subset of rules of *Elevator* consisting of *call_request* and *stop_request*. This subset of rules is a dependency-free system. It is not possible to find any critical sequence via the rules *call_request* and *stop_request*. This means that the order of consecutive recordings of an internal stop or external call request does not matter. On the other hand, there does not exist any subsystem of *Elevator* that is conflict-free. Namely, for each rule a pair of direct transformations via the same rule can be constructed that is conflicting.

2.8 Independence, Conflicts and Causal Dependencies for Rules

We now shift the notions of parallel and sequential independency as well as conflicts and causal dependencies for transformations to the rule-level. This will allow static analysis techniques such as, for example, investigations on rule sequence applicability in the next section.

2.8.1 Independence for Rules

We define parallel (resp. sequential) independency for rules by demanding that the corresponding transformations are independent. Analogously, it is possible to define rules that are in conflict (resp. rules that depend on each other).

2.8.1 Definition (parallel independent rules). Rules r_1 and r_2 are *parallel independent* if every pair of transformations $G \stackrel{(r_1,m_1)}{\Longrightarrow} H_1$ via r_1 with NAC_{r_1} and $G \stackrel{(r_2,m_2)}{\Longrightarrow} H_2$ via r_2 with NAC_{r_2} is parallel independent as defined in Def. 2.4.1.

2.8.2 Definition (sequentially independent rules). The pair of rules (r_1, r_2) is *sequentially independent* if every sequence of transformations $G \stackrel{(r_1,m_1)}{\Longrightarrow} H_1$ via r_1 with NAC_{r_1} followed by $H_1 \stackrel{(r_2,m_2)}{\Longrightarrow} H$ via r_2 with NAC_{r_2} is sequentially independent as defined in Def. 2.4.1.

2.8.3 Corollary (characterization of parallel independent rules). *Rules r_1 and r_2 are parallel independent if and only if there exist no critical pairs $P_1 \stackrel{(r_1,m_1)}{\Longleftarrow} K \stackrel{(r_2,m_2)}{\Longrightarrow} P_2$.*

Proof. Follows from Fact 3.2.15 and Corollary 3.8.3 in Chapter 3. □

2.8.4 Corollary (characterization of sequentially independent rules). *The pair of rules (r_1, r_2) is sequentially independent if and only if there exist no critical sequences $K \stackrel{(r_1,m_1)}{\Longrightarrow} P_1 \stackrel{(r_2,m_2)}{\Longrightarrow} P_2$.*

Proof. Follows from Fact 3.2.15 and Corollary 3.8.3 in Chapter 3. □

Analogous to Remark 2.4.2, we can relate parallel and sequential independency for rules instead of transformations.

2.8.5 Corollary (relating parallel and sequential independency for rules). *The rule pair (r_1, r_2) is sequentially independent if and only if r_1^{-1} and r_2 are parallel independent. The rules r_1 and r_2 are parallel independent if and only if the rule pair (r_1^{-1}, r_2) is sequentially independent if and only if the rule pair (r_2^{-1}, r_1) is sequentially independent.*

Proof. Follows from Fact 3.2.15 and Corollary 3.8.5 in Chapter 3. □

2.8.6 Example (independent rules for *Elevator*). Rules *process_stop_down* and *stop_request* (as presented in Fig. 2.18, resp. in Fig. 2.6) are parallel independent. It is not possible to construct any critical pair for them. Consider some system state for *Elevator* such that, on the one hand, some stop request r is processed and, on the other hand, some stop request r' for some floor f is generated. Then because of parallel independency we know that, on the one hand, the stop request r' can still be generated for floor f, and, on the other hand, the stop request r can still be processed. Note that although rules *process_stop_down* and *stop_request* are parallel independent, rules (*stop_request,process_stop_down*) are not sequentially independent. This is because rule *stop_request* might trigger rule *process_stop_down* by generating a stop request on the elevator floor, which can then be processed by *process_stop_down*. Moreover, in the same context rule *stop_request* is irreversible after *process_stop_down*. Rules (*call_request*, *stop_request*), as presented in Fig. 2.6 and in Fig. 2.12, are sequentially independent. It is not possible to construct any critical sequence for them. Consider some system state for *Elevator* such that at first some call request, and afterwards some stop request is generated. Then, because of sequential independency, we know that these requests could also have been generated the other way round.

2.8. INDEPENDENCE, CONFLICTS AND CAUSAL DEPENDENCIES FOR RULES

2.8.2 Conflicts and Causal Dependencies for Rules

We defined parallel (resp. sequential) independency for rules by demanding that the corresponding transformations are independent. Analogously, it is possible to define rules that are in conflict (resp. rules that depend on each other).

2.8.7 Definition (conflicting rules). Rules r_1 and r_2 are *in conflict* if there exists a pair of transformations $G \stackrel{p_1,m_1}{\Longrightarrow} H_1$ with NAC_{p_1} and $G \stackrel{p_2,m_2}{\Longrightarrow} H_2$ with NAC_{p_2} that are in conflict according to Def. 2.6.1.

2.8.8 Definition (causally dependent rules). Given a pair of rules (r_1, r_2), then rules r_1 and r_2 are *causally dependent* if there exists a sequence of two direct transformations $G \stackrel{p_1,m_1}{\Longrightarrow} H_1 \stackrel{p_2,m_2}{\Longrightarrow} H_2$ with NAC_{p_1} and NAC_{p_2} that are *causally dependent* according to Def. 2.6.2.

2.8.9 Corollary (characterization of conflicting rules). *Two rules r_1 and r_2 are in conflict according to Def. 2.8.7 if and only if there exists at least one critical pair $P_1 \stackrel{(r_1,m_1)}{\Longleftarrow} K \stackrel{(r_2,m_2)}{\Longrightarrow} P_2$.*

Proof. Follows from Fact 3.2.15 and Corollary 3.8.8 in Chapter 3. □

2.8.10 Corollary (characterization of causally dependent rules). *Given a pair of rules (r_1, r_2), then they are causally dependent according to Def. 2.8.8 if and only if there exists at least one critical sequence $K \stackrel{(r_1,m_1)}{\Longrightarrow} P_1 \stackrel{(r_2,m_2)}{\Longrightarrow} P_2$.*

Proof. Follows from Fact 3.2.15 and Corollary 3.8.9 in Chapter 3. □

Analogous to the conflict and causal dependency characterizations for transformations in Def. 2.6.6 (resp. 2.6.8), we can characterize conflicts and causal dependencies between rules as well.

2.8.11 Definition (rule r_1 causes a delete-use (resp. produce-forbid) conflict with rule r_2). Rule r_1 *causes a delete-use (resp. produce-forbid) conflict* with rule r_2 if there is a transformation $G \stackrel{(r_1,m_1)}{\Longrightarrow} H_1$ via r_1 with NAC_{r_1} that causes a delete-use (resp. produce-forbid) conflict with $G \stackrel{(r_2,m_2)}{\Longrightarrow} H_2$ via r_2 with NAC_{r_2} as defined in Def. 2.6.6. In general, we say that r_1 *causes a conflict* with r_2.

2.8.12 Definition (rule pair (r_1, r_2) is in produce-use (resp. delete-use) dependency). A rule pair (r_1, r_2) is in *produce-use (resp. delete-use) dependency* if there is a transformation sequence $G \stackrel{(r_1,m_1)}{\Longrightarrow} H_1 \stackrel{(r_2,m_2)}{\Longrightarrow} H_2$ such that $G \stackrel{(r_1,m_1)}{\Longrightarrow} H_1$ is in produce-use (resp. delete-use) dependency with $H_1 \stackrel{(r_2,m_2)}{\Longrightarrow} H_2$ according to Def. 2.6.8. In general, we say that r_2 is *triggered by* r_1.

2.8.13 Definition (rule pair (r_1, r_2) is in deliver-delete (resp. forbid-produce) dependency). A rule pair (r_1, r_2) is in *deliver-delete (resp. forbid-produce) dependency* if there is a transformation sequence $G \stackrel{(r_1,m_1)}{\Longrightarrow} H_1 \stackrel{(r_2,m_2)}{\Longrightarrow} H_2$ such that $G \stackrel{(r_1,m_1)}{\Longrightarrow} H_1$ is in deliver-delete (resp. forbid-produce) dependency with $H_1 \stackrel{(r_2,m_2)}{\Longrightarrow} H_2$ according to Def. 2.6.8. In general, we say that r_1 is *irreversible after* r_2.

2.8.14 Remark. Note that the following correspondences exist. Rules r_1 and r_2 are parallel independent if and only if r_1 does not cause a conflict with r_2 and r_2 does not cause a conflict with r_1. Rule pair (r_1, r_2) is sequentially independent if and only if r_2 is not triggered by r_1 and r_1 is not irreversible after r_2.

CHAPTER 2. RULE-BASED MODELING USING GRAPH TRANSFORMATION

Analogous to Corollary 2.8.5, we can also relate conflicts and causal dependencies for rules.

2.8.15 Corollary (relating conflicts and causal dependencies for rules). *Rule r_1 causes a conflict with r_2 if and only if r_2 is triggered by r_1^{-1} if and only if r_2^{-1} is irreversible after r_1. Given rule pair (r_1, r_2), r_2 is triggered by r_1 if and only if r^{-1} causes a conflict with r_2. Moreover, r_1 is irreversible after r_2 if and only if r_2 causes a conflict with r_1^{-1}.*

Proof. Follows from Fact 3.2.15 and Corollary 3.8.14 in Chapter 3. □

2.8.16 Example (conflicting and dependent rules for *Elevator*). Rule *call_request* causes a produce-forbid conflict with rule *set_direction_up*. A corresponding pair of transformations in conflict is shown in Fig. 2.25. Rule *process_call_down* causes a delete-use conflict with rule *process_stop_and_call* and the other way round. A corresponding pair of transformations in conflict is shown in Fig. 2.26. Rule *move_up* is triggered by *stop_request* by a produce-use dependency. A corresponding transformation sequence is shown in Fig. 2.27. Rule *move_up* is triggered by rule *process_stop_up* by a delete-forbid dependency. A corresponding transformation sequence is shown in Fig. 2.28. Moreover, rule *process_stop_up* is irreversible after rule *move_up*. This is because of a deliver-delete dependency, and it can be recognized as well on the transformation in Fig. 2.28. Since the elevator has moved to the second floor, the inverse rule of *process_stop_up* cannot be applied on the first floor anymore. Rule *call_request* is irreversible after *process_call_down* because of a deliver-delete dependency. A corresponding transformation sequence is shown in Fig. 2.29. Moreover, *process_call_down* is triggered by rule *call_request* because of a produce-use dependency. This can be recognized as well on the transformation in Fig. 2.29. A call request is produced that is processed immediately by rule *process_call_down*. Rule *process_stop_up* is irreversible after *call_request* because of a forbid-produce dependency. A corresponding transformation sequence is shown in Fig. 2.30.

If neighbored rules in a rule sequence are sequentially independent, then they can be switched as well. We say that such sequences are shift-equivalent.

2.8.17 Definition (shift-equivalent rule sequences). A rule sequence s' is *shift-equivalent* to a rule sequence $s : r_1, r_2, \ldots, r_m$ if the pair (s, s') belongs to the reflexive, symmetric, and transitive closure of the shift-equivalent relation S: a pair of rule sequences (s, s') belongs to the shift relation S if s' can be deduced from s by switching the rules r_j with r_{j+1} and the switching is allowed only if (r_j, r_{j+1}) and (r_{j+1}, r_j) are sequentially independent according to Def. 2.8.2.

If neighbored rules in a rule sequence are sequentially independent only in one order, then we say that they are just shift-related. These notions are used in Theorem 2.9.11, 2.9.14, and Corollary 2.9.15 to define rule sequence reductions with regard to their applicability resp. non-applicability.

2.8.18 Definition (shift-related rule sequences). A rule sequence s' is *shift-related* to a rule sequence $s : r_1, r_2, \ldots, r_m$ if the pair (s, s') belongs to the reflexive and transitive closure of the shift-relation S: a pair of rule sequences (s, s') belongs to the shift-relation S if s' can be deduced from s by switching the rules r_j with r_{j+1} and the switching is allowed only if the rule pair (r_{j+1}, r_j) is sequentially independent according to Def. 2.8.2.

2.8.19 Remark. Note that because of Theorem 2.8.5 rule pair (r_1, r_2) is sequentially independent if and only if r_2 and r_1^{-1} are parallel independent rules.

2.8. INDEPENDENCE, CONFLICTS AND CAUSAL DEPENDENCIES FOR RULES

We can distinguish a special case of causal dependency for the case without NACs. It is possible that a rule r_1 produces everything that is needed by r_2 regardless of what is already present in the corresponding transformations. This so-called pure dependency will be used for the applicability criteria of rule sequences in Section 2.9. Note that if r_2 is a rule with NACs, then it could be the case that r_1 produces everything that is needed by r_2, but also that r_1 produces something that is forbidden by r_1. Therefore, here we first restrict to the case without NACs.

2.8.20 Definition (rule r_1 purely enables r_2). A rule $r_2 : L_2 \leftarrow K_2 \to R_2$ is *purely enabled* by $r_1 : L_1 \leftarrow K_1 \to R_1$ if r_2 is a rule without NACs and there exists an injective morphism $l_{21} : L_2 \to R_1$.

2.8.21 Remark. Rule r_2 without NACs is triggered by rule r_1 according to Def. 2.8.12, if r_2 is purely enabled by r_1 and the following mild assumptions are satisfied: a morphism $k_{21} : L_2 \to K_1$ does not exist such that $r_1 \circ k_{21} = l_{21}$, match l_{21} fulfills the gluing condition for r_2, and $id : L_1 \to L_1 \models NAC_{r_1}$.

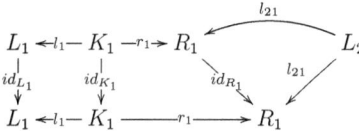

2.8.22 Example (purely enabled rule for *Elevator_alarm*). Suppose that the elevator control in our running example *Elevator* is extended by a fire-alarm control [10] operating the elevator cabin to the ground floor as soon as the fire alarm is released. The elevator car then stays in this position until the fire alarm is unset. We call this extended elevator control *Elevator_alarm*, and modify and extend the graph transformation system $GTS_{Elevator}$ to $GTS_{ElevatorAlarm}$ as follows. First, we add a node of type *alarm* to the type graph of *Elevator* (see Fig. 2.1). We then add the rules *set_alarm* and *unset_alarm* as shown in Fig. 2.37. They model that a fire alarm is set (resp. unset). Note that rule *unset_alarm* is purely enabled by *set_alarm*. Now we modify each rule of *Elevator* as follows: we add a NAC *no_alarm* consisting of the left-hand side of the rule and an extra node of type *alarm*. Thus, these rules cannot be applied anymore once the fire alarm is released. Finally, we add a rule *move_down_alarm* modeling the fact that the elevator car should move downward as soon as a fire alarm is present. Note that one should moreover add rules setting the elevator into an initial state again before the alarm is unset, but we do not depict these rules here.

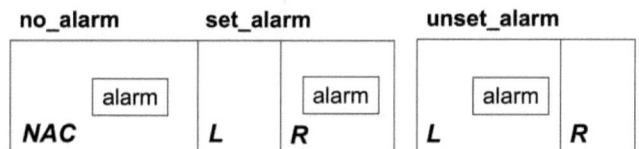

Figure 2.37: rules *set_alarm* and *unset_alarm* for *Elevator*

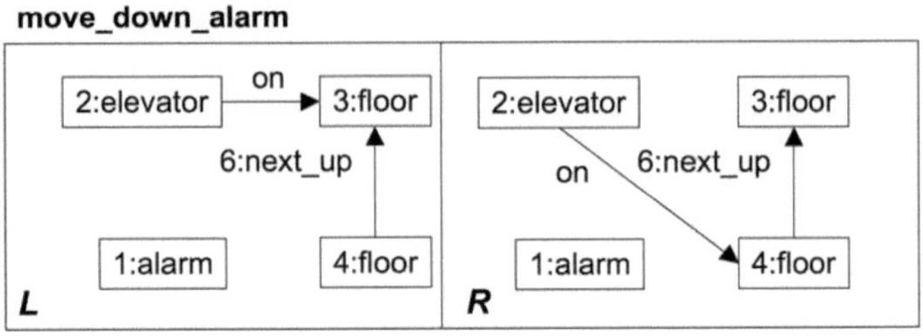

move_down_alarm

L: 2:elevator —on→ 3:floor, 6:next_up (3:floor → 4:floor), 1:alarm, 4:floor

R: 2:elevator, 3:floor, 6:next_up (3:floor → 4:floor), 2:elevator —on→ 1:alarm, 4:floor

Figure 2.38: rule *move_down_alarm* for *Elevator*

2.8.3 Independence of Concurrent Rules

This section describes that independency for concurrent rules can be derived from independency of their single rules.

2.8.23 Theorem (independence of concurrent and single rule). *Consider a concurrent rule r_c for some sequence of rules $r_1, r_2 \ldots, r_n$ and some rule r. r_c and r are parallel independent $((r_c, r)$ resp. (r, r_c) are sequentially independent) if r_i and r are parallel independent $((r_i, r)$ resp. (r, r_i) are sequentially independent) for $1 \leq i \leq n$.*

Proof. Follows from Fact 3.2.15 and Theorem 3.8.21 in Chapter 3. □

2.8.24 Theorem (independence of concurrent rules). *Consider a concurrent rule r_c (resp. r'_c) for some sequence of rules $r_1, r_2 \ldots r_n$ (resp. $r'_1, r'_2, \ldots, r'_m$). r_c and r'_c are parallel independent $((r_c, r'_c)$ resp. (r'_c, r_c) are sequentially independent) if r_i and r'_j are parallel independent $((r_i, r'_j)$ resp. (r'_j, r_i) are sequentially independent) for $1 \leq i \leq n$ and $1 \leq j \leq m$.*

Proof. Follows from Fact 3.2.15 and Theorem 3.8.22 in Chapter 3. □

2.8.25 Example. Consider the concurrent rule of *process_stop_down* and *process_call_down* processing a stop request and a call request on the elevator floor. Moreover, consider the concurrent rule of *stop_request* and *call_request* generating a stop request and a call request for the same floor. This rule then holds two NACs expressing that neither a stop request nor a call request should be present on the floor. These concurrent rules are parallel independent according to Theorem 2.8.24 since their single rules are. Consider some system state of *Elevator* such that, on the one hand, a stop request and a call request can be processed in downward mode for some floor f and, on the other hand, a stop request and a call request can be generated for another floor. Then, on the one hand it is possible to generate the stop and call request for floor f' and on the other hand it is possible to process the stop and call request on floor f.

Consider the concurrent rule of *call_request* and *call_request* generating a call request for two floors. This rule holds a set of NACs expressing that this rule can only be applied in an injective way on both floors and forbidding any call request on each of the floors. Analogously, consider the concurrent rule of *stop_request* and *stop_request*. These concurrent rules are sequentially independent according to Theorem 2.8.24 since their single rules are. Consider some system state of *Elevator* such that first a call request is generated on two floors, and afterwards a stop request is generated on two floors. Then because of sequential independence it is possible to generate the stop requests first, and afterwards generate the call requests.

2.8.26 Corollary (parallel (resp. sequentially) independent rules and concurrency). *Given a conflict-free (resp. dependency-free) graph transformation system GTS with NACs as given in Def. 2.7.17 (resp. Def. 2.7.19), then the graph transformation system GTS' with NACs equal to GTS, but holding in addition concurrent rules for sequences of rules in GTS, is conflict-free (resp. dependency-free) as well.*

Proof. Follows from Fact 3.2.15 and Corollary 3.8.23 in Chapter 3. □

2.9 Applicability (Non-Applicability) of Rule Sequences

In this section, we first introduce some reductions of rule sequences allowing us to conclude applicability (resp. non-applicability) of the original rule sequences from the applicability (resp. non-applicability) of the reduced sequences. Thereafter, we present sufficient criteria for the applicability and for the non-applicability of a rule sequence to a graph. These criteria are based mainly on the causal dependencies and conflicts between rules as presented in Section 2.8. Moreover, the non-satisfaction of one of the criteria may give a hint to the reason for a rule sequence to be applicable or inapplicable. In Chapter 4, it is explained with regard to the certification of property *Applicability* that this applicability analysis is implemented in AGG. Note that applicability criteria have been studied also in [118] for simple digraphs using matrix graph grammars.

Before starting this section though we make the following assumption. It ensures that as soon as a suitable match is found for a rule into some host graph, the gluing condition (see Def. 2.3.6) is always fulfilled. Moreover, some first results concerning applicability and non-applicability of rules can be deduced from this assumption (see Corrs .2.9.3, 2.9.5 and Theorem 2.9.7). Note that a match m fulfills the gluing condition for some rule p if the identification and dangling edge conditions are fulfilled. The *identification condition* ensures that no graph elements are glued by m such that one or both elements should be deleted by p. The *dangling edge condition* ensures that no nodes are deleted from the graph G to which p is applied without deleting all adjacent edges in G with them.

2.9.1 Assumption (gluing condition always fulfilled). In this section, we restrict ourselves to transformations via injective matches. Therefore, the identification condition is always fulfilled. Moreover, we restrict ourselves to a set of rules such that each rule is either non-deleting on nodes (dangling edge condition automatically fulfilled) or the dangling edge condition is fulfilled because nodes are deleted by rules only together with all possible incoming/outgoing edges. Thereby, note that NACs do not necessarily need to be fulfilled.

2.9.2 Example (gluing condition for *Elevator*). Rules *move_up* and *move_down* are the only rules in *Elevator* that can be applied in a non-injective way. In order to apply the theory in this chapter, we replace the rule *move_up* (resp. *move_down*) in *Elevator* by two move rules that can be applied in an injective way with the same effect as applying the original rule in a non-injective way (see Fig. 2.39 depicting the equivalent rules for *move_up*). Analogously, both rules for *move_down* can be derived. Moreover, we have the node-deleting rules *set_direction_up*, *set_direction_down*, and all *process* rules in *Elevator*. We have to argue that they fulfill the dangling condition in any circumstance. Since the type graph of *Elevator* (see Fig. 2.1) does not allow any incoming or outgoing edge for nodes of type *up* or *down*, the dangling edge condition for rules *set_direction_up* and *set_direction_down* is always fulfilled. Moreover, each

CHAPTER 2. RULE-BASED MODELING USING GRAPH TRANSFORMATION

process rule deletes a *request* node together with either a *call* loop or a *stop* loop. Since the rules *call_request* and *stop_request* generate *request* nodes either with a call or with a *stop* loop, the initial system state does not hold any requests, and no other rules generate requests, then the dangling edge condition is fulfilled for each *process* rule.

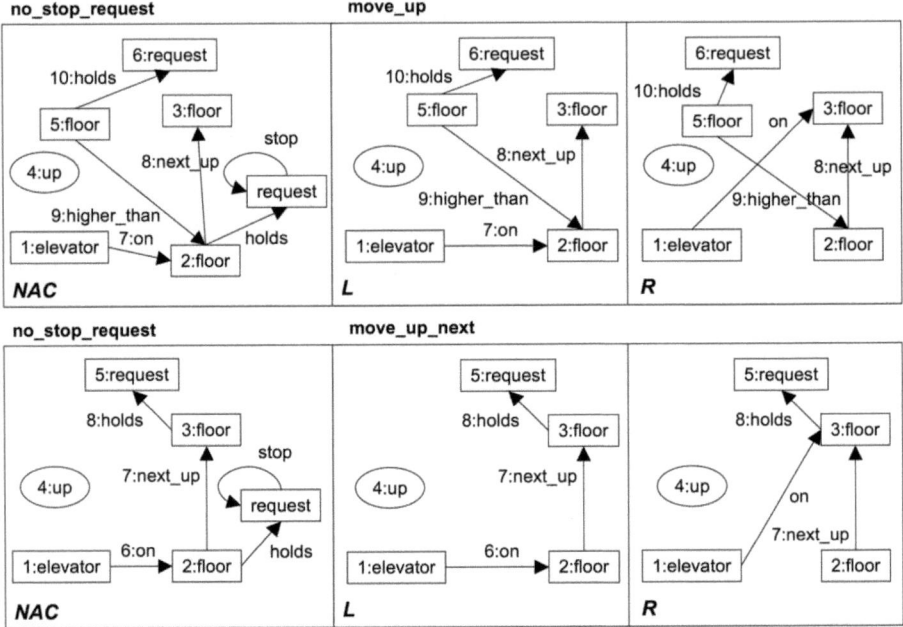

Figure 2.39: equivalent *move_up* rules for *Elevator*

Based on Assumption 2.9.1, it is possible to express the applicability of some rule p with at most one $NAC(n)$ to graph G, by the satisfaction and non-satisfaction of a specific constraint (as given in Corollary 2.9.3) derived from rule p. Analogously, the non-applicability of p with at most one $NAC(n)$ to a graph G is equivalent to the satisfaction of a specific constraint (as given in Corollary 2.9.5) derived from p. Note that Def. 2.2.13 reintroduces the notion of graph constraints. It is part of future work to generalize the following corollaries to nested application conditions and constraints as presented in [46]. With these more general constraints it will also be possible to express the applicability (resp. non-applicability) of rules with more than one $NAC(n)$. Note that Corollary 2.9.5 is used in Chapter 4 in order to certify Property *Constraint Guaranteed*. Moreover, it could be used as a basis for certifying deadlock-freeness. In particular, a constraint can be computed expressing that none of the rules is applicable anymore. If this constraint is equivalent to false, then a deadlock cannot occur. It is part of future work to describe this topic in more detail.

2.9.3 Corollary (rule applicability and constraints). *Given a rule* $p : L \leftarrow K \rightarrow R$ *without NACs and a graph* G, *then* p *is applicable to* G *if and only if* G *satisfies* $C_{appl}(p) = PC(L)$. *Given a rule* $p : L \leftarrow K \rightarrow R$ *with single* $NAC(n)$ *and a graph* G, *then* p *is applicable to*

2.9. APPLICABILITY AND NON-APPLICABILITY OF RULE SEQUENCES

G if and only if G satisfies $PC(L)$ and G does not satisfy $PC(n : L \to N)$ i.e. G satisfies $C_{appl}(p) = PC(L) \wedge \neg PC(n)$.

Proof. Some rule p without NACs is applicable to G if and only if an injective match morphism $m : L \to G$ exists i.e. $G \models PC(L)$. Rule p with $NAC(n)$ is applicable to G because of two reasons. First, there should exist some injective match morphism $m : L \to G$. Moreover, if such a match morphism m exists, then $m \models NAC(n)$ if and only if it holds that no injective morphism $q : N \to G$ exists such that $q \circ n = m$. This means that $PC(n : L \to N)$ should not be fulfilled by G. Note that since m automatically fulfills the gluing condition (see Assumption 2.9.1), there is no third reason for p to be applicable. □

2.9.4 Example (applicability of rule *move_up* of *Elevator*). Consider rule *move_up* as depicted in Fig. 2.39. It is applicable to each system state of *Elevator* such that the elevator is in upward mode, some request is available on a higher floor than the elevator floor that is different from the next floor, and the elevator floor does not hold any stop request. This is expressed by the constraint $PC(L) \wedge \neg PC(n)$ with L the left-hand side of *move_up* and n the morphism of NAC *no_stop_request*.

2.9.5 Corollary (rule non-applicability and constraints). *Given a rule* $p : L \leftarrow K \to R$ *without NACs and a graph* G, *then* p *is not applicable to* G *if and only if* G *satisfies* $C_{applNot}(p) = NC(L)$. *Given a rule* $p : L \leftarrow K \to R$ *with single* $NAC(n)$ *and a graph* G, *then* p *is not applicable to* G *if and only if* G *satisfies* $NC(L)$ *or* $PC(n : L \to N)$ *i.e.* G *satisfies* $C_{applNot}(p) = NC(L) \vee PC(n)$.

Proof. This follows because of Corollary 2.9.3 or because of the following argumentation: Some rule p without NACs is not applicable to G if and only if no injective match morphism $m : L \to G$ exists i.e. $G \models NC(L)$. If p is not applicable to G, then this can have exactly two reasons. The first one is that no match is found from L to G. In this case, G satisfies $NC(L)$. The second reason is that for each existing match $m : L \to G$, $NAC(n)$ is not fulfilled, i.e. there exists some injective morphism $q : N \to G$ such that $q \circ n = m$. This corresponds to the fact that G satisfies $PC(n : L \to N)$. Note that since m automatically fulfills the gluing condition (see Assumption 2.9.1), there is no third reason for p to be non-applicable. □

2.9.6 Example (non-applicability of rule *process_stop_down* of *Elevator*). Consider rule *process_stop_down* as depicted in Fig. 2.18. It is not applicable to each system state of *Elevator* such that no elevator in downward mode is present on a floor with a stop request. This is expressed by the constraint $NC(L)$ with L the left-hand side of *process_stop_down*.

Based on Assumption 2.9.1 and the conflict and dependency characterizations (see Def. 2.6.6 and Def. 2.6.8), we can formulate a weaker version of the Local Church-Rosser Theorem with NACs (see Theorem 2.4.3). It characterizes what it means for a transformation not to cause a conflict with another transformation (resp. not to depend on another transformation). Namely, it is possible to derive different new kinds of rule applicabilities. The following cases occur: If two rules p_1 and p_2 are applicable to the same graph G and the direct transformation $G \Rightarrow H_1$ via p_1 does not cause a conflict with the direct transformation $G \Rightarrow H_2$ via p_2, then it is possible to apply p_2 on the result of the first transformation H_1. If a sequence of rules p_1, p_2 is applicable to G and the first transformation $G \Rightarrow H_1$ via p_1 is reversible after $H_1 \Rightarrow G'$ via p_2, then it is possible to apply p_1^{-1} to G'. If a sequence of rules p_1, p_2 is applicable to G and the second transformation $H_1 \Rightarrow G'$ via p_2 is not triggered by the first one $G \Rightarrow H_1$ via p_1, then it is possible to apply p_2 also to G.

CHAPTER 2. RULE-BASED MODELING USING GRAPH TRANSFORMATION

2.9.7 Theorem (weak local Church-Rosser Theorem with NACs). *Given a graph transformation system GTS with NACs and two direct transformations with NACs $H_1 \stackrel{p_1,m_1}{\Leftarrow} G \stackrel{p_2,m_2}{\Rightarrow} H_2$ such that $G \stackrel{p_1,m_1}{\Rightarrow} H_1$ does not cause a conflict with $G \stackrel{p_2,m_2}{\Rightarrow} H_2$ (as defined in Def. 2.6.6), then there is a graph G' and a direct transformation $H_1 \stackrel{p_2,m'_2}{\Rightarrow} G'$. Vice versa, given two direct transformations with NACs $G \stackrel{p_1,m_1}{\Rightarrow} H_1 \stackrel{p_2,m'_2}{\Rightarrow} G'$ such that $G \stackrel{p_1,m_1}{\Rightarrow} H_1$ is reversible after $H_1 \stackrel{p_2,m'_2}{\Rightarrow} G'$ (as defined in Def. 2.6.8), then there is a graph H_2 and a direct transformation $H_2 \stackrel{p_1,m'_1}{\Rightarrow} G'$. Finally, if $H_1 \stackrel{p_2,m'_2}{\Rightarrow} G'$ is not triggered by $G \stackrel{p_1,m_1}{\Rightarrow} H_1$ (as defined in Def. 2.6.8), then there is a graph H_2 and a direct transformation $G \stackrel{p_2,m_2}{\Rightarrow} H_2$.*

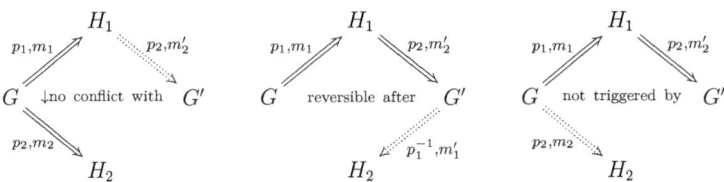

Proof. Follows from Fact 3.2.15 and Theorem 3.9.2 in Chapter 3. □

2.9.8 Example (weak local Church-Rosser property for *Elevator*). Consider a system state of *Elevator* such that the elevator is on the first floor holding a stop request. Now, on the one hand, rule *process_stop_up* can be applied, processing the stop request on the first floor . On the other hand, rule *call_request* can be applied, generating a call request on the first floor. The transformation via *process_stop_up* does not cause a conflict with the transformation via *call_request*. Therefore, it is possible according to Theorem 2.9.7 to apply *call_request* to the first floor after the stop request has been processed. Note that the other way round it is not possible to apply *process_stop_up* on the first floor after a call request has been generated for the first floor. This is because *process_stop_up* holds a NAC *no_call* forbidding a call request. Consider another system state of *Elevator* such that the elevator is in upward mode on the second floor holding a stop request. Now at first rule *process_stop_up* can be applied processing the stop request on the elevator floor. Afterwards it is possible to apply rule *stop_request* on the ground floor. The transformation via *process_stop_up* is reversible after *stop_request*. Therefore, according to Theorem 2.9.7 it is possible to apply the inverse rule of *process_stop_up* to the second floor after a stop request has been generated by *stop_request* on the ground floor. Moreover, the transformation via *stop_request* is not triggered by the transformation via *process_stop_up* since we consider requests on different floors. Note that this would be different if we were to process a stop request on a certain floor, and afterwards generate a stop request for the same floor. In this case though, according to Theorem 2.9.7, it is possible to apply *stop_request* at first on the ground floor, and afterwards process the stop request on the elevator floor.

2.9.1 Reduction of Rule Sequences

Most of the reductions that follow in this section (summary reduction, repeated elements reduction, and loop reduction) reduce a rule sequence to a shorter one under specific conditions. These conditions ensure that the longer sequence is applicable if the short one can be shown to be applicable. These reductions together with the shift-equivalent reduction can also be used

2.9. APPLICABILITY AND NON-APPLICABILITY OF RULE SEQUENCES

to reduce a set of rule sequences to a smaller set of rule sequences. Thereby, the applicability of each rule sequence in the original set follows from the applicability of each rule sequence in the smaller set. The reduced set of rule sequences is obtained by applying the reductions to single rule sequences in this set. Thereby, reduced rule sequences may be equal to already present rule sequences, and therefore, the size of the original set of rule sequences may be reduced. Moreover, by applying summary reduction, repeated elements reduction, or loop reduction to single rule sequences also the length of the rule sequences may be reduced. First, we present a reduction of rule sequences summarizing neighbored rules into concurrent rules (summary reduction), and thereby, show that applicability is not affected.

2.9.9 Theorem (summary reduction). *Consider $s : r_1, r_2, \ldots, r_n$, a sequence of n rules, a graph G_0, and a rule sequence $s' : r'_1, r'_2, \ldots, r'_m$ with $m < n$ in which neighbored rules $r_i, r_{i+1}, \ldots r_{i+k}$ with $k > 0$ in s are summarized by some concurrent rule for $r_i, r_{i+1}, \ldots r_{i+k}$. If the summarized rule sequence s' is applicable to G_0 with injective matching, then the original rule sequence s is applicable to G_0 with injective matching and the same result.*

Proof. Follows from Fact 3.2.15 and Theorem 3.9.3 in Chapter 3. □

2.9.10 Example (summary reduction for *Elevator*). Consider the rule sequence s : *stop_request*, *stop_request*, *call_request*, and the summarized rule sequence s' : *stop_request*, *stop_request* * *call_request* in which the last two rules are summarized into one concurrent rule generating a call and stop request for the same floor. According to Theorem 2.9.9, s is applicable to some G_0 if s' is applicable to G_0. Consider, for example, the initial system state of *Elevator* (see Fig. 2.2) and the following application of s' to this initial state. First, a stop request is generated for the third floor, and afterwards a stop and a call request are generated for the second floor. Then it is possible to generate a stop request for the third floor first, then generate a stop request for the second floor, and afterwards generate a call request for the second floor. Note that the other way round this does not have to be the case. Consider a system state of *Elevator* in which each floor except for the second floor already holds a call request, and the second floor holds a stop request. It is possible to apply s on this state in the following way. First, a stop request is generated for the third floor, then a stop request is generated for the first floor, and afterwards a call request is generated for the second floor. Now s' is not applicable since each floor holds at least one type of request already. Therefore, rule *stop_request* * *call_request* will not be applicable since it holds NACs expressing that neither a call request, nor a stop request can be already present on the floor.

In shift-equivalent rule sequences (see Def. 2.8.17) rule r_j in s is switched with rule r_{j+1} repeatedly under the condition that the pairs of rules (r_j, r_{j+1}) and (r_{j+1}, r_j) are sequentially independent. We show in the following reduction of rule sequences that switching such pairs of sequentially independent rules does not affect applicability. Note that this is a bidirectional reduction. We then also formulate a somewhat weaker unidirectional shift reduction, where we don't require that (r_j, r_{j+1}) is sequentially independent. Note that in [51] a weaker kind of equivalence, so-called permutation equivalence, is introduced for the framework of subobject transformation systems.

2.9.11 Theorem (bidirectional shift-equivalence reduction). *Rule sequence $s : r_1, r_2, \ldots, r_n$ is applicable to graph G_0 if and only if all shift-equivalent rule sequences as defined in Def. 2.8.17 are applicable to G_0 with the same result.*

CHAPTER 2. RULE-BASED MODELING USING GRAPH TRANSFORMATION

Proof. Follows from Fact 3.2.15 and Theorem 3.9.4 in Chapter 3. □

Analogously to Theorem 2.9.11, we can formulate the following reduction, expressing that all shift-equivalent rule sequences are *not* applicable to G_0 as soon as one of them appears to be non-applicable.

2.9.12 Corollary (bidirectional shift-equivalent reduction: non-applicability). *A rule sequence $s : r_1, r_2, \ldots, r_n$ is not applicable to graph G_0 if and only if none of the shift-equivalent rule sequences as defined in Def. 2.8.17 is applicable to G_0 either.*

Proof. Follows from Fact 3.2.15 and Theorem 3.9.5 in Chapter 3. □

2.9.13 Example (shift-equivalent reduction for *Elevator*). As partly shown in Example 2.8.6, rules (*stop_request*, *call_request*) as well as (*call_request*, *stop_request*) are sequentially independent. Therefore, the set of three rule sequences consisting of two times *stop_request* and one *call_request* in any order is applicable to some graph G_0 if and only if one of these rule sequences is applicable. Consider, for example, the initial system state of *Elevator* as depicted in Fig. 2.2. Rule sequence *stop_request*, *stop_request*, *call_request* is applicable to this state and, therefore, the other sequences in which *call_request* comes as first or second rule are applicable as well. Consider, on the other hand, a system state of *Elevator* in which each floor holds already a stop request and a call request. Then, no sequence is applicable since *stop_request*, *stop_request*, *call_request* cannot be applied .

Based on the weaker notion of shift-related rule sequences as given in Def. 2.8.18, we can formulate the following unidirectional reductions with regard to applicability (resp. non-applicability).

2.9.14 Theorem (unidirectional shift reduction). *Consider some rule sequence $s : r_1, r_2, \ldots, r_n$, start graph G_0, and rule sequence s' such that s' is shift-related to s. If s' is applicable to G_0, then s is applicable to graph G_0.*

Proof. Follows from Fact 3.2.15 and Theorem 3.9.6 in Chapter 3. □

2.9.15 Corollary (unidirectional shift reduction: non-applicability). *Consider some rule sequence $s : r_1, r_2, \ldots, r_n$, start graph G_0, and rule sequence s' such that s is shift-related to s'. If s' is not applicable to G_0, then s is not applicable to G_0 either.*

Proof. Follows from Fact 3.2.15 and Corollary 3.9.7 in Chapter 3. □

In order to prove, in Chapter 3, the correctness of some more unidirectional reductions, we introduce two lemmas. In addition, we use these lemmas in Chapter 3 to show the correctness of the applicability criteria in Theorem 2.9.25. The first lemma describes under which conditions an existing transformation sequence can be elongated by a rule that is applicable to one of the intermediate graphs in this sequence. The second lemma can be derived from the first one, and describes under which conditions an applicable rule sequence can be elongated by a rule that has occurred in the rule sequence before.

2.9.16 Lemma (elongate by rule applicable to intermediate graph). *Consider a transformation sequence $t : G_0 \overset{r_1}{\Rightarrow} G_1 \ldots G_{n-1} \overset{r_n}{\Rightarrow} G_n$ via the rule sequence $r_1, r_2, \ldots, r_n$. Rule r is applicable with injective matching to G_n whenever r is applicable with injective matching to some intermediate graph G_j with $0 \leq j \leq n$ in the transformation sequence t, and each r_i with $j+1 \leq i \leq n$ causes no conflict with r.*

2.9. APPLICABILITY AND NON-APPLICABILITY OF RULE SEQUENCES

Proof. Follows from Fact 3.2.15 and Lemma 3.9.8 in Chapter 3. □

2.9.17 Lemma (elongate by occurring rule). *Given a rule sequence $r_1, r_2, \ldots, r_n$ that is applicable to some G_0 with monomorphic matching, then the extended rule sequence $r_1, r_2, \ldots, r_n, r_j$ with $1 \leq j \leq n$ is applicable with injective matching to G_0 if r_i with $j \leq i \leq n$ causes no conflict with r_j.*

Proof. Follows from Fact 3.2.15 and Lemma 3.9.9 in Chapter 3. □

Now, we show another unidirectional reduction for rule sequences in which a subsequence of identical rules occurs such that this rule does not cause any conflict with itself. The applicability of these rule sequences can be deduced from the applicability of the same rule sequence in which this subsequence is reduced to only one occurrence of the rule.

2.9.18 Theorem (repeated elements reduction). *Consider a rule sequence $s : q, r^n, q'$ consisting of a rule sequence q followed by n (with $(n > 1)$) times r followed by a rule sequence q'. Sequence s is applicable to G_0 with injective matching if sequence $s' : q, r, q'$ is applicable to G_0 with injective matching, and r does not cause any conflict with itself, and in addition for each r' in q' one of the following cases holds:*

- *r' is equal to some predecessor rule r'' in s', and r'' together with all intermediate rules of r'' and r' in s' do not cause a conflict with r'*

- *r' is purely enabled as given in Def. 2.8.20 by some predecessor r'' in s', and all intermediate rules of r'' and r' in s' do not cause a conflict with r'*

- *r' is applicable to the start graph G_0 and all predecessor rules of r' in s' do not cause a conflict with r'.*

Proof. Follows from Fact 3.2.15 and Theorem 3.9.10 in Chapter 3. □

2.9.19 Example (repeated elements reduction for *Elevator*). In our running example, all rules are conflicting with themselves. Therefore, it is difficult to find a suitable repeated elements reduction with these rules as an example. Imagine though that we have a rule *add_person_to_floor* generating a person who is present on a specific floor. We can add this rule to the generating grammar $GG_{ElevatorGen}$ as introduced in Example 2.3.16. Therefore, we need to enrich the type graph of *Elevator* by a node type *person* and edge type *present_on* from *person* to *floor*. The rule *add_person_to_floor* then has in its left-hand side a *floor* node. In its right-hand side it has the same *floor* node together with a new edge of type *present_on* from a new node of type *person* to the *floor*. This rule can be used to generate a graph modeling not only how many floors the elevator should serve, but also how many persons are present on each floor. This would enable to also design rules that model the passenger traffic of an elevator with regard to model animation, for example. Now suppose that we have a rule sequence $s' : qrq'$ with $q = $ *add_floor, add_floor*, q' the empty subsequence, and $r =$ *add_person_to_floor*. Consider again the start graph $S_{ElevatorGen}$ as presented in Fig. 2.9 and described in Example 2.3.16. It should be possible to generate with the rule *add_person_to_floor* as many persons as desired to each floor in the building. Now we can deduce because of the above repeated elements reduction that $s : qr^nq'$ is applicable to $S_{ElevatorGen}$ if s' is applicable to it. This is because *add_person_to_floor* is not in conflict with itself. Since s' is applicable to $S_{ElevatorGen}$ generating two more floors in the building, we can conclude that also s is generating n persons on different floors in the building.

It is not only possible to reduce repeated elements of some sequence, but also to reduce repeated subsequences. We call this reduction loop reduction since the loop body should be repeated only once. Note that the loop body is fixed i.e. some subsequence is repeated identically. For this loop reduction in addition to the repeated elements reduction the rules belonging to the loop body should be pairwise parallel independent.

2.9.20 Theorem (loop reduction). *Consider a rule sequence $s : q, (r_1, r_2, \ldots, r_m)^n, q'$ consisting of a rule sequence q followed by n (with $(n > 1)$) times sequence $r_1, r_2, \ldots, r_m$ followed by a rule sequence q'. Sequence s is applicable to G_0 with injective matching if sequence $s' : q, r_1, r_2, \ldots, r_m, q'$ is applicable to G_0 with injective matching, and r_i and r_j are parallel independent for $1 \leq i, j \leq m$, and in addition for each r' in q belonging to s' one of the following cases holds:*

- *r' is equal to some predecessor rule r'' in s', and r'' together with all intermediate rules of r'' and r' in s' do not cause a conflict with r'*

- *r' is purely enabled as given in Def.2.8.20 by some predecessor r'' in s', and all intermediate rules of r'' and r' in s' do not cause a conflict with r'*

- *r' is applicable to the start graph G_0 and all predecessor rules of r' in s' do not cause a conflict with r'.*

Proof. Follows from Fact 3.2.15 and Theorem 3.9.11 in Chapter 3. □

2.9.21 Remark. Note that the repeated elements reduction is a special case of the loop reduction.

2.9.22 Example (loop reduction for *Elevator*). We continue with considering the rule *add_person_to_floor* as introduced in Example 2.9.19. Now, suppose that we have a rule sequence $s' : qr_1r_2q'$ with q empty, r_1 =*add_floor*, r_2 =*add_person_to_floor* and q' empty. Rules *add_floor* and *add_person_to_floor* are parallel independent, and they are also parallel independent with themselves. Therefore, as soon as rule sequence s' is applicable to some graph G_0 also the rule sequence $s : (r_1r_2)^n$ with $n > 1$ will be applicable. Thus, we can add a floor to the building, and afterwards add a person to some floor in the building – for example, to the new floor – as many times as desired.

2.9.2 Applicability Criteria

Let $s : r_1r_2 \ldots r_n$ be a sequence of n rules and G_0 a graph on which this sequence should be applied. The criteria defined in the following definition guarantee this applicability. Note that these criteria are sufficient, but not necessary. The reductions presented in the previous section can help if the criteria appear to be not sufficient enough. The *initialization* criterion is trivial since it just requires the first rule being applicable to G_0. The *no impeding predecessors* criterion ensures that the applicability of a rule r_i is not impeded by one of the predecessor rules r_j of r_i. Criterion *pure enabling predecessor* will be satisfied if rule r_i is purely enabled by some predecessor rule r_j in the sequence s. In this case r_j triggers the applicability of r_i regardless of what is present already in the start graph G_0. The *not-needed enabling predecessor* criterion applies to rules that are already applicable to the start graph G_0, and do not need to be triggered by some predecessor rule. The correctness of the criteria is proven in Theorem 2.9.25.

2.9. APPLICABILITY AND NON-APPLICABILITY OF RULE SEQUENCES

2.9.23 Definition (applicability criteria). Given a sequence $s : r_1 r_2 \ldots r_n$ of n rules and a graph G_0, then we define the following applicability criteria for s on G_0:

initialization r_1 is applicable to G_0 via some injective match $m_1 : L_1 \to G_0$

no impeding predecessors $\forall r_i, r_j$ in s with $1 \leq j < i \leq n$, r_j does not cause a conflict with r_i

enabling predecessor $\forall r_i$ in s with $1 < i \leq n$ one of the following cases holds

> **pure** there exists a rule r_j in s with $1 \leq j < i \leq n$ and r_i is purely enabled by r_j, which especially means that r_i has no NACs
>
> **not needed** rule r_i itself is applicable to G_0 via some injective match. We say that r_i is *self-enabled*.

2.9.24 Remark (partial rule dependencies). Note that these applicability criteria as well as the non-applicability criteria (as presented in the next section) are only sufficient for applicability (resp. non-applicability). For example, the no impeding predecessor criterion forbids each kind of conflict that might be caused by some predecessor rule. It might be the case though that the matches of the corresponding transformation can be chosen in such a way that these potential conflicts do not occur. It is part of future work to consider these eventualities in improved criteria. The notion of partial rule dependencies as introduced in [55] should support this development. They express which nodes (or also edges) should be reused within the graph transformation when applying the rule sequence.

2.9.25 Theorem (correctness of applicability criteria). *Consider $s : r_1, r_2, \ldots, r_n$ a sequence of n rules and a graph G_0. If the criteria in Def. 2.9.23 are satisfied for rule sequence s and graph G_0, then this rule sequence is applicable to G_0 with injective matching i.e. there exists a transformation $G_0 \overset{r_1}{\Rightarrow} G_1 \ldots G_{n-1} \overset{r_n}{\Rightarrow} G_n$ with injective matching.*

Proof. Follows from Fact 3.2.15 and Theorem 3.9.14 in Chapter 3. □

2.9.26 Example (applicable rule sequence for *Elevator*). Consider rule sequence s : *stop_request, call_request* and the initial system state of *Elevator* as G_0 and depicted in Fig. 2.2. This rule sequence is applicable to G_0 since *stop_request* can be applied to G_0 (initialization), *stop_request* does not cause any conflict with *call_request* (no impeding predecessors), and *call_request* is applicable to G_0 (not needed). Note that according to the applicability criteria above, this rule sequence is applicable to each system state G_0 to which *stop_request* and *call_request* are applicable.

The pure enabling predecessor criterion is only sufficient for the case that some rule r does not need anything from the start graph G_0, for example. The more general criterion *direct enabling predecessor* ensures the applicability of a rule r_i causally dependent on a direct predecessor rule together with the start graph G_0. This is expressed by the fact that a concurrent rule r_c of r_{i-1} and r_i exists that is applicable to the start graph G_0. The construction of a concurrent rule with NACs is explained in Section 2.5. The correctness of this new criterion can be shown by using the summary reduction introduced in the previous section.

2.9.27 Definition (direct enabling predecessor criterion). Given a sequence $s : r_1, r_2, \ldots, r_n$ of n rules and a graph G_0, then we define the *direct enabling predecessor criterion* for s on G_0 as follows:

CHAPTER 2. RULE-BASED MODELING USING GRAPH TRANSFORMATION

direct there exists a concurrent rule r_c of r_{i-1} and r_i such that r_c is applicable via some injective match on G_0 and r_j does not cause a conflict with r_c for $j < (i-1)$. We say that r_i is *directly enabled*.

2.9.28 Theorem (direct enabling predecessor criterion). *Theorem 2.9.25 (correctness of applicability criteria) still holds if the enabling predecessor in Def. 2.9.23 is extended by the direct enabling predecessor criterion as given in Def. 2.9.27. Thus, a rule can be also directly enabled in order to fulfill the enabling predecessor criterion.*

Proof. Follows from Fact 3.2.15 and Theorem 3.9.16 in Chapter 3. □

2.9.29 Remark. Please note that r_c can be matched to G_0 in a different way to how r_{n-1} was related to G_0 during the checking procedure of the applicability criteria. Thus, the last step in the transformation sequence that arose for rule sequence $r_1 \ldots r_{n-1}$ can be overwritten when checking the criteria for rule r_n. This is avoided by Def. 2.9.34 of forwarded concurrent matches.

2.9.30 Example (direct enabling predecessor in *Elevator*). Consider rule sequence s : *stop_request, call_request, process_call_down* (see Fig. 2.39) and the system state G_0 of *Elevator* as depicted in Fig. 2.40, expressing that the elevator car is on the highest floor in downward direction without any requests. Analogously to Example 2.9.26, we can conclude that the first

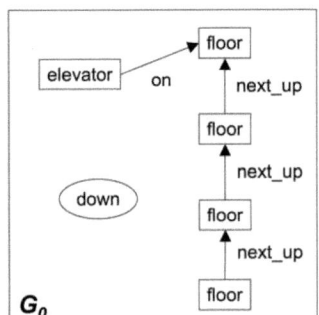

Figure 2.40: elevator on highest floor

two rules of s are applicable to G_0. We check at first the no impeding predecessor criterion for rule *process_call_down*. Since rule *process_call_down* does not forbid anything, no conflicts occur with its predecessor rules *stop_request* and *call_request*. We then show that rule *process_call_down* is directly enabled by *call_request*. The following concurrent rule of *call_request* and *process_call_down* can be applied to G_0. It consists of the identical rule checking for the existence of an elevator cabin in downward direction on some floor, and thereby, forbidding the presence of a call request on this floor. This concurrent rule expresses the situation that an external call for the elevator in downward direction is registered on the elevator floor, which can then be processed immediately. It is applicable to G_0 in which the elevator is on the highest floor and no requests are present at all. Note that according to the criteria rule sequence s is applicable to each system state G_0 such that a stop request can be generated on some floor, the elevator car is in downward mode, and the elevator car is on a floor without call request.

2.9. APPLICABILITY AND NON-APPLICABILITY OF RULE SEQUENCES

2.9.31 Definition (multiple direct enabling predecessors criterion). Given a sequence s : $r_1, r_2, \ldots, r_n$ of n rules and a graph G_0, then we define the *multiple direct enabling predecessors criterion* for s on G_0 as follows:

multiple direct there exists a concurrent rule r_c of r'_c and r_i such that r'_c is a concurrent rule of $r_{i-k}, r_{i-k+1}, \ldots, r_{i-1}$ with $k > 1$, r_c is applicable via some injective match on G_0 and r_j does not cause a conflict with r_c for $j < (i - k)$. We say that r_i is *multiple directly enabled*.

2.9.32 Theorem (multiple direct enabling predecessors criterion). *Theorem 2.9.25 (correctness of applicability criteria) still holds if the enabling predecessor in Def. 2.9.23 is extended by the multiple direct enabling predecessors criterion as given in Def. 2.9.27. Thus, a rule can also be multiple directly enabled in order to fulfill the enabling predecessor criterion.*

Proof. Follows from Fact 3.2.15 and Theorem 3.9.19 in Chapter 3. □

2.9.33 Example (multiple direct enabling predecessor in *Elevator*). Consider rule sequence s : *stop_request, call_request, process_stop_and_call*. We show that this rule sequence is applicable to the initial system state G_0 of *Elevator*. As explained in Example 2.9.26 it is possible to apply *stop_request* and *call_request* to G_0. Now *process_stop_and_call* is multiple directly enabled by *stop_request* and *call_request* by means of the following concurrent rule. It checks for the existence of an elevator standing on a certain floor (identical rule) with a NAC checking if neither a stop nor a call request is present for the elevator floor. This rule is applicable to the initial system state G_0 of *Elevator* with an elevator car on the ground floor without any requests. In general, it follows from the criteria that s is applicable to each system state G_0 where the elevator floor holds neither a stop nor a call request.

The following definition of forwarded concurrent match ensures that when matching a rule (resp. concurrent rule) to some graph G_0 the same match is continued to be used when extending it to a concurrent (resp. longer concurrent) rule.

2.9.34 Definition (forwarded concurrent match). Consider a concurrent rule $r_c = r'_c *_E r_n$ of a sequence of rules $r_0, \ldots, r_n$ as defined in Def. 2.5.2 and matches $m_c : L_c \to G_0$ and $m'_c : L'_c \to G_0$ from the LHS of r_c (resp. r'_c) into G_0. Let l_c be the lhs-match of r_c. We say that m'_c is *forwarded* to m_c if $m_c \circ l_c = m'_c$ as shown on the right. We say that m_c is a *forwarded concurrent match*.

We can formulate yet another enabling predecessor criterion for the case that the enabling predecessor is not direct.

2.9.35 Definition (partial enabling predecessor criterion). Given a sequence $s : r_1, r_2, \ldots, r_n$ of n rules and a graph G_0, then we define the *partial enabling predecessor criterion* for s on G_0 as follows:

partial there exists a concurrent rule $r_c = r_j *_E r_i$ of rule r_i and a not necessarily direct predecessor rule r_j with $1 \leq j < i$ such that r_c is applicable via some injective match m_{r_c} to G_0. Moreover, all predecessors r_k with $1 \leq k < j$ of r_c do not cause a conflict with r_c. In addition, the following *forward condition* should hold: r_j was self-enabled via some m_{r_j} such that m_{r_j} is forwarded to m_{r_c} as in Def. 2.9.34. We say that r_i is *partially enabled* by r_j via r_c and m_{r_c}.

CHAPTER 2. RULE-BASED MODELING USING GRAPH TRANSFORMATION

2.9.36 Remark. Please note that the difference of the partial enabling predecessor criterion and the direct enabling predecessor criterion in Def. 2.9.23 is that the partial enabling predecessor does not need to be direct, but in return fulfills the *forward condition*. Moreover, note that if r_i fulfills the partial enabling predecessor criterion without any intermediate rule between r_i and r_j (i.e. $j = i - 1$), then r_i is *directly enabled*.

2.9.37 Theorem (partial enabling predecessor criterion). *Theorem 2.9.25 (correctness of applicability criteria) still holds if the enabling predecessor criterion in Def. 2.9.23 is extended by the partial enabling predecessor criterion as given in Def. 2.9.35. Thus, a rule can be also partially enabled in order to fulfill the enabling predecessor criterion.*

Proof. Follows from Fact 3.2.15 and Theorem 3.9.23 in Chapter 3. □

2.9.38 Example (partial enabling predecessor in *Elevator*). Consider rule sequence s : *stop_request*, *call_request*, *process_stop_down* and the system state G_0 of *Elevator* as depicted in Fig. 2.40, expressing that the elevator car is in downward direction on the highest floor without any requests. Analogous to Example 2.9.26, we can conclude that the first two rules of s are applicable to G_0. We show as a next step that the no impeding predecessor criterion holds for *process_stop_down*. This is the case since it does not forbid anything that could have been produced by its predecessors. We now show that *process_stop_down* is partially enabled by *stop_request* under the following conditions. Consider the following concurrent rule of *stop_request* and *process_stop_down*. It is an identical rule checking for the existence of an elevator cabin in downward direction on some floor without stop request. This concurrent rule expresses that on an elevator floor without stop request a stop request can be generated that is immediately processed afterwards. Note that *stop_request* is self-enabled such that its match can be forwarded to a match for this concurrent rule. This is the case if we apply *stop_request* to the elevator floor. The same match will be 'reused' by the concurrent rule. Note that *call_request* is self-enabled in this case since it can be applied on any floor without a call request. Note that, in general, according to the above criteria s is applicable to any system state G_0 of *Elevator* where the elevator car is in downward mode, no stop request is already present on the elevator floor, and a floor is present for which a call request can be generated.

From the applicability criteria for a rule sequence, we can deduce some specific conditions under which a rule of a conflict-free grammar is always applicable. This leads in addition to a sufficient and necessary condition for non-termination of conflict-free grammars.

2.9.39 Corollary (necessary and sufficient condition for rule applicability in (resp. non-termination of) conflict-free grammar). *Consider a conflict-free (according to Def. 2.7.17) graph grammar with NACs* $GR = (P, S)$ *with start graph S. Rule p in P is applicable to each graph belonging to $\mathcal{L}(GR)$ if and only if p is applicable to the start graph S. This means in particular that a conflict-free grammar (P, S) is non-terminating if and only if at least one rule p in P is applicable to the start graph S.*

Proof. Follows from Fact 3.2.15 and Corollary 3.9.24 in Chapter 3. □

If in a regular grammar no rule causes a conflict with some rule p, then p is always applicable if and only if it is applicable to the start graph. Therefrom we can deduce another sufficient condition for non-termination of grammars.

2.9. APPLICABILITY AND NON-APPLICABILITY OF RULE SEQUENCES

2.9.40 Corollary (necessary and sufficient (resp. sufficient) condition for rule applicability in (resp. non-termination of) grammar). *Consider a graph grammar with NACs* $GR = (P, S)$ *with start graph S such that each rule in P does not cause any conflict according to Def. 2.8.11 with some particular rule p in P. Rule p is applicable to each graph belonging to $\mathcal{L}(GR)$ if and only if it is applicable to the start graph S. In particular, this means that a grammar (P, S) is non-terminating as soon as at least one rule p in P is applicable to the start graph S such that p does not cause any conflict with itself.*

Proof. Follows from Fact 3.2.15 and Corollary 3.9.25 in Chapter 3. □

2.9.41 Example (*Elevator* is non-terminating). Consider rule sequence s : *stop_request, call_request, process_stop_and_call* of *Elevator*. Consider the concurrent rule of this rule sequence as introduced in Example 2.9.33. It checks for the existence of an elevator standing on a certain floor (identical rule) with a NAC checking if neither a stop nor a call request is present for the elevator floor. This concurrent rule expresses the situation that on the elevator floor an internal stop and an external call is registered that can then be processed immediately. We call this concurrent rule *stop_call_process*. Consider now graph grammar $GG_{Elevator} = (GTS_{Elevator}, S_{Elevator})$ as introduced in Example 2.3.5. We can add rule *stop_call_process* to this grammar obtaining $GG_{ElevatorExt}$. Since rule *stop_call_process* is non-conflicting with itself, and since *stop_call_process* is applicable to $S_{Elevator}$, we have that $GG_{ElevatorExt}$ is non-terminating. It follows straightforwardly from Theorem 2.5.9 that the languages generated by $GG_{Elevator}$ and $GG_{ElevatorExt}$ are equal. This is because each transformation via the concurrent rule *stop_call_process* can be decomposed in a transformation via the single rules *stop_request, call_request,* and *process_stop_and_call*. Therefore, we can conclude that also $GG_{Elevator}$ is non-terminating.

2.9.3 Non-Applicability Criteria

Let $s : r_1, r_2, \ldots, r_n$ be a sequence of n rules and G_0 a graph. The satisfaction of the following criteria for s and G_0 guarantee that s will not be applicable to G_0. The *initialization error* is trivial since it just requires the first rule being non-applicable to G_0. Criterion *no enabling predecessor* checks if predecessors for a rule r_i, which is not applicable already on G_0, are present in the sequence that can trigger the applicability of r_i. If not, r_i will not be applicable, and therefore, neither will the rule sequence be applicable.

2.9.42 Definition (non-applicability criteria). Given $s : r_1, r_2, \ldots, r_n$ a sequence of n rules and a graph G_0, then we define the following non-applicability criteria for s on G_0:

initialization error r_1 is not applicable to G_0

no enabling predecessor $\exists r_i$ in s with $1 < i \leq n$ such that r_i is not applicable to G_0 and for all rules r_j in s with $1 \leq j < i \leq n$, r_i is not triggered by r_j.

2.9.43 Theorem (correctness of non-applicability criteria). *Consider a sequence $s : r_1, r_2, \ldots, r_n$ of n rules and a graph G_0. If the initialization error or no enabling predecessor criterion in Def. 2.9.42 is satisfied for rule sequence s and graph G_0, then this rule sequence is not applicable to G_0 i.e. there exists no transformation $G_0 \overset{r_1}{\Rightarrow} G_1 \ldots G_{n-1} \overset{r_n}{\Rightarrow} G_n$.*

Proof. Follows from Fact 3.2.15 and Theorem 3.9.27 in Chapter 3. □

2.9.44 Remark. Please note that this theorem holds for general matching.

2.9.45 Example (non-applicable rule sequences for *Elevator*). Consider the initial system state G_0 of *Elevator* as depicted in Fig. 2.2. Each sequence starting with rule *move_up* is not applicable because of an initialization error. Rule *move_up* cannot be applied as long as no request is present. Moreover, consider rule sequence s : *call_request, stop_request, move_up, move_down*. Rule *move_down* is not applicable to G_0 since it expects the elevator to be in downward mode. Therefore, s is not applicable to G_0 because rule *move_down* has no enabling predecessor. The elevator should at first change its direction mode before being able to move down.

From the non-applicability criteria for a rule sequence we can deduce some sufficient and necessary condition under which a rule of a dependency-free grammar is never applicable. This leads in addition to a sufficient condition for rules to be superfluous in a dependency-free grammar.

2.9.46 Corollary (necessary and sufficient (resp. sufficient) condition for rule non-applicability (resp. superfluity) in dependency-free grammar). *Consider a dependency-free (according to Def. 2.7.19) graph grammar with NACs* GR $= (P, S)$ *with start graph S. Rule p in P is not applicable to the start graph S if and only if it is not applicable to any graph belonging to $\mathcal{L}(GR)$. If rule p in P is not applicable to the start graph S, then $\mathcal{L}$(GR) $= \mathcal{L}$(GR') where GR' is GR with a new set of rules $P' = P \setminus \{p\}$.*

Proof. Follows from Fact 3.2.15 and Corollary 3.9.28 in Chapter 3. □

2.9.47 Corollary (necessary and sufficient (resp. sufficient) condition for rule non-applicability (resp. superfluity) in grammar). *Consider a graph grammar with NACs* GR $= (P, S)$ *with start graph S such that p cannot be triggered by any rule in $P \setminus \{p\}$. Rule p in P is not applicable to the start graph S if and only if it is not applicable to any graph belonging to $\mathcal{L}(GR)$. If rule p in P is not applicable to the start graph S, then $\mathcal{L}$(GR) $= \mathcal{L}$(GR') where GR' is GR with a new set of rules $P' = P \setminus \{p\}$.*

Proof. Follows from Fact 3.2.15 and Corollary 3.9.29 in Chapter 3. □

2.9.48 Example (no superfluous rules in *Elevator*). In *Elevator*, we cannot deduce from the above corollary that any rule is superfluous. This is because each rule that is not applicable to the initial system state (see Fig. 2.2) of *Elevator* is triggered by at least some other rule. Suppose though that we were to delete the rules *stop_request* and *move_down* from the rules in *Elevator*. Then, the rule *process_stop_down* would be superfluous in *Elevator* since it can no longer be triggered by any rule.

2.10 Embedding and Confluence

In Section 2.5 we have defined the concurrent rule p_c with NACs (resp. match g_c) induced by a transformation t. We need this definition in order to define NAC consistency, which is an extra condition needed on top of boundary consistency to generalize the Embedding and Extension Theorem to transformations with NACs. Having generalized the notion of critical pairs, completeness, embedding and extension to transformations with NACs, it is now possible

2.10. EMBEDDING AND CONFLUENCE

to formulate a sufficient condition on the critical pairs with NACs in order to obtain local confluence of a graph transformation system with NACs, i.e. to formulate the Critical Pair Lemma with NACs.

We start though with the definition of NAC consistency for an extension morphism k_0 w.r.t. a transformation t. It expresses that the extended concurrent match induced by t should fulfill the concurrent NAC induced by t.

2.10.1 Definition (NAC consistency). A morphism $k_0 : G_0 \to G'_0$ is called NAC consistent w.r.t. a transformation $t : G_0 \Rightarrow^* G_n$ if $k_0 \circ g_c \models NAC_{p_c}$ with NAC_{p_c} the *concurrent NAC* and g_c the *concurrent match induced by t*.

The Embedding Theorem for rules with NACs requires as extra condition on the extension morphism k_0 NAC consistency. Note the following renaming in order to be able to distinguish better NAC consistency from the consistency needed for the Embedding Theorem without NACs. In the following we speak about *boundary consistency* when we mean *consistency* as in Def. 6.12 of [29]. For readability reasons, we reintroduce the definition of boundary consistency. Intuitively, it means that the boundary graph B (see Construction 2.6.10) of the extension morphism k_0 is preserved by the transformation t.

2.10.2 Definition (boundary consistency). Given a transformation $t : G_0 \overset{*}{\Rightarrow} G_n$ with a derived span $der(t) = (G_0 \overset{d_0}{\leftarrow} D \overset{d_n}{\to} G_n)$ (see Def. 6.9 in [29]), then a morphism $k_0 : G_0 \to G'_0$ is called *boundary consistent* with respect to t if there exist an initial pushout (1) (see Construction 2.6.10) over k_0 and an injective morphism b with $d_0 \circ b = b_0$:

$$\begin{array}{c} B \overset{b_0}{\to} G_0 \overset{d_0}{\leftarrow} D \overset{d_n}{\to} G_n \\ \downarrow \quad (1) \quad \downarrow k_0 \\ C \longrightarrow G'_0 \end{array}$$

2.10.3 Theorem (embedding theorem with NACs). *Consider a transformation $t : G_0 \Rightarrow^n G_n$ with NACs. If $k_0 : G_0 \to G'_0$ is boundary consistent and NAC consistent w.r.t. t, then there exists an extension diagram with NACs over t and k_0.*

Proof. Follows from Fact 3.2.15 and Theorem 3.10.3 in Chapter 3. □

2.10.4 Example (embedding a transformation for *Elevator*). Consider the transformation as depicted in Fig. 2.41. It adds a stop request on the elevator floor for an elevator in upward direction, and immediately afterwards processes this request such that the elevator can continue moving upward. Note that we again omit depicting the arrows of type *higher_than* since they would make the picture too complex. The concurrent rule induced by this transformation consists of the following parts. Its left-hand side holds an elevator standing on a certain floor connected to the next upward floor and a floor that is higher than the elevator floor holding a request. The right-hand side is identical to the left-hand side except for the elevator having moved to the next upward floor. Moreover, the induced concurrent rule holds the following NACs. The first NAC stems from *stop_request* and already forbids the elevator floor to hold a stop request. The second NAC forbids this as well for the case that the next upward floor to the elevator floor is the same as the floor with the triggering request for the *move_up* rule. The third NAC stems from NAC *no_call* of rule *process_stop_up*. It forbids the elevator floor to hold a call request. The fourth NAC forbids this as well for the case again that the next upward floor to the elevator floor is the same as the floor with the triggering request. The next NAC stems from NAC *no_stop_request* of rule *move_up*, and already forbids the elevator floor to hold a stop request. This NAC is identical to the first one, and thus, can be omitted. The next NAC stems from NAC *no_stop_request_glue*, and forbids the elevator floor to hold a stop request already for the case that the next upward floor and the floor holding the triggering upward request are the same. This NAC is identical to the second one, and thus, can be omitted. Now consider both graphs G'_0 and G''_0 in Fig. 2.42. From G_0 to G'_0 there is an extension morphism k_0 embedding the system state of *Elevator* into a building with one more higher floor. Can the above sequence be embedded into this bigger context? First, we check if k_0 is boundary consistent. The boundary consists in this case of the highest floor in the old building since a new higher floor is attached to it by k_0. The interface D of the derived span of $G_0 \Rightarrow^3 G_3$ consists of the intersection of G_0 and G_3. The highest floor in the old building is contained in D, and therefore, k_0 is boundary consistent. Now we check if k_0 is also NAC consistent. We see that there is neither a stop request nor a call request on the elevator floor. Therefore, the transformation can be embedded into G'_0, and can be repeated in the higher building. Now we consider the embedding morphism k'_0 from G_0 into G'''_0 adding a call request on the elevator floor. We now see that k_0 is not NAC consistent since call requests are forbidden by the induced concurrent rule on the elevator floor. Therefore, it is not possible to embed the transformation into G'''_0.

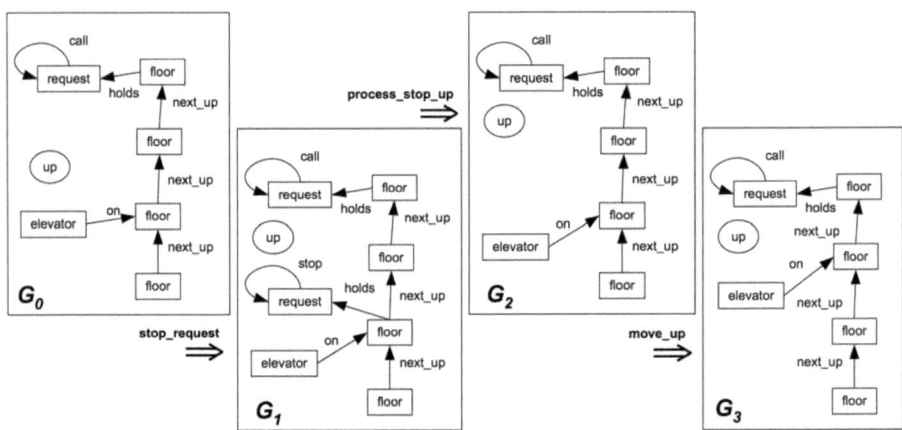

Figure 2.41: transformation for *Elevator*

The following Extension Theorem with NACs describes the fact that boundary and NAC consistency are not only sufficient, but also necessary conditions for the construction of extension diagrams for transformations with NACs.

2.10.5 Theorem (extension theorem with NACs). *Given a transformation $t : G_0 \Rightarrow^n G_n$ with NACs with a derived span $der(t) = (G_0 \xleftarrow{d_0} D_n \xrightarrow{d_n} G_n)$ and an extension diagram (1) as in the*

2.10. EMBEDDING AND CONFLUENCE

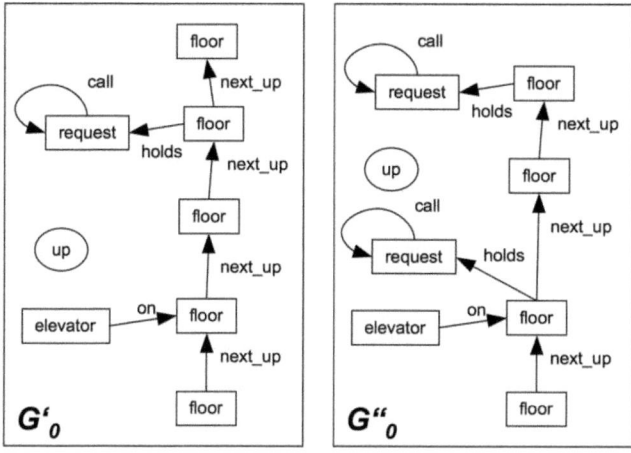

Figure 2.42: embedding *Elevator* transformation in Fig. 2.41 into G'_0 or G''_0

following picture:

$$B \xrightarrow{b_0} G_0 \xRightarrow{t} {}^* G_n$$
$$\quad\quad (2)\ k_0 \downarrow \quad (1) \quad \downarrow k_n$$
$$C \longrightarrow G'_0 \xRightarrow{t'} {}^* G'_n$$

then

- $k_0 : G_0 \to G'_0$ is boundary consistent w.r.t. t, with the morphism $b : B \to D_n$.

- $k_0 : G_0 \to G'_0$ is NAC consistent w.r.t. t.

- Let $p_c : L_c \leftarrow K_c \to R_c$ (resp. $g_c : L_c \to G_0$) be the concurrent rule with NAC_{p_c} (resp. concurrent match) induced by t. There is a direct transformation $G'_0 \Rightarrow G'_n$ via $der(t)$ with $NAC_{der(t)} = D_{g_c}(NAC_{p_c})$ and match k_0 given by pushouts (3) and (4) with h and k_n injective.

- There are initial pushouts (5) and (6) over h injective and k_n injective, respectively, with the same boundary-context morphism $B \to C$.

$$G_0 \xleftarrow{d_0} D_n \xrightarrow{d_n} G_n \quad B \xrightarrow{b} D_n \quad B \xrightarrow{d_n \circ b} G_n$$
$$k_0 \downarrow (3) \quad h \downarrow (4) \quad \downarrow k_n \quad \downarrow (5) \quad \downarrow h \quad \downarrow (6) \quad \downarrow k_n$$
$$G'_0 \leftarrow D'_n \longrightarrow G'_n \quad C \longrightarrow D'_n \quad C \longrightarrow G'_n$$

Proof. Follows from Fact 3.2.15 and Theorem 3.10.4 in Chapter 3. □

For the Critical Pair Lemma with NACs, we need a stronger condition as in the case without NACs in order to obtain local confluence of the graph transformation system. In addition to strict confluence of the set of critical pairs, we also need NAC confluence. If a critical pair is strictly confluent via some transformations t_1 and t_2, we call t_1 and t_2 a *strict solution* of the critical pair. NAC confluence of a critical pair expresses that the NAC consistency of an

CHAPTER 2. RULE-BASED MODELING USING GRAPH TRANSFORMATION

extension morphism w.r.t. a strict solution of the critical pair follows from the NAC consistency of the extension morphism w.r.t. the critical pair itself.

We reintroduce the definition of strict confluence first. Intuitively, it means that the common graph part, which is preserved by the critical pair, is also preserved by the strict solution of the critical pair.

2.10.6 Definition (strict confluence of critical pairs). A critical pair $P_1 \overset{p_1,g_1}{\Leftarrow} K \overset{p_2,g_2}{\Rightarrow} P_2$ is called *strictly confluent*, if we have the following:

Confluence The critical pair is confluent, i.e. there are transformations $t_1 : P_1 \overset{*}{\Rightarrow} K'$, $t_2 : P_2 \overset{*}{\Rightarrow} K'$ with derived spans $der(P_i \overset{*}{\Rightarrow} K') = (P_i \overset{v_{i+2}}{\Leftarrow} N_{i+2} \overset{w_{i+2}}{\to} K')$ for $i = 1, 2$.

Strictness Let $der(K \overset{p_i,o_i}{\Rightarrow} P_i) = (K \overset{v_i}{\leftarrow} N_i \overset{w_i}{\to} P_i)$ for $i = 1, 2$, and let N be the pullback object of the pullback (1). Then, there are morphisms z_3 and z_4 such that (2),(3), and (4) commute:

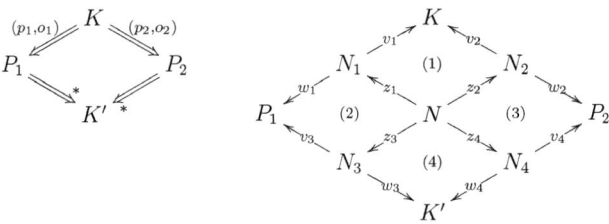

2.10.7 Definition (strictly NAC confluent). A critical pair $P_1 \overset{p_1,g_1}{\Leftarrow} K \overset{p_2,g_2}{\Rightarrow} P_2$ is *strictly NAC confluent* if and only if

- it is *strictly confluent* via some transformations $t_1 : K \overset{p_1,g_1}{\Rightarrow} P_1 \Rightarrow^* X$ and $t_2 : K \overset{p_2,g_2}{\Rightarrow} P_2 \Rightarrow^* X$

- and it is *NAC confluent for t_1 and t_2*, i.e. for every injective morphism $k_0 : K \to G$ that is NAC consistent w.r.t. $K \overset{p_1,g_1}{\Rightarrow} P_1$ and $K \overset{p_2,g_2}{\Rightarrow} P_2$ it follows that k_0 is NAC consistent w.r.t. t_1 and t_2.

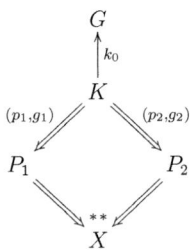

A sufficient condition for local confluence that is easy to check is described in the following fact.

2.10.8 Fact (no critical pairs). *A graph transformation system with NACs is locally confluent if there are no critical pairs for this graph transformation system with NACs.*

Proof. Follows from Fact 3.2.15 and Fact 3.10.7 in Chapter 3. □

2.10. EMBEDDING AND CONFLUENCE

2.10.9 Theorem (local confluence theorem – critical pair lemma with NACs). *Given a graph transformation system with NACs, it is locally confluent if all its critical pairs are strictly NAC confluent.*

Proof. Follows from Fact 3.2.15 and Theorem 3.10.8 in Chapter 3. □

Given a critical pair and a strict solution for it, it is in general difficult to check for NAC confluence of this solution. It would be desirable to have a constructive method to check for NAC confluence. Therefore, the following theorem formulates a constructive sufficient condition (called implication condition) for a critical pair $P_1 \overset{p_1}{\Leftarrow} K \overset{p_2}{\Rightarrow} P_2$ that is strictly confluent via some transformations $t_1 : K \overset{p_1,g_1}{\Rightarrow} P_1 \Rightarrow^* X$ and $t_2 : K \overset{p_2,g_2}{\Rightarrow} P_2 \Rightarrow^* X$ to be also NAC confluent for t_1 and t_2. This means by definition that for every extension morphism $k_0 : K \to G$ that is injective and NAC consistent w.r.t. $K \overset{p_1,g_1}{\Rightarrow} P_1$ and $K \overset{p_2,g_2}{\Rightarrow} P_2$ it follows that k_0 is also NAC consistent w.r.t. t_1 and t_2. In the following theorem two different conditions on each single $NAC(n_{1,j})$ (resp. $NAC(n_{2,j})$) of the concurrent NAC induced by transformation t_1 (resp. t_2) are given leading to NAC confluence if one of them is satisfied. The first condition expresses that there exists a suitable NAC on p_1 (resp. p_2) evoking the satisfaction of $NAC(n_{1,j})$ (resp. $NAC(n_{2,j})$). The second condition first asks for a suitable morphism between the LHS's of the concurrent rules induced by both transformations t_1 and t_2. Moreover, it expresses that there exists a suitable NAC on p_2 (resp. p_1) evoking the satisfaction of $NAC(n_{1,j})$ (resp. $NAC(n_{2,j})$).

2.10.10 Theorem (implication condition for NAC confluence). *Consider a critical pair $P_1 \overset{p_1}{\Leftarrow} K \overset{p_2}{\Rightarrow} P_2$ that is strictly confluent via the transformations $t_1 : K \overset{p_1,g_1}{\Rightarrow} P_1 \Rightarrow^* X$ and $t_2 : K \overset{p_2,g_2}{\Rightarrow} P_2 \Rightarrow^* X$. Let $L_{c,1}$ (resp. $L_{c,2}$) be the left-hand side of the concurrent rule $p_{c,1}$ (resp. $p_{c,2}$) and $m_1 : L_1 \to L_{c,1}$ (resp. $m_2 : L_2 \to L_{c,2}$) the lhs-match induced by t_1 (resp. t_2). Then the critical pair $P_1 \overset{p_1}{\Leftarrow} K \overset{p_2}{\Rightarrow} P_2$ is also NAC confluent for t_1 and t_2, and thus, strictly NA confluent if one of the following implication conditions holds for each $NAC(n_{1,j}) : L_{c,1} \to N_{1,j}$ (resp. $NAC(n_{2,j}) : L_{c,2} \to N_{2,j}$) of the concurrent $NAC_{p_{c,1}}$ induced by t_1 (resp. $NAC_{p_{c,2}}$ induced by t_2):*

- *there exists a $NAC(n'_{1,i}) : L_{c,1} \to N'_{1,i}$ (resp. $NAC(n'_{2,i}) : L_{c,2} \to N'_{2,i}$) in $D_{m_1}(NAC_{p_1})$ (resp. $D_{m_2}(NAC_{p_2})$) and an injective morphism $d_{ij} : N'_{1,i} \to N_{1,j}$ (resp. $d_{ij} : N'_{2,i} \to N_{2,j}$) such that (1) (resp. (1')) commutes.*

- *there exists a morphism $l_{21} : L_{c,2} \to L_{c,1}$ (resp. $l_{12} : L_{c,1} \to L_{c,2}$) s.t. (2) (resp. (2')) commutes and in addition a $NAC(n'_{2,i}) : L_{c,2} \to N'_{2,i}$ (resp. $n'_{1,i} : L_{c,1} \to N'_{1,i}$) in $D_{m_2}(NAC_{p_2})$ (resp. $D_{m_1}(NAC_{p_1})$) with an injective morphism $m_{ij} : N'_{2,i} \to N_{1,j}$ (resp. $m_{ij} : N'_{1,i} \to N_{2,j}$) s.t. $n_{1,j} \circ l_{21} = m_{ij} \circ n'_{2,i}$ (resp. $n_{2,j} \circ l_{12} = m_{ij} \circ n'_{1,i}$).*

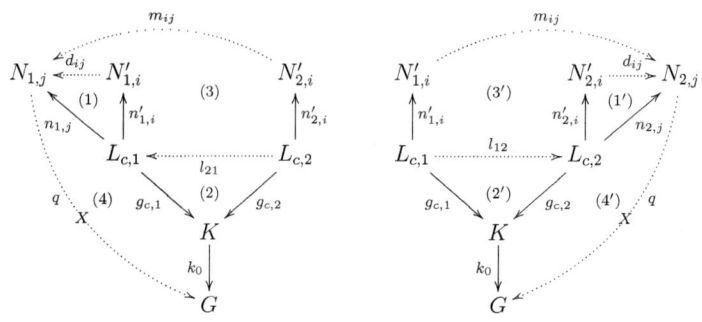

Proof. Follows from Fact 3.2.15 and Theorem 3.10.9 in Chapter 3. □

The following corollary follows directly from this theorem.

2.10.11 Corollary (critical pair solution without NACs). *A critical pair $P_1 \overset{p_1}{\Leftarrow} K \overset{p_2}{\Rightarrow} P_2$ is strictly NAC confluent if*

- *it is strictly confluent via the transformations $t_1 : K \overset{p_1,g_1}{\Rightarrow} P_1 \Rightarrow^* X$ (resp. $t_2 : K \overset{p_2,g_2}{\Rightarrow} P_2 \Rightarrow^* X$) and both $P_1 \Rightarrow^* X$ and $P_2 \Rightarrow^* X$ are transformation sequences without NACs.*

Proof. Follows from Fact 3.2.15 and Corollary 3.10.10 in Chapter 3. □

2.10.12 Example. Consider at first the critical pair $P_1 \Leftarrow K \Rightarrow P_2$ as depicted in Fig. 2.32 via the rules *process_stop_and_call* and *process_stop_down*. These rules are without NACs and also the following strict solution is without NACs. Apply rule *process_call_down* to P_2 in order to obtain P_1. This solution is strict since an elevator node linked to the elevator floor and the node down is preserved by the critical pair and also by the solution. This critical pair is trivially NAC confluent since it holds no NACs at all. Consider now the critical pair $P_1 \Leftarrow K \Rightarrow P_2$ as

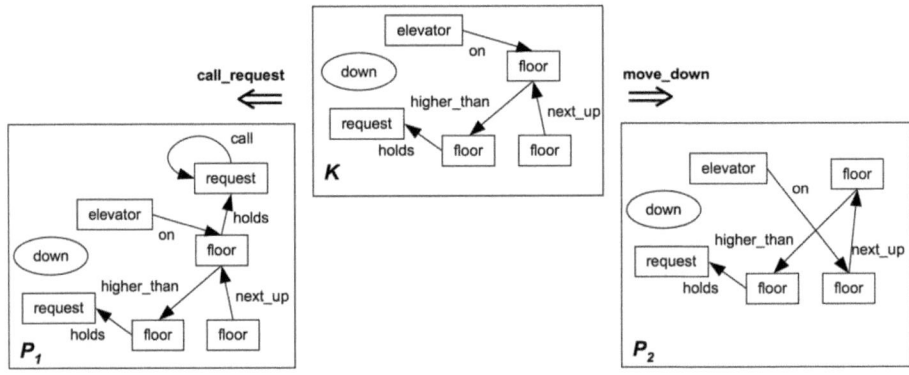

Figure 2.43: critical pair for *Elevator*

depicted in Fig. 2.43 via the rules *call_request* and *move_down*. A strict solution for this pair consists of applying *process_call_down* to P_1 obtaining K again to which in turn *move_down* can be applied to obtain P_2. Thus, t_1 of the solution consists of three direct transformations, and t_2 consists only of $K \Rightarrow P_2$. We need to show that the implication condition is fulfilled for this solution. Thus, we check if the NACs on $P_1 \Leftarrow K \Rightarrow P_2$ imply the ones present in t_1. Rule *process_call_down* does not hold any NACs. The satisfaction of the NACs of rule *move_down* in t_1 of the solution is implied by the satisfaction of the NACs of the same rule *move_down* in the critical pair. This corresponds to the second case in Theorem 2.10.10. Therefore, also the critical pair in Fig. 2.43 is strictly NAC confluent. Finally, consider the critical pair $P_1 \Leftarrow K \Rightarrow P_2$ as depicted in Fig. 2.44 via the rules *call_request* and *process_stop_up*. A solution of this pair consists of applying *process_stop_and_call* to P_1 obtaining P_2. It is strict and also NAC confluent since *process_stop_and_call* is a rule without NACs (see Corollary 2.10.11).

In order to formulate not only a sufficient, but also a necessary and sufficient condition for local confluence of a graph transformation system with NACs, we define the so-called set of extended critical pairs.

2.10. EMBEDDING AND CONFLUENCE

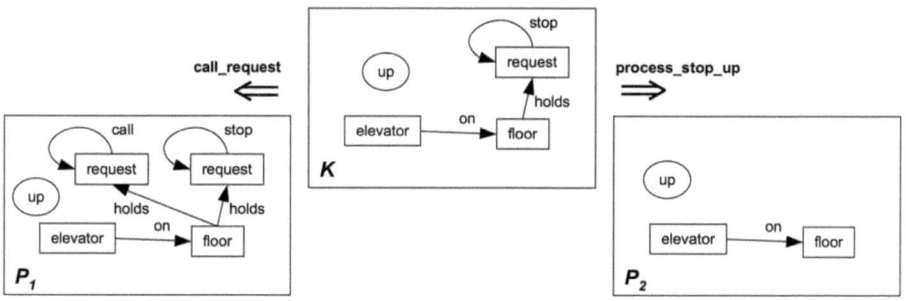

Figure 2.44: critical pair for *Elevator*

2.10.13 Definition (extended critical pair). For each critical pair $P_1 \Leftarrow K \Rightarrow P_2$ that is not strictly NAC confluent, an *extended critical pair* is a pair of direct transformations $H_1 \Leftarrow G \Rightarrow H_2$ as in the following figure, with $k_0 : K \to G$ a NAC consistent and boundary consistent injective morphism w.r.t. $K \Rightarrow P_1$ and $K \Rightarrow P_2$:

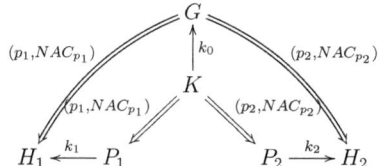

2.10.14 Remark. If we take $k_0 = id$, then each critical pair that is not strictly NAC confluent belongs to the set of its extended critical pairs.

2.10.15 Theorem (extended critical pair lemma). *A graph transformation system with NACs is locally confluent if and only if all its extended critical pairs are locally confluent.*

Proof. Follows from Fact 3.2.15 and Theorem 3.10.13 in Chapter 3. □

2.10.16 Example (extended critical pair for *Elevator*). Consider the critical pair $P_1 \Leftarrow K \Rightarrow P_2$ as depicted in Fig. 2.45 via the rules *stop_request* and *move_up*. The left transformation

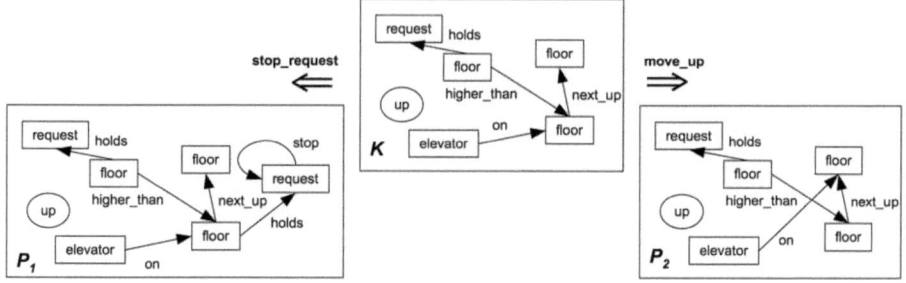

Figure 2.45: critical pair for *Elevator* to be extended

causes a produce-forbid conflict with the right one because for the elevator floor on the left a stop request is generated that is forbidden by the right transformation. Now this critical pair is strictly confluent in the following way. It is possible to apply rule *process_stop_up*, and afterwards *move_up* to P_1 arriving at P_2. This transformation is shown in Fig. 2.46. It

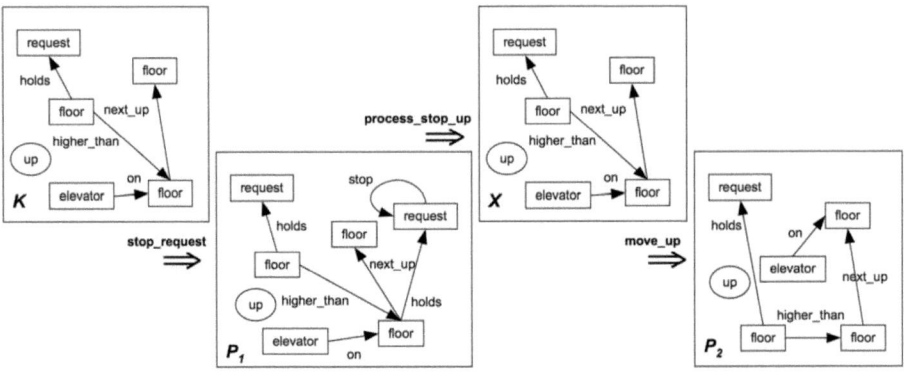

Figure 2.46: strict, but not NAC confluent solution for critical pair in Fig. 2.45

is a strict solution for the critical pair since everything that is preserved from $K \Rightarrow P_1$ and $K \Rightarrow P_2$ (everything from K except for *on* edge) is preserved also by the proposed solution. The induced concurrent NAC of the transformation, however, forbids a stop request as well as a call request on the elevator floor. A NAC consistent extension morphism $k_0 : K \to G$ w.r.t. $K \Rightarrow P_1$ and $K \Rightarrow P_2$ forbids a stop request on the elevator floor as well, since *stop_request* as well as *move_up* also do. In general though, a call request on the elevator floor for a NAC consistent extension morphism k_0 w.r.t. $K \Rightarrow P_1$ and $K \Rightarrow P_2$ is not forbidden. Thus, we cannot conclude that this critical pair is strictly NAC confluent and, therefore, consider the corresponding extended critical pairs. Thereby, we distinguish two cases. In the first case, k_0 is an extension morphism embedding K into some G without any call request for the elevator floor. In the second case, on the other hand, k_0 adds a call request to the elevator floor in G. In the first case the above-described solution is valid for the corresponding extended critical pairs. In the second case we consider another solution. Instead of applying *process_stop_up* to P_1, now t_1 consists of applying *process_stop_and_call* and then *move_up* again. In this case the induced NAC of t_1 merely forbids a stop request on the elevator floor, which is fulfilled by the implication condition. Therefore, also this second type of extended critical pairs is locally confluent.

Finally, we consider the following critical pairs for *Elevator* for which local confluence analysis becomes rather complex. The critical pairs for the rules *call_request* and *stop_request* causing produce-forbid conflicts with the rules *set_direction_up* and *set_direction_down* need quite a few types of extensions in order to be able to conclude local confluence. Consider, in particular, the critical pair representing a produce-forbid conflict in a minimal way caused by rule *call_request* with *set_direction_up* as depicted in Fig. 2.31. A call request is generated on a lower floor than the elevator floor such that afterwards it is not longer possible for the elevator to change its direction mode. First the new call request should be processed in order for the elevator to be able to change its direction. Note at first that it is not possible to conclude local confluence of this critical pair without considering extra context. We need to know how many floors there are in between the elevator floor and the floor with the generated call request. Therefore, we need to consider at least as many types of extended critical pairs as the number of possible intermediate floors. The argumentation that all these types of extended critical pairs are locally confluent is then analog for each of them[5]. We know that the NAC *no_lower_request* needs to be fulfilled when applying the rule *set_direction_up*. Thus, we only need to extend K in a way that in G lower floors do not hold any requests. Therefore, the only request that can be found on a floor lower than the elevator floor in the extended graph H_2 of P_2 is the call request generated just now. Now we can argue that rule *move_down* is applicable to H_2. On the elevator floor in H_2 there is no request because there was no request on the elevator floor in G (NAC *no_request* and NAC *no_request_glue* of rule *set_direction_up* are fulfilled on G). We can now apply rule *move_down* as often as necessary to reach the floor with the call request. This depends on the type of extended critical pair, and thus, on the number of intermediate floors between the elevator floor and the lower floor with the call request. Having reached this floor rule *process_call_down* can be applied. Afterwards rule *set_direction_up* can be applied since this was the only request for this floor. Finally, rule *move_up* should be applied as long as necessary in order to reach the original elevator floor again. This is possible since we know that all the intermediate floors do not hold any request.

In Chapter 4, it is described how to conclude local confluence for (parts of) *Elevator* based on the local confluence analysis of critical pairs. To this end, as a first step the automatic critical pair detection in **AGG** is used. Moreover, guidelines are introduced for automatizing not only conflict detection, but also local confluence analysis of critical pairs.

Since the set of extended critical pairs can become infinitely big, the necessary and sufficient condition based on the extended critical pairs is difficult to check. Therefore, we still introduce a necessary condition for local confluence that can be checked statically. In the case that this condition is not fulfilled, it demonstrates easily that a graph transformation system is not locally confluent.

2.10.17 Theorem (necessary condition for local confluence)**.** *If a graph transformation system with NACs is locally confluent, then there exists no critical pair $P_1 \Leftarrow K \Rightarrow P_2$ such that no rule of the graph transformation system is applicable to P_1 (resp. P_2), and thereby, P_1 and P_2 are not isomorphic.*

Proof. Follows from Fact 3.2.15 and Theorem 3.10.14 in Chapter 3. □

2.11 Efficient Conflict and Causal Dependency Detection

The notion of critical pairs (resp. critical sequences) already allows a static conflict (resp. causal dependency) detection, which is important for all kinds of applications and already implemented in **AGG**. Unfortunately the standard construction is not very efficient. In this section we present two alternative solutions making the static conflict and causal dependency

---

[5]Proving that it is enough to consider only these types of extended critical pairs and, thus, that they are complete, is beyond the scope of this thesis. It is part of future work to relate constraints and local confluence in order to obtain a more precise notion of (extended) critical pairs.

detection more efficient. The first solution presents a way to utilize negative constraints holding for every potential system state under consideration, ruling out critical pairs (resp. sequences) not satisfying these constraints. The second alternative solution introduces the concept of essential critical pairs and sequences based on conflict resp. causal dependency reasons. In both cases, efficiency is obtained because the set of critical pairs resp. sequences is reduced significantly. Therefore, the set of representative conflicts (resp. causal dependencies) to be computed statically diminishes. Moreover, it is more efficient to analyze the reduced sets of critical pairs for strict confluence than it is for the larger set of critical pairs. Thus, not only conflict detection, but also conflict analysis becomes more efficient. Both more efficient ways of static conflict (resp. causal dependency) detection are implemented in AGG.

2.11.1 Critical Pairs and Sequences satisfying Negative Constraints

Recall that negative constraints are defined in Section 2.2 (see Def. 2.2.9). We consider here negative constraints of the form $NC(C)$ with C a graph. Negative constraints of this form are very similar to negative application conditions since they also check for the non-existence of a certain graph pattern. In this case it is checked for the non-existence of C. The difference is that a negative constraint can be checked against each graph representing a system state. A negative application condition on the contrary is formulated for a specific rule, and checked for satisfaction before or after applying this rule. The following example illustrates that the set of critical pairs is reduced significantly, when only the critical pairs satisfying a specific set of negative constraints is considered.

2.11.1 Example (critical pairs (resp. sequences) satisfying negative constraints for *Elevator*). AGG computes 60 critical pairs for rule *move_up* with itself. This is because each overlap of the left-hand side of *move_up* with itself leads to a critical pair. The set of critical pairs, on the contrary, consists of only three pairs. All the others do not fulfill the negative constraints (see Fig. 2.5) or maximal multiplicities (see Fig. 2.1), which can be expressed as negative constraints, of *Elevator*. Analogously, we can consider at first the set of critical sequences for rule pair (*set_direction_up*, *move_up*). AGG computes 88 critical sequences for them. The set of critical sequences satisfying negative constraints consists of only 12 sequences. All the others do not fulfill the negative constraints or multiplicities of *Elevator*.

The following theorem states that it is sufficient to consider the subset of critical pairs, satisfying the set of negative constraints $\mathcal{NC} = \{NC(C) | C \text{ a graph}\}$, if each graph representing a potential system state satisfies them. Note that it is part of future work to discover which kind of nested constraints (see [46]) can reduce the set of critical pairs (resp. sequence) to consider with regard to critical pair (resp. critical sequence) detection.

2.11.2 Theorem (completeness of critical pairs satisfying negative constraints). *For each pair of direct transformations $H_1 \stackrel{p_1,m_1'}{\Longleftarrow} G \stackrel{p_2,m_2'}{\Longrightarrow} H_2$ in conflict such that G, H_1, and H_2 satisfy a set of negative constraints $\mathcal{NC} = \{NC(C) | C \text{ a graph}\}$ there is a critical pair $P_1 \stackrel{p_1}{\Longleftarrow} K \stackrel{p_2}{\Longrightarrow} P_2$ with extension diagrams (1) and (2) and m injective such that K, P_1, and P_2 satisfy $\mathcal{NC}$ as well. We say in this case that this critical pair satisfies the negative constraints $\mathcal{NC}$.*

$$\begin{array}{ccc} P_1 & \Longleftarrow K \Longrightarrow & P_2 \\ \downarrow & {\scriptstyle (1)\ m\ \downarrow\ (2)} & \downarrow \\ H_1 & \Longleftarrow G \Longrightarrow & H_2 \end{array}$$

2.11. EFFICIENT CONFLICT AND CAUSAL DEPENDENCY DETECTION

Proof. From Theorem 2.7.8 it follows directly that the critical pair $P_1 \stackrel{p_1}{\Leftarrow} K \stackrel{p_2}{\Rightarrow} P_2$ with extension diagrams (1) and (2) and m injective exists. Consider a $NC(C)$ from the set $\mathcal{NC}$. Suppose that K does not satisfy $NC(C)$. Then there would exist some injective morphism $q : C \to K$. Because of composition of monomorphisms, then there exists a monomorphism $m \circ q : C \to G$. This is a contradiction, and therefore, K satisfies $\mathcal{NC}$ as well. Analogously, it follows that also P_1 and P_2 satisfy $\mathcal{NC}$. □

2.11.3 Theorem (completeness of critical sequences satisfying negative constraints). *For each sequence of causally dependent direct transformations $G \stackrel{p_1,m_1'}{\Longrightarrow} H_1 \stackrel{p_2,m_2'}{\Longrightarrow} H_2$ such that $G, H_1,$ and H_2 satisfy $\mathcal{NC}$, there is a critical sequence $K \stackrel{p_1}{\Longrightarrow} P_1 \stackrel{p_2}{\Longrightarrow} P_2$ with extension diagrams (1) and (2) and m injective such that also $K, P_1,$ and P_2 satisfy $\mathcal{NC}$. We say in this case that this critical sequence satisfies the negative constraints $\mathcal{NC}$.*

$$\begin{array}{ccccc} K & \Longrightarrow & P_1 & \Longrightarrow & P_2 \\ \downarrow & (1) \; m \downarrow & & (2) & \downarrow \\ G & \Longrightarrow & H_1 & \Longrightarrow & H_2 \end{array}$$

Proof. As noted already in Remark 2.4.2, $G \stackrel{p_1}{\Longrightarrow} H_1 \stackrel{p_2}{\Longrightarrow} H_2$ are sequentially independent if and only if $G \stackrel{p_1^{-1}}{\Longleftarrow} H_1 \stackrel{p_2}{\Longrightarrow} H_2$ are parallel independent. Therefore, the above assumption follows directly from this remark and Theorem 2.11.2. □

Finally, it follows that a pair of transformations $H_1 \Leftarrow G \Rightarrow H_2$ in conflict satisfying $\mathcal{NC}$ is locally confluent via transformations satisfying $\mathcal{NC}$ as well, if the corresponding critical pair $P_1 \Leftarrow K \Rightarrow P_2$ representing the same conflict in a minimal context is strictly NAC confluent (see Def. 2.10.7) via some solution $t_1' : P_1 \stackrel{*}{\Rightarrow} K'$ and $t_2' : P_2 \stackrel{*}{\Rightarrow} K'$. Moreover, the rules occurring in this solution (i.e. in t_1' and t_2') preserve the constraints in $\mathcal{NC}$. We demand the satisfaction of this extra condition in order to ensure that the transformations making $H_1 \Leftarrow G \Rightarrow H_2$ locally confluent satisfy $\mathcal{NC}$ as well. Note that a rule p preserves a constraint $NC(C)$, if for every direct transformation $G \stackrel{p}{\Rightarrow} H$ such that $G \models NC(C)$, it holds that also $H \models NC(C)$. In Section 4.3.9, it is explained how it is possible to verify that a rule is constraint-preserving.

2.11.4 Theorem (critical pair lemma with negative constraints). *Consider a graph transformation system with NACs, a set of negative constraints $\mathcal{NC} = \{NC(C)|C \text{ a graph}\}$, and a pair of direct transformations $H_1 \stackrel{p_1,m_1'}{\Longleftarrow} G \stackrel{p_2,m_2'}{\Longrightarrow} H_2$ such that $G, H_1,$ and H_2 satisfy $\mathcal{NC} = \{NC(C)|C \text{ a graph}\}$. The pair of transformations $H_1 \stackrel{p_1,m_1'}{\Longleftarrow} G \stackrel{p_2,m_2'}{\Longrightarrow} H_2$ is locally confluent via transformations $t_1 : H_1 \stackrel{*}{\Rightarrow} X$ and $t_2 : H_2 \stackrel{*}{\Rightarrow} X$ such that each graph belonging to t_1 and t_2 satisfies $\mathcal{NC} = \{NC(C)|C \text{ a graph}\}$, if p_1 and p_2 are rules preserving $\mathcal{NC}$, and in addition all critical pairs satisfying $\mathcal{NC}$ are strictly NAC confluent via some solution $t_1' : P_1 \stackrel{*}{\Rightarrow} K'$ and $t_2' : P_2 \stackrel{*}{\Rightarrow} K'$, consisting of rules preserving $\mathcal{NC}$.*

Proof. If $H_1 \stackrel{p_1,m_1'}{\Longleftarrow} G \stackrel{p_2,m_2'}{\Longrightarrow} H_2$ are parallel independent, then it follows because of Theorem 2.4.3 that $H_1 \stackrel{p_2}{\Rightarrow} X \stackrel{p_1}{\Leftarrow} H_2$ exist. Therefore, this pair of transformations is locally confluent, and since p_1 and p_2 preserve $\mathcal{NC}$, it follows that X preserves $\mathcal{NC}$ as well. Let $H_1 \stackrel{p_1,m_1'}{\Longleftarrow} G \stackrel{p_2,m_2'}{\Longrightarrow} H_2$ be conflicting. Then it follows from Theorem 2.11.2 that a critical pair satisfying $\mathcal{NC}$ exists, representing the same conflict, in a minimal context. Because of 2.10.9, the assumption that each critical pair satisfying $\mathcal{NC}$ is strictly NAC confluent via some solution with $\mathcal{NC}$-preserving rules, then there exist transformations $t_1 : H_1 \overset{*}{\Rightarrow} X$ and $t_2 : H_2 \overset{*}{\Rightarrow} X$ such that each graph belonging to t_1 and t_2 satisfy $\mathcal{NC}$. □

2.11.2 Essential Critical Pairs and Sequences

We introduce the concept of essential critical pairs (still smaller as introduced in [71], see Remark 2.11.5), allowing for a more efficient conflict detection. This is based on the conflict characterization (see Theorem 2.6.13) (resp. causal dependency characterization as presented in Theorem 2.6.14) in Section 2.6, which determines for each conflict (resp. causal dependency) occurring between two rules the exact conflict reason. This new notion of conflict reason leads us to an optimization of conflict (resp. causal dependency) detection. Note that this conflict (resp. causal dependency) characterization with reason is formulated for transformations without NACs, and therefore, only delete-use conflicts (resp. produce-use dependencies and deliver-delete dependencies) will be captured by essential critical pairs. It is part of future work to characterize conflicts and causal dependencies caused by NACs in the transformations. In this section, we show that indeed for each conflict (resp. causal dependency) in the system, there exists an essential critical pair (resp. sequence) representing it. Finally, a local confluence lemma based on essential critical pairs is shown.

First, we introduce the notion of essential critical pairs. The idea behind this notion is that for each conflict reason (as given in Def. 2.6.11) we have an essential critical pair, expressing the conflict caused by exactly this conflict reason in a minimal context. Analogously, essential critical sequences can be defined based on the notion of causal dependency reason span (as given in Def. 2.6.12). Note that for Def. 2.6.11 and 2.6.12 we need initial pushouts over graph morphisms, general PBs, and in addition for the essential critical pairs and sequences we need general pushouts of graph morphisms that are constructed componentwise in **Sets**.

2.11.5 Remark. Note that in [71], reasons for symmetrical conflicts have been constructed separately. Here we show that without considering these reasons separately, the resulting set of essential critical pairs is still complete in the sense of Theorem 2.11.9.

2.11.6 Definition (essential critical pair). A pair of direct transformations $P_1 \overset{p_1,m_1}{\Longleftarrow} K \overset{p_2,m_2}{\Longrightarrow} P_2$ is an *essential critical pair* for the pair of rules (p_1, p_2) if the following holds: $K \overset{p_1,m_1}{\Longrightarrow} P_1$ causes a delete-use conflict with $K \overset{p_2,m_2}{\Longrightarrow} P_2$ or the other way round and (K, m_1, m_2) is a pushout of the causal dependency reason $(S_1, g_1 \circ o_1, q_{12})$ or $(S_2, q_{21}, g_2 \circ o_2)$ of $P_1 \overset{p_1,m_1}{\Longleftarrow} K \overset{p_2,m_2}{\Longrightarrow} P_2$ according to Definition 2.6.11.

2.11.7 Definition (essential critical sequence). A sequence of direct transformations $K \overset{p_1,m_1}{\Longrightarrow} P_1 \overset{p_2,m_2}{\Longrightarrow} P_2$ is an *essential critical sequence* for the sequence of rules (p_1, p_2) if the following holds: $K \overset{p_1,m_1}{\Longrightarrow} P_1$ is in produce-use dependency or deliver-delete dependency with $P_1 \overset{p_2,m_2}{\Longrightarrow} P_2$ and (K, m_1', m_2) is a pushout of the conflict reason $(S_1, g_1 \circ o_1, q_{12})$ or $(S_2, q_{21}, g_2 \circ o_2)$ of $K \overset{p_1,m_1}{\Longleftarrow} P_1 \overset{p_2,m_2}{\Longrightarrow} P_2$ according to Definition 2.6.12.

2.11.8 Example (essential critical pairs (resp. sequences) for *Elevator*). AGG computes 60 critical pairs expressing delete-use conflicts in some minimal context for rule *move_up* with itself. This is because each overlap of the left-hand side of *move_up* with itself leads to a critical pair. The set of essential critical pairs, on the contrary, consists of only one pair (depicted in Fig. 2.47) since there is only one reason to be in conflict with itself. This reason consists of the edge *on* from the *elevator* node to the elevator *floor* because it is deleted and used (in order to delete as well). The conflict expresses that the elevator cannot be moved from some floor to another one twice one after the other. Analogously, we can consider the set of critical sequences

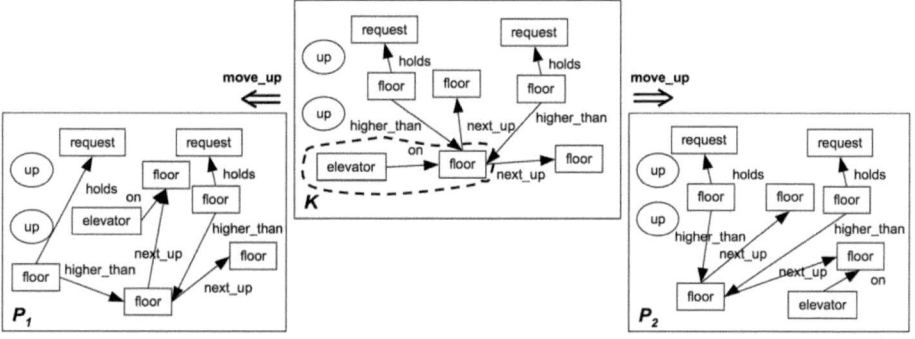

Figure 2.47: essential critical pair for *Elevator*

for rule pair (*set_direction_up*, *move_up*). AGG computes 88 critical sequences for these rules. 68 of them express produce-use dependencies in some minimal context. The other 20 express deliver-delete dependencies in some minimal context. The set of essential critical sequences consists of two sequences (one of them depicted in Fig. 2.48) since there are two reasons for this sequence to be dependent. The first reason consists of the node *up*. This is because the presence of this node triggers the application of *move_up*. The second reason consists of the elevator standing on the floor from which it moves one floor upward. This is because after moving the elevator car upward it is on another floor such that it becomes impossible to undo the previous application of *set_direction_up*.

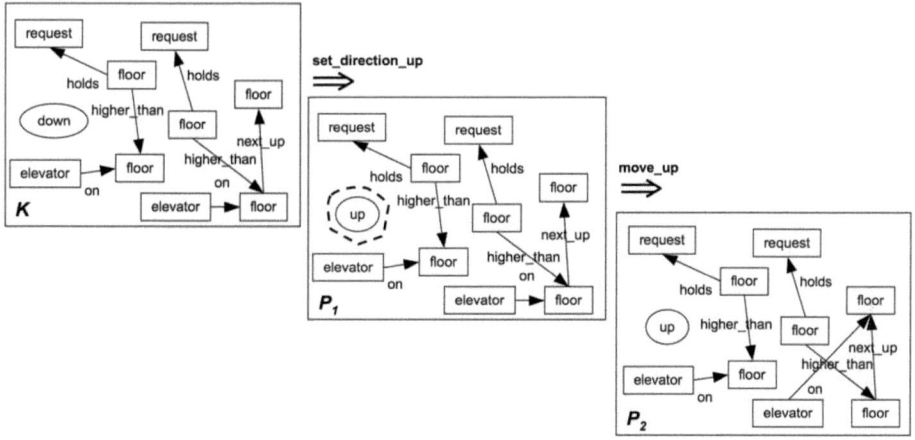

Figure 2.48: essential critical sequence for *Elevator*

CHAPTER 2. RULE-BASED MODELING USING GRAPH TRANSFORMATION

2.11.9 Theorem (completeness of essential critical pairs). *For each critical pair $P_1' \overset{p_1,m_1'}{\Leftarrow} K' \overset{p_2,m_2'}{\Rightarrow} P_2'$ of (p_1,p_2) such that $K' \overset{p_1,m_1'}{\Rightarrow} P_1'$ causes a delete-use conflict with $K' \overset{p_2,m_2'}{\Rightarrow} P_2'$ or the other way round, there exists an essential critical pair $P_1 \overset{p_1,m_1}{\Leftarrow} K \overset{p_2,m_2}{\Rightarrow} P_2$ of (p_1,p_2) with the same conflict reason and extension diagrams (1) and (2).*

$$
\begin{array}{ccccc}
P_1 & \Longleftarrow & K & \Longrightarrow & P_2 \\
\downarrow & (1) & \downarrow m & (2) & \downarrow \\
P_1' & \Longleftarrow & K' & \Longrightarrow & P_2'
\end{array}
$$

Remark: $m : K \to K'$ is surjective, but not necessarily injective.

Proof. For the critical pair $P_1' \overset{p_1,m_1'}{\Leftarrow} K' \overset{p_2,m_2'}{\Rightarrow} P_2'$ according to Theorem 2.6.13 the following cases can occur:

1. $(S_1, g_1 \circ o_1, q_{12})$ is a conflict reason
2. $(S_2, q_{21}, g_2 \circ o_2)$ is a conflict reason

with $(S_1, o_1 : S_1 \to C_2, q_{12} : S_1 \to L_2)$ the pullback of $(m_1' \circ g_1, m_2')$, $(S_2, q_{21} : S_2 \to L_1, o_2 : S_2 \to C_2)$ the pullback of $(m_1', m_2' \circ g_2)$.

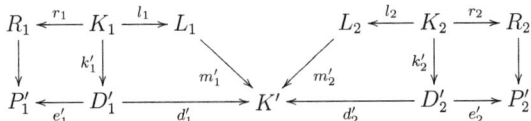

1. Analogous to the following case.

2. Construct the pushout (9) $(K, m_1 : L_1 \to K, m_2 : L_2 \to K)$ of the conflict reason $(S_2, q_{21}, g_2 \circ o_2)$.

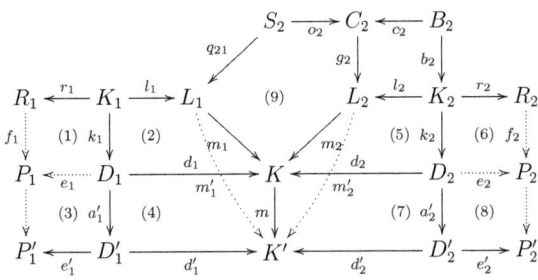

Since (9) is a pushout and $m_1' \circ q_{21} = m_2' \circ g_2 \circ o_2$, a unique morphism $m : K \to K'$ exists such that $m_1' = m \circ m_1$ and $m_2' = m \circ m_2$. Now we can construct the pullback (4) $(D_1, d_1 : D_1 \to K, a_1' : D_1 \to D_1')$ of (d_1', m) and the pullback (7) $(D_2, d_2 : D_2 \to K, a_2' : D_2 \to D_2')$ of (d_2', m). Since (4) (resp. (7)) is a pullback and $d_1' \circ k_1' = m \circ m_1 \circ l_1$ (resp. $d_2' \circ k_2' = m \circ m_2 \circ l_2$), a morphism $k_1 : K_1 \to D_1$ resp. ($k_2 : K_2 \to D_2$) exists s.t. $a_1' \circ k_1 = k_1'$ (resp. $a_2' \circ k_2 = k_2'$) and $d_1 \circ k_1 = m_1 \circ l_1$ (resp. $d_2 \circ k_2 = m_2 \circ l_2$). Now we prove that (d_1, m_1) and (d_2, m_2) are jointly surjective.

(a) We start with proving that (d_1, m_1) is jointly surjective. Since (m_1, m_2) are jointly surjective, K can also be written as $K = K_{L_2 \setminus L_1} \cup K_{L_1}$ with $K_{L_2 \setminus L_1} = m_2(L_2) \setminus m_1(L_1)$ and $K_{L_1} = m_1(L_1)$. For all $x \in K_{L_2 \setminus L_1}$ we have to prove that they have a preimage in D_1. So, we assume that $\exists y_2 \in L_2 : m_2(y_2) = x$ and $\not\exists y_1 \in L_1 : m_1(y_1) = x$. Since (m'_1, m'_2) are also jointly surjective, $K' = K'_{L_2 \setminus L_1} \cup K'_{L_1}$ with $K'_{L_2 \setminus L_1} = m'_2(L_2) \setminus m'_1(L_1)$ and $K'_{L_1} = m'_1(L_1)$.

- $m(x) \in K'_{L_2 \setminus L_1}$ implies that $m(x)$ doesn't have a preimage in L_1. But since (m'_1, d'_1) jointly surjective, $\exists x_1 \in D'_1 : d'_1(x_1) = m(x)$ and since (4) is a pullback we have $(x_1, x) \in D_1$ with $d_1(x_1, x) = x$.

- $m(x) \in K'_{L_1}$ implies that there exists an $y_1 \in L_1$ s.t. $m'_1(y_1) = m(x)$. Now again we distinguish two cases:

  – Let $y_1 \in L_1 \setminus C_1$. Then $\exists x_1 \in K_1 : l_1(x_1) = y_1$ and $m(x) = m'_1(y_1) = m'_1(l_1(x_1)) = m(m_1(l_1(x_1))) = d'_1(a'_1(k_1(x_1)))$. This implies that $(a'_1(k_1(x_1)), x) \in D_1$ with $d_1(a'_1(k_1(x_1)), x) = x$ since (4) is a pullback.

  – On the other hand, if $y_2 \in C_2$ then $g_2(y_2) = y_2$ and $m'_2(g_2(y_2)) = m'_2(y_2) = m(x) = m(m_1(y_1)) = m'_1(y_1)$ and since (S_2, q_{21}, o_2) is a pullback of $(m'_1, m'_2 \circ g_2)$ it follows that $(y_1, y_2) \in S_2$. But since (9) is a pushout this implies $m_1(y_1) = m_1(q_{21}(y_1, y_2)) = m_2(g_2(o_2(y_1, y_2))) = m_2(y_2)$. This is a contradiction since now $m_1(y_1) = m_2(y_2) = x$, but $\not\exists y_1 \in L_1 : m_1(y_1) = x$.

(b) Now we prove that (d_2, m_2) are jointly surjective. Since (m_1, m_2) are jointly surjective, $K = K_{L_1 \setminus L_2} \cup K_{L_2}$. It suffices to show that for each $x \in K_{L_1 \setminus L_2}$ there exists $y'_2 \in D_2 : d_2(y'_2) = x$. So, we assume that $\exists y_1 \in L_1 : m_1(y_1) = x$ and $\not\exists y_2 \in L_2 : m_2(y_2) = x$. Since also (m'_1, m'_2) are jointly surjective, $K' = K'_{L_1 \setminus L_2} \cup K'_{L_2}$, and we distinguish the following two cases:

- $m(x) \in K'_{L_1 \setminus L_2}$ implies that $m(x)$ doesn't have a preimage in L_2. Since (m'_2, d'_2) are jointly surjective, there exists $x_2 \in D'_2 : d'_2(x_2) = m(x)$. Because (7) is a pullback $(x_2, x) \in D_2$ with $d_2(x_2, x) = x$.

- $m(x) \in K'_{L_2}$ implies that there exists $y_2 \in L_2 : m'_2(y_2) = m(x)$. Now again we distinguish two cases:

  – Let $y_2 \in L_2 \setminus C_2$. Then $\exists x_2 \in K_2 : l_2(x_2) = y_2$ and $m(x) = m'_2(y_2) = m'_2(l_2(x_2)) = m(m_2(l_2(x_2))) = d'_2(a'_2(k_2(x_2)))$. This implies that $(a'_2(k_2(x_2)), x) \in D_2$ with $d_2(a'_2(k_2(x_2)), x) = x$ since (7) is a pullback.

  – On the other hand, if $y_2 \in C_2$ then $g_2(y_2) = y_2$ and $m'_2(g_2(y_2)) = m'_2(y_2) = m(x) = m(m_1(y_1)) = m'_1(y_1)$ and since (S_2, q_{21}, o_2) is a pullback of $(m'_1, m'_2 \circ g_2)$ it follows that $(y_1, y_2) \in S_2$. But since (9) is a pushout this implies $m_1(y_1) = m_1(q_{21}(y_1, y_2)) = m_2(g_2(o_2(y_1, y_2))) = m_2(y_2)$. This is a contradiction since now $m_1(y_1) = x = m_2(y_2)$, but $\not\exists y_2 \in L_2 : m_2(y_2) = x$.

Now we know that if we build (K, m_1, m_2) as a pushout of the conflict reason of $P'_1 \stackrel{p_1, m'_1}{\Leftarrow} K' \stackrel{p_2, m'_2}{\Rightarrow} P'_2$, (d_1, m_1) and (d_2, m_2) are jointly surjective. Now we can conclude that (2) (resp. (5)) is a pullback since (d_1, m_1) (resp.(d_2, m_2)) are jointly surjective, (4) (resp. (7)) is a pullback and (2)+(4) (resp. (5)+(7)) is a pushout and also a pullback. Since l_1 (resp. l_2) is injective, (2)+(4) (resp. (5)+(7)) is a pushout and (2),(4) (resp.(5),(7)) are pullbacks, this implies that (2),(4) (resp.(5),(7)) are also pushouts. Then we can construct P_1 and P_2 as pushouts of (r_1, k_1)

resp. (r_2, k_2) and because of the pushout property the two lacking morphisms f_1 and f_2 for the essential critical pair are constructed. Because of pushout-pushout decomposition, now we can deduce that (1),(3),(6) and (8) are pushouts. Now we know that $P_1 \overset{p_1,m_1}{\Leftarrow} K \overset{p_2,m_2}{\Rightarrow} P_2$ is a pair of direct transformations.

Since (K, m_1, m_2) was constructed as a pushout over the conflict reason of $P'_1 \overset{p_1,m'_1}{\Leftarrow} K' \overset{p_2,m'_2}{\Rightarrow} P_2$, we still have to prove that the conflict reason stays the same for $P_1 \overset{p_1,m_1}{\Leftarrow} K \overset{p_2,m_2}{\Rightarrow} P_2$. Therefore, first, we have to show that if (S_2, q_{21}, o_2) is a pullback of $(m'_1, m'_2 \circ g_2)$ then it is also a pullback of $(m_1, m_2 \circ g_2)$.

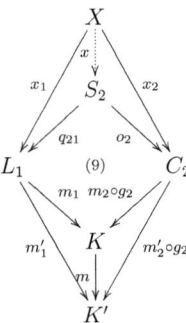

$m_1 \circ q_{21} = m_2 \circ g_2 \circ o_2$ because (9) is a pushout. Moreover, if we take another graph X and morphisms $x_1 : X \to L_1$ and $x_2 : X \to C_2$ such that $m_1 \circ x_1 = m_2 \circ g_2 \circ x_2$, this implies $m'_1 \circ x_1 = m \circ m_1 \circ x_1 = m \circ m_2 \circ g_2 \circ x_2 = m'_2 \circ g_2 \circ x_2$ and because of the pullback property of the outer pullback a unique morphism $x : X \to S_2$ exists s.t. $q_{21} \circ x = x_1$ and $o_2 \circ x = x_2$. Thus, (S_2, q_{21}, o_2) is also a pullback of $(m_1, m_2 \circ g_2)$. Analogously, we can prove that (S_1, q_{12}, o_1) is also a pullback of $(m_1 \circ g_1, m_2)$. Therefore, we know that the conflict reason $(S1, g_1 \circ o_1, q_{12})$ (resp. $(S2, q_{21}, g_2 \circ o_2)$) stays the same for $P_1 \overset{p_1,m_1}{\Leftarrow} K \overset{p_2,m_2}{\Rightarrow} P_2$, which implies by Theorem 2.6.13 that also $P_1 \overset{p_1,m_1}{\Leftarrow} K \overset{p_2,m_2}{\Rightarrow} P_2$ is in conflict. Now we have constructed an essential critical pair $P_1 \overset{p_1,m_1}{\Leftarrow} K \overset{p_2,m_2}{\Rightarrow} P_2$ with extension morphism $m : K \to K'$. □

2.11.10 Theorem (completeness of essential critical sequences). *For each critical sequence $K' \overset{p_1,m'_1}{\Rightarrow} P'_1 \overset{p_2,m'_2}{\Rightarrow} P'_2$ of (p_1, p_2) such that they are in produce-use dependency or deliver-delete dependency, there exists an essential critical sequence $K \overset{p_1,m_1}{\Rightarrow} P_1 \overset{p_2,m_2}{\Rightarrow} P_2$ of (p_1, p_2) with the same causal dependency reason and extension diagrams (1) and (2).*

$$
\begin{array}{ccccc}
K & \Longrightarrow & P_1 & \Longrightarrow & P_2 \\
\downarrow & (1) \ m & \downarrow & (2) & \downarrow \\
K' & \Longrightarrow & P'_1 & \Longrightarrow & P'_2
\end{array}
$$

Proof. This follows directly from Theorem 2.11.9 and Remark 2.4.2. □

2.11.11 Remark. Note that the following combination of critical pairs (resp. sequences) satisfying negative constraints and essential critical pairs (resp. sequences) can be made. It is possible to reduce the set of essential critical pairs (resp. sequences) to a subset of essential critical pairs (resp. sequences) satisfying negative constraints that are checked for non-injective satisfaction. Non-injective means that the morphism q as given in Def. 2.2.9 is non-injective instead of injective. In our running example *Elevator* the set of negative constraints that are also satisfied when checked in a non-injective way consists of *no_up_and_down*, *higher_is_not_next*, *higher_is_not_opposite*, *next_is_not_opposite*, *no_stop_and_call*, and *no_intermediate* as depicted in Fig. 2.5. They can, therefore, be used to reduce the set of essential critical pairs and sequences even more. Moreover, having maximal multiplicities or negative constraints checked for satisfaction in an injective way (as introduced in Def. 2.2.9) the following check can be done: try and glue the graphs K, P_1, and P_2 of the essential critical pair $P_1 \Leftarrow K \Rightarrow P_2$ (resp. sequence $K \Rightarrow P_1 \Rightarrow P_2$) in such a way that the maximal multiplicity or negative constraint, when checked in an injective way, is fulfilled. If no gluing exists such that the constraint with injective satisfaction is fulfilled, then probably the essential critical pair can be omitted. It is part of future work to formulate these ideas more precisely and supply tool support.

Finally, we can also formulate a Local Confluence Theorem for essential critical pairs as follows.

2.11.12 Theorem (essential critical pair lemma). *If all essential critical pairs of a graph transformation system are strictly confluent, then this graph transformation system is locally confluent.*

Proof. In the proof of the critical pair lemma in [29] for adhesive HLR systems it is demanded that the extension morphism m belongs to the special subset of monomorphisms $\mathcal{M}'$ in the corresponding adhesive HLR category. For the proof of this lemma though it is sufficient to demand the existence of an initial pushout over the extension morphism m. In the case of essential critical pairs m is not necessarily an injective morphism, as shown in Theorem 2.11.9, but an initial pushout over a non-injective morphism m in the category **Graphs** (or also **Graphs**$_{TG}$) always exists. Therefore, the proof of the critical pair lemma can be repeated, restricting the set of critical pairs to the set of essential critical pairs. □

Chapter 3

Rule-Based Modeling using High-Level Transformation

3.1 Introduction

In the previous chapter, graphs have been introduced to represent system states of rule-based models. Moreover, graph transformation formalizes the rule-based manipulation, evolution, reconfiguration, etc. of models. Graphs consist of a set of nodes and edges, and two mappings, describing source and target of these edges. However, as soon as rule-based models need to describe more complex concepts like, for example, attribution or inheritance, it is not that easy anymore to formalize these models. Category theory offers the opportunity to abstract from the internal details of models, which might become quite complex. Instead, it is investigated if and how models are related to each other. A category consists of objects and morphisms between objects. Thereby, objects play the role of opaque models, and morphisms can be interpreted as relations between models. In category theory, the only possibility to get to know something about a specific object is to investigate how it is related by specific morphisms to other objects in the category. For example, in the category of graphs, the object that is the empty graph is identifiable because there exists a unique graph morphism of the empty graph in any other graph. Note that in order to identify the empty graph in this way, it was not necessary to have a look into the internals of this object. Analogously, it is possible to define with categorical means the concept of rules and transformations of objects via rules. Such a *categorical approach* has the advantage that proof reasoning abstracts from fine-grained internals. Instead, a categorical proof is concerned with finding specific morphisms between specific objects. This technique is often called diagram chasing.

A *categorical framework* is based on a predefined category in which a set of assumptions hold for specific classes of morphisms. The objects and morphisms of such a predefined category might be graphs resp. graph morphisms, but also some other kinds of high-level structures resp. morphisms fulfilling the assumptions. For each instance fitting into such a categorical framework, specific properties can be derived. In this thesis, we are interested mainly in a framework that applies particularly well to deriving properties important for rule-based transformation systems. Using such a categorical framework has the advantage that theory can be developed on such an abstract level that it applies to several possible instances of transformation systems at once. Therefore, we call such a categorical framework for transformation systems *high-level transformation systems* and the corresponding transformations *high-level transformations*.

In particular, *adhesive High-Level Replacement (HLR) categories*, as introduced in [29], provide a formal method to describe transformation systems. The development of adhesive HLR categories was inspired by the notion of HLR-systems [36] and the notion of adhesive categories as introduced in [65]. The resulting framework is called adhesive HLR systems. These systems are based on rules that describe in an abstract way how objects in adhesive HLR categories can be transformed. Moreover, in [29], it is explained how to define application conditions for rules, restricting the application of a rule. However, in [29], most of the theoretical results are formulated for adhesive HLR systems based on rules without application conditions. Thus, these results should be generalized to adhesive HLR systems based on rules holding application conditions. The most frequently used kind of application condition is the so-called negative application condition (NAC), as introduced in [44] and used, for example, in [19, 59, 84, 116]. It forbids a certain structure to be present before or after applying a rule. Therefore, in this chapter, we concentrate on generalizing the theoretical results, formulated for adhesive HLR systems based on rules without application conditions, to adhesive HLR systems based on rules holding NACs. To this end, in Section 3.2, we introduce a new kind of category, called *NAC-adhesive HLR*. Based on this category, in Section 3.3, we will introduce *adhesive HLR systems with NACs*.

A lot of theoretical results for the particular case of (typed) graph transformation with NACs have already been presented in Chapter 2. The overall goal of this theory is to come up with practical analysis techniques for rule-based models. In practice though, most of these results are needed for the instantiation of typed *attributed* graph transformation systems with application conditions. This more general kind of graph transformation technique is most significant for modeling and meta-modeling in software engineering and visual languages. In [29], it has already been proven that such a typed attributed graph transformation system is a valid instantiation of adhesive HLR systems. In this chapter, we show that typed attributed graph transformation systems are also a valid instantiation of adhesive HLR systems with NACs. This is one of the most important motivations for lifting the theory of graph transformation with NACs to the level of adhesive HLR transformation with NACs. Moreover, results within adhesive HLR systems can be applied to all other instantiations of adhesive HLR systems such as, for example, hypergraph, algebraic signature, or specification transformations with NACs. In order to allow more instantiations, so-called weak adhesive HLR categories and systems are defined in [29]. In this slightly weaker framework all important theoretical results still hold. For example, Petri net transformation is an instantiation of weak adhesive HLR systems.

Summarizing, this chapter lifts the results presented in Chapter 2 for the case of (typed) graph transformation with NACs to the level of adhesive HLR systems with NACs. Therefore, the structure of this chapter is completely analogous to the structure of Chapter 2. The proofs for the theorems presented in Chapter 2 can be found in the corresponding sections of this chapter on the level of NAC-adhesive HLR categories. For a detailed introduction to the results of Chapter 2, for (typed) graph transformation with NACs, we refer to Section 2.1. Here, we merely give a brief overview of the results for adhesive HLR systems with NACs, as presented in this chapter. Section 3.2 introduces NAC-adhesive HLR categories, and in particular, it shows that the category of **Graphs**, **Graphs**$_{TG}$ (typed graphs), and **AGraphs**$_{TG}$ (typed attributed graphs) are NAC-adhesive HLR. Based on NAC-adhesive HLR categories, we define the framework of adhesive HLR systems with NACs in Section 3.3. Independence and parallelism for adhesive HLR transformations with NACs are handled in Section 3.4. The main results in this section are the Local Church-Rosser Theorem and Parallelism Theorem for adhesive HLR systems with NACs. In Section 3.5, concurrent adhesive HLR transformations with NACs are defined and a corresponding Concurrency Theorem for adhesive HLR systems with NACs is proven. Section 3.6 is concerned with characterizing conflicts and causal dependencies between adhesive HLR transformations with NACs. Section 3.7 introduces the theory of critical pairs and sequences for adhesive HLR systems with NACs. It formulates the Restriction Theorem for adhesive HLR transformations with NACs and a Completeness Theorem for critical pairs and sequences. In Section 3.8, the notion of conflict and causal dependency are considered on the rule level instead of the transformation level. This enables us to deduce properties of the adhesive HLR system with NACs by analyzing the corresponding rules. In Section 3.9, sufficient criteria are introduced leading to applicability (resp. non-applicability) of a rule sequence to an object in the NAC-adhesive HLR category. Moreover, a number of reductions for rule sequences is introduced preserving applicability (resp. non-applicability). Finally, based on the assumption in this section that the gluing condition is always fulfilled, a weak Local Church-Rosser Theorem is formulated. Section 3.10 is concerned with embedding and confluence of adhesive HLR transformations with NACs. A corresponding Embedding and Extension Theorem, and Critical Pair Lemma (Local Confluence Theorem) are formulated. Finally, Section 2.11 in Chapter 2 is not lifted to the level of NAC-adhesive HLR categories. It is merely explained which expectations are present concerning the success of lifting also the theory of essential critical pairs (resp. sequences) and critical pairs (resp. sequences) satisfying negative constraints[1].

3.2 Modeling with High-Level Structures

In this section, we introduce NAC-adhesive HLR categories. This kind of categories can describe all kinds of high-level structures such as graph-like structures, but also Petri net structures. Moreover, there are special morphism classes in NAC-adhesive HLR categories, allowing for rich theory regarding transformation of such high-level structures. NACs are an important feature for the modeling of transformation systems, expressing that a certain structure is not present when performing the transformation [44], and thus, enhancing the expressiveness of the transformation. In order to provide a rich theory for such transformations with NACs, they are integrated into the framework of adhesive HLR systems as presented in [29]. For this integration, mainly some new morphism classes have to be defined, which are necessary for successful adaption of the theory.

First we repeat the notion of weak adhesive HLR categories as introduced in [29]. The intuitive idea of adhesive categories is that suitable pushouts and pullbacks in these categories are compatible with each other. This property is expressed by so-called van Kampen (VK) squares. The idea of these squares is that of a pushout that is stable under pullbacks, and, vice versa, that pullbacks are stable under combined pushouts and pullbacks. The name "van Kampen" originates from the relationship between these squares and the Van Kampen Theorem in topology (see [20]).

3.2.1 Definition ((weak) van Kampen square). A pushout (1) is a *van Kampen square* if, for any commutative cube (2) with (1) in the bottom and where the back faces are pullbacks, the

---
[1]Note that, the results on constraints and applicability, as presented in Section 2.9, are not formulated for NAC-adhesive HLR systems either. It is part of future work to generalize these results as well.

CHAPTER 3. RULE-BASED MODELING USING HIGH-LEVEL TRANSFORMATION

following statement holds: the top face is a pushout iff the front faces are pullbacks:

$$
\begin{array}{ccc} A & \xrightarrow{m} & B \\ \downarrow & (1) & \downarrow \\ C & \xrightarrow{n} & D \end{array}
\qquad (1)
$$

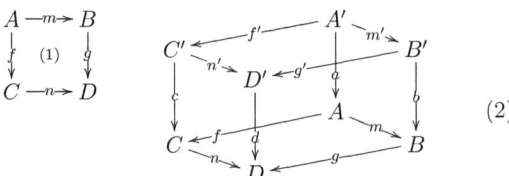

(2)

Consider a special morphism class $\mathcal{M}$. A pushout (1) is a *weak van Kampen square* if the above property holds for any commutative cube (2) with $m \in \mathcal{M}$ and ($f \in \mathcal{M}$ or $b, c, d \in \mathcal{M}$).

In [29] it is shown that in **Sets** regular pushouts are not necessarily van Kampen squares, but at least pushouts along monomorphisms are. In [64], adhesive categories are introduced in which pushouts along monomorphisms and pullbacks exist, and in particular, pushouts along monomorphisms are VK squares. In [29], it is shown that the categories **Sets**, **Graphs** and **Typed Graphs** are adhesive. Moreover, it is motivated that the notion of adhesive categories should be weakened to adhesive HLR categories in order to handle high-level structures, including several kinds of graphs and Petri nets as well as algebraic specifications. In [37] it has been shown that weak adhesive HLR categories based on weak van Kampen squares are suitable for describing place/transition nets and algebraic high-level nets.

3.2.2 Definition ((weak) adhesive HLR category). A category **C** with a morphism class $\mathcal{M}$ is called a *weak adhesive HLR category*, if

1. $\mathcal{M}$ is a class of monomorphisms closed under isomorphisms, composition and decomposition,

2. **C** has pushouts (PO) and pullbacks (PB) along $\mathcal{M}$-morphisms and $\mathcal{M}$-morphisms are closed under pushouts and pullbacks,

3. pushouts in **C** along $\mathcal{M}$-morphisms are (weak) Van Kampen squares.

For a *NAC-adhesive HLR category* we demand in addition to an adhesive HLR category some additional properties on special morphism classes in the category in order to be able to generalize all of the results. We distinguish three classes of morphisms, namely $\mathcal{M}, \mathcal{M}'$ and $\mathcal{Q}$, and a class of pairs of morphisms $\mathcal{E}'$. $\mathcal{M}$ is a subset of the class of all monomorphisms as given in [29], and the rule morphisms are always in $\mathcal{M}$. The non-existing morphism q in Def. 3.3.1 for NACs is an element of the morphism class $\mathcal{Q}$. Moreover, for pair factorization in Def. 5.25 in [29] we need the classes $\mathcal{M}'$ and $\mathcal{E}'$. First we (re-)introduce some definitions for properties that the morphism classes $\mathcal{M}, \mathcal{E}', \mathcal{M}'$ and $\mathcal{Q}$ should have. Thereafter all needed properties are listed in the definition for adhesive HLR categories with NACs.

We repeat the following definitions of properties introduced in [29] for an $\mathcal{E}' - \mathcal{M}'$ pair factorization (see Def. 5.25 in [29]), $\mathcal{M} - \mathcal{M}'$ PO-PB decomposition (see Def. 5.27 in [29]), $\mathcal{M}'$ is closed under PO's and PB's along $\mathcal{M}$ - morphims, and initial PO over $\mathcal{M}'$ - morphisms (see Def. 6.1 in [29]). Moreover, we introduce the definitions for epi - $\mathcal{M}$ factorization, and induced PB-PO for $\mathcal{M}$ and $\mathcal{Q}$.

3.2.3 Property ((unique) $\mathcal{E}' - \mathcal{M}'$ pair factorization). A category with special class of morphism pairs $\mathcal{E}'$ with the same codomain and special morphism class $\mathcal{M}'$, has an $\mathcal{E}' - \mathcal{M}'$ pair *factorization* if, for each pair of morphisms $f_1 : A_1 \to C$ and $f_2 : A_2 \to C$, there exists an object K and morphisms $e_1 : A_1 \to K$, $e_2 : A_2 \to K$, and $m : K \to C$ with $(e_1, e_2) \in \mathcal{E}'$ and $m \in \mathcal{M}'$ such that $m \circ e_1 = f_1$ and $m \circ e_2 = f_2$:

$$A_1 \xrightarrow{e_1} K \xrightarrow{m} C, \quad A_2 \xrightarrow{e_2} K, \quad f_1, f_2$$

An $\mathcal{E}' - \mathcal{M}'$ pair factorization is *unique* if two $\mathcal{E}' - \mathcal{M}'$ pair factorizations of f_1 and f_2 are isomorphic.

3.2.4 Property ($\mathcal{M} - \mathcal{M}'$ PO-PB decomposition). Given a category with special morphism classes $\mathcal{M}$ and $\mathcal{M}'$, it has the $\mathcal{M} - \mathcal{M}'$ *PO-PB decomposition property* if the following property holds. Given the following commutative diagram with $l \in \mathcal{M}$ and $w \in \mathcal{M}'$, and where (1) + (2) is a pushout and (2) a pullback, then (1) and (2) are pushouts and also pullbacks:

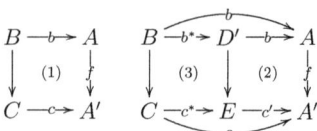

3.2.5 Definition (initial pushout, boundary, context). Consider a morphism $f : A \to A'$. A morphism $b : B \to A$ with $b \in \mathcal{M}$ is called the *boundary* over f if there is a pushout complement of f and b such that (1) is a pushout that is *initial* over f. (1) is initial over f if for every pushout (2) with $b' \in \mathcal{M}$ there exist unique morphisms $b^* : B \to D$ and $c^* : C \to E$ with $b^*, c^* \in \mathcal{M}$ such that $b' \circ b^* = b$, $c' \circ c^* = c$ and (3) is a pushout. B is then called the *boundary object* and C the *context* with respect to f.

$$B \xrightarrow{b} A \qquad B \xrightarrow{b^*} D' \xrightarrow{b'} A$$
$$\downarrow (1) \downarrow \qquad \downarrow (3) \downarrow (2) \downarrow$$
$$C \xrightarrow{c} A' \qquad C \xrightarrow{c^*} E \xrightarrow{c'} A'$$

3.2.6 Property (initial PO over $\mathcal{M}'$ - morphisms). A category with special morphism class $\mathcal{M}'$ has initial PO over $\mathcal{M}'$ - morphisms if the following property holds. For each morphism $f \in \mathcal{M}'$ an initial PO over f as given in Def.3.2.5 exists.

3.2.7 Property ((unique) epi - $\mathcal{M}$ factorization). A category with special morphism class $\mathcal{M}$ has an *epi-$\mathcal{M}$ factorization* if for each morphism $f : A \to C$ there exists some object B, an epimorphism $e : A \to B$, and morphism $m : B \to C \in \mathcal{M}$ such that $m \circ e = f$. An epi-$\mathcal{M}$ factorization is *unique* if two epi-$\mathcal{M}$ factorizations of f are isomorphic.

3.2.8 Property ($\mathcal{M}'$ is closed under PO's and PB's along $\mathcal{M}$ - morphims). Given a category with special morphism classes $\mathcal{M}$ and $\mathcal{M}'$, then $\mathcal{M}'$ is *closed under PO's and PB's along $\mathcal{M}$ - morphisms* if the following holds. Given (1) with $m, n \in \mathcal{M}$, we have that:

- if (1) is a pushout and $f \in \mathcal{M}'$, then $g \in \mathcal{M}'$ also and

- if (1) is a pullback and $g \in \mathcal{M}'$, then $f \in \mathcal{M}'$ also:

$$\begin{array}{ccc} A & \xrightarrow{m} & B \\ f \downarrow & (1) & \downarrow g \\ C & \xrightarrow{n} & D \end{array}$$

3.2.9 Property (induced PB-PO for $\mathcal{M}$ and $\mathcal{Q}$). Given $a : A \to C \in \mathcal{Q}$ and $b : B \to C \in \mathcal{M}$ and the following PB and PO,

$$\begin{array}{ccc} D & \xrightarrow{d_2} & B \\ d_1 \downarrow & (PB) & \downarrow b \\ A & \xrightarrow{a} & C \end{array} \qquad \begin{array}{ccc} D & \xrightarrow{d_2} & B \\ d_1 \downarrow & (PO) & \downarrow e_1 \\ A & \xrightarrow{e_2} & E \end{array}$$

then the induced morphism $x : E \to C$ with $x \circ e_1 = b$ and $x \circ e_2 = a$ is a monomorphism in $\mathcal{Q}$.

3.2.10 Remark. Theorem 5.1 in [65] proves the induced PB-PO property in adhesive categories for a,b being mono with the result that x is also mono. The proof is based on the fact that general PBs exist in adhesive categories.

3.2.11 Definition (NAC-adhesive HLR category). A *NAC-adhesive HLR category* is a weak adhesive HLR category **C** with special morphism class $\mathcal{M}$ and in addition three morphism classes $\mathcal{M}', \mathcal{E}'$ and $\mathcal{Q}$ with the following properties:

1. unique $\mathcal{E}' - \mathcal{M}'$ pair factorization (see Prop. 3.2.3)

2. unique epi - $\mathcal{M}$ factorization (see Prop. 3.2.7)

3. $\mathcal{M} - \mathcal{M}'$ PO-PB decomposition (see Prop. 3.2.4)

4. $\mathcal{M} - \mathcal{Q}$ PO-PB decomposition (see Prop. 3.2.4)

5. initial PO over $\mathcal{M}'$ - morphisms (see Prop. 3.2.6)

6. $\mathcal{M}'$ is closed under PO's and PB's along $\mathcal{M}$ - morphims (see Prop. 3.2.8)

7. $\mathcal{Q}$ is closed under PO's and PB's along $\mathcal{M}$ - morphisms (see Prop. 3.2.8)

8. induced PB-PO for $\mathcal{M}$ and $\mathcal{Q}$ (see Prop. 3.2.9)

9. If $f : A \to B \in \mathcal{Q}$ and $g : B \to C \in \mathcal{M}'$ then $g \circ f \in \mathcal{Q}$.
   Composition of morphisms in $\mathcal{M}'$ and $\mathcal{Q}$

10. If $g \circ f \in \mathcal{Q}$ and $g \in \mathcal{M}'$ then $f \in \mathcal{Q}$.
    Decomposition of morphisms in $\mathcal{M}'$ and $\mathcal{Q}$

11. If g and $f \in \mathcal{Q}$ then $g \circ f \in \mathcal{Q}$.
    Composition of morphisms in $\mathcal{Q}$

12. If $g \circ f \in \mathcal{Q}$ and $g \in \mathcal{Q}$ then $f \in \mathcal{Q}$.
    Decomposition of morphisms in $\mathcal{Q}$

3.2.12 Remark. Property 1 is needed for Theorem 3.7.6, Definition 3.5.3, Theorem 3.10.3. Property 2 is needed for Lemma 3.3.13. Property 3 is needed for Theorem 3.7.5, Definition 3.5.3, Theorem 3.10.3. Property 4 is needed for Lemma 3.3.7. Property 5 is needed for Theorem 3.10.4. Property 6 is needed for Theorem 3.7.6, Theorem 3.10.4. Property 7 is needed for Lemma 3.3.7, Lemma 3.3.13. Property 8 is needed for Lemma 3.3.13. Property 9 is needed for Theorem 3.7.5. Property 10 is needed for Theorem 3.7.6. Property 11 is needed for Lemma 3.3.13, Lemma 3.3.7, Theorem 3.10.9. Property 12 is needed for Lemma 3.3.7.

It can be shown that the following property holds in each NAC-adhesive HLR category (in particular, it follows from Prop. 3.2.7). It is needed in order to prove Theorem 3.8.21.

3.2.13 Property (diagonal morphism). Given the following commuting diagram such that $a : A \to B$ is an epimorphism and $d : C \to D$ in $\mathcal{M}$, then there exists a *diagonal morphism* $f : B \to C$ such that $f \circ a = c$ and $d \circ f = b$.

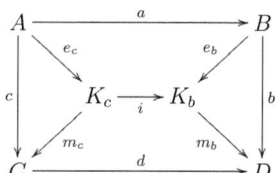

3.2.14 Corollary. *Given a NAC-adhesive HLR category, then the diagonal morphism property as given in Prop. 3.2.13 holds.*

Proof. Consider morphisms b, c, an epimorphism a, and a morphism $d \in \mathcal{M}$ such that the following diagram commutes:

$$\begin{array}{ccc} A & \xrightarrow{a} & B \\ \downarrow^{e_c} & \searrow^{e_b} & \\ c \downarrow & K_c \xrightarrow{i} K_b & \downarrow b \\ & \swarrow^{m_c} \quad \searrow^{m_b} & \\ C & \xrightarrow{d} & D \end{array}$$

Since in a NAC-adhesive HLR category we have a unique epi-$\mathcal{M}$ factorization, we have $c = m_c \circ e_c$ with $m_c \in \mathcal{M} : A \to K_c$ and $e_c : K_c \to C$ an epimorphism, and $b = m_b \circ e_b$ with $m_b \in \mathcal{M} : B \to K_b$ and $e_b : K_b \to D$ an epimorphism. Now $d \circ m_c \circ e_c$ and $m_b \circ e_b \circ a$ are epi-$\mathcal{M}$ factorizations of $d \circ c = b \circ a$. Since epi-$\mathcal{M}$ factorizations are unique, we have an isomorphism $i : K_c \to K_b$ such that a morphism $f = m_c \circ i^{-1} \circ e_b : B \to C$ exists with $f \circ a = c$ and $d \circ f = b$. □

3.2.15 Fact (**Graphs** (resp. **Graphs**$_{TG}$) is a NAC-adhesive HLR category). *The category* **Graphs** *(resp.* **Graphs**$_{TG}$ *of typed graphs) with* $\mathcal{M} = \mathcal{M}' = \mathcal{Q}$ *the set of all injective graph morphisms (resp. typed over TG), and $\mathcal{E}'$ the set of jointly surjective graph morphisms (resp. typed over TG) is NAC-adhesive HLR.*

Proof. Property 1-7 have been shown in [29]. Property 8 holds, because of Remark 3.2.10 and the fact that **Graphs** (resp. **Graphs**$_{TG}$) is adhesive. Property 9-12 corresponds to the regular composition and decomposition property of injective graph morphisms. □

3.2.16 Fact (**AGraphs**$_{TG}$ is a NAC-adhesive HLR category). *The category* **AGraphs**$_{TG}$ *of typed attributed graphs with $\mathcal{M}$ injective, and in addition isomorphic on the data type part, $\mathcal{M}' = \mathcal{Q}$ and $\mathcal{E}'$ as presented in [29] is NAC-adhesive HLR.*

CHAPTER 3. RULE-BASED MODELING USING HIGH-LEVEL TRANSFORMATION

Proof. Property 8 holds, since as described in Remark 3.2.10 it is based on the existence of general PBs. As remarked in [29], although not required, general PBs exist in **AGraphs**$_{TG}$. Properties $1 - 7$ and $9 - 12$ have been shown in [29] for **AGraphs**$_{TG}$. □

In this thesis we are interested mainly in graph-like instantiations. In [101, 102] though it is proven that the category of Petri nets and Algebraic High-Level Systems is also NAC-adhesive HLR.

3.3 Rule-Based Modeling using High-Level Transformation

Adhesive HLR systems are introduced in [29] as transformation systems for high-level structures based on adhesive HLR categories. The rules of these abstract transformation systems do not hold any application conditions. In this section we add negative application conditions to the rules. NACs are an important feature for the modeling of transformation systems, expressing that a certain structure is not present when performing the transformation [44], and thus, enhancing the expressiveness of the transformation. In the former section, we defined NAC-adhesive HLR categories paving the ground for adhesive HLR systems with NACs. The extra properties holding in NAC-adhesive HLR categories enable us to extend all main results presented in [29] for adhesive HLR systems without NACs.

3.3.1 Definition (negative application condition, rule with NACs).

- A *negative application condition* or $NAC(n)$ on L is an arbitrary morphism $n : L \to N$. A morphism $g : L \to G$ satisfies $NAC(n)$ on L, written $g \models NAC(n)$, if and only if $\nexists\, q : N \to G \in \mathcal{Q}$ such that $q \circ n = g$.

$$L \xrightarrow{n} N$$
$$\downarrow g \quad \quad \stackrel{q}{\cdots}$$
$$G \;\longleftarrow\;$$

A set of NACs on L is denoted by $NAC_L = \{NAC(n_i) | i \in I\}$. A morphism $g : L \to G$ satisfies NAC_L if and only if g satisfies all single NACs on L i.e. $g \models NAC(n_i)\ \forall i \in I$.

- Similarly, a *negative application condition* or $NAC(n)$ on R is an arbitrary graph morphism $n : R \to N$. A graph morphism $h : R \to H$ satisfies $NAC(n)$ on R, written $h \models NAC(n)$, if and only if $\nexists\, q : N \to H$ such that q is injective and $q \circ n = h$.

- A set of NACs NAC_L (resp. NAC_R) on L (resp. R) for a rule $p : L \xleftarrow{l} K \xrightarrow{r} R$ (with $l, r \in \mathcal{M}$) is called *left* (resp. *right*) NAC on p. $NAC_p = (NAC_L, NAC_R)$, consisting of a set of left and a set of right NACs on p is called a *set of NACs on p*. A *rule (p, NAC_p) with NACs* is a rule $p : L \xleftarrow{l} K \xrightarrow{r} R$ (with $l, r \in \mathcal{M}$) with a set of NACs on p. We call L (resp. R), the left-hand side (LHS) (resp. right-hand side (RHS)) of rule p.

3.3.2 Definition (adhesive HLR system, grammar, transformation, language with NACs).

- An *adhesive HLR system with NACs* AHS $= (\mathbf{C}, \mathcal{M}, \mathcal{M}', \mathcal{E}', \mathcal{Q}, P)$ consists of a NAC-adhesive HLR category $(\mathbf{C}, \mathcal{M}, \mathcal{M}', \mathcal{E}', \mathcal{Q})$ and a set of rules with NACs P. An *adhesive*

3.3. RULE-BASED MODELING USING HIGH-LEVEL TRANSFORMATION

HLR grammar with NACs $AHG = (AHS, S) = ((\mathbf{C}, \mathcal{M}, \mathcal{M}', \mathcal{E}', \mathcal{Q}, P), S)$ consists of an adhesive HLR system with NACs $(\mathbf{C}, \mathcal{M}, \mathcal{M}', \mathcal{E}', \mathcal{Q}, P)$ and a start object S belonging to $\mathbf{C}$.

- A *direct transformation* $G \stackrel{p,g}{\Rightarrow} H$ from G to H via a rule $p : L \leftarrow K \rightarrow R$ with $NAC_p = (NAC_L, NAC_R)$ and a match $g : L \rightarrow G$ consists of the double pushout (DPO) [23]

$$\begin{array}{ccccc} L & \longleftarrow & K & \longrightarrow & R \\ {\scriptstyle g}\downarrow & & \downarrow & & \downarrow{\scriptstyle h} \\ G & \longleftarrow & D & \longrightarrow & H \end{array}$$

where g satisfies NAC_L, written $g \models NAC_L$ and $h : R \rightarrow H$ satisfies NAC_R, written $h \models NAC_R$. Since pushouts along $\mathcal{M}$-morphisms in an adhesive HLR category always exist, the DPO can be constructed if the pushout complement of $K \rightarrow L \rightarrow G$ exists. If so, we say that the match g satisfies the *gluing condition* of rule p. A *transformation*, denoted as $G_0 \stackrel{*}{\Rightarrow} G_n$, is a sequence $G_0 \Rightarrow G_1 \Rightarrow \cdots \Rightarrow G_n$ of direct transformations. For $n = 0$, we have the identical transformation $G_0 \Rightarrow G_0$. Moreover, for $n = 0$ we also allow isomorphisms $G_0 \cong G_0'$, because pushouts, and hence also direct transformations, are only unique up to isomorphism.

- An *adhesive HLR language* $\mathcal{L}(AHG)$ consists of S and all objects G such that there exists a transformation from S to G via rules in P.

3.3.3 Remark (instantiations of adhesive HLR systems with NACs). As noted in Fact 3.2.15 **Graphs** (resp. **Graphs**$_{TG}$, **AGraphs**$_{TG}$) is a NAC-adhesive HLR category. Based on these categories, therefore, we can build (typed, attributed) graph transformation systems with NACs as adhesive HLR systems with NACs. In this thesis we are interested mainly in graph-like instantiations. In [101, 102] though it is proven that the category of Petri nets and Algebraic High-Level Systems is NAC-adhesive HLR, and therefore, the corresponding transformation systems are adhesive HLR systems with NACs.

3.3.4 Assumption (left NACs). From now on we consider only adhesive HLR systems with rules having an empty set of right negative application conditions.

This assumption is without loss of generality, because each right NAC can be shifted over a rule to an equivalent left NAC as explained in [34] and [29], where Def. 7.16 and Theorem 7.17 can be specialized to NACs as shown in the following construction and lemma. Note that [46] presents this result for more general nested application conditions.

3.3.5 Definition (construction of left from right NACs). For each $NAC(n_i)$ on R with $n_i : R \rightarrow N_i$ of a rule $p = (L \leftarrow K \rightarrow R)$, the equivalent left application condition $L_p(NAC(n_i))$ is defined in the following way:

$$\begin{array}{ccccc} L & \longleftarrow & K & \longrightarrow & R \\ {\scriptstyle n_i'}\downarrow & (2) & \downarrow & (1) & \downarrow{\scriptstyle n_i} \\ N_i' & \longleftarrow & Z & \longrightarrow & N_i \end{array}$$

- If the pair $(K \rightarrow R, R \rightarrow N_i)$ has a pushout complement, we construct $(K \rightarrow Z, Z \rightarrow N_i)$ as the pushout complement (1). Then we construct pushout (2) with the morphism $n_i' : L \rightarrow N_i'$. Now we define $L_p(NAC(n_i)) = NAC(n_i')$.

- If the pair $(K \to R, R \to N_i)$ does not have a pushout complement, we define $L_p(NAC(n_i)) = true$.

For each set of NACs on R, $NAC_R = \cup_{i \in I} NAC(n_i)$ we define the following set of left NACs:

$$L_p(NAC_R) = \cup_{i \in I'} L_p(NAC(n'_i))$$

with $i \in I'$ if and only if the pair $(K \to R, R \to N_i)$ has a pushout complement.

3.3.6 Remark. Note that Z is unique since pushout complements along $\mathcal{M}$-morphisms are unique up to isomorphism in adhesive HLR categories [29].

3.3.7 Lemma (equivalence of left and right NACs). *For every rule p with NAC_R a set of right NACs on p, $L_p(NAC_R)$ as defined in Def. 3.3.5 is a set of left NACs on p such that for all direct transformations $G \overset{p,g}{\Rightarrow} H$ with comatch h,*

$$g \models L_p(NAC_R) \Leftrightarrow h \models NAC_R$$

Proof. The proof corresponds to case 1 and 3 in the proof of Theorem 7.17 in [29]. □

Since we have assumed without loss of generality that NAC_p consists only of a set of NACs on its left-hand side, we can define applicability of a rule with NACs as follows. The construction of a direct transformation remains the same as for adhesive HLR systems without NACs [29].

3.3.8 Definition (applicability of rule). Let $p : L \overset{l}{\leftarrow} K \overset{r}{\to} R$ be a rule with NAC_p. For an object G and a match $m : L \to G$, p is *applicable* via m if the pushout complement for $K \overset{l}{\to} L \overset{m}{\to} G$ exists (i.e. m fulfills the gluing condition), and in addition m satisfies NAC_p.

3.3.9 Fact (construction of direct transformations). *Given rule p and match $m : L \to G$ such that p is applicable to G via m as given in Def. 3.3.8, then a direct transformation can be constructed in two steps:*

1. *Construct the pushout complement $K \overset{k}{\to} D \overset{f}{\to} G$ of $K \overset{l}{\to} L \overset{m}{\to} G$ in diagram (1) below.*

2. *Construct the pushout $D \overset{g}{\to} H \overset{n}{\leftarrow} R$ of $D \overset{k}{\leftarrow} K \overset{r}{\to} R$ in diagram (2). This construction is unique up to isomorphism.*

$$\begin{array}{ccccc} L & \xleftarrow{l} & K & \xrightarrow{r} & R \\ {\scriptstyle m}\downarrow & (1) & {\scriptstyle k}\downarrow & (2) & {\scriptstyle n}\downarrow \\ G & \xleftarrow{f} & D & \xrightarrow{g} & H \end{array}$$

Proof. As given in Def. 3.3.2 we have a direct transformation via rule p and match m if $m \models NAC_p$ and a double pushout (DPO) exists. From Def. 3.3.8 it follows that $m \models NAC_p$ and a pushout complement for $K \overset{l}{\to} L \overset{m}{\to} G$ exists. Since $r \in \mathcal{M}$, pushout (2) can be constructed as well. Uniqueness is proven in [29]. □

By means of the following definition and theorem, we show that it is possible to apply a rule inversely. It is based on the shifting of NACs over a rule as presented in Def. 3.3.5. Inverse transformations will be used, for example, in Section 3.6 to define causal dependencies (see Def. 3.6.2) between transformations. In particular, it is shown that a transformation can become irreversible, after applying an intermediate transformation.

3.3. RULE-BASED MODELING USING HIGH-LEVEL TRANSFORMATION

3.3.10 Definition (inverse rule with NACs). For a rule $p : L \leftarrow K \rightarrow R$ with $NAC_p = (NAC_L, \emptyset)$, the inverse rule is defined by $p^{-1} = R \leftarrow K \rightarrow L$ with $NAC_{p^{-1}} = (L_{p^{-1}}(NAC_L), \emptyset)$.

3.3.11 Theorem (inverse direct transformation with NACs). *For each direct transformation with NACs $G \Rightarrow H$ via a rule $p : L \leftarrow K \rightarrow R$ with NAC_p a set of left NACs on p, there exists an inverse direct transformation with NACs $H \Rightarrow G$ via the inverse rule p^{-1} with $NAC_{p^{-1}}$.*

$$\begin{array}{ccccc}
N & & & & N' \\
\uparrow & & & & \uparrow \\
L & \leftarrow K \rightarrow & R & R \leftarrow K \rightarrow & L \\
\downarrow \;(2)\; \downarrow \;(1)\; \downarrow & & \downarrow \;(1)\; \downarrow \;(2)\; \downarrow \\
G & \leftarrow D \rightarrow & H & H \leftarrow D \rightarrow & G
\end{array}$$

Proof. This follows directly from Def. 3.3.10 and Lemma 3.3.7. □

Finally, the following definition introduces how to shift NACs over a morphism. In particular, it is shown how to construct for an object A with NACs a set of equivalent NACs on an object B via some morphism $m : A \rightarrow B$. In Section 3.5, we use this construction to define concurrent rules with NACs. Note that [46] presents the following result for more general nested application conditions.

3.3.12 Definition (construction of NACs on B from NACs on A with $m : A \rightarrow B$). Consider the following diagram:

$$\begin{array}{ccc}
N'_j & \xrightarrow{e_{ji}} & N_i \\
n'_j \uparrow & (1) & \uparrow n_i \\
A & \xrightarrow{m} & B
\end{array}$$

For each $NAC(n'_j)$ on A with $n'_j : A \rightarrow N'_j$ and $m : A \rightarrow B$, let

$$D_m(NAC(n'_j)) = \{NAC(n_i) | i \in I, n_i : B \rightarrow N_i\}$$

where I and n_i are constructed as follows: $i \in I$ if and only if (e_{ji}, n_i) with $e_{ji} : N'_j \rightarrow N_i$ jointly epimorphic, $e_{ji} \circ n'_j = n_i \circ m$ and $e_{ji} \in \mathcal{Q}$.
For each set of NACs $NAC_A = \{NAC(n_j) | j \in J\}$ on A the downward shift of NAC_A is then defined as:

$$D_m(NAC_A) = \cup_{j \in J} D_m(NAC(n'_j))$$

3.3.13 Lemma (equivalence of set of NACs on A and set of NACs on B with $m : A \rightarrow B$). *Given $g : A \rightarrow G_0$, $m : A \rightarrow B$ with NAC_A and $g' = g \circ m$ as in the following diagram:*

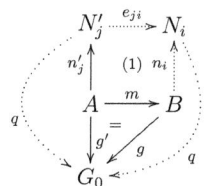

CHAPTER 3. RULE-BASED MODELING USING HIGH-LEVEL TRANSFORMATION

then the following holds :
$$g' \models NAC_A \Leftrightarrow g \models D_m(NAC_A).$$

Proof. • ($\Rightarrow$) Let $g \not\models D_m(NAC(A)) = \cup_{j \in J} D_m(NAC(n'_j))$ with $NAC_A = \{NAC(n'_j) | j \in J\}$. Then for some $j \in J$ there is a NAC $n_i : B \to N_i \in D_m(NAC(n'_j))$ and $e_{ji} : N'_j \to N_i$ for which holds that $g \not\models NAC(n_i)$, (e_{ji}, n_i) jointly epi, $e_{ji} \in \mathcal{Q}$ and $e_{ji} \circ n'_j = n_i \circ m$. Consequently there exists a morphism $q : N_i \to G_0 \in \mathcal{Q}$ such that $q \circ n_i = g$. Since $g' = g \circ m = q \circ n_i \circ m = q \circ e_{ji} \circ n'_j$, there exists a morphism $q' : N'_j \to G_0$ defined by $q' = q \circ e_{ji}$ s.t. $q' \circ n'_j = q \circ e_{ji} \circ n'_j = g'$. Because of the composition property for morphisms in $\mathcal{Q}$, we have $q' \in \mathcal{Q}$ since $q \in \mathcal{Q}$ and e_{ji} in $\mathcal{Q}$. Hence $g' \not\models NAC(n'_j) \Rightarrow g' \not\models NAC_A$, and therefore, ($\Rightarrow$) of the above equivalence holds.

• ($\Leftarrow$) Let $g' \not\models NAC_A$ with $NAC_A = \{NAC(n'_j)|j \in J\}$. Then for some $j \in J$ a morphism $q' : N'_j \to G_0 \in \mathcal{Q}$ exists such that $q' \circ n'_j = g'$. Let (e^*, m^*) be an epi-$\mathcal{M}$-factorization of g. Construct X with $p_1 : X \to E$ and $m_1 : X \to N'_j$ as pullback of m^* and q (PBs along $\mathcal{M}$-morphisms exist).

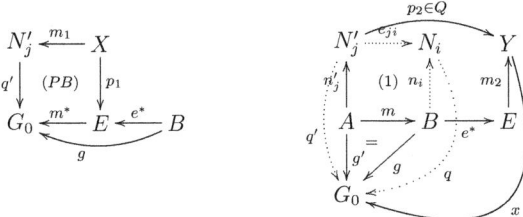

Then we have $m_1 \in \mathcal{M}$ and $p_1 \in \mathcal{Q}$, since $m^* \in \mathcal{M}$ and $q' \in \mathcal{Q}$, PBs preserve $\mathcal{M}$ and PBs along $\mathcal{M}$ preserve $\mathcal{Q}$. Now construct Y with $m_2 : E \to Y$ and $p_2 : N'_j \to Y$ as pushout of m_1 and p_1. Then we have $m_2 \in \mathcal{M}$, $p_2 \in \mathcal{Q}$, since $m_1 \in \mathcal{M}$, $p_1 \in \mathcal{Q}$, POs preserve $\mathcal{M}$ and POs along $\mathcal{M}$ preserve $\mathcal{Q}$ Because of the induced PB-PO property, the induced morphism $x : Y \to G_0$ with $x \circ m_2 = m^*$ and $x \circ p_2 = q'$ is a monomorphism in $\mathcal{Q}$.

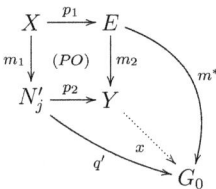

Moreover, it holds that $p_2, m_2 \circ e^*$ jointly epimorphic because e^* epimorphic and p_2, m_2 jointly epimorphic. Summarizing we have the following equations: $x \circ m_2 \circ e^* \circ m = m^* \circ e^* \circ m = g \circ m = g' = q' \circ n'_j = x \circ p_2 \circ n'_j$ and since x mono we have $m_2 \circ e^* \circ m = p_2 \circ n'_j$. Since $m_2 \circ e^*$ and p_2 are jointly epimorphic, $p_2 \circ n'_j = (m_2 \circ e^*) \circ m$ and $p_2 \in \mathcal{Q}$ we can conclude that $m_2 \circ e^* : L_c \to Y$ equals one of the morphisms $n_i : B \to N_i \in D_m(NAC(n'_j))$. Moreover, since $x \circ m_2 \circ e^* = m^* \circ e^* = g$ and $x \in \mathcal{Q}$ it holds that $g \not\models NAC(m_2 \circ e^*) = NAC(n_i)$, and consequently $g \not\models NAC(n_i) \Rightarrow g \not\models D_m(NAC(n'_j)) \Rightarrow g \not\models D_m(NAC_A)$. Hence ($\Leftarrow$) of the above equivalence holds.

□

3.3.14 Remark. Assuming that $\mathcal{Q}$ is the set of all morphisms in the NAC-adhesive HLR category, and each NAC-morphism n is in $\mathcal{M}$ (or each match is in $\mathcal{M}$), a more simple construction of a set of NACs on the domain of a morphism m into an equivalent set of NACs on the codomain of m is possible. In this case it is not necessary to consider a set of jointly epimorphic morphisms (e_{ji}, n'_i) such that (1) commutes. It would be sufficient to construct the PO of each (n'_j, m) for each $j \in J$. The proof of this more simple construction is omitted here. Different kinds of satisfiability of NACs and translations of one kind of satisfiability into the other one can be found in [46].

3.4 Independence and Parallelism

In order to generalize the notion of parallelism to adhesive HLR systems with NACs, it is first necessary to define when two direct transformations with NACs are parallel and sequentially independent. For a pair of transformations with NACs it is not only possible that one transformation deletes a structure that is needed by the other one, but also that one transformation produces a structure that is forbidden by the other one. Moreover, for a sequence of two direct transformations with NACs it is not only possible that the first transformation produces a structure that is needed by the second one, but also that the first transformation deletes a structure that is forbidden by the second one. For this new notion of parallel and sequential independence we formulate the local Church-Rosser property with NACs and also a Parallelism Theorem with NACs.

3.4.1 Definition (parallel and sequential independence). Two direct transformations $G \stackrel{p_1,m_1}{\Longrightarrow} H_1$ with NAC_{p_1} and $G \stackrel{p_2,m_2}{\Longrightarrow} H_2$ with NAC_{p_2} are *parallel independent* if

$$\exists h_{12} : L_1 \to D_2 \text{ s.t. } (d_2 \circ h_{12} = m_1 \text{ and } e_2 \circ h_{12} \models NAC_{p_1})$$

and

$$\exists h_{21} : L_2 \to D_1 \text{ s.t. } (d_1 \circ h_{21} = m_2 \text{ and } e_1 \circ h_{21} \models NAC_{p_2})$$

as in the following diagram:

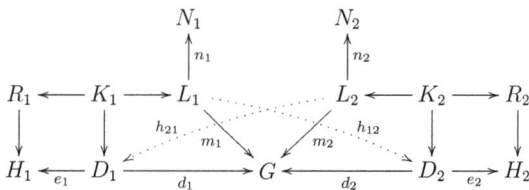

Two direct transformations $G \stackrel{p_1,m_1}{\Longrightarrow} H_1$ with NAC_{p_1} and $H_1 \stackrel{p_2,m_2}{\Longrightarrow} H_2$ with NAC_{p_2} are *sequentially independent* if

$$\exists h_{12} : R_1 \to D_2 \text{ s.t. } (d_2 \circ h_{12} = m'_1 \text{ and } e_2 \circ h_{12} \models NAC_{p_1^{-1}})$$

and

$$\exists h_{21} : L_2 \to D_1 \text{ s.t. } (e_1 \circ h_{21} = m_2 \text{ and } d_1 \circ h_{21} \models NAC_{p_2})$$

as in the following diagram:

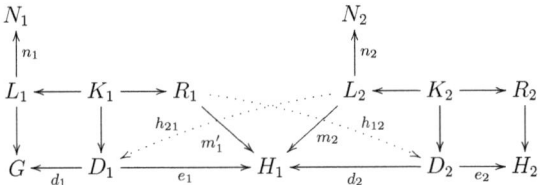

3.4.2 Remark. Note that as for the case without NACs we have the following relationship between parallel and sequential independence: $G \overset{p_1}{\Rightarrow} H_1 \overset{p_2}{\Rightarrow} H_2$ are sequentially independent iff $G \overset{p_1^{-1}}{\Leftarrow} H_1 \overset{p_2}{\Rightarrow} H_2$ are parallel independent.

3.4.3 Theorem (local Church-Rosser theorem with NACs). *Given an adhesive HLR system with NACs AHS and two parallel independent direct transformations with NACs $H_1 \overset{p_1,m_1}{\Leftarrow} G \overset{p_2,m_2}{\Rightarrow} H_2$, there are an object G' and direct transformations $H_1 \overset{p_2,m_2'}{\Rightarrow} G'$ and $H_2 \overset{p_1,m_1'}{\Rightarrow} G'$ such that $G \overset{p_1,m_1}{\Rightarrow} H_1 \overset{p_2,m_2'}{\Rightarrow} G'$ and $G \overset{p_2,m_2}{\Rightarrow} H_2 \overset{p_1,m_1'}{\Rightarrow} G'$ are sequentially independent. Vice versa, given two sequentially independent direct transformations with NACs $G \overset{p_1,m_1}{\Rightarrow} H_1 \overset{p_2,m_2'}{\Rightarrow} G'$ there are an object H_2 and sequentially independent direct transformations $G \overset{p_2,m_2}{\Rightarrow} H_2 \overset{p_1,m_1'}{\Rightarrow} G'$ such that $H_1 \overset{p_1,m_1}{\Leftarrow} G \overset{p_2,m_2}{\Rightarrow} H_2$ are parallel independent:*

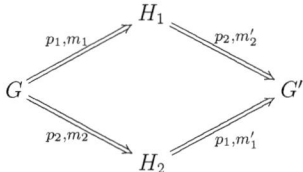

Proof. 1. Consider the parallel independent transformations $H_1 \overset{p_1,m_1}{\Leftarrow} G \overset{p_2,m_2}{\Rightarrow} H_2$:

$$\begin{array}{ccccc} L_1 & \leftarrow K_1 \rightarrow & R_1 & & \\ m_1 \downarrow & \downarrow & \downarrow n_1 & & \\ G & \leftarrow D_1 \rightarrow & H_1 & & \end{array} \quad \begin{array}{ccc} L_2 \leftarrow K_2 \rightarrow R_2 \\ m_2 \downarrow \quad \downarrow \quad \downarrow n_2 \\ G \leftarrow D_2 \rightarrow H_2 \end{array}$$

Because of Def. 3.4.1 and the parallel independence with NACs of $H_1 \overset{p_1,m_1}{\Leftarrow} G \overset{p_2,m_2}{\Rightarrow} H_2$, we know that there exists $i_2 : L_2 \to D_1$ (resp. $i_1 : L_1 \to D_2$) s.t. $f_1 \circ i_2 = m_2$ (resp. $f_2 \circ i_1 = m_1$) and moreover, $g_1 \circ i_2 \models NAC_{p_2}$ (resp. $g_2 \circ i_1 \models NAC_{p_1}$). Because of the Local Church-Rosser Theorem for parallel independent transformations without NACs, all necessary pushouts in $H_1 \overset{p_2}{\Rightarrow} G'$ and $H_2 \overset{p_1}{\Rightarrow} G'$ can be constructed s.t. $G \overset{p_1}{\Rightarrow} H_1 \overset{p_2}{\Rightarrow} G'$ and $G \overset{p_2}{\Rightarrow} H_2 \overset{p_1}{\Rightarrow} G'$ are sequentially independent according to Def. 5.9 in [29] for direct transformations without NACs. In particular, this means that $t_1 : R_1 \to D_2'$ (resp. $t_2 : R_2 \to D_1'$) exist s.t. $s_1 \circ t_1 = n_1$ (resp. $s_2 \circ t_2 = n_2$) and the following diagrams exist in which each square is a pushout:

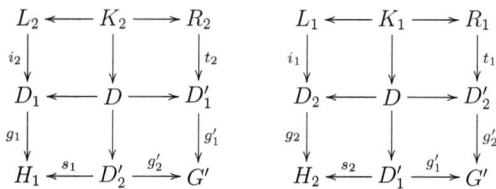

Since $g_1 \circ i_2 \models NAC_{p_2}$ and $g_2 \circ i_1 \models NAC_{p_1}$, $H_1 \overset{p_2}{\Rightarrow} G'$ and $H_2 \overset{p_1}{\Rightarrow} G'$ are valid direct transformations with NACs. For the sequential independence with NACs of $G \overset{p_1}{\Rightarrow} H_1 \overset{p_2}{\Rightarrow} G'$ we have to show that i_2, t_1 are the required morphisms. For i_2 we have $f_1 \circ i_2 = m_2$, and therefore, $f_1 \circ i_2 \models NAC_{p_2}$ follows by assumption. Now we investigate $g'_2 \circ t_1$. Because of Theorem 3.3.11 and the fact that $g_2 \circ i_1 \models NAC_{p_1}$, it follows directly that also $g'_2 \circ t_1 \models NAC_{p_1^{-1}}$. Analogously, the sequential independence of $G \overset{p_2}{\Rightarrow} H_2 \overset{p_1}{\Rightarrow} G'$ can be proven.

2. Given sequentially independent direct transformations with NACs $G \overset{p_1,m_1}{\Rightarrow} H_1 \overset{p_2,m'_2}{\Rightarrow} G'$ with comatches n'_1 and n'_2, respectively, from Remark 3.4.2 we obtain parallel independent direct transformations with NACs $G \overset{p_1,n_1}{\Leftarrow} H_1 \overset{p_2,m'_2}{\Rightarrow} G'$. Now part (i) of the proof gives us sequentially independent direct transformations with NACs $H_1 \overset{p_1^{-1},n_1}{\Rightarrow} G \overset{p_2,m_2}{\Rightarrow} H_2$ and $H_1 \overset{p_2,m'_2}{\Rightarrow} G' \overset{p_1^{-1},n'_1}{\Rightarrow} H_2$. Applying again Remark 3.4.2 to the first transformation we obtain parallel independent direct transformations with NACs $H_1 \overset{p_1,m_1}{\Leftarrow} G \overset{p_2,m_2}{\Rightarrow} H_2$:

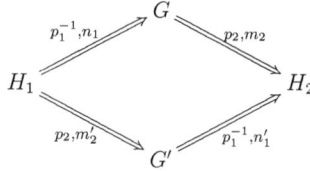

□

Now we can generalize the notion of parallelism to adhesive HLR systems with NACs. In order to build parallel rules, we need binary coproducts. Therefore, we make the following assumption.

3.4.4 Assumption (binary coproducts exist). Let for Definition 3.4.5 and Theorem 3.4.7 $AHS = (\mathbf{C}, \mathcal{M}, \mathcal{M}', \mathcal{E}', \mathcal{Q}, P)$ be an adhesive HLR system with NACs, where $\mathbf{C}$ has binary coproducts.

Recall that in Def. 3.3.12, a construction is given to shift NACs on some object A into a set of equivalent NACs on some object B over some morphism $m : A \to B$. Moreover, recall that in Def. 3.3.5, it is explained how to construct an equivalent set of left NACs from a set of right NACs on a rule. In the following definition we use these constructions to define a set of NACs on the parallel rule $p_1 + p_2$.

3.4.5 Definition (parallel rule and transformation with NAC). Given two rules $p_1 = (L_1 \xleftarrow{l_1} K_1 \xrightarrow{r_1} R_1)$ with NAC_{p_1} and $p_2 = (L_2 \xleftarrow{l_2} K_2 \xrightarrow{r_2} R_2)$ with NAC_{p_2}, the *parallel rule* $p_1 + p_2$ with $NAC_{p_1+p_2}$ is defined by the coproduct constructions over the corresponding objects and morphisms: $p_1 + p_2 = (L_1 + L_2 \xleftarrow{l_1+l_2} K_1 + K_2 \xrightarrow{r_1+r_2} R_1 + R_2)$ and $NAC_{p_1+p_2} = D_{i_1}(NAC_{p_1}) \cup D_{i_2}(NAC_{p_2}) \cup L_{p_{1,2fix}}(D_{i'_2}(NAC_{p_2})) \cup L_{p_{1fix,2}}(D_{i'_1}(NAC_{p_1}))$ with $p_{1,2fix} = L_1 + L_2 \leftarrow K_1 + L_2 \rightarrow R_1 + L_2$ and $p_{1fix,2} = L_1 + L_2 \leftarrow L_1 + K_2 \rightarrow L_1 + R_2$.

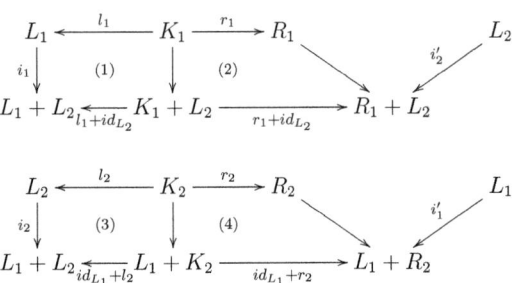

A direct transformation $G \Rightarrow G'$ via $p_1 + p_2$ with $NAC_{p_1+p_2}$ and a match $m : L_1 + L_2 \rightarrow G$ satisfying $NAC_{p_1+p_2}$ is a *direct parallel transformation with NAC* or *parallel transformation with NAC* for short.

3.4.6 Remark. Note that (1),(2),(3) and (4) in the above diagram are pushouts. Moreover, note that it is not necessary to require that coproducts are compatible with $\mathcal{M}$ as assumed in Def. 5.14 in [29]. This is because of the following argumentation. Assume that $m_1 : A_1 \rightarrow B_1$ and $m_2 : A_2 \rightarrow B_2$ are both in $\mathcal{M}$. We can then conclude that $m_1 + m_2 = (m_1 + id_{B_2}) \circ (id_{A_1} + m_2)$ is in $\mathcal{M}$ since $\mathcal{M}$-morphisms are closed under pushouts and composition.

The following theorem describes that two sequentially independent transformations with NACs can be synthesized to a parallel transformation with NACs, and the other way around that a parallel transformation with NACs can be analyzed to two sequentially independent transformations with NACs.

3.4.7 Theorem (parallelism theorem with NACs). **Synthesis.** *Given a sequentially independent direct transformation sequence with NACs $G \Rightarrow H_1 \Rightarrow G'$ via p_1, m_1 (resp. p_2, m'_2) with NAC_{p_1} (resp. NAC_{p_2}), there is a construction leading to a parallel transformation with NACs $G \Rightarrow G'$ via $[m_1, m_2]$ and the parallel rule $p_1 + p_2$ with $NAC_{p_1+p_2}$, called a synthesis construction.*

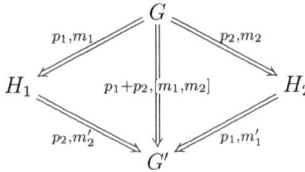

Analysis. *Given a direct parallel transformation with NACs $G \Rightarrow G'$ via $m : L_1 + L_2 \rightarrow G$ and the parallel rule $p_1 + p_2$ with $NAC_{p_1+p_2}$, then there is a construction leading to two sequentially independent transformation sequences with NACs $G \Rightarrow H_1 \Rightarrow G'$ via p_1, m_1*

3.4. INDEPENDENCE AND PARALLELISM

and p_2, m'_2 and $G \Rightarrow H_2 \Rightarrow G'$ via p_2, m_2 and p_1, m'_1, called an analysis construction.

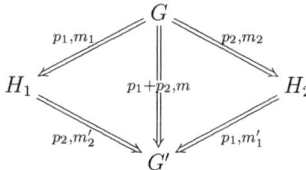

Bijective Correspondence. *The synthesis analysis construction are inverse to each other up to isomorphism.*

Proof. **Synthesis.** Given the sequentially independent direct transformations with NACs $G \overset{p_1,m_1}{\Rightarrow} H_1 \overset{p_2,m'_2}{\Rightarrow} G'$, using the Parallelism Theorem (Theorem 5.18 in [29]) without NACs we can construct the following double pushout:

$$
\begin{array}{ccccc}
L_1 + L_2 & \longleftarrow & K_1 + K_2 & \longrightarrow & R_1 + R_2 \\
{\scriptstyle [m_1,m_2]}\downarrow & & \downarrow & & \downarrow \\
G & \longleftarrow & D & \longrightarrow & G'
\end{array}
$$

Because of Theorem 3.4.3, we know that also the sequentially independent direct transformations with NACs $G \overset{p_2,m_2}{\Rightarrow} H_2 \overset{p_1,m'_1}{\Rightarrow} G'$ exist. Now we have to prove that $[m_1, m_2] \models NAC_{p_1+p_2}$ such that according to Def. 3.4.5 the above double pushout becomes a direct parallel transformation with NACs. Let us start with proving that $[m_1, m_2] \models D_{i_1}(NAC_{p_1}) \cup L_{p_1,2fix}(D_{i'_2}(NAC_{p_2}))$. Consider, therefore, the following diagrams.

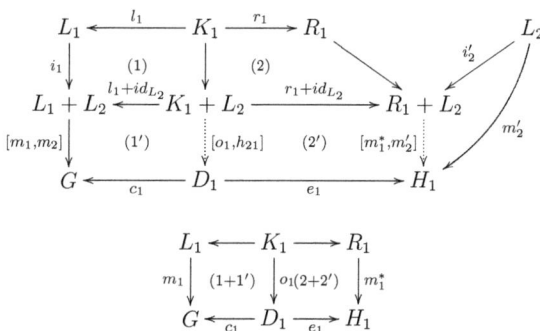

According to Lemma 3.3.13 it can be followed directly that $[m_1, m_2] \models D_{i_1}(NAC_{p_1})$. Because of sequential independence of $G \overset{p_1,m_1}{\Rightarrow} H_1 \overset{p_2,m'_2}{\Rightarrow} G'$, there exists a morphism $h_{21} : L_2 \to D_1$ such that $e_1 \circ h_{21} = m'_2$ with $m'_2 \models NAC_{p_2}$. Therefore, morphism $[o_1, h_{21}]$ exists. Since (1') and (2') commute, (1),(2),(1+1') and (2+2') are pushouts because of decomposition of pushouts also (1') and (2') are pushouts. Now because of Lemma 3.3.13 and $m'_2 \models NAC_{p_2}$ it holds that $[m^*_1, m'_2] \models D_{i'_2}(NAC_{p_2})$ and because of Lemma 3.3.7 $[m_1, m_2] \models L_{p_1,2fix}(D_{i'_2}(NAC_{p_2}))$. Analogously, we can argue to prove in addition $[m_1, m_2] \models D_{i_2}(NAC_{p_2}) \cup L_{p_1fix,2}(D_{i'_1}(NAC_{p_1}))$.

Analysis. Given a parallel transformation $G \overset{p_1+p_2,m}{\Longrightarrow} G'$ with $m \models NAC_{p_1+p_2}$, then because of the Parallelism Theorem without NACs (Theorem 5.18 in [29]) it follows that $G \Rightarrow H_1$ and $G \Rightarrow H_2$ are parallel independent without NACs and moreover, the necessary double pushouts for $G \Rightarrow H_1 \Rightarrow G'$ via p_1, m_1 and p_2, m_2' and $G \Rightarrow H_2 \Rightarrow G'$ via p_2, m_2 and p_1, m_1' can be constructed s.t. they are sequentially independent without NACs. Thereby, the match morphism m is identical to $[m_1, m_2]$. Note that we again have that the above diagrams with pushouts (1),(1'),(2),(2') exist. Now from $[m_1, m_2] \models D_{i_1}(NAC_{p_1})$ and Lemma 3.3.13 we can follow immediately that $m_1 \models NAC_{p_1}$. Moreover, since $[m_1, m_2] \models L_{p_{1,2fix}}(D_{i_2'}(NAC_{p_2}))$ we can follow from Lemma 3.3.7 that $[m_1^*, m_2'] \models D_{i_2'}(NAC_{p_2})$. Consequently because of Lemma 3.3.13 $m_2' \models NAC_{p_2}$. Analogously, one can prove that $m_1' \models NAC_{p_1}$ and $m_2 \models NAC_{p_2}$. Therefore, $G \Rightarrow H_1$ and $G \Rightarrow H_2$ are parallel independent as transformations with NACs as defined in Def. 3.4.1. From Theorem 3.4.3 it follows that $G \Rightarrow H_1 \Rightarrow G'$ and $G \Rightarrow H_2 \Rightarrow G'$ are then sequentially independent with NACs.

Bijective Correspondence. Because of the uniqueness of pushouts and pushout complements [29], the constructions are inverse to each other up to isomorphism. □

3.4.8 Remark. Note that in [72], $NAC_{p_1+p_2}$ is defined differently. It contains fewer single NACs as contained in $NAC_{p_1+p_2}$ in Def. 3.4.5. Therefore, the analysis part of the Parallelism Theorem with NACs in [72] needs an extra compatibility condition.

3.5 Concurrency

Let t be a transformation via some rule sequence $p_0, \ldots, p_{n-1}, p_n$ with NACs and matches $g_0, \ldots, g_{n-1}, g_n$. In general there will be causal dependencies between several direct transformations in this transformation sequence. Therefore, it is not possible to apply the Parallelism Theorem in order to summarize the transformation sequence successively into one equivalent transformation step. It is possible, however, to formulate a Concurrency Theorem expressing how to summarize such a sequence into one equivalent transformation step anyway via some induced concurrent rule. Vice versa, it is possible to split up a transformation via such a concurrent rule into a sequence via single rules. In order to develop the corresponding theory we build on the notion of concurrent rules without NACs as introduced in [29]. Moreover, we have to shift all the NACs occurring in the rule sequence $p_0, \ldots, p_{n-1}, p_n$ backward into an equivalent set of NACs on the concurrent rule p_c of this rule sequence. This means that we are looking for a set NAC_{p_c} for the concurrent rule p_c that is equivalent to $NAC_{p_0}, \ldots, NAC_{p_{n-1}}, NAC_{p_n}$ for the transformation rules in t. This section gradually describes how to obtain this concurrent NAC and then generalizes then the Concurrency Theorem to transformations with NACs.

First, we define how concurrent rules for rule sequences without NACs can be constructed. This definition corresponds to the definition of concurrent rules in [29]. However, we generalize this definition to rule sequences containing more than two rules. Then we reintroduce the Concurrency Theorem for transformations without NACs, and thereby, define what a concurrent rule *induced by* a transformation t is. Note that in comparison to [29] we do not demand explicitly a transformation to be $E-$related. Each transformation t defined by some adhesive HLR system with NACs is automatically $E-$related since each NAC-adhesive HLR category has an

3.5. CONCURRENCY

$\mathcal{E}' - \mathcal{M}'$ pair factorization and the $\mathcal{M} - \mathcal{M}'$ PO-PB decomposition property automatically holds (this follows directly from Fact 5.29 in [29]). After that, we also introduce concurrent rules with NACs for rule sequences with NACs. This definition is based on the shifting of all NACs on the rules in a rule sequence to an equivalent set of NACs on its concurrent rule. Finally, a Concurrency Theorem for transformations with NACs is formulated.

3.5.1 Definition (concurrent rule for a rule sequence). $n = 0$ The *concurrent rule* p_c for rule p_0 is p_c itself.

$n \geq 1$ A *concurrent rule* p_c for the rule sequence $p_0, \ldots p_n$ is defined by $p_c = (L_c \xleftarrow{lok'_c} K \xrightarrow{rok_n} R)$ as shown in the following diagram where $p'_c : L'_c \leftarrow K'_c \to R'_c$ is a concurrent rule for the rule sequence $p_0, \ldots p_{n-1}$, $(e'_c, e_n) \in \mathcal{E}'$, (1),(2), (3) and (4) are pushouts and (5) is a pullback. We denote the concurrent rule p_c also as $p'_c *_E p_n$.

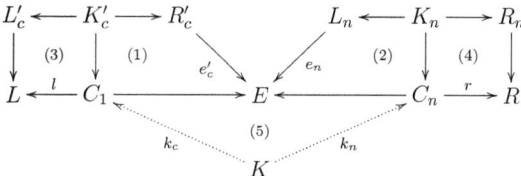

3.5.2 Remark. Since pullbacks, pushouts and pushout complements are unique in adhesive HLR categories [29] a concurrent rule for $n \geq 1$ is uniquely determined by its E-dependency relations (e'_c, e_n) as defined in [29].

3.5.3 Definition (concurrent rule, concurrent (co-, lhs-)match *induced by* $G_0 \xRightarrow{n+1} G_{n+1}$).

$n = 0$ For a direct transformation $G_0 \Rightarrow G_1$ via match $g_0 : L_0 \to G_0$, comatch $g_1 : R_1 \to G_1$, and rule $p_0 : L_0 \leftarrow K_0 \to R_0$, the *concurrent rule* p_c for p_0 induced by $G_0 \Rightarrow G_1$ is defined by $p_c = p_0$, the *concurrent comatch* h_c is defined by $h_c = g_1$, the *concurrent lhs-match* by $id : L_0 \to L_0$, and the *concurrent match* g_c by $g_c = g_0 : L_0 \to G_0$.

$n \geq 1$ Consider $p'_c : L'_c \leftarrow K'_c \to R'_c$ (resp. $g'_c : L'_c \to G_0$, $h'_c : R'_c \to G_n, m'_c : L_0 \to L'_c$), the concurrent rule (resp. concurrent match, comatch, lhs-match) for $p_0, \ldots, p_{n-1}$ induced by $G_0 \xRightarrow{n} G_n$. Let $((e'_c, e_n), h)$ be the $\mathcal{E}' - \mathcal{M}'$ pair factorization of the comatch h'_c and match g_n of $G_n \Rightarrow G_{n+1}$. Then the diagram below can be constructed as explained in Remark 3.5.4, where is a pullback and all other squares are pushouts:

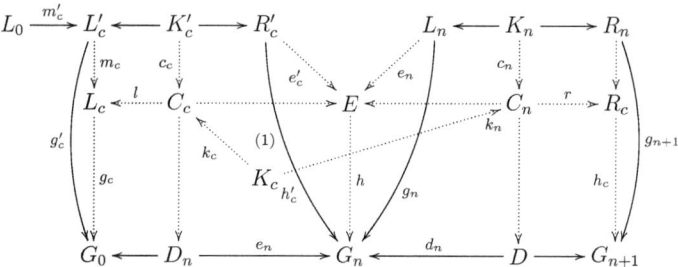

CHAPTER 3. RULE-BASED MODELING USING HIGH-LEVEL TRANSFORMATION

For a transformation sequence $G_0 \overset{n+1}{\Longrightarrow} G_{n+1}$, the *concurrent rule* p_c (resp. concurrent match, comatch, lhs-match) for $p_0, \ldots, p_n$ induced by $G_0 \overset{n+1}{\Longrightarrow} G_{n+1}$ is defined by $p_c = L_c \overset{l \circ k_c}{\leftarrow} K_c \overset{r \circ k_n}{\rightarrow} R_c$ $(g_c : L_c \to G_0,\ h_c : R_c \to G_{n+1},\ m_c \circ m'_c : L_0 \to L_c)$.

3.5.4 Remark. Since PBs via morphisms in $\mathcal{M}$ exist, and e_n (resp. d_n) is in $\mathcal{M}$ because it is closed under pushouts, the second and third square in the lower row of the above diagram can be constructed as PBs via h and e_n (resp. h and d_n). Because of the universal property of PBs, the morphisms c_c and c_n can be constructed such that the second and third square in the upper row commute. Because of $\mathcal{M} - \mathcal{M}'$ PO-PB decomposition, it follows that the second and third square in the upper and lower row are POs. Now the first square and last square in the upper row can be constructed as POs, since POs exist via morphisms in $\mathcal{M}$, and rules consist of a pair of morphisms in $\mathcal{M}$. Because of the universal property of POs, then also the first and last square of the second row can be constructed such that they commute. Because of PO decomposition, then also the first and last square of the lower row are POs. Finally, since $\mathcal{M}$-morphisms are closed under POs, and PBs exist via $\mathcal{M}$-morphisms (1) can be constructed as a PB. Note that the concurrent rule induced by some transformation t is uniquely determined because of the uniqueness of the $\mathcal{E}' - \mathcal{M}'$ pair factorization, PBs, and POs, and the universal property of PBs and POs.

3.5.5 Theorem (concurrency theorem without NACs).

1. Synthesis. *Given a transformation sequence $t : G_0 \overset{*}{\Longrightarrow} G_{n+1}$ via a sequence of rules $p_0, p_1, \ldots, p_n$, then there is a* synthesis construction *leading to a direct transformation $G_0 \Rightarrow G_{n+1}$ via the induced concurrent rule $p_c : L_c \leftarrow K_c \to R_c$, match $g_c : L_c \to G_0$ and comatch $h_c : R_c \to G_{n+1}$ induced by $t : G_0 \overset{*}{\Longrightarrow} G_{n+1}$.*

2. Analysis. *Given a direct transformation $G_0 \Rightarrow G_{n+1}$ via some concurrent rule $p_c : L_c \leftarrow K_c \to R_c$ of rules $p_0, p_1, \ldots, p_n$, then there is an* analysis construction *leading to a transformation sequence $t : G_0 \overset{*}{\Longrightarrow} G_{n+1}$ via $p_0, p_1, \ldots, p_n$.*

Proof. **Synthesis.** Case $n = 0$ is trivial. Case $n \geq 1$ can be directly derived from the construction of the induced concurrent rule in Def.3.5.3 and the proof of the Synthesis part in Theorem 5.23 in [29].

Analysis. Case $n = 0$ is trivial. Case $n \geq 1$ can be directly derived from the proof of the Analysis part in Theorem 5.23 in [29].

□

Now, we present a construction that we use to shift a set of NACs on some rule occurring in a transformation t to a set of equivalent NACs on the concurrent rule induced by t. Recall that in Def. 3.3.12, a construction is already given to shift NACs on some object A into a set of equivalent NACs on some object B via some morphism $m : A \to B$. Moreover, recall that in Def. 3.3.5, it is explained how to construct an equivalent set of left NACs from a set of right NACs on a rule. A combination of these constructions leads to a construction of a set of equivalent NACs on the LHS of a concurrent rule for a rule sequence from the set of NACs on each rule in this sequence.

3.5.6 Definition (concurrent rule with NACs for a rule sequence).

$n = 0$ The *concurrent rule* p_c with NACs for rule p_0 with NACs is p_0 with NACs itself.

$n \geq 1$ A *concurrent rule* $p_c = p'_c *_E p_n$ with NACs for the rule sequence $p_0, \ldots p_n$ with NACs is defined recursively as in Def. 3.5.1 and equals $p_c = (L_c \xleftarrow{l \circ k_c} K \xrightarrow{r \circ k_n} R)$ as shown in the following diagram in which (1)-(4) are POs and (5) is a PB

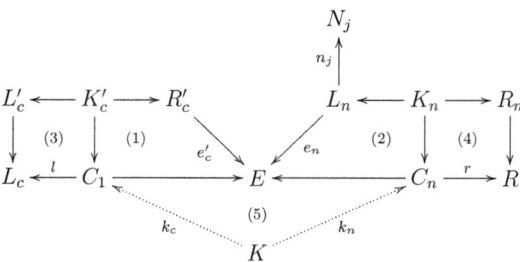

with $NAC_{p_c} = DL_{p_c}(NAC_{L_n}) \cup D_{m_c}(NAC_{L'_c})$ with D_{m_c} according to Def. 3.3.12 and $DL_{p_c}(NAC_{L_n})$ with $NAC_{L_n} = \{NAC(n_j) | j \in J\}$ constructed as follows:

$$DL_{p_c}(NAC_{L_n}) = \cup_{j \in J} DL_{p_c}(NAC(n_j)) = \cup_{j \in J} L_p(D_{e_n}(NAC(n_j)))$$

with $p : L_c \leftarrow C_1 \to E$ and D_{e_n} (resp. L_p) according to Def. 3.3.12 (resp. Def. 3.3.5).

3.5.7 Definition (concurrent rule with NAC, concurrent (co-, lhs-)match induced by $G_0 \overset{n+1}{\Longrightarrow} G_{n+1}$).

$n = 0$ For a direct transformation $G_0 \Rightarrow G_1$ via match $g_0 : L_0 \to G_0$, comatch $g_1 : R_1 \to G_1$, and rule $p_0 : L_0 \leftarrow K_0 \to R_0$ with NAC_{p_0} the *concurrent rule p_c with NAC* induced by $G_0 \Rightarrow G_1$ is defined by $p_c = p_0$ with $NAC_{p_c} = NAC_{p_0}$, the *concurrent comatch* h_c is defined by $h_c = g_1$, the *concurrent lhs-match* by $id : L_0 \to L_0$, and the *concurrent match* g_c by $g_c = g_0 : L_0 \to G_0$.

$n \geq 1$ Consider $p'_c : L'_c \leftarrow K'_c \to R'_c$ (resp. $g'_c : L'_c \to G_0$, $h'_c : R'_c \to G_n, m'_c : L_0 \to L'_c$), the concurrent rule with NACs (resp. concurrent match, comatch, lhs-match) induced by $G_0 \overset{n}{\Longrightarrow} G_n$. For a transformation sequence $G_0 \overset{n+1}{\Longrightarrow} G_{n+1}$ the *concurrent rule p_c with NACs* (resp. concurrent match, comatch, lhs-match) induced by $G_0 \overset{n+1}{\Longrightarrow} G_{n+1}$ is defined by $p_c = L_c \leftarrow K_c \to R_c$ ($g_c : L_c \to G_0$, $h_c : R_c \to G_{n+1}$, $m_c \circ m'_c : L_0 \to L_c$) the induced concurrent rule p_c (resp. concurrent match, comatch, lhs-match) as defined in Def.3.5.3 for transformations without NACs. Thereby, NAC_{p_c} is defined by $NAC_{p_c} = DL_{p_c}(NAC_{L_n}) \cup D_{m_c}(NAC_{L'_c})$.

3.5.8 Theorem (concurrency theorem with NACs).

1. *Synthesis.* Given a transformation sequence $t : G_0 \overset{*}{\Longrightarrow} G_{n+1}$ via a sequence of rules $p_0, p_1, \ldots, p_n$, then there is a synthesis construction *leading to a direct transformation* $G_0 \Rightarrow G_{n+1}$ via the concurrent rule $p_c : L_c \leftarrow K_c \to R_c$ with NAC_{p_c}, match $g_c : L_c \to G_0$ and comatch $h_c : R_c \to G_{n+1}$ induced by $t : G_0 \overset{*}{\Longrightarrow} G_{n+1}$.

2. *Analysis.* Given a direct transformation $G_0 \Rightarrow G_{n+1}$ via some concurrent rule $p_c : L_c \leftarrow K_c \to R_c$ with NAC_{p_c} for a sequence of rules $p_0, p_1, \ldots, p_n$, then there is an analysis construction *leading to a transformation sequence* $t : G_0 \overset{*}{\Longrightarrow} G_{n+1}$ with NACs via $p_0, p_1, \ldots, p_n$.

CHAPTER 3. RULE-BASED MODELING USING HIGH-LEVEL TRANSFORMATION

Proof. We prove this theorem by induction over the number of transformation steps $n + 1$.

1. *Synthesis.*

    Basis. n=0. For a direct transformation $t : G_0 \stackrel{p_0,g_0}{\Longrightarrow} G_1$ via match $g_0 : L_0 \to G_0$ and rule $p_0 : L_0 \leftarrow K_0 \to R_0$ with NAC_{p_0} the *concurrent rule* p_c *with NAC* induced by $G_0 \Rightarrow G_1$ is defined by $p_c = p_0$ with $NAC_{p_c} = NAC_{p_0}$ and the *concurrent match* g_c is defined by $g_c = g_0 : L_0 \to G_0$. Therefore, the synthesis construction is equal to $G_0 \stackrel{p_c,g_c}{\Longrightarrow} G_1$.

    Induction Step. Consider $t : G_0 \stackrel{n}{\Longrightarrow} G_n \Rightarrow G_{n+1}$ via the rules $p_0, p_1 \ldots, p_n$. Let $p'_c : L'_c \leftarrow K'_c \to R'_c$ (resp. $g'_c : L'_c \to G_0$, $h'_c : R'_c \to G_n$), be the concurrent rule with NACs (resp. concurrent match, comatch) induced by $G_0 \stackrel{n}{\Longrightarrow} G_n$. Because of the induction hypothesis, $G_0 \stackrel{p'_c,g'_c}{\Longrightarrow} G_n$ is a direct transformation with NACs in which p'_c with NACs is the concurrent rule induced by $G_0 \stackrel{n}{\Longrightarrow} G_n$ as defined in Def. 3.5.7. The *concurrent rule* p_c *with NACs* (resp. concurrent match, comatch) induced by $G_0 \stackrel{n+1}{\Longrightarrow} G_{n+1}$ is according to Def. 3.5.7 and as depicted in the following diagram $p_c = L_c \stackrel{l \circ k_c}{\leftarrow} K_c \stackrel{r \circ k_n}{\to} R_c$ ($g_c : L_c \to G_0$, $h_c : R_c \to G_{n+1}$) with $NAC_{p_c} = DL_{p_c}(NAC_{L_n}) \cup D_{m_c}(NAC_{L'_c})$.

    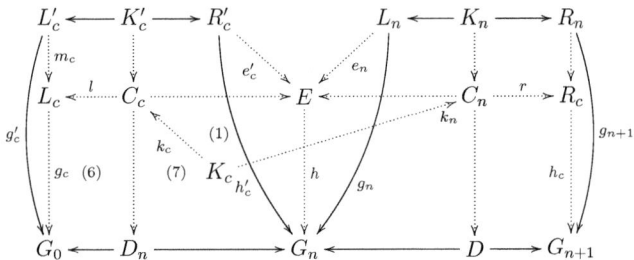

    According to Theorem 3.5.5 $G_0 \stackrel{p_c,g_c}{\Longrightarrow} G_{n+1}$ is a valid transformation without considering the NACs. We should prove that $G_0 \stackrel{p_c,g_c}{\Longrightarrow} G_{n+1}$ is also a valid direct transformation with NACs. We show that g_c satisfies NAC_{p_c}. Since g'_c satisfies $NAC_{p'_c}$ and $g_c \circ m_c = g'_c$, because of Lemma 3.3.13 it holds that $g_c \models D_{m_c}(NAC_{L'_c})$. Moreover, since g_n satisfies NAC_{p_n} and $g_n = h \circ e_n$ because of Lemma 3.3.13 again it holds that $h \models D_{e_n}(NAC_{L'_c})$. Now because of Lemma 3.3.7 and the fact that PO along $\mathcal{M}$ preserve $\mathcal{M}$ such that $L_c \leftarrow C_c \to E$ is a rule, which we call p, and (6) and (7) are POs, it follows that $g_c \models L_p(D_{e_n}(NAC_{L_n})) = DL_{p_c}(NAC_{L_n})$ as defined in Def. 3.5.6.

2. *Analysis.*

    Basis. n=0. For a direct transformation $G_0 \Rightarrow G_1$ via the concurrent rule $p_c = p_0$ with $NAC_{p_c} = NAC_{p_0}$ the analysis construction is equal to $G_0 \Rightarrow G_1$.

    Induction Step. Consider a direct transformation $G_0 \Rightarrow G_{n+1}$ via some concurrent rule $p_c : L_c \leftarrow K_c \to R_c$ with NAC_{p_c} for a sequence of rules $p_0, p_1, \ldots, p_n$. According to the Analysis part of Theorem 3.5.5 the following diagram can be constructed with

3.5. CONCURRENCY

$G_0 \Rightarrow G_n$ via $p'_c : L'_c \leftarrow K'_c \rightarrow R'_c$ and $G_n \Rightarrow G_{n+1}$ via p_n.

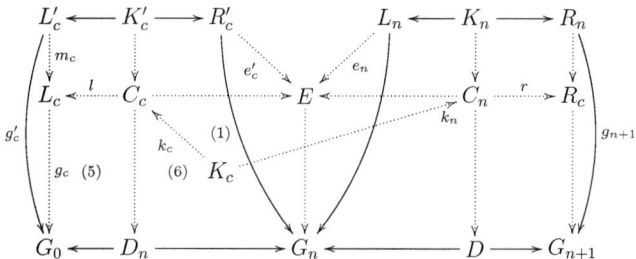

We know by assumption that match g satisfies NAC_{p_c}. We should show that g'_c satisfies $NAC_{p'_c}$ and g_n satisfies NAC_{p_n}. Since g_c satisfies $NAC_{p_c} = DL_{p_c}(NAC_{L_n}) \cup D_{m_c}(NAC_{L'_c})$ and $g_c \circ m_c = g'_c$, because of Lemma 3.3.13 it holds that $g'_c \models NAC_{L'_c}$. Moreover, since g_c satisfies $NAC_{p_c} = DL_{p_c}(NAC_{L_n}) \cup D_{m_c}(NAC_{L'_c})$, (5) and (6) are POs, POs along $\mathcal{M}$-morphisms are compatible with $\mathcal{M}$ and, therefore, $p : L_c \leftarrow C_c \rightarrow E$ is a rule it holds because of Lemma 3.3.7 and the fact that $DL_{p_c}(NAC_{L_n}) = L_p(D_{e_n}(NAC_{L_n}))$ that h satisfies $D_{e_n}(NAC_{L_n})$. Finally, since $h \circ e_n = g_n$ because of Lemma 3.3.13 it holds that $g_n \models NAC_{L_n}$. Therefore, $G_0 \Rightarrow G_n \Rightarrow G_{n+1}$ is a valid transformation sequence with NACs. Because of the induction hypothesis, there exists an analysis construction $G_0 \Rightarrow G_1 \Rightarrow \ldots G_n$ via $p_0, p_1, \ldots, p_{n-1}$ for $G_0 \Rightarrow G_n$ via p'_c. Thus, we obtain a transformation sequence with NACs $G_0 \Rightarrow G_1 \Rightarrow \ldots G_{n+1}$ via $p_0, p_1, \ldots, p_n$ for the direct transformation $G_0 \Rightarrow G_{n+1}$ via the concurrent rule $p_c : L_c \leftarrow K_c \rightarrow R_c$ with NAC_{p_c}.

□

Finally, we can characterize the notion of parallelism for rules and transformations, as given in Def. 3.4.5, by describing it by means of concurrency as in the following theorem.

3.5.9 Theorem (characterization of parallelism via concurrency). *A direct parallel transformation with NACs $G \Rightarrow G'$ via $m : L_1 + L_2 \rightarrow G$ and the parallel rule $p_1 + p_2$ with $NAC_{p_1+p_2}$ exist if and only if $G \Rightarrow G'$ is a direct transformation with NACs via $m : L_1 + L_2 \rightarrow G$ and the concurrent rule $p_1 *_{R_1+L_2} p_2$ with $NAC_{p_1*R_1+L_2 p_2}$ and $G \Rightarrow G'$ is a direct transformation with NACs via $m : L_1 + L_2 \rightarrow G$ and the concurrent rule $p_2 *_{R_2+L_1} p_1$ with $NAC_{p_2*R_2+L_1 p_1}$.*

Proof. Recall that
$NAC_{p_1+p_2} = D_{i_1}(NAC_{p_1}) \cup D_{i_2}(NAC_{p_2}) \cup L_{p_{1,2fix}}(D_{i'_2}(NAC_{p_2})) \cup L_{p_{1fix,2}}(D_{i'_1}(NAC_{p_1}))$ with $p_{1,2fix} = L_1 + L_2 \leftarrow K_1 + L_2 \rightarrow R_1 + L_2$ and $p_{1fix,2} = L_1 + L_2 \leftarrow L_1 + K_2 \rightarrow L_1 + R_2$ (see Definition 3.4.5). Note that $p_1 *_{R_1+L_2} p_2 = p_2 *_{R_2+L_1} p_1 = p_1 + p_2$ without considering NACs. Moreover, $NAC_{p_1+p_2} = NAC_{p_1*R_1+L_2 p_2} \cup NAC_{p_2*R_2+L_1 p_1}$.

- Suppose that a direct parallel transformation with NACs $G \Rightarrow G'$ via $m : L_1 + L_2 \rightarrow G$ and the parallel rule $p_1 + p_2$ with $NAC_{p_1+p_2}$ exists. In Theorem 3.4.7 it is proven that the following diagram with (1),(1'),(2), and (2') POs can then be constructed. This is possible because $G \Rightarrow G'$ can be analyzed into sequentially independent transformations $G \Rightarrow H_1 \Rightarrow G'$. We can complete this diagram by constructing (3),(3'),(4),(4') in an analogous way.

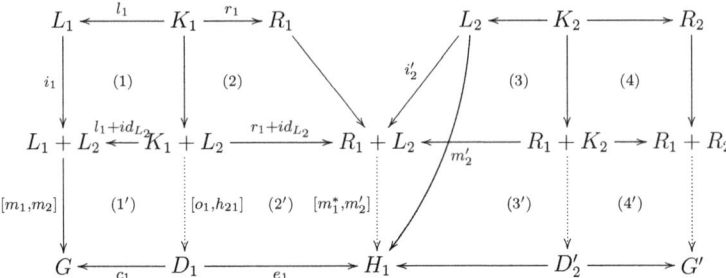

Analogously, because $G \Rightarrow G'$ can be analyzed into sequentially independent transformations $G \Rightarrow H_2 \Rightarrow G'$, it is possible to construct the following diagram with (1-4) and (1'-4') POs.

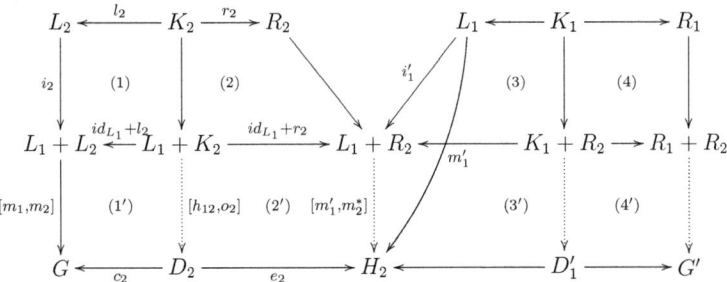

Because of Lemma 3.3.13 and 3.3.7, we can follow that $G \Rightarrow G'$ is a direct transformation with NACs via $m : L_1 + L_2 \to G$ and the concurrent rule $p_1 *_{R_1+L_2} p_2$ with $NAC_{p_1*_{R_1+L_2}p_2}$ and $G \Rightarrow G'$ is a direct transformation with NACs via the concurrent rule $p_2 *_{R_2+L_1} p_1$ with $NAC_{p_2*_{R_2+L_1}p_1}$.

- Suppose that $G \Rightarrow G'$ is a direct transformation with NACs via $m : L_1 + L_2 \to G$ and the concurrent rule $p_1 *_{R_1+L_2} p_2$ with $NAC_{p_1*_{R_1+L_2}p_2}$ and $G \Rightarrow G'$ is a direct transformation with NACs via the concurrent rule $p_2 *_{R_2+L_1} p_1$ with $NAC_{p_2*_{R_2+L_1}p_1}$. Therefore, $G \Rightarrow G'$ is a direct transformation with NACs via $m : L_1 + L_2 \to G$ and the parallel rule $p_1 + p_2$ with $NAC_{p_1+p_2}$.

□

3.6 Conflicts and Causal Dependencies for Transformations

Two transformations in adhesive HLR systems are not always parallel or sequentially independent. In this section, we explain what it means for two direct transformations to be in conflict (resp. to depend on each other), i.e. not being parallel independent (resp. not being sequentially independent).

3.6. CONFLICTS AND CAUSAL DEPENDENCIES FOR TRANSFORMATIONS

3.6.1 Definition (conflict). Two direct transformations $G \stackrel{p_1,m_1}{\Longrightarrow} H_1$ with NAC_{p_1} and $G \stackrel{p_2,m_2}{\Longrightarrow} H_2$ with NAC_{p_2} are *in conflict* if they are not parallel independent i.e. if

$$\not\exists h_{12} : L_1 \to D_2 \text{ s.t. } (d_2 \circ h_{12} = m_1 \text{ and } e_2 \circ h_{12} \models NAC_{p_1})$$

or

$$\not\exists h_{21} : L_2 \to D_1 \text{ s.t. } (d_1 \circ h_{21} = m_2 \text{ and } e_1 \circ h_{21} \models NAC_{p_2}).$$

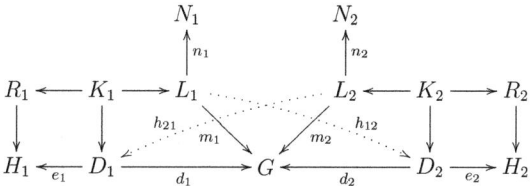

3.6.2 Definition (causal dependency). Given a sequence of two direct transformations $G \stackrel{p_1,m_1}{\Longrightarrow} H_1 \stackrel{p_2,m_2}{\Longrightarrow} H_2$ with NAC_{p_1} and NAC_{p_2}, these transformations are *causally dependent* if they are not sequentially independent i.e. if

$$\not\exists h_{12} : R_1 \to D_2 \text{ s.t. } (d_2 \circ h_{12} = m'_1 \text{ and } e_2 \circ h_{12} \models NAC_{p_1^{-1}})$$

or

$$\not\exists h_{21} : L_2 \to D_1 \text{ s.t. } (e_1 \circ h_{21} = m_2 \text{ and } d_1 \circ h_{21} \models NAC_{p_2}).$$

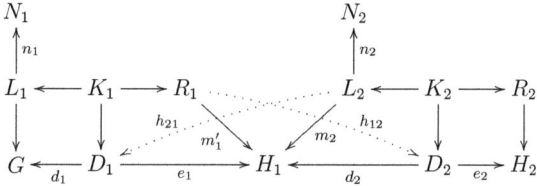

The following lemmata allow an elegant characterization of conflicts and causal dependencies in Theorem 3.6.5 and Theorem 3.6.7. They state that if a morphism exists that potentially leads to parallel or sequential independence of two direct transformations, then it is unique.

3.6.3 Lemma. *Given two direct transformations $G \stackrel{p_1,m_1}{\Longrightarrow} H_1$ with NAC_{p_1} and $G \stackrel{p_2,m_2}{\Longrightarrow} H_2$ with NAC_{p_2}, then the following holds:*

- *if $\exists h_{12} : L_1 \to D_2$ s.t. $d_2 \circ h_{12} = m_1$ then h_{12} is unique,*
- *if $\exists h_{21} : L_2 \to D_1$ s.t. $d_1 \circ h_{21} = m_2$ then h_{21} is unique.*

Moreover, if the match morphism m_1 (resp. m_2) is monomorphic, then also h_{12} (resp. h_{21}) is monomorphic.

Proof. Since each rule consists of two morphisms in $\mathcal{M}$ and $\mathcal{M}$-morphisms are closed under pushouts, d_1 and d_2 are in $\mathcal{M}$ as well. Suppose there exists $h'_{12} : L_1 \to D_2 : d_2 \circ h'_{12} = m_1$ then because of d_2 in $\mathcal{M}$ and thus, a monomorphism and $d_2 \circ h'_{12} = d_2 \circ h_{12} = m_1$ it follows that $h'_{12} = h_{12}$. Analogously, one can prove that h_{21} is unique. The monomorphic property follows from the decomposition property of monomorphisms. □

CHAPTER 3. RULE-BASED MODELING USING HIGH-LEVEL TRANSFORMATION

3.6.4 Lemma. *Given a sequence of two direct transformations $G \stackrel{p_1,m_1}{\Longrightarrow} H_1$ with NAC_{p_1} and $H_1 \stackrel{p_2,m_2}{\Longrightarrow} H_2$ with NAC_{p_2}, then the following holds:*

- *if $\exists h_{12} : R_1 \to D_2$ s.t. $d_2 \circ h_{12} = m'_1$ then h_{12} is unique,*
- *if $\exists h_{21} : L_2 \to D_1$ s.t. $e_1 \circ h_{21} = m_2$ then h_{21} is unique.*

Proof. As noted already in Remark 3.4.2 $G \stackrel{p_1}{\Longrightarrow} H_1 \stackrel{p_2}{\Longrightarrow} H_2$ are sequentially independent if and only if $G \stackrel{p_1^{-1}}{\Longleftarrow} H_1 \stackrel{p_2}{\Longrightarrow} H_2$ are parallel independent. Therefore, the above assumption follows directly from this remark and Lemma 3.6.3. □

In the following conflict characterization it is described which types of conflicts may arise between a pair of direct transformations $G \stackrel{p_1,m_1}{\Longrightarrow} H_1$ and $G \stackrel{p_2,m_2}{\Longrightarrow} H_2$. In particular, $G \stackrel{p_1,m_1}{\Longrightarrow} H_1$ causes a so-called delete-use conflict with $G \stackrel{p_2,m_2}{\Longrightarrow} H_2$ if rule p_1 deletes something that is used by p_2. $G \stackrel{p_1,m_1}{\Longrightarrow} H_1$ causes a so-called produce-forbid conflict with $G \stackrel{p_2,m_2}{\Longrightarrow} H_2$ if rule p_1 produces something forbidden by NAC_{p_2} of p_2. Analogously, $G \stackrel{p_2,m_2}{\Longrightarrow} H_2$ can cause a delete-use conflict (resp. produce-forbid conflict) with $G \stackrel{p_1,m_1}{\Longrightarrow} H_1$.

3.6.5 Theorem (conflict characterization). *Two direct transformations $G \stackrel{p_1,m_1}{\Longrightarrow} H_1$ with NAC_{p_1} and $G \stackrel{p_2,m_2}{\Longrightarrow} H_2$ with NAC_{p_2} are in conflict if and only if at least one of the following assumptions holds:*

1. *$\nexists h_{12} : L_1 \to D_2 : d_2 \circ h_{12} = m_1$,*
2. *there exists a unique $h_{12} : L_1 \to D_2 : d_2 \circ h_{12} = m_1$, but $e_2 \circ h_{12} \not\models NAC_{p_1}$,*
3. *$\nexists h_{21} : L_2 \to D_1 : d_1 \circ h_{21} = m_2$,*
4. *there exists a unique $h_{21} : L_2 \to D_1 : d_1 \circ h_{21} = m_2$, but $e_1 \circ h_{21} \not\models NAC_{p_2}$.*

Proof. $G \stackrel{p_1,m_1}{\Longrightarrow} H_1$ with NAC_{p_1} and $G \stackrel{p_2,m_2}{\Longrightarrow} H_2$ with NAC_{p_2} are *in conflict* if

$$\nexists h_{12} : L_1 \to D_2 \text{ s.t. } (d_2 \circ h_{12} = m_1 \text{ and } e_2 \circ h_{12} \models NAC_{p_1})$$

or

$$\nexists h_{21} : L_2 \to D_1 \text{ s.t. } (d_1 \circ h_{21} = m_2 \text{ and } e_1 \circ h_{21} \models NAC_{p_2})$$

We consider first the first line of this disjunction. Let $A(h_{12}) := d_2 \circ h_{12} = m_1$, $B(h_{12}) := e_2 \circ h_{12} \models NAC_{p_1}$, $P(h_{12}) := (A(h_{12}) \wedge B(h_{12}))$ and $\mathcal{M}_{12}$ be the set of all morphisms from L_1 to D_2. Then the first line is equivalent to

$$\nexists h_{12} \in \mathcal{M}_{12} : (A(h_{12}) \wedge B(h_{12})) \equiv \nexists h_{12} \in \mathcal{M}_{12} : P(h_{12})$$

This is equivalent to

$$\forall h_{12} \in \mathcal{M}_{12} : \neg P(h_{12}) \equiv (\mathcal{M}_{12} = \emptyset) \vee (\mathcal{M}_{12} \neq \emptyset \wedge \forall h_{12} \in \mathcal{M}_{12} : \neg P(h_{12}))$$

Moreover, $P \equiv A \wedge B \equiv A \wedge (A \Rightarrow B)$ and thus, $\neg P \equiv \neg(A \wedge B) \equiv \neg(A \wedge (A \Rightarrow B)) \equiv \neg A \vee \neg(A \Rightarrow B) \equiv \neg A \vee \neg(\neg A \vee B) \equiv \neg A \vee (A \wedge \neg B)$. This implies that $(\mathcal{M}_{12} = \emptyset) \vee (\mathcal{M}_{12} \neq \emptyset \wedge \forall h_{12} \in \mathcal{M}_{12} : \neg P(h_{12})) \equiv$

$$(\mathcal{M}_{12} = \emptyset) \vee (\mathcal{M}_{12} \neq \emptyset \wedge \forall h_{12} \in \mathcal{M}_{12} : \neg A(h_{12}) \vee (A(h_{12}) \wedge \neg B(h_{12})))$$

3.6. CONFLICTS AND CAUSAL DEPENDENCIES FOR TRANSFORMATIONS

Because of Lemma 3.6.3 and because the disjunction holding for each morphism in $\mathcal{M}_{12}$ is an exclusive one, this is equivalent to

$$(\mathcal{M}_{12} = \emptyset) \vee (\mathcal{M}_{12} \neq \emptyset \wedge \forall h_{12} \in \mathcal{M}_{12} : \neg A(h_{12})) \vee (\exists! h_{12} \in \mathcal{M}_{12} : (A(h_{12}) \wedge \neg B(h_{12})))$$

Now $(\mathcal{M}_{12} = \emptyset) \vee (\mathcal{M}_{12} \neq \emptyset \wedge \forall h_{12} \in \mathcal{M}_{12} : \neg A(h_{12})) \equiv \forall h_{12} \in \mathcal{M}_{12} : \neg A(h_{12}) \equiv \nexists h_{12} \in \mathcal{M}_{12} : A(h_{12})$. This implies finally that $\nexists h_{12} : L_1 \to D_2$ s.t. $(d_2 \circ h_{12} = m_1$ and $e_2 \circ h_{12} \models NAC_{p_1})$ is equivalent to

$$(\nexists h_{12} \in \mathcal{M}_{12} : d_2 \circ h_{12} = m_1) \vee (\exists! h_{12} \in \mathcal{M}_{12} : (d_2 \circ h_{12} = m_1 \wedge e_2 \circ h_{12} \not\models NAC_{p_1}))$$

is equivalent to

1. $\nexists h_{12} : L_1 \to D_2 : d_2 \circ h_{12} = m_1$
   or
2. there exists a unique $h_{12} : L_1 \to D_2 : d_2 \circ h_{12} = m_1$, but $e_2 \circ h_{12} \not\models NAC_{p_1}$.

Analogously, we can proceed for the second part of the disjunction. $\square$

3.6.6 Definition (conflict characterization). Consider two direct transformations $G \stackrel{p_1,m_1}{\Longrightarrow} H_1$ with NAC_{p_1} and $G \stackrel{p_2,m_2}{\Longrightarrow} H_2$ with NAC_{p_2} that are in conflict. If case (1) in Theorem 3.6.5 occurs, we say that $G \stackrel{p_2,m_2}{\Longrightarrow} H_2$ *causes a delete-use conflict with* $G \stackrel{p_1,m_1}{\Longrightarrow} H_1$. If case (2) occurs, we say that $G \stackrel{p_2,m_2}{\Longrightarrow} H_2$ *causes a produce-forbid conflict with* $G \stackrel{p_1,m_1}{\Longrightarrow} H_1$. If cases (1) or (2) occur, we say in general that $G \stackrel{p_2,m_2}{\Longrightarrow} H_2$ *causes a conflict with* $G \stackrel{p_1,m_1}{\Longrightarrow} H_1$. If case (3) occurs, we say that $G \stackrel{p_1,m_1}{\Longrightarrow} H_1$ *causes a delete-use conflict with* $G \stackrel{p_2,m_2}{\Longrightarrow} H_2$. If case (4) occurs, we say that $G \stackrel{p_1,m_1}{\Longrightarrow} H_1$ *causes a produce-forbid conflict with* $G \stackrel{p_2,m_2}{\Longrightarrow} H_2$. If cases (3) or (4) occur, we say in general that $G \stackrel{p_1,m_1}{\Longrightarrow} H_1$ *causes a conflict with* $G \stackrel{p_2,m_2}{\Longrightarrow} H_2$.

Note that case (1) (resp. case (3)) cannot occur simultaneously to case (2) (resp. case (4)) in Theorem 3.6.5, since $1 \Rightarrow \neg 2$ (resp. $3 \Rightarrow \neg 4$). This means that $G \stackrel{p_2,m_2}{\Longrightarrow} H_2$ (resp. $G \stackrel{p_1,m_1}{\Longrightarrow} H_1$) can only cause a produce-forbid conflict with $G \stackrel{p_1,m_1}{\Longrightarrow} H_1$ (resp. $G \stackrel{p_2,m_2}{\Longrightarrow} H_2$) if it does not cause a delete-use conflict. All other cases can occur simultaneously. This means that $G \stackrel{p_2,m_2}{\Longrightarrow} H_2$ can cause a delete-use conflict or produce-forbid conflict with $G \stackrel{p_1,m_1}{\Longrightarrow} H_1$ and simultaneously $G \stackrel{p_1,m_1}{\Longrightarrow} H_1$ can cause a delete-use conflict or produce-forbid conflict with $G \stackrel{p_2,m_2}{\Longrightarrow} H_2$.

In the following causal dependency characterization it is described which types of causal dependencies may arise between $G \stackrel{p_1,m_1}{\Longrightarrow} H_1$ and $H_1 \stackrel{p_2,m_2}{\Longrightarrow} H_2$ in a sequence of two direct transformations. In particular, $G \stackrel{p_1,m_1}{\Longrightarrow} H_1$ is in a *produce-use dependency* with $H_1 \stackrel{p_2,m_2}{\Longrightarrow} H_2$ if rule p_1 produces something that is used by p_2. $G \stackrel{p_1,m_1}{\Longrightarrow} H_1$ is in a *delete-forbid dependency* with $H_1 \stackrel{p_2,m_2}{\Longrightarrow} H_2$ if rule p_1 deletes something forbidden by NAC_{p_2} of p_2. These causal dependencies express that the application of rule p_2 is triggered by the application of rule p_1. Moreover, $G \stackrel{p_1,m_1}{\Longrightarrow} H_1$ is in a *deliver-delete dependency* with $H_1 \stackrel{p_2,m_2}{\Longrightarrow} H_2$ if rule p_1 preserves or produces something that is thereafter deleted by p_2. $G \stackrel{p_1,m_1}{\Longrightarrow} H_1$ is in a *forbid-produce dependency* with $H_1 \stackrel{p_2,m_2}{\Longrightarrow} H_2$ if rule p_2 produces something forbidden by $NAC_{p_1^{-1}}$. These causal dependencies express that the application of p_1 can no longer be made irreversible after applying p_2 by applying thereafter p_1^{-1}.

3.6.7 Theorem (dependency characterization). *Given a sequence of two direct transformations $G \stackrel{p_1,m_1}{\Longrightarrow} H_1 \stackrel{p_2,m_2}{\Longrightarrow} H_2$ with NAC_{p_1} and NAC_{p_2}, then they are causally dependent if and only if at least one of the following assumptions holds:*

1. $\nexists h_{12} : R_1 \to D_2 : d_2 \circ h_{12} = m'_1$,

2. there exists a unique $h_{12} : R_1 \to D_2 : d_2 \circ h_{12} = m'_1$, but $e_2 \circ h_{12} \not\models NAC_{p_1^{-1}}$,

3. $\nexists h_{21} : L_2 \to D_1 : e_1 \circ h_{21} = m_2$,

4. there exists a unique $h_{21} : L_2 \to D_1 : e_1 \circ h_{21} = m_2$, but $d_1 \circ h_{21} \not\models NAC_{p_2}$.

Proof. As noted already in Remark 3.4.2 $G \stackrel{p_1}{\Longrightarrow} H_1 \stackrel{p_2}{\Longrightarrow} H_2$ are sequentially independent if and only if $G \stackrel{p_1^{-1}}{\Longleftarrow} H_1 \stackrel{p_2}{\Longrightarrow} H_2$ are parallel independent. Therefore, the above assumption follows directly from this remark and Theorem 3.6.5. □

3.6.8 Definition (causal dependency characterization). Consider a sequence of two direct transformations $G \stackrel{p_1,m_1}{\Longrightarrow} H_1 \stackrel{p_2,m_2}{\Longrightarrow} H_2$ with NAC_{p_1} and NAC_{p_2} such that $G \stackrel{p_1,m_1}{\Longrightarrow} H_1$ and $H_1 \stackrel{p_2,m_2}{\Longrightarrow} H_2$ are causally dependent. If case (1) in Theorem 3.6.7 occurs, we say that $G \stackrel{p_1,m_1}{\Longrightarrow} H_1$ is in a *deliver-delete dependency* with $H_1 \stackrel{p_2,m_2}{\Longrightarrow} H_2$. If case (2) occurs, we say that $G \stackrel{p_1,m_1}{\Longrightarrow} H_1$ is in *forbid-produce dependency* with $H_1 \stackrel{p_2,m_2}{\Longrightarrow} H_2$. If cases (1) or (2) occur, we say in general that $G \stackrel{p_1,m_1}{\Longrightarrow} H_1$ is *irreversible after* $H_1 \stackrel{p_2,m_2}{\Longrightarrow} H_2$. If case (3) occurs, we say that $H_1 \stackrel{p_2,m_2}{\Longrightarrow} H_2$ is in *produce-use dependency* with $G \stackrel{p_1,m_1}{\Longrightarrow} H_1$. If case (4) occurs, we say that $H_1 \stackrel{p_2,m_2}{\Longrightarrow} H_2$ is in *delete-forbid dependency* with $G \stackrel{p_1,m_1}{\Longrightarrow} H_1$. If cases (3) or (4) occur, we say in general that $H_1 \stackrel{p_2,m_2}{\Longrightarrow} H_2$ is *triggered by* $G \stackrel{p_1,m_1}{\Longrightarrow} H_1$.

Note that analogous to the conflict cases, case (1) (resp. case (3)) cannot occur simultaneously to case (2) (resp. case (4)) in Theorem 3.6.7. This means that $G \stackrel{p_1,m_1}{\Longrightarrow} H_1$ can only be in forbid-produce dependency (resp. delete-forbid dependency) with $H_1 \stackrel{p_2,m_2}{\Longrightarrow} H_2$ if it is not in deliver-delete dependency (resp. produce-use dependency). All other cases can occur simultaneously. This means that $G \stackrel{p_1,m_1}{\Longrightarrow} H_1$ can be irreversible after $H_1 \stackrel{p_2,m_2}{\Longrightarrow} H_2$ and simultaneously $H_1 \stackrel{p_2,m_2}{\Longrightarrow} H_2$ can be triggered by $G \stackrel{p_1,m_1}{\Longrightarrow} H_1$.

In the last part of this section, we give yet another characterization of conflicts and causal dependencies. The following definitions of conflict and causal dependency condition emphasize in a more constructive way the reasons for conflicts and causal dependencies. By means of specific pullback constructions objects are distinguished that may constitute the reason for a conflict or causal dependency between transformations. For example, if there exist two transformations on G, then an object S_1 can be constructed that contains deleted parts of the first transformation and used parts of the second transformation. We restrict ourselves here to characterizing delete-use conflicts, produce-use dependencies and deliver-delete dependencies. It is part of future work to characterize in an analogous way conflicts and causal dependencies caused by NACs in the transformations.

3.6.9 Assumption (general PBs exist, existence initial PO over $\mathcal{M}$- morphism). For the rest of this section, we assume that pullbacks of regular morphisms always exist. Moreover, we assume that initial POs as given in Def. 3.2.5 over $\mathcal{M}$-morphisms exist.

3.6.10 Definition (conflict reason). Given a pair of direct transformations $H_1 \stackrel{p_1,m_1}{\Longleftarrow} G \stackrel{p_2,m_2}{\Longrightarrow} H_2$ with $p_1 : L_1 \stackrel{l_1}{\leftarrow} K_1 \stackrel{r_1}{\to} R_1$ (resp. $p_2 : L_2 \stackrel{l_2}{\leftarrow} K_2 \stackrel{r_2}{\to} R_2$) and (2_1) (resp. (2_2)) the initial pushout over l_1 (resp. l_2), then

- if $(S_1, o_1 : S_1 \to C_1, q_{12} : S_1 \to L_2)$ is the pullback of $(m_1 \circ g_1, m_2)$, and if $\nexists s_1 : S_1 \to B_1 \in \mathcal{M}$ such that $c_1 \circ s_1 = o_1$, then $(S_1, g_1 \circ o_1, q_{12})$ is called a *conflict reason* for

3.6. CONFLICTS AND CAUSAL DEPENDENCIES FOR TRANSFORMATIONS

$H_1 \overset{p_1,m_1}{\Leftarrow} G \overset{p_2,m_2}{\Rightarrow} H_2$.

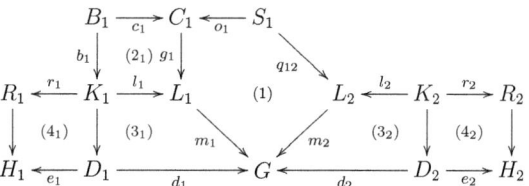

- if $(S_2, q_{21} : S_2 \to L_1, o_2 : S_2 \to C_2)$ is the pullback of $(m_1, m_2 \circ g_2)$, and if $\not\exists s_2 : S_2 \to B_2 \in \mathcal{M}$ such that $c_2 \circ s_2 = o_2$, then $(S_2, q_{21}, g_2 \circ o_2)$ is called a *conflict reason* for $H_1 \overset{p_1,m_1}{\Leftarrow} G \overset{p_2,m_2}{\Rightarrow} H_2$.

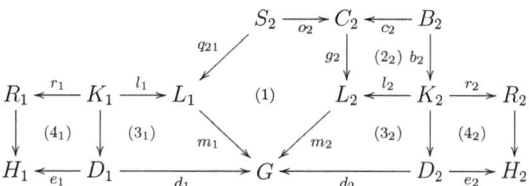

3.6.11 Definition (causal dependency reason). Given a sequence of two direct transformations $G \overset{p_1,m_1}{\Rightarrow} H_1 \overset{p_2,m_2}{\Rightarrow} H_2$ with $p_1 : L_1 \overset{l_1}{\leftarrow} K_1 \overset{r_1}{\to} R_1$ (resp. $p_2 : L_2 \overset{l_2}{\leftarrow} K_2 \overset{r_2}{\to} R_2$) and (2_1) (resp. (2_2)) the initial pushout over r_1 (resp. l_2), then

- if $(S_1, o_1 : S_1 \to C_1, q_{12} : S_1 \to L_2)$ is the pullback of $(m'_1 \circ g_1, m_2)$, and if: $\not\exists s_1 : S_1 \to B_1 \in \mathcal{M}$ such that $c_1 \circ s_1 = o_1$, then $(S_1, g_1 \circ o_1, q_{12})$ is called a *causal dependency reason* for $G \overset{p_1,m_1}{\Rightarrow} H_1 \overset{p_2,m_2}{\Rightarrow} H_2$.

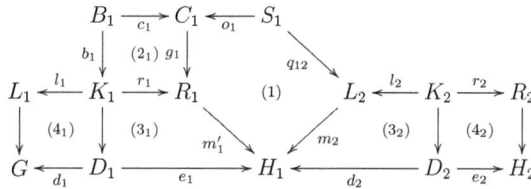

- if $(S_2, q_{21} : S_2 \to L_1, o_2 : S_2 \to C_2)$ is the pullback of $(m'_1, m_2 \circ g_2)$, and if $\not\exists s_2 : S_2 \to B_2 \in \mathcal{M}$ such that $c_2 \circ s_2 = o_2$, then $(S_2, q_{21}, g_2 \circ o_2)$ is called a *causal dependency reason* for $G \overset{p_1,m_1}{\Rightarrow} H_1 \overset{p_2,m_2}{\Rightarrow} H_2$.

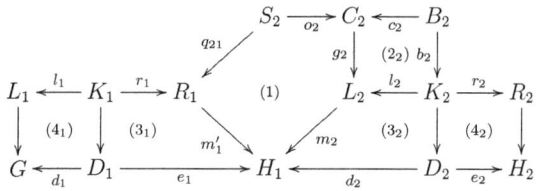

CHAPTER 3. RULE-BASED MODELING USING HIGH-LEVEL TRANSFORMATION

The following theorems now state that a conflict (resp. causal dependency) occurs between transformations if and only if a corresponding conflict reason (resp. causal dependency reason) exists.

3.6.12 Theorem (conflict characterization with reason). *Given a pair of direct transformations* $H_1 \overset{p_1,m_1}{\Leftarrow} G \overset{p_2,m_2}{\Rightarrow} H_2$, *then the following equivalences hold:*

- $G \overset{p_1,m_1}{\Rightarrow} H_1$ *causes a delete-use conflict with* $G \overset{p_2,m_2}{\Rightarrow} H_2$

$$\Leftrightarrow$$

$(S_1, g_1 \circ o_1, q_{12})$ *as given in Def. 3.6.10 is a conflict reason for* $H_1 \overset{p_1,m_1}{\Leftarrow} G \overset{p_2,m_2}{\Rightarrow} H_2$.

- $G \overset{p_2,m_2}{\Rightarrow} H_2$ *causes a delete-use conflict with* $G \overset{p_1,m_1}{\Rightarrow} H_1$

$$\Leftrightarrow$$

$(S_2, q_{21}, g_2 \circ o_2)$ *as given in Def. 3.6.10 is a conflict reason for* $H_1 \overset{p_1,m_1}{\Leftarrow} G \overset{p_2,m_2}{\Rightarrow} H_2$.

Proof. • Consider $(S_2, q_{21}, g_2 \circ o_2)$ as conflict reason for $H_1 \overset{p_1,m_1}{\Leftarrow} G \overset{p_2,m_2}{\Rightarrow} H_2$. We need to show that $G \overset{p_2,m_2}{\Rightarrow} H_2$ causes a delete-use conflict with $G \overset{p_1,m_1}{\Rightarrow} H_1$. Assume that $G \overset{p_2,m_2}{\Rightarrow} H_2$ does not cause a delete-use conflict with $G \overset{p_1,m_1}{\Rightarrow} H_1$. Consequently we have $h_{12} : L_1 \to D_2$ with $d_2 \circ h_{12} = m_1$. It suffices to construct $s_2 : S_2 \to B_2 \in \mathcal{M}$ with $c_2 \circ s_2 = o_2$.

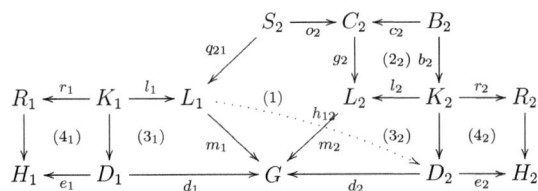

We have pushout along $\mathcal{M}$-morphism, and hence also a pullback $(2_2) + (3_2)$, $o_2 : S_2 \to C_2$ and $h_{12} \circ q_{21} : S_2 \to D_2$ with $m_2 \circ g_2 \circ o_2 = m_1 \circ q_{21} = d_2 \circ h_{12} \circ q_{21}$, implying by the pullback property a unique $s_2 : S_2 \to B_2$ with $c_2 \circ s_2 = o_2$ and $k_2 \circ b_2 \circ s_2 = h_{12} \circ q_{21}$. Now $o_2, c_2 \in \mathcal{M}$ implies $s_2 \in \mathcal{M}$, because $\mathcal{M}$ is closed under decomposition.

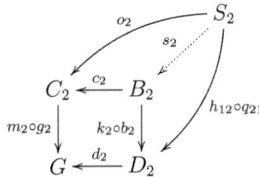

Analogously, we can construct $s_1 : S_1 \to B_1 \in \mathcal{M}$ s.t. $c_1 \circ s_1 = o_1$ assuming that $G \overset{p_1,m_1}{\Rightarrow} H_1$ does not cause a delete-use conflict with $G \overset{p_2,m_2}{\Rightarrow} H_2$. These are two contradictions, and therefore, $G \overset{p_2,m_2}{\Rightarrow} H_2$ causes a delete-use conflict with $G \overset{p_1,m_1}{\Rightarrow} H_1$. Analogously, we can prove that $G \overset{p_1,m_1}{\Rightarrow} H_1$ causes a delete-use conflict with $G \overset{p_2,m_2}{\Rightarrow} H_2$ if $(S_1, g_1 \circ o_1, q_{12})$ is a conflict reason.

3.6. CONFLICTS AND CAUSAL DEPENDENCIES FOR TRANSFORMATIONS

- Consider $G \overset{p_2,m_2}{\Longrightarrow} H_2$ that causes a delete-use conflict with $G \overset{p_1,m_1}{\Longrightarrow} H_1$, and assume that $(S_2, q_{21}, g_2 \circ o_2)$ is not a conflict reason. Then there exists a morphism $s_2 : S_2 \to B_2 \in \mathcal{M}$ with $c_2 \circ s_2 = o_2$. It suffices to show that $G \overset{p_2,m_2}{\Longrightarrow} H_2$ does not cause a delete-use conflict with $G \overset{p_1,m_1}{\Longrightarrow} H_1$. This is equivalent to constructing $h_{12} : L_1 \to D_2$ with $d_2 \circ h_{12} = m_1$. Therefore, consider the following picture:

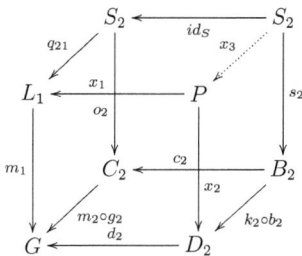

Let (P, x_1, x_2) be the pullback of (G, m_1, d_2) in the front square. The left square is a pullback by construction. Recall that POs along $\mathcal{M}$-morphisms are also PBs (see Theorem 4.26 in [29]). Then c_2 is a monomorphism since (2_2) is a PO along morphism b_2 in $\mathcal{M}$, and therefore, (2_2) is also a PB along $\mathcal{M}$-morphism l_2 inducing that c_2 is also in $\mathcal{M}$. Thus, the back square is a pullback because c_2 is a monomorphism. The front pullback leads to a unique morphism $x_3 : S_2 \to P$ s.t. $q_{21} = x_1 \circ x_3$ and $x_2 \circ x_3 = k_2 \circ b_2 \circ s_2$. The top square is a pullback because x_1 is a monomorphism. The bottom square is a pushout by construction along $\mathcal{M}$, and hence also pullback. This implies by pullback composition and decomposition that also the right square is a pullback. Now the Van Kampen property with bottom pushout and $c_2 \in \mathcal{M}$ implies that the top is a pushout as well. This implies x_1 is an isomorphism. Now let $h_{12} = x_2 \circ (x_1)^{-1} : L_1 \to D_2$, then $d_2 \circ h_{12} = d_2 \circ x_2 \circ (x_1)^{-1} = m_1 \circ x_1 \circ (x_1)^{-1} = m_1$. Consider $G \overset{p_1,m_1}{\Longrightarrow} H_1$ that causes a delete-use conflict with $G \overset{p_2,m_2}{\Longrightarrow} H_2$, then analogously, we can construct h_{21} with $d_1 \circ h_{21} = m_2$ assuming that $(S_2, q_{21}, g_2 \circ o_2)$ is no conflict reason. These are two contradictions, and therefore, it holds that if $G \overset{p_1,m_1}{\Longrightarrow} H_1$ (resp. $G \overset{p_2,m_2}{\Longrightarrow} H_2$) causes a delete-use conflict with $G \overset{p_2,m_2}{\Longrightarrow} H_2$ (resp. $G \overset{p_1,m_1}{\Longrightarrow} H_1$) then $(S_1, g_1 \circ o_1, q_{12})$ (resp. $(S_2, q_{21}, g_2 \circ o_2)$) is a conflict reason.

□

Note that S_1 represents in case 1 what is deleted by rule p_1 and used by rule p_2. Thus, S_1 represents the reason for the conflict with $G \overset{p_2,m_2}{\Longrightarrow} H_2$ caused by $G \overset{p_1,m_1}{\Longrightarrow} H_1$. Analogously, S_2 represents in case 2 what is deleted by rule p_2 and used by rule p_1. Thus, S_2 represents the reason for the conflict with $G \overset{p_1,m_1}{\Longrightarrow} H_1$ caused by $G \overset{p_2,m_2}{\Longrightarrow} H_2$.

3.6.13 Theorem (causal dependency characterization with reason). *Given a sequence of two direct transformations $G \overset{p_1,m_1}{\Longrightarrow} H_1 \overset{p_2,m_2}{\Longrightarrow} H_2$, then the following equivalences hold:*

- $G \overset{p_1,m_1}{\Longrightarrow} H_1$ *is in produce-use dependency with* $H_1 \overset{p_2,m_2}{\Longrightarrow} H_2$

⇔

$(S_1, g_1 \circ o_1, q_{12})$ *as given in Def. 3.6.11 is a causal dependency reason.*

- $G \stackrel{p_1,m_1}{\Rightarrow} H_1$ is in deliver-delete dependency with $H_1 \stackrel{p_2,m_2}{\Rightarrow} H_2$

$$\Leftrightarrow$$

$(S_2, q_{21}, g_2 \circ o_2)$ as given in Def. 3.6.11 is a causal dependency reason.

Proof. As noted already in Remark 3.4.2, $G \stackrel{p_1}{\Rightarrow} H_1 \stackrel{p_2}{\Rightarrow} H_2$ are sequentially independent if and only if $G \stackrel{p_1^{-1}}{\Leftarrow} H_1 \stackrel{p_2}{\Rightarrow} H_2$ are parallel independent. Therefore, the above assumption follows directly from this remark and Theorem 3.6.12. □

Note that in the first case S_1 represents what is produced by rule p_1 and used by rule p_2. Thus, S_1 represents the reason for the triggering of $H_1 \stackrel{p_2,m_2}{\Rightarrow} H_2$ by $G \stackrel{p_1,m_1}{\Rightarrow} H_1$. Analogously, in the second case S_2 represents what is preserved or produced by rule p_1 and deleted by p_2. Thus, S_2 represents the reason for the irreversibility of $G \stackrel{p_1,m_1}{\Rightarrow} H_1$ after $H_1 \stackrel{p_2,m_2}{\Rightarrow} H_2$.

3.7 Critical Pairs and Critical Sequences

The conflict (resp. causal dependency) characterization formulated in Theorem 3.6.5 (resp. Theorem 3.6.7) leads to a new critical pair (resp. so-called critical sequence) notion for transformations with NACs. A critical pair (resp. critical sequence) describes a conflict (resp. causal dependency) between two rules in a minimal context. In this section we introduce a critical pair (resp. sequence) definition with $\mathcal{E}'$ expressing this minimal context. Moreover, it is proven in this section that the new critical pair (resp. sequence) definition satisfies completeness. This means that for each conflict (resp. causal dependency) occurring between two direct transformations with NACs there is a critical pair (resp. sequence) expressing the same conflict (resp. causal dependency) in a minimal context. At the end of this section, it is proven that if there are no critical pairs (resp. sequences) for a given transformation system, then all direct transformations are parallel (resp. sequentially) independent. Such kinds of systems is called conflict-free (resp. dependency-free).

3.7.1 Definition (critical pair). A *critical pair* is a pair of direct transformations $K \stackrel{p_1,m_1}{\Rightarrow} P_1$ with NAC_{p_1} and $K \stackrel{p_2,m_2}{\Rightarrow} P_2$ with NAC_{p_2} such that:

1. (a) $\nexists h_{12} : L_1 \to D_2 : d_2 \circ h_{12} = m_1$ and (m_1, m_2) in $\mathcal{E}'$
   (delete-use conflict)

   or

   (b) there exists $h_{12} : L_1 \to D_2$ s.t. $d_2 \circ h_{12} = m_1$, but for one of the NACs $n_1 : L_1 \to N_1$ of p_1 there exists a morphism $q_{12} : N_1 \to P_2 \in \mathcal{Q}$ s.t. $q_{12} \circ n_1 = e_2 \circ h_{12}$, and thus, $e_2 \circ h_{12} \not\models NAC_{n_1}$, and (q_{12}, m_2') in $\mathcal{E}'$ (produce-forbid conflict)

   or

2. (a) $\nexists h_{21} : L_2 \to D_1 : d_1 \circ h_{21} = m_2$ and (m_1, m_2) in $\mathcal{E}'$
   (delete-use conflict)

   or

   (b) there exists $h_{21} : L_2 \to D_1$ s.t. $d_1 \circ h_{21} = m_2$, but for one of the NACs $n_2 : L_2 \to N_2$ of p_2 there exists a morphism $q_{21} : N_2 \to P_1 \in \mathcal{Q}$ s.t. $q_{21} \circ n_2 = e_1 \circ h_{21}$, and thus, $e_1 \circ h_{21} \not\models NAC_{n_2}$, and (q_{21}, m_1') in $\mathcal{E}'$ (produce-forbid conflict)

3.7. CRITICAL PAIRS AND CRITICAL SEQUENCES

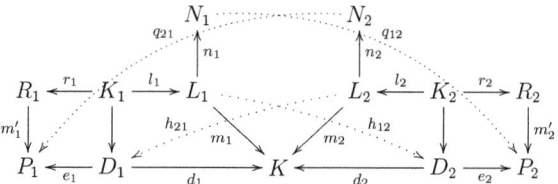

3.7.2 Definition (critical sequence). A *critical sequence* is a sequence of direct transformations $K \overset{p_1,m_1}{\Rightarrow} P_1$ with NAC_{p_1} and $P_1 \overset{p_2,m_2}{\Rightarrow} P_2$ with NAC_{p_2} such that at least one of the following four assumptions holds:

1. $\nexists h_{12} : R_1 \to D_2 : d_2 \circ h_{12} = m_1'$ and (m_1', m_2) in $\mathcal{E}'$,

2. there exists $h_{12} : R_1 \to D_2$ s.t. $d_2 \circ h_{12} = m_1'$, but for one of the NACs $n_1 : R_1 \to N_1$ of $NAC_{p_1^{-1}}$ there exists a morphism $q_{12} : N_1 \to P_2 \in \mathcal{Q}$ s.t. $q_{12} \circ n_1 = e_2 \circ h_{12}$ and (q_{12}, m_2') in $\mathcal{E}'$,

3. $\nexists h_{21} : L_2 \to D_1 : e_1 \circ h_{21} = m_2$ and (m_1', m_2) in $\mathcal{E}'$

4. there exists $h_{21} : L_2 \to D_1$ s.t. $e_1 \circ h_{21} = m_2$, but for one of the NACs $n_2 : L_2 \to N_2$ of p_2 there exists a morphism $q_{21} : N_2 \to P_1 \in \mathcal{Q}$ s.t. $q_{21} \circ n_2 = d_1 \circ h_{21}$ and (q_{21}, m_1') in $\mathcal{E}'$ (produce-forbid conflict)

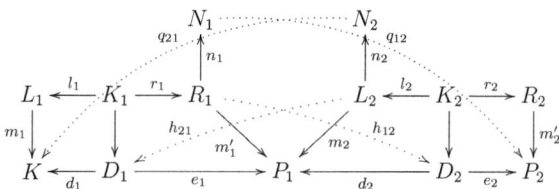

3.7.3 Remark. As noted already in Remark 3.4.2, $K \overset{p_1}{\Rightarrow} P_1 \overset{p_2}{\Rightarrow} P_2$ are sequentially independent if and only if $K \overset{p_1^{-1}}{\Leftarrow} P_1 \overset{p_2}{\Rightarrow} P_2$ are parallel independent. Thus, the above critical sequence definition is obtained by Def. 3.7.1 for the pair $K \overset{p_1^{-1}}{\Leftarrow} P_1 \overset{p_2}{\Rightarrow} P_2$.

Now we prove that Def. 3.7.1 (resp. 3.7.2) of critical pairs (resp. sequences) leads to completeness. Therefore, we need the following definition and theorem first. In particular, an extension diagram with NACs describes how a transformation $t : G_0 \Rightarrow^* G_n$ with NACs can be extended to a transformation $t' : G_0' \Rightarrow^* G_n'$ with NACs via an extension morphism $k_0 : G_0 \to G_0'$. On the other hand, the restriction theorem with NACs states that a direct transformation with NACs can be restricted to a direct transformation with NACs, starting with a smaller context.

3.7.4 Definition (extension diagram with NACs). An *extension diagram* is a diagram (1),

$$\begin{array}{ccc} G_0 & \overset{t}{\Longrightarrow^*} & G_n \\ k_0 \downarrow & (1) & \downarrow k_n \\ G_0' & \overset{t'}{\Longrightarrow^*} & G_n' \end{array}$$

CHAPTER 3. RULE-BASED MODELING USING HIGH-LEVEL TRANSFORMATION

where, $k_0 : G_0 \to G'_0$ is a morphism, called extension morphism, and $t : G_0 \overset{*}{\Rightarrow} G_n$ and $t' : G'_0 \overset{*}{\Rightarrow} G'_n$ are transformations with NACs via the same rules $(p_0, \cdots, p_{n-1})$, and matches $(m_0, \cdots, m_{n-1})$ and extended matches $(k_0 \circ m_0, \cdots, k_{n-1} \circ m_{n-1})$, respectively, defined by the following DPO diagrams :

$$p_i : \begin{array}{ccccc} L_i & \overset{l_i}{\leftarrow} & K_i & \overset{r_i}{\to} & R_i \\ m_i \downarrow & & j_i \downarrow & & n_i \downarrow \\ G_i & \overset{f_i}{\leftarrow} & D_i & \overset{g_i}{\to} & G_{i+1} \\ k_i \downarrow & & d_i \downarrow & & k_{i+1} \downarrow \\ G'_i & \overset{f'_i}{\leftarrow} & D'_i & \overset{g'_i}{\to} & G'_{i+1} \end{array}$$

3.7.5 Theorem (restriction theorem with NACs). *Given a direct transformation $G' \overset{p,m'}{\Rightarrow} H'$ with NACs, a morphism $s : G \to G' \in \mathcal{M}'$, and a match $m : L \to G$ such that $s \circ m = m'$, then there is a direct transformation $G \overset{p,m}{\Rightarrow} H$ with NACs leading to the following extension diagram:*

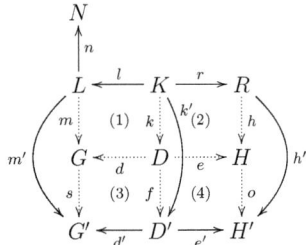

Proof. Consider $G \overset{p}{\Rightarrow} H$ with NAC n as shown above. Because the $\mathcal{M} - \mathcal{M}'$ pushout-pullback decomposition property holds in an adhesive HLR category with NACs and because of the Restriction Theorem without NACs (Theorem 6.18 in [29]), the above extension diagram without NACs exists. It remains to show that m satisfies the NACs of p. Suppose that m doesn't satisfy some $NAC(n)$ of p, then there exists a morphism $q : N \to G \in \mathcal{Q}$ s.t. $q \circ n = m$, but this implies $s \circ q \circ n = s \circ m = m'$ with $q \in \mathcal{Q}$, $s \in \mathcal{M}'$ and because of the composition property $s \circ q \in \mathcal{Q}$, and this is a contradiction. □

Now, we are ready to formulate the completeness theorem for critical pairs with NACs, stating that each potential conflict is represented in a minimal context by some critical pair.

3.7.6 Theorem (completeness of critical pairs with NACs). *For each pair of direct transformations $H_1 \overset{p_1,m'_1}{\Leftarrow} G \overset{p_2,m'_2}{\Rightarrow} H_2$ in conflict, there is a critical pair $P_1 \overset{p_1}{\Leftarrow} K \overset{p_2}{\Rightarrow} P_2$ with extension diagrams (1) and (2) and $m \in \mathcal{M}'$.*

$$\begin{array}{ccc} P_1 & \Leftarrow K \Rightarrow & P_2 \\ \downarrow & (1) \; m \downarrow \; (2) & \downarrow \\ H_1 & \Leftarrow G \Rightarrow & H_2 \end{array}$$

Proof. According to Theorem 3.6.5 at least one of the following reasons is responsible for a pair of direct transformations $G \overset{p_1,m'_1}{\Rightarrow} H_1$ with NAC_{p_1} and $G \overset{p_2,m'_2}{\Rightarrow} H_2$ with NAC_{p_2} to be *in conflict*:

1. $\nexists h'_{12} : L_1 \to D'_2 : d'_2 \circ h'_{12} = m'_1$,

2. there exists a unique $h'_{12} : L_1 \to D'_2 : d'_2 \circ h'_{12} = m'_1$, but $e'_2 \circ h'_{12} \not\models NAC_{p_1}$,

3. $\nexists h'_{21} : L_2 \to D_1 : d'_1 \circ h'_{21} = m'_2$,

4. there exists a unique $h'_{21} : L_2 \to D_1 : d'_1 \circ h'_{21} = m'_2$, but $e'_1 \circ h'_{21} \not\models NAC_{p_2}$.

It is possible that 2 and 4 are both false. In this case, 1 or 3 have to be true corresponding to the type of conflict for transformations without NACs and in [29] it is described how to embed a critical pair into this pair of direct transformations. This critical pair fulfills the NACs because of Theorem 3.7.5. In the other case, 2 or 4 are true. First let 2 be true. This means that there exists a unique $h'_{12} : L_1 \to D'_2 : d'_2 \circ h'_{12} = m'_1$, but $e'_2 \circ h'_{12} \not\models NAC_{p_1}$. Thus, for one of the NACs $n_1 : L_1 \to N_1$ of p_1 there exists a morphism $q'_{12} : N_1 \to H_2 \in \mathcal{Q}$ such that $q'_{12} \circ n_1 = e'_2 \circ h'_{12}$. For each pair of morphisms with the same codomain, we have an $\mathcal{E}' - \mathcal{M}'$ pair factorization. Thus, for $q'_{12} : N_1 \to H_2$ and $h'_2 : R_2 \to H_2$ we obtain an object P_2 and morphisms $h_2 : R_2 \to P_2$, $q_{12} : N_1 \to P_2$ and $o_2 : P_2 \to H_2$ with $(h_2, q_{12}) \in \mathcal{E}'$ and $o_2 \in \mathcal{M}'$ such that $o_2 \circ h_2 = h'_2$ and $o_2 \circ q_{12} = q'_{12}$. Considering that $H_2 \Rightarrow G$ is a direct transformation via p_2^{-1} (see Theorem 3.3.11), $o_2 \circ h_2 = h'_2$ and $o_2 \in \mathcal{M}'$ we can apply Theorem 3.7.5. It follows that the extension diagram with NACs via p_2^{-1} consisting of pushouts (5) - (8) can be constructed. Because of Theorem 3.3.11, m_2 satisfies NAC_{p_2}. Since $o_2 \in \mathcal{M}'$ and (7) and (8) are pushouts along $\mathcal{M}$-morphisms, also $f_2 \in \mathcal{M}'$ and $m \in \mathcal{M}'$. Now we have the first half $K \Rightarrow P_2$ of the critical pair under construction. Then we can start constructing the second half of the critical pair. Since (8) is a pullback and $o_2 \circ q_{12} \circ n_1 = q'_{12} \circ n_1 = e'_2 \circ h'_{12}$, there exists a morphism $h_{12} : L_1 \to D_2$, with $e_2 \circ h_{12} = q_{12} \circ n_1$ and $f_2 \circ h_{12} = h'_{12}$. Let m_1 be the morphism $d_2 \circ h_{12}$, then the following holds: $m \circ m_1 = m \circ d_2 \circ h_{12} = d'_2 \circ f_2 \circ h_{12} = d'_2 \circ h'_{12} = m'_1$. Because of Theorem 3.7.5, $m \circ m_1 = m'_1$ and $m \in \mathcal{M}'$ the extension diagram with NACs consisting of pushouts (1) - (4) with m_1 satisfying the NACs of p_1.
We still have to check if $P_1 \Leftarrow K \Rightarrow P_2$ shows a conflict of type 2 as well. We have that $e_2 \circ h_{12} = q_{12} \circ n_1$ and because of the decomposition property $q'_{12} = o_2 \circ q_{12} \in \mathcal{Q}$ and $o_2 \in \mathcal{M}'$ we have $q_{12} \in \mathcal{Q}$. This means that $e_2 \circ h_{12}$ does not satisfy NAC $n_1 : L_1 \to N_1$ either.
Thus, finally we obtain a critical pair according to Def. 3.7.1 of type 2 because we have h_{12} with $d_2 \circ h_{12} = m_1$. Moreover, there is $q_{12} \in \mathcal{Q}$ with $(q_{12}, h_2) \in \mathcal{E}'$ and $e_2 \circ h_{12} = q_{12} \circ n_1$.

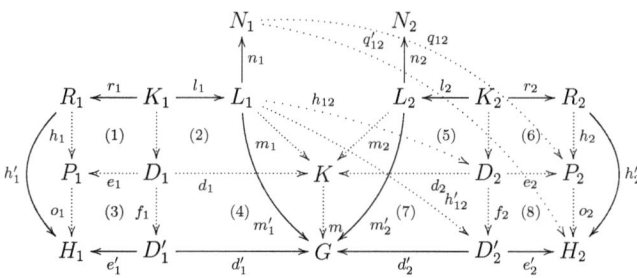

Analogously, we can proceed for case 4 being true, leading to a critical pair of type 4 according to Def. 3.7.1. $\square$

3.7.7 Remark. Note that the critical pair that is constructed in the proof exhibits the same type of conflict (see Def. 3.6.6) as the pair of conflicting direct transformations.

CHAPTER 3. RULE-BASED MODELING USING HIGH-LEVEL TRANSFORMATION

As for the conflict case, we can now formulate the completeness theorem for critical sequences with NACs, stating that each potential causal dependency is represented in a minimal context by some critical sequence.

3.7.8 Theorem (completeness of critical sequences with NACs). *For each sequence of causally dependent direct transformations* $G \stackrel{p_1,m_1'}{\Longrightarrow} H_1 \stackrel{p_2,m_2'}{\Longrightarrow} H_2$, *there is a critical sequence* $K \stackrel{p_1}{\Longrightarrow} P_1 \stackrel{p_2}{\Longrightarrow} P_2$ *with extension diagrams (1) and (2) and* $m \in \mathcal{M}'$.

$$\begin{array}{ccc} K \Longrightarrow P_1 \Longrightarrow P_2 \\ \downarrow \quad (1) \; m \downarrow \quad (2) \quad \downarrow \\ G \Longrightarrow H_1 \Longrightarrow H_2 \end{array}$$

Proof. As noted already in Remark 3.4.2 $G \stackrel{p_1}{\Longrightarrow} H_1 \stackrel{p_2}{\Longrightarrow} H_2$ are sequentially independent if and only if $G \stackrel{p_1^{-1}}{\Longleftarrow} H_1 \stackrel{p_2}{\Longrightarrow} H_2$ are parallel independent. Therefore, the above assumption follows directly from this remark and Theorem 3.7.6. □

3.7.9 Remark. Note that, analogous to Remark 3.7.7, the constructed critical sequence exhibits the same type of dependency (see Def. 3.6.8) as the sequence of causally dependent direct transformations.

The following fact characterizes that each pair of direct graph transformations is not in conflict if the corresponding graph transformation system has an empty set of critical pairs. Such a system is called conflict-free. Thereby, note that a pair of direct transformations via the same rule must be non-conflicting as well.

3.7.10 Fact (necessary and sufficient condition for parallel independence). *Each pair of direct transformations* $H_1 \Leftarrow G \Rightarrow H_2$ *in an adhesive HLR system with NACs is parallel independent if and only if there are no critical pairs for this adhesive HLR system with NACs.*

Proof.
- Consider an adhesive HLR system with NACs with an empty set of critical pairs and let $H_1 \Leftarrow G \Rightarrow H_2$ be a pair of direct transformations in conflict for this adhesive HLR system with NACs. This is a contradiction, since then there would exist a critical pair that can be embedded into this pair of direct transformations, as shown in Theorem 3.7.6.

- Consider an adhesive HLR system with NACs with only parallel independent pairs of direct transformations $H_1 \Leftarrow G \Rightarrow H_2$. Then, the set of critical pairs has to be empty, otherwise a critical pair would be a pair of direct transformations in conflict.

□

3.7.11 Definition (conflict-free system). *An adhesive HLR system with NACs in which each pair of direct transformations* $H_1 \Leftarrow G \Rightarrow H_2$ *is parallel independent is called* conflict-free.

Analogously, we have a fact characterizing that a sequence of two direct graph transformations is not causally dependent if the corresponding graph transformation system has an empty set of critical sequences. Such a system is called dependency-free. Thereby, note that a sequence of two direct transformations via the same rule must be independent as well.

3.8. INDEPENDENCE, CONFLICTS AND CAUSAL DEPENDENCIES FOR RULES

3.7.12 Fact (a necessary and sufficient condition for sequential independence). *Each sequence of direct transformations $G \Rightarrow H_1 \Rightarrow H_2$ in an adhesive HLR system with NACs is sequentially independent if and only if there are no critical sequences for this adhesive HLR system with NACs.*

Proof. As noted already in Remark 3.4.2 $G \overset{p_1}{\Rightarrow} H_1 \overset{p_2}{\Rightarrow} H_2$ are sequentially independent if and only if $G \overset{p_1^{-1}}{\Leftarrow} H_1 \overset{p_2}{\Rightarrow} H_2$ are parallel independent. Therefore, the above assumption follows directly from this remark and Fact 3.7.10. □

3.7.13 Definition (dependency-free system). An adhesive HLR system with NACs in which each sequence of direct transformations $G \Rightarrow H_1 \Rightarrow H_2$ is sequentially independent is called *dependency-free*.

3.8 Independence, Conflicts and Causal Dependencies for Rules

We now shift the notions of parallel and sequential independency as well as conflicts and causal dependencies for transformations to the rule level. This will allow static analysis techniques such as, for example, investigations on rule sequence applicability in the next section.

3.8.1 Independence for Rules

We define parallel (resp. sequential) independency for rules by demanding that the corresponding transformations are independent. Analogously, it is possible to define rules that are in conflict (resp. rules that depend on each other).

3.8.1 Definition (parallel independent rules). Rules r_1 and r_2 are *parallel independent* if every pair of transformations $G \overset{(r_1,m_1)}{\Rightarrow} H_1$ via r_1 with NAC_{r_1} and $G \overset{(r_2,m_2)}{\Rightarrow} H_2$ via r_2 with NAC_{r_2} is parallel independent as defined in Def. 3.4.1.

3.8.2 Definition (sequentially independent rules). The pair of rules (r_1, r_2) is *sequentially independent* if every sequence of transformations $G \overset{(r_1,m_1)}{\Rightarrow} H_1$ via r_1 with NAC_{r_1} followed by $H_1 \overset{(r_2,m_2)}{\Rightarrow} H$ via r_2 with NAC_{r_2} is sequentially independent as defined in Def. 3.4.1.

3.8.3 Corollary (characterization of parallel independent rules). *Rules r_1 and r_2 are parallel independent if and only if there exist no critical pairs $P_1 \overset{(r_1,m_1)}{\Leftarrow} K \overset{(r_2,m_2)}{\Rightarrow} P_2$.*

Proof. This follows directly from Def. 3.8.1 and Theorem 3.7.10. □

3.8.4 Corollary (characterization of sequentially independent rules). *The pair of rules (r_1, r_2) is sequentially independent if and only if there exist no critical sequences $K \overset{(r_1,m_1)}{\Rightarrow} P_1 \overset{(r_2,m_2)}{\Rightarrow} P_2$.*

Proof. This follows directly from Def. 3.8.2 and Theorem 3.7.12. □

Analogous to Remark 3.4.2, we can relate parallel and sequential independency for rules instead of transformations.

3.8.5 Corollary (relating parallel and sequential independency for rules). *The rule pair* (r_1, r_2) *is sequentially independent if and only if* r_1^{-1} *and* r_2 *are parallel independent. The rules* r_1 *and* r_2 *are parallel independent if and only if the rule pair* (r_1^{-1}, r_2) *is sequentially independent if and only if the rule pair* (r_2^{-1}, r_1) *is sequentially independent.*

Proof. This follows directly from Def. 3.8.1 and Def. 3.8.2. □

3.8.2 Conflicts and Causal Dependencies for Rules

We defined parallel (resp. sequential) independency for rules by demanding that the corresponding transformations are independent. Analogously, it is possible to define rules that are in conflict (resp. rules that depend on each other).

3.8.6 Definition (conflicting rules). Rules r_1 and r_2 are *in conflict* if there exists a pair of transformations $G \overset{p_1,m_1}{\Longrightarrow} H_1$ with NAC_{p_1} and $G \overset{p_2,m_2}{\Longrightarrow} H_2$ with NAC_{p_2} that are in conflict according to Def. 3.6.1.

3.8.7 Definition (causally dependent rules). Given a pair of rules (r_1, r_2), then rules r_1 and r_2 are *causally dependent* if there exists a sequence of two direct transformations $G \overset{p_1,m_1}{\Longrightarrow} H_1 \overset{p_2,m_2}{\Longrightarrow} H_2$ with NAC_{p_1} and NAC_{p_2} that are *causally dependent* according to Def. 3.6.2.

3.8.8 Corollary (characterization of conflicting rules). *Two rules* r_1 *and* r_2 *are in conflict according to Def. 3.8.6 if and only if there exists at least one critical pair* $P_1 \overset{(r_1,m_1)}{\Longleftarrow} K \overset{(r_2,m_2)}{\Longrightarrow} P_2$.

Proof. This follows directly from Def. 3.8.6 and Theorem 3.7.6. □

3.8.9 Corollary (characterization of causally dependent rules). *Given a pair of rules* (r_1, r_2), *then they are causally dependent according to Def. 3.8.7 if and only if there exists at least one critical sequence* $K \overset{(r_1,m_1)}{\Longrightarrow} P_1 \overset{(r_2,m_2)}{\Longrightarrow} P_2$.

Proof. This follows directly from Def. 3.8.7 and Theorem 3.7.8. □

Analogous to the conflict and causal dependency characterizations for transformations in Def. 3.6.6 (resp. 3.6.8), we can characterize conflicts and causal dependencies between rules as well.

3.8.10 Definition (rule r_1 causes a delete-use (resp. produce-forbid) conflict with rule r_2). Rule r_1 *causes a delete-use (resp. produce-forbid) conflict* with rule r_2 if there is a transformation $G \overset{(r_1,m_1)}{\Longrightarrow} H_1$ via r_1 with NAC_{r_1} that causes a delete-use (resp. produce-forbid) conflict with $G \overset{(r_2,m_2)}{\Longrightarrow} H_2$ via r_2 with NAC_{r_2} as defined in Def. 3.6.6. In general, we say that r_1 *causes a conflict with* r_2.

3.8.11 Definition (rule pair (r_1, r_2) is in produce-use (resp. delete-use) dependency). A rule pair (r_1, r_2) is in *produce-use (resp. delete-use) dependency* if there is a transformation sequence $G \overset{(r_1,m_1)}{\Longrightarrow} H_1 \overset{(r_2,m_2)}{\Longrightarrow} H_2$ such that $G \overset{(r_1,m_1)}{\Longrightarrow} H_1$ is in produce-use (resp. delete-use) dependency with $H_1 \overset{(r_2,m_2)}{\Longrightarrow} H_2$ according to Def. 3.6.8. In general, we say that r_2 is *triggered by* r_1.

3.8.12 Definition (rule pair (r_1, r_2) is in deliver-delete (resp. forbid-produce) dependency). A rule pair (r_1, r_2) is in *deliver-delete (resp. forbid-produce) dependency* if there is a transformation sequence $G \overset{(r_1,m_1)}{\Longrightarrow} H_1 \overset{(r_2,m_2)}{\Longrightarrow} H_2$ such that $G \overset{(r_1,m_1)}{\Longrightarrow} H_1$ is in deliver-delete (resp. forbid-produce) dependency with $H_1 \overset{(r_2,m_2)}{\Longrightarrow} H_2$ according to Def. 3.6.8. In general, we say that r_1 is *irreversible after* r_2.

3.8. INDEPENDENCE, CONFLICTS AND CAUSAL DEPENDENCIES FOR RULES

3.8.13 Remark. Note that the following correspondences exist. Rules r_1 and r_2 are parallel independent if and only if r_1 does not cause a conflict with r_2 and r_2 does not cause a conflict with r_1. Rule pair (r_1, r_2) is sequentially independent if and only if r_2 is not triggered by r_1 and r_1 is not irreversible after r_2.

Analogous to Corollary 3.8.5, we can also relate conflicts and causal dependencies for rules.

3.8.14 Corollary (relating conflicts and causal dependencies for rules). *Rule r_1 causes a conflict with r_2 if and only if r_2 is triggered by r_1^{-1} if and only if r_2^{-1} is irreversible after r_1. Given rule pair (r_1, r_2), then r_2 is triggered by r_1 if and only if r^{-1} causes a conflict with r_2. Moreover, r_1 is irreversible after r_2 if and only if r_2 causes a conflict with r_1^{-1}.*

Proof. This follows directly from Def. 3.8.10, Def. 3.8.11 and Def. 3.8.12. □

If neighbored rules in a rule sequence are sequentially independent, then they can be switched as well. We say that such sequences are shift-equivalent.

3.8.15 Definition (shift-equivalent rule sequences). A rule sequence s' is *shift-equivalent* to a rule sequence $s : r_1, r_2, \ldots, r_m$ if the pair (s, s') belongs to the reflexive, symmetric, and transitive closure of the shift-equivalent relation S: a pair of rule sequences (s, s') belongs to the shift-relation S if s' can be deduced from s by switching the rules r_j with r_{j+1} and the switching is allowed only if (r_j, r_{j+1}) and (r_{j+1}, r_j) are sequentially independent according to Def. 3.8.2.

If neighbored rules in a rule sequence are sequentially independent only in one order, then we say that they are just shift-related. These notions are used in Theorems 3.9.4, 3.9.6, and Corollary 3.9.7 to define rule sequence reductions with regard to their applicability resp. non-applicability.

3.8.16 Definition (shift-related rule sequences). A rule sequence s' is *shift-related* to a rule sequence $s : r_1, r_2, \ldots, r_m$ if the pair (s, s') belongs to the reflexive and transitive closure of the shift relation S: a pair of rule sequences (s, s') belongs to the shift-relation S if s' can be deduced from s by switching the rules r_j with r_{j+1} and the switching is allowed only if the rule pair (r_{j+1}, r_j) is sequentially independent according to Def. 3.8.2.

3.8.17 Remark. Note that because of Theorem 3.8.5 rule pair (r_1, r_2) is sequentially independent if and only if r_2 and r_1^{-1} are parallel independent rules.

We can distinguish a special case of causal dependency for the case without NACs. It is possible that a rule r_1 produces everything that is needed by r_2 regardless of what is already present in the corresponding transformations. This so-called pure dependency will be used for the applicability criteria of rule sequences in Section 3.9. Note that if r_2 was a rule with NACs, then it could be the case that r_1 produces everything that is needed by r_2, but also that r_1 produces something that is forbidden by r_1. Therefore, here we at first restrict ourselves to the case without NACs.

3.8.18 Definition (rule r_1 purely enables r_2). A rule $r_2 : L_2 \leftarrow K_2 \to R_2$ is *purely enabled* by $r_1 : L_1 \leftarrow K_1 \to R_1$ if r_2 is a rule without NACs and there exists a monomorphism $l_{21} : L_2 \to R_1$.

3.8.19 Remark. Rule r_2 without NACs is triggered by rule r_1, if r_2 is purely enabled by r_1 and the following mild assumptions are satisfied: a morphism $k_{21} : L_2 \to K_1$ does not exist such that $r_1 \circ k_{21} = l_{21}$, match l_{21} fulfills the gluing condition for r_2, and $id : L_1 \to L_1 \models NAC_{r_1}$.

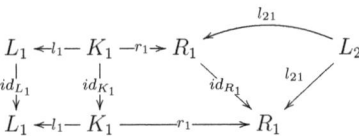

3.8.3 Independence of Concurrent Rules

This section describes that independency for concurrent rules can be derived from independency of their single rules. In order to prove this fact we need to assume the existence of binary coproducts.

3.8.20 Assumption (binary coproducts exist, $\mathcal{E}'$ is joint epi, $\mathcal{M} - \mathcal{M}'$ decomposition). Let for Theorem 3.8.21, Theorem 3.8.22, and Corollary 3.8.23 AHS $= (\mathbf{C}, \mathcal{M}, \mathcal{M}', \mathcal{E}', \mathcal{Q}, P)$ be an adhesive HLR system with NACs, where $\mathbf{C}$ has binary coproducts. In addition, let each pair of morphisms in $\mathcal{E}'$ as defined in Property 3.2.3 be jointly epimorphic. Moreover, the $\mathcal{M} - \mathcal{M}'$ decomposition property holds. This means that if $g \circ f$ belongs to $\mathcal{M}'$ and g belongs to $\mathcal{M}$, then f belongs to $\mathcal{M}'$.

3.8.21 Theorem (independence of concurrent and single rule). *Consider a concurrent rule r_c for some sequence of rules $r_1, r_2 \ldots r_n$ and some rule r. r_c and r are parallel independent $((r_c, r)$ resp. (r, r_c) are sequentially independent) if r_i and r are parallel independent $((r_i, r)$ resp. (r, r_i) are sequentially independent) for $1 \leq i \leq n$.*

Proof. We argue by induction over the length of the rule sequence n. If $n = 1$, then r_1 is a regular rule and it follows by assumption that $r_c = r_1$ and r are not in conflict. Let $n > 1$, and suppose that the above assumption holds for any rule r and concurrent rule r'_c for a sequence of rules $r_1, r_2 \ldots r_{n-1}$. In the following diagram, we have on the left a direct transformation via r on G. On the right, we have a direct transformation via r_c on G, which can be analyzed according to Theorem 3.5.8 and the recursive Def. 3.5.7 into a direct transformation via r'_c and r_n. Thereby, r'_c is a concurrent rule via $r_1, r_2 \ldots r_{n-1}$, (1) and (2) are PBs, and all other squares are POs.

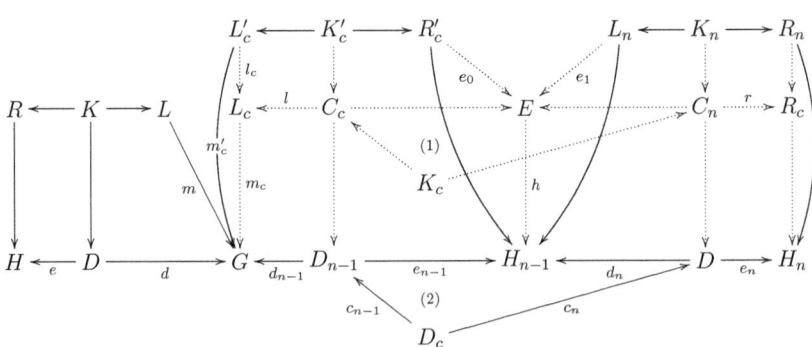

3.8. INDEPENDENCE, CONFLICTS AND CAUSAL DEPENDENCIES FOR RULES

- We at first prove that r_c does not cause any conflict with r. Thus, we have to show that there exists some morphism $h_c : L \to D_c$ such that $d_{n-1} \circ c_{n-1} \circ h_c = m$ and $e_n \circ c_n \circ h_c \models NAC_r$. Therefore, we first consider only the following part of the above diagram.

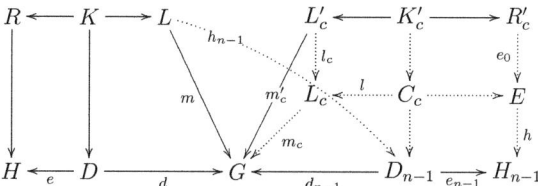

Since r'_c by induction hypothesis does not cause any conflict with r, there exists a morphism $h_{n-1} : L \to D_{n-1}$ such that $d_{n-1} \circ h_{n-1} = m$ and $e_{n-1} \circ h_{n-1} \models NAC_L$. Since r'_c and r are not in conflict by induction hypothesis, the above pair of direct transformations $H \Leftarrow G \Rightarrow H_{n-1}$ is parallel independent. This means that we can apply Theorem 3.4.3 and construct the left direct transformation $H_{n-1} \Rightarrow X$ of the following diagram. The right part depicts the direct transformation $H_{n-1} \Rightarrow H_n$ via r_n.

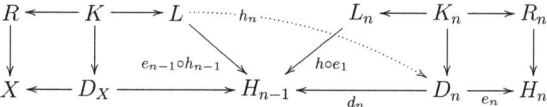

Since r and r_n are not in conflict by assumption, the above pair of direct transformations is not in conflict either. Therefore, there exists some morphism h_n such that $d_n \circ h_n = e_{n-1} \circ h_{n-1}$ and $e_n \circ h_n \models NAC_r$. Now consider the following diagram in which (2) is a PB:

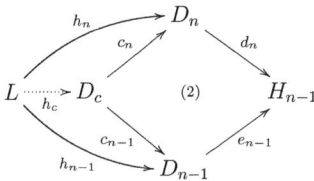

Since (2) is a PB and $d_n \circ h_n = e_{n-1} \circ h_{n-1}$, there exists a unique morphism $h_c : L \to D_c$ such that $c_n \circ h_c = h_n$ and $c_{n-1} \circ h_c = h_{n-1}$. Now $d_{n-1} \circ c_{n-1} \circ h_c = d_{n-1} \circ h_{n-1} = m$ and $e_n \circ c_n \circ h_c = e_n \circ h_n \models NAC_r$. Thus, it follows that r_c does not cause any conflict with r.

- Now we prove that r does not cause any conflict with r_c. We consider again

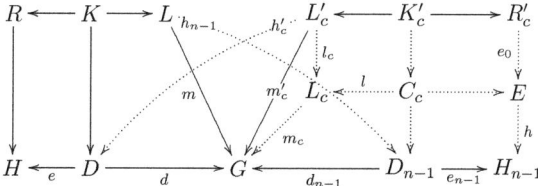

Since r and r'_c are not in conflict, it is possible to apply Theorem 3.4.3 on this pair of transformations and, therefore, the following diagrams depicting $H_{n-1} \Rightarrow X$ via r and $H \Rightarrow X$ via r'_c can be constructed:

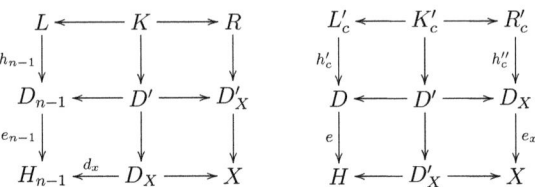

Note that thereby, $d_x \circ h''_c = h \circ e_0$. Moreover, consider the following diagram again:

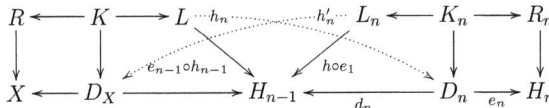

Since r and r_n are not in conflict, also h'_n exists such that $d_x \circ h'_n = h \circ e_1$. Applying Theorem 3.4.3 again, the following diagrams depicting $H_n \Rightarrow Y$ via r and $X \Rightarrow Y$ via r_n can be constructed:

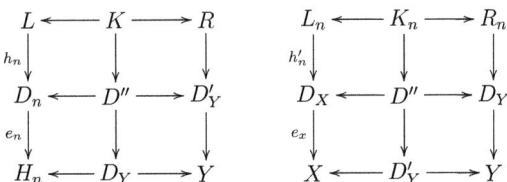

Note that thereby, $e_x \circ h'_n \models NAC_{L_n}$. Now we can construct the following diagram:

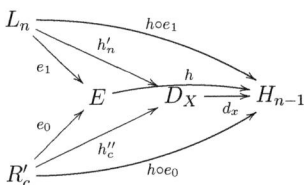

Note that thereby, as shown before the outer triangles commute. Moreover, d_x belongs to $\mathcal{M}$. Considering the coproduct $R'_c + L_n$ we can construct the following diagram:

$$R'_c + L_n \xrightarrow{[e_0, e_1]} E$$
$$[h''_c, h'_n] \downarrow \quad e_d \searrow \quad \downarrow h$$
$$D_X \xrightarrow{d_x} H_{n-1}$$

In a NAC-adhesive HLR category the diagonal morphism property (see Prop. 3.2.13)

3.8. INDEPENDENCE, CONFLICTS AND CAUSAL DEPENDENCIES FOR RULES

holds as proven in Corr. 3.2.14. Therefore, some morphism $e_d : E \to D_X$ exists such that $d_x \circ e_d = h$ and $e_d \circ [e_0, e_1] = [h''_c, h'_n]$. Moreover, since h belongs to $\mathcal{M}'$ and d_x to $\mathcal{M}$ also e_d is in $\mathcal{M}'$. This means that we can construct the following diagram by means of the $\mathcal{M} - \mathcal{M}'$ PO-PB decomposition property, the existence of POs over $\mathcal{M}$-morphisms, and PO-decomposition.

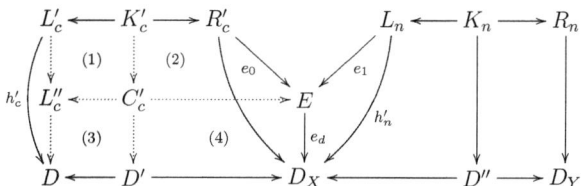

Because of uniqueness of PO-complements (see Remark 3.3.6) and PO-objects, it can be followed that diagrams (1),(2),(3), and (4) equal (1),(2),(3), and (4) in the following diagram:

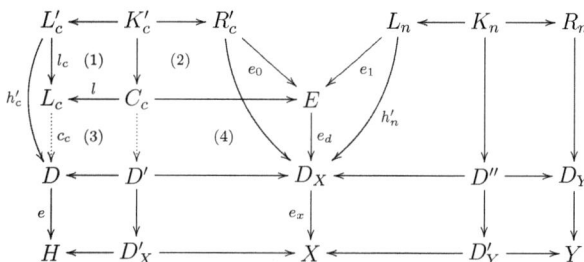

Therefore, there exists some $h_c : L_c \to H$ with $h_c = e \circ c_c$ such that $h_c \models NAC_{L_c}$ with $NAC_{L_c} = DL_{r_c}(NAC_{L_n}) \cup D_{l_c}(NAC_{L'_c})$. This is because $h_c \circ l_c = e \circ c_c \circ l_c = e \circ h'_c \models NAC_{L'_c}$ and $e_x \circ e_d \circ e_1 = e_x \circ h'_n \models NAC_{L_n}$.

Because of Remark 3.4.2, the case that some rule and a concurrent rule are sequentially independent can be reduced to the former case. □

3.8.22 Theorem (independence of concurrent rules). *Consider a concurrent rule r_c (resp. r'_c) for some sequence of rules $r_1, r_2 \ldots r_n$ (resp. $r'_1, r'_2, \ldots, r'_m$). r_c and r'_c are parallel independent ((r_c, r'_c) resp. (r'_c, r_c) are sequentially independent) if r_i and r'_j are parallel independent ((r_i, r'_j) resp. (r'_j, r_i) are sequentially independent) for $1 \leq i \leq n$ and $1 \leq j \leq m$.*

Proof. We argue by induction over n. If $n = 1$, we have $r_c = r_1$ and r'_c such that r_1 is not in conflict with each single rule in r'_c. By Theorem 3.8.21 we can conclude that r_c is not in conflict with r'_c. Suppose that the above assumption holds for some $r_{c,n-1}$ constructed from a sequence of $n-1$ rules. Now we prove that r_c and r'_c are not in conflict. By Def. 3.5.6 we know that r_c is a concurrent rule of some $r_{c,n-1}$ and r_n with $r_{c,n-1}$ the concurrent rule for $r_1, r_2, \ldots r_{n-1}$. By induction hypothesis we know that $r_{c,n-1}$ is not in conflict with r'_c. Moreover, r_n is not in conflict with r'_c because of Theorem 3.8.21. Therefore, it follows again from Theorem 3.8.21 that r_c as concurrent rule of $r_{c,n-1}$ and r_n is not in conflict with r'_c. Because of Remark 3.4.2, the case that two concurrent rules are sequentially independent can be reduced to the former case. □

CHAPTER 3. RULE-BASED MODELING USING HIGH-LEVEL TRANSFORMATION

3.8.23 Corollary (parallel (resp. sequentially) independent rules and concurrency). *Given a conflict-free (resp. dependency-free) adhesive HLR system* AHS *with NACs as given in Def. 3.7.11 (resp. Def. 3.7.13), then the adhesive HLR system* AHS' *with NACs equal to* AHS, *but holding in addition concurrent rules for sequences of rules in* AHS, *is conflict-free (resp. dependency-free) as well.*

Proof. In a conflict-free (resp. dependency-free) system each pair of rules is parallel (resp. sequentially) independent. Otherwise, there would exist at least one pair of transformations in conflict (resp. causally dependent transformations), and this is a contradiction with Def. 3.7.11 (resp. 3.7.13). Because of Theorem 3.8.22, it can be followed directly that each pair of concurrent rules will be parallel independent (resp. sequentially independent) as well. □

3.9 Applicability (Non-Applicability) of Rule Sequences

In this section, we first introduce some reductions of rule sequences allowing to conclude applicability (resp. non-applicability) of the original rule sequences from the applicability (resp. non-applicability) of the reduced sequences. Thereafter, we present sufficient criteria for the applicability and for the non-applicability of a rule sequence to an object. These criteria are based mainly on the causal dependencies and conflicts between rules as presented in Section 3.8. Moreover, the non-satisfaction of one of the criteria may give a hint to the reason for a rule sequence to be applicable or inapplicable. Applicability criteria have also been studied in [118] for simple digraphs using matrix graph grammars.

Before starting this section though, we make the following assumption. It ensures that as soon as a suitable match is found for a rule into some host object, the gluing condition is always fulfilled.

3.9.1 Assumption (gluing condition always fulfilled). In this section, we restrict ourselves to transformations via monomorphic matches. Moreover, we restrict ourselves to a set of rules such that the gluing condition via rules and monomorphic matches is always fulfilled. Thereby, note that NACs do not necessarily need to be fulfilled.

As noted in Assumption 2.9.1 in Chapter 2 for non-node-deleting graph transformation rules and injective matches the gluing condition is always fulfilled.

Based on this assumption and the conflict and dependency characterizations (see Def. 3.6.6 and Def. 3.6.8), we can formulate a weaker version of the Local Church-Rosser Theorem with NACs (see Thm 3.4.3). It characterizes what it means for a transformation not to cause a conflict with another transformation (resp. not to depend on another transformation). Namely, it is possible to derive different new kinds of rule applicabilities. The following cases occur: If two rules p_1 and p_2 are applicable to the same object G and the direct transformation $G \Rightarrow H_1$ via p_1 does not cause a conflict with the direct transformation $G \Rightarrow H_2$ via p_2, then it is possible to apply p_2 on the result of the first transformation H_1. If a sequence of rules p_1, p_2 is applicable to G and the first transformation $G \Rightarrow H_1$ via p_1 is reversible after $H_1 \Rightarrow G'$ via p_2, then it is possible to apply p_1^{-1} to G'. If a sequence of rules p_1, p_2 is applicable to G and the second transformation $H_1 \Rightarrow G'$ via p_2 is not triggered by the first one $G \Rightarrow H_1$ via p_1, then it is possible to apply p_2 also to G.

3.9.2 Theorem (weak local Church-Rosser theorem with NACs). *Given an adhesive HLR system* AHS *with NACs and two direct transformations with NACs* $H_1 \overset{p_1,m_1}{\Leftarrow} G \overset{p_2,m_2}{\Rightarrow} H_2$ *such that*

3.9. APPLICABILITY AND NON-APPLICABILITY OF RULE SEQUENCES

$G \stackrel{p_1,m_1}{\Rightarrow} H_1$ does not cause a conflict with $G \stackrel{p_2,m_2}{\Rightarrow} H_2$ (as defined in Def. 3.6.6), then there is an object G' and a direct transformation $H_1 \stackrel{p_2,m_2'}{\Rightarrow} G'$. Vice versa, given two direct transformations with NACs $G \stackrel{p_1,m_1}{\Rightarrow} H_1 \stackrel{p_2,m_2'}{\Rightarrow} G'$ such that $G \stackrel{p_1,m_1}{\Rightarrow} H_1$ is reversible after $H_1 \stackrel{p_2,m_2'}{\Rightarrow} G'$ (as defined in Def. 3.6.8), then there is an object H_2 and a direct transformation $H_2 \stackrel{p_1,m_1'}{\Rightarrow} G'$. Finally, if $H_1 \stackrel{p_2,m_2'}{\Rightarrow} G'$ is not triggered by $G \stackrel{p_1,m_1}{\Rightarrow} H_1$ (as defined in Def. 3.6.8), then there is an object H_2 and a direct transformation $G \stackrel{p_2,m_2}{\Rightarrow} H_2$.

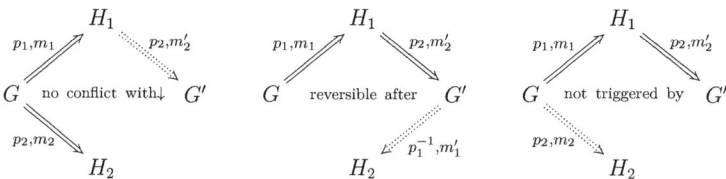

Proof. In the first case, it follows from Def. 3.6.6 that a morphism $m_2' : L_2 \to H_1$ with $m_2' \models NAC_{p_2}$ exists. By Assumption 3.9.1 we can follow that therefore, p_2 is applicable to H_1 such that $H_1 \Rightarrow G'$ can be constructed. In the second case, it follows from Def. 3.6.8 that a morphism $m_1' : R_1 \to G'$ with $m_1' \models NAC_{p_1^{-1}}$ exists. By Assumption 3.9.1 we can follow that therefore, p_1^{-1} is applicable to G' such that $G' \Rightarrow H_2$ can be constructed. In the third case, it follows from Def. 3.6.8 that a morphism $m_2 : L_1 \to G$ with $m_2 \models NAC_{p_1}$ exists. By Assumption 3.9.1 we can follow that therefore, p_1 is applicable to G such that $G \Rightarrow H_2$ can be constructed. □

Reduction of Rule Sequences Most of the reductions that follow in this section (summary reduction, repeated elements reduction, and loop reduction) reduce a rule sequence to a shorter one under specific conditions. These conditions ensure that the longer sequence is applicable if the shorter one can be shown to be applicable. These reductions together with the shift-equivalent reduction can also be used to reduce a set of rule sequences to a smaller set of rule sequences. Thereby, the applicability of each rule sequence in the original set follows from the applicability of each rule sequence in the smaller set. The reduced set of rule sequences is obtained by applying the reductions to single rule sequences in this set. Thereby, reduced rule sequences may be equal to already present rule sequences, and, therefore, the size of the original set of rule sequences may be reduced. Moreover, by applying summary reduction, repeated elements reduction, or loop reduction to single rule sequences also the length of the rule sequences may be reduced. At first, we present a reduction of rule sequences summarizing neighbored rules into concurrent rules, and show that thereby, applicability is not affected.

3.9.3 Theorem (summary reduction). *Consider $s : r_1, r_2, \ldots, r_n$, a sequence of n rules, an object G_0, and a rule sequence $s' : r_1', r_2', \ldots, r_m'$ with $m < n$ in which neighbored rules $r_i, r_{i+1}, \ldots r_{i+k}$ with $k > 0$ in s are summarized by some concurrent rule for $r_i, r_{i+1}, \ldots r_{i+k}$. If the summarized rule sequence s' is applicable to G_0 with monomorphic matching, then the original rule sequence s is applicable to G_0 with monomorphic matching and the same result.*

Proof. This follows directly from the Concurrency Theorem with NACs (Theorem 3.5.8). □

In shift-equivalent rule sequences (see Def. 3.8.15) rule r_j in s is switched with rule r_{j+1} repeatedly under the condition that the pairs of rules (r_j, r_{j+1}) and (r_{j+1}, r_j) are sequentially independent. We show in the following reduction of rule sequences that switching such pairs of sequentially independent rules does not affect applicability. Note that this is a bidirectional reduction. We then also formulate a somewhat weaker unidirectional shift reduction, where we don't require that (r_j, r_{j+1}) is sequentially independent.

3.9.4 Theorem (bidirectional shift-equivalence reduction). *Rule sequence $s : r_1, r_2, \ldots, r_n$ is applicable to object G_0 if and only if all shift-equivalent rule sequences as defined in Def. 3.8.15 are applicable to G_0 with the same result.*

Proof. This follows directly from Def. 3.8.15, the Local Church-Rosser Theorem with NACs (Theorem 3.4.3), and Def. 3.8.2. □

Analogous to Theorem 3.9.4, we can formulate the following reduction, expressing that all shift-equivalent rule sequences are *not* applicable to G_0 as soon as one of them appears to be non-applicable.

3.9.5 Corollary (bidirectional shift-equivalent reduction: non-applicability). *A rule sequence $s : r_1, r_2, \ldots, r_n$ is not applicable to object G_0 if and only if none of the shift-equivalent rule sequences as defined in Def. 3.8.15 is applicable to G_0 either.*

Proof. This is a negation of Theorem 3.9.4. □

Based on the weaker notion of shift-related rule sequences as given in Def. 3.8.16, we can formulate the following unidirectional reductions with regard to applicability (resp. non-applicability).

3.9.6 Theorem (unidirectional shift reduction). *Consider some rule sequence $s : r_1, r_2, \ldots, r_n$, start object G_0, and rule sequence s' such that s' is shift-related to s. If s' is applicable to G_0, then s is applicable to G_0.*

Proof. This follows directly from Def. 3.8.16, the Local Church-Rosser Theorem with NACs (Theorem 3.4.3), and Def. 3.8.2. □

3.9.7 Corollary (unidirectional shift reduction: non-applicability). *Consider some rule sequence $s : r_1, r_2, \ldots, r_n$, start object G_0, and rule sequence s' such that s is shift-related to s'. If s' is not applicable to G_0, then s is not applicable to G_0 either.*

Proof. This follows by contraposition from Theorem 3.9.6. □

In order to prove the correctness of some more unidirectional reductions, we introduce two lemmas. We also use these lemmas to show the correctness of the applicability criteria in Theorem 3.9.14. The first lemma describes under which conditions an existing transformation sequence can be elongated by a rule that is applicable to one of the intermediate objects in this sequence. The second lemma can be derived from the first one and describes under which conditions an applicable rule sequence can be elongated by a rule that has occurred in the rule sequence before.

3.9.8 Lemma (elongate by rule applicable to intermediate object). *Consider a transformation sequence $t : G_0 \overset{r_1}{\Rightarrow} G_1 \ldots G_{n-1} \overset{r_n}{\Rightarrow} G_n$ via the rule sequence $r_1, r_2, \ldots, r_n$. Then, r is applicable with monomorphic matching to G_n whenever r is applicable with monomorphic matching to some intermediate object G_j with $0 \leq j \leq n$ in the transformation sequence t, and each r_i with $j + 1 \leq i \leq n$ causes no conflict with r.*

3.9. APPLICABILITY AND NON-APPLICABILITY OF RULE SEQUENCES

Proof. Let G_j with $1 \leq j \leq n$ be the intermediate object in t to which r is applicable via match m. Consider now the transformation sequence $t' : G_j \Rightarrow^* G_n$ via $r_{j+1}, \ldots, r_n$ arising by cutting off the first j steps of transformation sequence t. Consider then the following diagram:

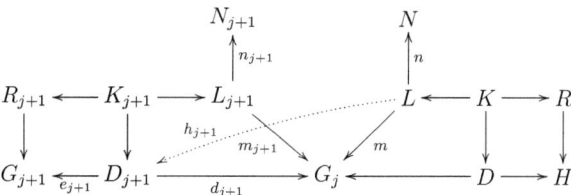

Since r_{j+1} does not cause a conflict with r, the morphism $e_{j+1} \circ h_{j+1}$ exists satisfying NAC_r. This makes r applicable with monomorphic matching (see Lemma 3.6.3) to G_{j+1} (see Theorem 3.9.2). We can iterate this argumentation up to the conclusion that r is applicable to G_n, and in the end a transformation sequence with monomorphic matching $t'' : G_0 \Rightarrow^* G_n \overset{r}{\Rightarrow} G_{n+1}$ exists via $r_1, r_2, \ldots, r_n, r$. □

3.9.9 Lemma (elongate by occurring rule). *Given a rule sequence $r_1, r_2, \ldots, r_n$ that is applicable to some G_0 with monomorphic matching, then the extended rule sequence $r_1, r_2, \ldots, r_n, r_j$ with $1 \leq j \leq n$ is applicable with monomorphic matching to G_0 if r_i with $j \leq i \leq n$ causes no conflict with r_j.*

Proof. This follows from the previous lemma because of the following argumentation. A transformation sequence $G_0 \overset{r_1}{\Rightarrow} G_1 \ldots G_{n-1} \overset{r_n}{\Rightarrow} G_n$ exists via rule sequence $r_1, r_2, \ldots, r_n$ to G_0. Rule r_j with $1 \leq j \leq n$ is applicable to the intermediate object G_{j-1} in this sequence. Moreover, by assumption each r_i with $j \leq i \leq n$ causes no conflict with r_j. Therefore, because of Lemma 3.9.8 a transformation sequence $G_0 \overset{r_1}{\Rightarrow} G_1 \ldots G_{n-1} \overset{r_n}{\Rightarrow} G_n \overset{r_j}{\Rightarrow} G_{n+1}$ exists with monomorphic matching. □

We show, on the basis of both previous lemmas, another unidirectional reduction for rule sequences in which a subsequence of identical rules occurs such that this rule does not cause any conflict with itself. The applicability of these rule sequences can be deduced from the applicability of the same rule sequence in which this subsequence is reduced to only one occurrence of the rule.

3.9.10 Theorem (repeated elements reduction). *Consider a rule sequence $s : q, r^n, q'$ consisting of a rule sequence q followed by n (with $(n > 1)$) times r followed by a rule sequence q'. Sequence s is applicable to G_0 with monomorphic matching if sequence $s' : q, r, q'$ is applicable to G_0 with monomorphic matching, and r does not cause any conflict with itself, and in addition for each r' in q' one of the following cases holds:*

- *r' is equal to some predecessor rule r'' in s' , and r'' together with all intermediate rules of r'' and r' in s' do not cause a conflict with r'*

- *r' is purely enabled as given in Def.3.8.18 by some predecessor r'' in s', and all intermediate rules of r'' and r' in s' do not cause a conflict with r'*

- *r' is applicable to the start object G_0 and all predecessor rules of r' in s' do not cause a conflict with r'.*

Proof. Rule r can be appended $n-1$ times to rule sequence $s' : q, r$ without influencing applicability to G_0 by applying $n-1$ times Lemma 3.9.9. This is because r does not cause a conflict with itself. Therefore, $s : q, r^n$ is applicable to G_0. Now we can append all rules r' of q' to q, r^n because of the following argumentation. If r' is equal to some predecessor rule r'' in s', we argue as follows: r' is then also equal to some predecessor rule r'' in s. In the case that $r'' = r$ we interpret the last occurrence of r in s as r''. Then the set of intermediate rules between r'' and r' in s' is the same as the set of intermediate rules between r'' and r' in s. Thus, we can apply Lemma 3.9.9. If r' is purely enabled by some predecessor rule r'' in s', we argue as follows: r' is then purely enabled by r'' in s as well. In the case that $r'' = r$ we interpret the last occurrence of r in s as r''. Then the set of intermediate rules between r'' and r' in s' is the same as the set of intermediate rules between r'' and r' in s. Since r' is applicable to the resulting object of its purely triggering predecessor r'', we can apply Lemma 3.9.8. If r' is applicable to G_0, we argue as follows. In particular, the intermediate object now equals G_0. Note that the set of predecessors of r' in s' is equal to the set of predecessors of r' in s. Since no predecessor rule of r' causes a conflict with r', Lemma 3.9.8 can be applied. □

It is not only possible to reduce repeated elements of some sequence, but also to reduce repeated subsequences. We call this reduction loop reduction, since the loop body should be repeated only once. Note that the loop body is fixed i.e. some subsequence is repeated identically. For this loop reduction in addition to the repeated elements reduction the rules belonging to the loop body should be pairwise parallel independent.

3.9.11 Theorem (loop reduction). *Consider a rule sequence $s : q, (r_1, r_2, \ldots, r_m)^n, q'$ consisting of a rule sequence q followed by n (with $(n > 1)$) times sequence $r_1, r_2, \ldots, r_m$ followed by a rule sequence q'. Sequence s is applicable to G_0 with monomorphic matching if sequence $s' : q, r_1, r_2, \ldots, r_m, q'$ is applicable to G_0 with monomorphic matching, and r_i and r_j are parallel independent for $1 \leq i, j \leq m$, and in addition for each r' in q' belonging to s' one of the following cases holds:*

- *r' is equal to some predecessor rule r'' in s', and r'' together with all intermediate rules of r'' and r' in s' do not cause a conflict with r'*

- *r' is purely enabled as given in Def. 3.8.18 by some predecessor r'' in s', and all intermediate rules of r'' and r' in s' do not cause a conflict with r'*

- *r' is applicable to the start object G_0 and all predecessor rules of r' in s' do not cause a conflict with r'.*

Proof. By assumption we know that $q, r_1, r_2, \ldots, r_m$ is applicable. Because of the Synthesis part of Theorem 3.5.8, we have then that also q, r is applicable with r some concurrent rule of $r_1, r_2, \ldots, r_m$. Recall that in Corollary 3.8.23 it is stated that a set of parallel independent rules leads to parallel independent concurrent rules. Thus, in this case r does not cause any conflict with r. Now consider rule sequence q, r^n. Because of Theorem 3.9.10, it holds that q, r^n is applicable if q, r is. Thus, we have that q, r^n is applicable and by Theorem 3.9.3 we can conclude that $q, (r_1, r_2, \ldots, r_m)^n$ is applicable as well. Now by an analogous argumentation as in Theorem 3.9.10 we can conclude that also the longer sequence $q, (r_1, r_2, \ldots, r_m)^n, q'$ is applicable. □

3.9.12 Remark. Note that the repeated elements reduction is a special case of the loop reduction.

3.9. APPLICABILITY AND NON-APPLICABILITY OF RULE SEQUENCES

Applicability Criteria Let $s : r_1, r_2, \ldots, r_n$ be a sequence of n rules and G_0 an object on which this sequence should be applied. The criteria defined in the following definition guarantee this applicability. Note that these criteria are sufficient, but not necessary. The reductions presented in the previous section can help if the criteria appear to be not sufficient enough. The *initialization* criterion is trivial since it just requires the first rule being applicable to G_0. The *no impeding predecessors* criterion ensures that the applicability of a rule r_i is not impeded by one of the predecessor rules r_j of r_i. Criterion *pure enabling predecessor* will be satisfied if rule r_i is purely enabled by some predecessor rule r_j in the sequence s. In this case r_j triggers the applicability of r_i regardless of what is present already in the start object G_0. The *not-needed enabling predecessor criterion* applies to rules that are already applicable to the start object G_0, and do not need to be triggered by some predecessor rule. The correctness of the criteria is proven in Theorem 3.9.14.

3.9.13 Definition (applicability criteria). Given a sequence $s : r_1, r_2, \ldots, r_n$ of n rules and an object G_0, then we define the following applicability criteria for s on G_0:

initialization r_1 is applicable to G_0 via some monomorphic match $m_1 : L_1 \to G_0$

no impeding predecessors $\forall r_i, r_j$ in s with $1 \leq j < i \leq n$, r_j does not cause a conflict with r_i

enabling predecessor $\forall r_i$ in s with $1 < i \leq n$ one of the following cases holds

    pure there exists a rule r_j in s with $1 \leq j < i \leq n$ and r_i is purely enabled by r_j, which especially means that r_i has no NACs

    not needed rule r_i itself is applicable to G_0 via some monomorphic match. We say that r_i is *self-enabled*.

3.9.14 Theorem (correctness of applicability criteria). *Consider $s : r_1, r_2, \ldots r_n$ a sequence of n rules and an object G_0. If the criteria in Def. 3.9.13 are satisfied for rule sequence s and object G_0, then this rule sequence is applicable to G_0 with monomorphic matching i.e. there exists a transformation $G_0 \overset{r_1}{\Rightarrow} G_1 \ldots G_{n-1} \overset{r_n}{\Rightarrow} G_n$ with monomorphic matching.*

Proof. Note that because of Assumption 3.9.1 it is always possible to construct the pushout complement of $G \overset{m}{\leftarrow} L \overset{l}{\leftarrow} K$ with m a monomorphic match and l the left-hand-side rule morphism. This means in particular that as soon as a match m is found for a rule r into an object G, this rule is applicable to G if the NAC is satisfied. Now we prove this theorem by induction over the number of rules in the rule sequence s.

- **(Basis.** $n = 1$) Criterion 1 ensures that a monomorphic match $m_1 : L_1 \to G_0$ exists. The fact that the gluing condition is always satisfied and m_1 satisfies NAC_{r_1} allows us to construct, therefore, the direct transformation $G_0 \overset{m_1}{\Rightarrow} G_1$.

- **(Induction Step.)** Consider the transformation $G_0 \overset{r_1}{\Rightarrow} G_1 \ldots \overset{r_{n-1}}{\Rightarrow} G_{n-1}$. We are now looking for a monomorphic match $m_n : L_n \to G_{n-1}$ such that also the direct transformation $G_{n-1} \overset{r_n}{\Rightarrow} G_n$ exists. We have the following two cases.

    – Rule r_n is purely enabled by some predecessor rule r_j in s such that $1 \leq j < n$ and r_n. This means that r_n does not have any NACs, and we have a monomorphic morphism

$l_{n,j} : L_n \to R_j$ according to Def. 3.8.18. Consider now the comatch $m'_j : R_j \to G_j$ of the direct transformation $G_{j-1} \stackrel{r_j}{\Rightarrow} G_j$ and the composition of morphisms $m'_j \circ l_{n,j}$. This is a monomorphic match $m'_j \circ l_{n,j} : L_n \to G_j$ for rule r_n into G_j. Thus, we can apply Lemma 3.9.8 because of the impeding predecessor criterion and conclude that the direct transformation $G_n \stackrel{r_n}{\Rightarrow} G_{n+1}$ exists.

– Rule r_n is applicable to G_0 via a monomorphic match m_n. We know because of the impeding predecessor criterion in Def. 3.9.13 that each rule r_j in the sequence s with $j < n$ does not cause any conflict with r_n. Therefore, we can apply Lemma 3.9.8, and it follows that transformation $G_n \stackrel{r_n}{\Rightarrow} G_{n+1}$ exists with monomorphic matching.

□

The pure enabling predecessor criterion is only sufficient for the case that some rule r does not need anything from the start object G_0 for example. The more general criterion *direct enabling predecessor* ensures the applicability of a rule r_i causally dependent on a direct predecessor rule together with the start object G_0. This is expressed by the fact that a concurrent rule r_c of r_{i-1} and r_i exists that is applicable to the start object G_0. The construction of a concurrent rule with NACs is explained in Section 3.5. The correctness of this new criterion can be shown by using the summary reduction introduced in the previous section.

3.9.15 Definition (direct enabling predecessor criterion). Consider a sequence $s : r_1, r_2, \ldots, r_n$ of n rules and an object G_0. Then we define the *direct enabling predecessor criterion* for s on G_0 as follows:

direct there exists a concurrent rule r_c of r_{i-1} and r_i such that r_c is applicable via some monomorphic match on G_0 and r_j does not cause a conflict with r_c for $j < (i-1)$. We say that r_i is *directly enabled*.

3.9.16 Theorem (direct enabling predecessor criterion). *Theorem 3.9.14 (correctness of applicability criteria) still holds if the enabling predecessor criterion in Def. 3.9.13 is extended by the direct enabling predecessor criterion as given in Def. 3.9.15. Thus, a rule can be also directly enabled in order to fulfill the enabling predecessor criterion.*

Proof. We prove the correctness of this criterion by induction. Suppose that $r_1, r_2, \ldots, r_{n-1}$ is applicable. We can apply the summary reduction (see Theorem 3.9.3) to $s : r_1, r_2, \ldots, r_{n-1}, r_n$, and consider $s' : r_1, r_2, \ldots, r_c$. If we can prove the applicability of s', also s is applicable. By assumption r_c is applicable to G_0, and thus, is self-enabled. Moreover, all predecessors of r_c are non-impeding. Therefore, s' is applicable, and thus, also s. □

3.9.17 Remark. Please note that r_c can be matched to G_0 in a different way as r_{n-1} was related to G_0 during the checking procedure of the applicability criteria. Thus, the last step in the transformation sequence that arose for rule sequence $r_1 \ldots r_{n-1}$ can be overwritten when checking the criteria for rule r_n. This is avoided by Def. 3.9.20 of forwarded concurrent matches.

3.9.18 Definition (multiple direct enabling predecessors criterion). Consider a sequence $s : r_1, r_2, \ldots, r_n$ of n rules and an object G_0. Then we define the *multiple direct enabling predecessors criterion* for s on G_0 as follows:

3.9. APPLICABILITY AND NON-APPLICABILITY OF RULE SEQUENCES

multiple direct there exists a concurrent rule r_c of r'_c and r_i such that r'_c is a concurrent rule of $r_{i-k}, r_{i-k+1}, \ldots, r_{i-1}$ with $k > 1$, r_c is applicable via some monomorphic match on G_0 and r_j does not cause a conflict with r_c for $j < (i - k)$. We say that r_i is *multiple directly enabled*.

3.9.19 Theorem (multiple direct enabling predecessors criterion). *Theorem 3.9.14 (correctness of applicability criteria) still holds if the enabling predecessor criterion in Def. 3.9.13 is extended by the multiple direct enabling predecessors criterion as given in Def. 3.9.15. Thus, a rule can be also multiple directly enabled to fulfill the enabling predecessor criterion.*

Proof. This follows directly by the summary reduction (see Theorem 3.9.3) and the correctness of the direct enabling predecessor criterion. □

The following definition of forwarded concurrent match ensures that when matching a rule (resp. concurrent rule) to some object G_0 the same match is continued to use when extending it to a concurrent (resp. longer concurrent) rule.

3.9.20 Definition (forwarded concurrent match).
Consider a concurrent rule $r_c = r'_c *_E r_n$ of a sequence of rules $r_0, \ldots, r_n$ as defined in Def. 3.5.1 and matches $m_c : L_c \to G_0$ and $m'_c : L'_c \to G_0$ from the LHS of r_c (resp. r'_c) into G_0. Let l_c be the lhs-match of r_c. Then, we say that m'_c is *forwarded* to m_c if $m_c \circ l_c = m'_c$ as shown on the right. We say that m_c is a forwarded concurrent match.

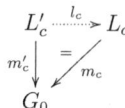

We can formulate yet another enabling predecessor criterion for the case that the enabling predecessor is not direct.

3.9.21 Definition (partial enabling predecessor criterion). Consider a sequence $s : r_1, r_2, \ldots, r_n$ of n rules and an object G_0. Then we define the *partial enabling predecessor criterion* for s on G_0 as follows:

partial there exists a concurrent rule $r_c = r_j *_E r_i$ of rule r_i and a not necessarily direct predecessor rule r_j with $1 \leq j < i$ such that r_c is applicable via some monomorphic match m_{r_c} to G_0. Moreover, all predecessors r_k with $1 \leq k < j$ of r_c do not cause a conflict with r_c. In addition the following *forward condition* should hold: r_j was self-enabled via some m_{r_j} such that m_{r_j} is forwarded to m_{r_c} as in Def. 3.9.20. We say that r_i is *partially enabled* by r_j via r_c and m_{r_c}.

3.9.22 Remark. Please note that the differences of the partial enabling predecessor criterion with the direct enabling predecessor criterion in Def. 3.9.13 is that the enabling predecessor does not need to be direct, but in return fulfills the *forward condition*. Moreover, note that if r_i fulfills the partial enabling predecessor criterion without any intermediate rule between r_i and r_j (i.e. $j = i - 1$), then r_i is *directly enabled*.

3.9.23 Theorem (partial enabling predecessor criterion). *Theorem 3.9.14 (correctness of applicability criteria) still holds if the enabling predecessor criterion in Def. 3.9.13 is extended by the partial enabling predecessor criterion as given in Def. 3.9.21. Thus, a rule can be also partially enabled in order to fulfill the enabling predecessor criterion.*

Proof. We show again as in Theorem 3.9.14 by induction that $s : r_1, \ldots, r_{n-1}, r_n$ is applicable to G_0. The induction hypothesis says that some transformation $t : G_0 \overset{r_1}{\Rightarrow} G_1 \ldots \overset{r_{n-1}}{\Rightarrow} G_{n-1}$ exists. We are looking for a monomorphic match $m_n : L_n \to G_{n-1}$ such that also the direct transformation $G_{n-1} \overset{r_n}{\Rightarrow} G_n$ exists. By assumption there exists a concurrent rule r_c of r_j and r_n with $1 \leq j < n$ such that r_c is applicable to G_0. Moreover, each predecessor of r_c does not cause any conflict with r_c. Consider the following diagram:

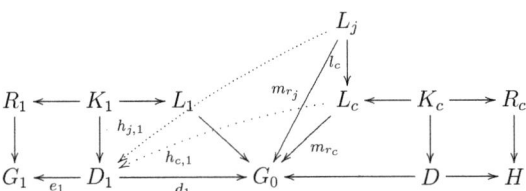

By assumption r_j is self-enabled, and the forward condition states that $m_{r_j} = m_{r_c} \circ l_c$ with $r_c = r_j * r_n$. We know that Lemma 3.9.8 was used in order to derive from m_{r_j} also matches of rule r_j into $G_1, G_2, \ldots, G_{j-1}$. First we prove that these derived matches of r_j can be forwarded to matches of r_c. The match of r_j into G_1 equals $e_1 \circ h_{j,1}$ of L_j into G_1 as depicted above with $d_1 \circ h_{j,1} = m_{r_j}$. Since by assumption r_1 does not cause any conflict with r_c either, analogously, we can derive because of Lemma 3.9.8 a match of L_c into G_1, which is equal to $e_1 \circ h_{c,1}$, such that $d_1 \circ h_{c,1} = m_{r_c}$. We now prove that match $e_1 \circ h_{j,1}$ is forwarded to $e_1 \circ h_{c,1}$ i.e. $e_1 \circ h_{j,1} = e_1 \circ h_{c,1} \circ l_c$. This is true if we can prove that $h_{j,1} = h_{c,1} \circ l_c$. Because of Lemma 3.6.3, it holds that $h_{j,1}$ is a unique morphism such that $d_1 \circ h_{j,1} = m_{r_j}$. Now also $d_1 \circ h_{c,1} \circ l_c = m_{r_j}$. This is because $m_{r_j} = m_{r_c} \circ l_c$ (forward condition) and $m_{r_c} = d_1 \circ h_{c,1}$. Thus, it holds that $h_{j,1} = h_{c,1} \circ l_c$. Continuing this argumentation iteratively, it follows that the derived match $m_j : L_j \to G_{j-1}$ is forwarded to $m_{c,j-1} : L_c \to G_{j-1}$ as depicted in the diagram on the right.

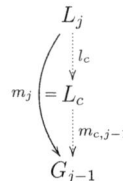

Thereafter, it follows that $G_0 \overset{r_1}{\Rightarrow} G_1 \ldots G_{j-1} \overset{r_c, m_{c,j-1}}{\Rightarrow} G'_n$ exists such that $G_{j-1} \overset{r_c, m_{c,j-1}}{\Rightarrow} G'_n$ can be decomposed into $G_{j-1} \overset{r_j, m_j}{\Rightarrow} G_j \overset{r_n, m_n}{\Rightarrow} G'_n$ because of the Concurrency Theorem with NACs (see Theorem 3.5.8). Now we know that $t : G_0 \overset{r_1}{\Rightarrow} G_1 \ldots \overset{r_{n-1}}{\Rightarrow} G_{n-1}$ exists. Since we have just shown that r_n is applicable to G_j, then by Lemma 3.9.8 we can conclude that also $G_{n-1} \overset{r_n}{\Rightarrow} G_n$ exists. □

From the applicability criteria for a rule sequence, we can deduce some specific conditions under which a rule of a conflict-free grammar is always applicable. This leads in addition to a sufficient and necessary condition for non-termination of conflict-free grammars.

3.9.24 Corollary (necessary and sufficient condition for rule applicability in (resp. non-termination of) conflict-free grammar). *Consider a conflict-free (according to Def. 3.7.11) adhesive HLR grammar with NACs* $AHG = (AHS, S) = (\mathbf{C}, \mathcal{M}, \mathcal{M}', \mathcal{E}', \mathcal{Q}, P, S)$ *with start object* S. *Rule* p *in* P *is applicable to each object belonging to* $\mathcal{L}(AHG)$ *if and only if* p *is applicable to the start object* S. *In particular, this means that a conflict-free grammar* (AHS, S) *is non-terminating if and only if at least one rule* p *in* P *is applicable to the start object* S.

Proof. This follows directly from Theorem 3.9.14. □

3.9. APPLICABILITY AND NON-APPLICABILITY OF RULE SEQUENCES

If in a regular grammar no rule causes a conflict with some rule p, then p is always applicable if and only if it was applicable to the start object. Therefrom we can deduce another sufficient condition for non-termination of grammars.

3.9.25 Corollary (necessary and sufficient (resp. sufficient) condition for rule applicability in (resp. non-termination of) grammar). *Consider an adhesive HLR grammar with NACs* AHG $= (\text{AHS}, S) = (\boldsymbol{C}, \mathcal{M}, \mathcal{M}', \mathcal{E}', \mathcal{Q}, P, S)$ *with start object S such that each rule in P does not cause any conflict according to Def. 3.8.10 with some particular rule p in P. Rule p is applicable to each object belonging to $\mathcal{L}(\text{AHG})$ if and only if it is applicable to the start object S. In particular, this means that a grammar (AHS, S) is non-terminating as soon as at least one rule p in P is applicable to the start object S such that p does not cause any conflict with itself.*

Proof. The first fact follows directly from Theorem 3.9.14. If, in particular, p is applicable to the start object S, we have the following non-terminating transformation sequence $S \stackrel{p}{\Rightarrow} S' \stackrel{p}{\Rightarrow} S'' \ldots$. □

Non-Applicability Criteria Let $s : r_1, r_2, \ldots, r_n$ be a sequence of n rules and G_0 an object. The satisfaction of the following criteria for s and G_0 guarantee that s will not be applicable to G_0. The *initialization error* is trivial since it just requires the first rule being non-applicable to G_0. Criterion *no enabling predecessor* checks if predecessors for a rule r_i, which is not applicable already on G_0, are present in the sequence that can trigger the applicability of r_i.

3.9.26 Definition (non-applicability criteria). Consider $s : r_1, r_2, \ldots, r_n$ a sequence of n rules and an object G_0. Then we define the following non-applicability criteria for s on G_0:

initialization error r_1 is not applicable to G_0

no enabling predecessor $\exists r_i$ in s with $1 < i \leq n$ such that r_i is not applicable to G_0 and for all rules r_j in s with $1 \leq j < i \leq n$, r_i is not triggered by r_j.

3.9.27 Theorem (correctness of non-applicability criteria). *Consider a sequence $s : r_1, r_2, \ldots, r_n$ of n rules and an object G_0. If the initialization error or no enabling predecessor criterion in Def. 3.9.26 is satisfied for rule sequence s and object G_0, then this rule sequence is not applicable to G_0 i.e. there exists no transformation $G_0 \stackrel{r_1}{\Rightarrow} G_1 \ldots G_{n-1} \stackrel{r_n}{\Rightarrow} G_n$.*

Proof.
- If the initialization error criterion 1 in Def. 3.9.26 is satisfied, then it is obvious that a transformation sequence cannot exist.

- If the no enabling predecessor criterion in Def. 3.9.26 is satisfied, then $\exists r_i$ in s with $1 < i \leq n$ such that there does not exist a match into G_0 satisfying NAC_{r_i} and for all rules r_j in s with $1 \leq j < i \leq n$, r_i is not triggered by r_j. Suppose that a transformation $G_0 \stackrel{r_1}{\Rightarrow} G_1 \ldots G_{n-1} \stackrel{r_n}{\Rightarrow} G_n$ exists. Then we have the following diagram:

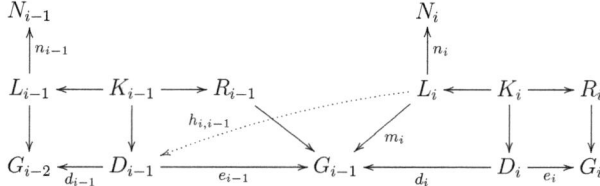

Because of the assumption and Def. 3.8.11, we know that $h_{i,i-1}$ exists such that $e_{i-1} \circ h_{i,i-1} = m_i$ and $d_{i-1} \circ h_{i,i-1} \models NAC_{r_i}$. Therefore, we can now construct the following diagram:

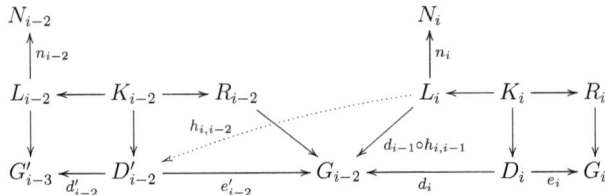

Again because of the assumption and Def. 3.8.11 we know that $h_{i,i-2}$ exists such that $e'_{i-2} \circ h_{i,i-2} = d_{i-1} \circ h_{i,i-1}$ and $d'_{i-2} \circ h_{i,i-2} \models NAC_{r_i}$. Iteratively, in the end we will find a match $m \models NAC_{r_i} : L_i \to G_0$ and this is a contradiction. Therefore, a transformation $G_0 \overset{r_1}{\Rightarrow} G_1 \ldots G_{n-1} \overset{r_n}{\Rightarrow} G_n$ cannot exist. □

From the non-applicability criteria for a rule sequence, we can deduce some sufficient and necessary condition under which a rule of a dependency-free grammar is never applicable. This leads in addition to a sufficient condition for rules to be superfluous in a dependency-free grammar.

3.9.28 Corollary (necessary and sufficient (resp. sufficient) condition for rule non-applicability (resp. superfluity) in dependency-free grammar). *Consider a dependency-free (according to Def. 3.7.13) adhesive HLR grammar with NACs AHG = (AHS, S) = ($\boldsymbol{C}, \mathcal{M}, \mathcal{M}', \mathcal{E}', \mathcal{Q}, P, S$) with start object S. Rule p in P is not applicable to the start object S if and only if it is not applicable to any object belonging to $\mathcal{L}(AHG)$. If rule p in P is not applicable to the start object S, then $\mathcal{L}(AHG) = \mathcal{L}(AHG')$ where AHG' is AHG with a new set of rules $P' = P \setminus \{p\}$.*

Proof. This follows directly from Theorem 3.9.27. □

3.9.29 Corollary (necessary and sufficient (resp. sufficient) condition for rule non-applicability (resp. superfluity) in grammar). *Consider an adhesive HLR grammar with NACs AHG = (AHS, S) = ($\boldsymbol{C}, \mathcal{M}, \mathcal{M}', \mathcal{E}', \mathcal{Q}, P, S$) with start object S such that p cannot be triggered by any rule in $P \setminus \{p\}$. Rule p in P is not applicable to the start object S if and only if it is not applicable to any object belonging to $\mathcal{L}(AHG)$. If rule p in P is not applicable to the start object S, then $\mathcal{L}(AHG) = \mathcal{L}(AHG')$ where AHG' is AHG with a new set of rules $P' = P \setminus \{p\}$.*

Proof. This follows directly from Theorem 3.9.27. □

3.10 Embedding and Confluence

In Section 3.5 we have defined the concurrent rule p_c with NACs (resp. match g_c) induced by a transformation t. We need this definition in order to define NAC consistency, which is an extra condition needed on top of boundary consistency to generalize the Embedding and Extension Theorem to transformations with NACs. Having generalized the notion of critical pairs, completeness, embedding and extension to transformations with NACs, it is now possible

3.10. EMBEDDING AND CONFLUENCE

to formulate a sufficient condition on the critical pairs with NACs in order to obtain local confluence of an adhesive HLR system with NACs, i.e. to formulate the Critical Pair Lemma with NACs.

We start, however, with the definition of NAC consistency for an extension morphism k_0 w.r.t. a transformation t. It expresses that the extended concurrent match induced by t should fulfill the concurrent NAC induced by t.

3.10.1 Definition (NAC consistency). A morphism $k_0 : G_0 \to G'_0$ is called NAC consistent w.r.t. a transformation $t : G_0 \Rightarrow^* G_n$ if $k_0 \circ g_c \models NAC_{p_c}$ with NAC_{p_c} the *concurrent NAC* and g_c the *concurrent match induced by t*.

The Embedding Theorem for rules with NACs requires as extra condition on the extension morphism k_0 NAC consistency. Note the following renaming in order to be able to distinguish better NAC consistency from the consistency needed for the Embedding Theorem without NACs. In the following we speak about *boundary consistency* when we mean *consistency* as in Def. 6.12 of [29]. For readability reasons we reintroduce the definition of boundary consistency. Intuitively, it means that the boundary object B of the extension morphism k_0 is preserved by the transformation t.

3.10.2 Definition (boundary consistency). Given a transformation $t : G_0 \stackrel{*}{\Rightarrow} G_n$ with a derived span $der(t) = (G_0 \stackrel{d_0}{\leftarrow} D \stackrel{d_n}{\to} G_n)$ (see Def. 6.9 in [29]), a morphism $k_0 : G_0 \to G'_0$ is called *boundary consistent* with respect to t if there exist an initial pushout (1) (see Def. 3.2.5) over k_0 and a morphism $b \in \mathcal{M}$ with $d_0 \circ b = b_0$:

$$B \xrightarrow{b_0} G_0 \xleftarrow{d_0} D \xrightarrow{d_n} G_n$$
$$\downarrow \quad (1) \quad \downarrow k_0$$
$$C \longrightarrow G'_0$$

3.10.3 Theorem (embedding theorem with NACs). *Consider a transformation $t : G_0 \Rightarrow^n G_n$ with NACs. If $k_0 : G_0 \to G'_0$ is boundary consistent and NAC consistent w.r.t. t, then there exists an extension diagram with NACs over t and k_0.*

Proof. We prove this theorem by induction over the number of direct transformation steps n.

Basis. n=1. Consider a direct transformation $t : G_0 \stackrel{p_0, g_0}{\Rightarrow} G_1$ via match $g_0 : L_0 \to G_0$ and rule $p_0 : L_0 \leftarrow K_0 \to R_0$ with NAC_{p_0} and extension morphism $k_0 : G_0 \to G'_0$. Because of NAC consistency, $k_0 \circ g_0 \models NAC_{L_0}$. This means that the extension diagram over k_0 and t without NACs as described in Theorem 6.14 in [29] is also an extension diagram over k_0 and t with NACs.

Induction Step. Consider $t : G_0 \Rightarrow^n G_n \stackrel{p_n, g_n}{\Rightarrow} G_{n+1}$ via the rules $p_0, p_1 \ldots, p_n$. Let $p'_c : L'_c \leftarrow K'_c \to R'_c$ (resp. $g'_c : L'_c \to G_0$, $h'_c : R'_c \to G_n$) be the concurrent rule with NACs (resp. concurrent match, comatch) induced by $G_0 \Rightarrow^n G_n$. The induction hypothesis says that there exists an extension diagram with NACs over $t' : G_0 \Rightarrow G_n$ and $k_0 : G_0 \to G'_0$. In particular, this means that $k_0 \circ g_0 \models NAC_{L_0}, k_1 \circ g_1 \models NAC_{L_1}, \ldots, k_{n-1} \circ g_{n-1} \models NAC_{L_{n-1}}$, i.e. each extended match of the extension diagram satisfies the NACs on the corresponding rule. Moreover, let $G'_0 \leftarrow D'_n \to G'_n$ be the derived span of the extension diagram $G'_0 \Rightarrow^n G'_n$ over t and k_0. In the proof of Theorem 6.14 in [29] it is described how to obtain an extension diagram without NACs over $t : G_0 \Rightarrow^n G_n \Rightarrow G_{n+1}$ and $k_0 : G_0 \to G'_0$. The same construction can be made since k_0 is boundary consistent. Now we still have to prove that the last extended match $k_n \circ g_n$ of the extension diagram without NACs satisfies the set of NACs on the last rule p_n of the transformation sequence. Let $((e'_c, e_n), h)$ be the $\mathcal{E}' - \mathcal{M}'$ pair factorization of the comatch h'_c of $G_0 \stackrel{p'_c}{\Rightarrow} G_n$ and match g_n of $G_n \Rightarrow G_{n+1}$. PO-PB decomposition, PO composition and decomposition lead to the diagram below as described in Fact 5.29 in [29] in which (1) is a pullback and all other squares are pushouts:

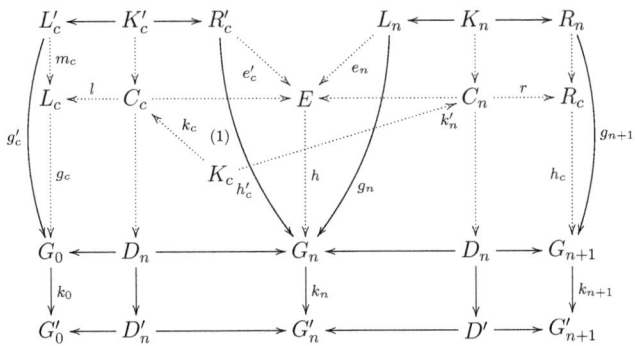

The *concurrent rule p_c with NACs* (resp. concurrent match, comatch) induced by $G_0 \Rightarrow^{n+1} G_{n+1}$ is $p_c = L_c \stackrel{l \circ k_c}{\leftarrow} K_c \stackrel{r \circ k'_n}{\to} R_c$ ($g_c : L_c \to G_0$, $h_c : R_c \to G_{n+1}$). Thereby, NAC_{p_c} is $NAC_{p_c} = DL_{p_c}(NAC_{L_n}) \cup D_{m_c}(NAC_{L'_c})$ and $G_0 \stackrel{p_c, g_c}{\Rightarrow} G_n$. Because of NAC consistency of k_0, we know that $k_0 \circ g_c \models NAC_{p_c} = DL_{p_c}(NAC_{L_n}) \cup D_{m_c}(NAC_{L'_c})$. Now because of Lemma 3.3.13 and Lemma 3.3.7, the fact that $k_0 \circ g_c \circ m_c = k_0 \circ g'_c$, $k_n \circ h \circ e_n = k_n \circ g_n$, and (5)-(8) are POs along $\mathcal{M}$ it follows that $k_n \circ g_n \models NAC_{L_n}$, and thus, we have an extension diagram with NACs over t and k_0.

$\square$

The following Extension Theorem with NACs describes the fact that boundary and NAC consistency are not only sufficient, but also necessary conditions for the construction of extension diagrams for transformations with NACs.

3.10.4 Theorem (extension theorem with NACs). *Given a transformation $t : G_0 \Rightarrow^n G_n$ with NACs with a derived span $der(t) = (G_0 \stackrel{d_0}{\leftarrow} D_n \stackrel{d_n}{\to} G_n)$ and an extension diagram (1) as in the following picture:*

$$\begin{array}{ccccc} B & \stackrel{b_0}{\longrightarrow} & G_0 & \stackrel{t}{\Longrightarrow}^* & G_n \\ \downarrow & (2)\ k_0 \downarrow & (1) & & \downarrow k_n \\ C & \longrightarrow & G'_0 & \stackrel{t'}{\Longrightarrow}^* & G'_n \end{array}$$

then

- $k_0 : G_0 \to G'_0$ *is boundary consistent w.r.t. t, with the morphism $b : B \to D_n$.*

- $k_0 : G_0 \to G'_0$ *is NAC consistent w.r.t. t.*

3.10. EMBEDDING AND CONFLUENCE

- Let $p_c : L_c \leftarrow K_c \rightarrow R_c$ (resp. $g_c : L_c \rightarrow G_0$) be the concurrent rule with NAC_{p_c} (resp. concurrent match) induced by t. There is a direct transformation $G'_0 \Rightarrow G'_n$ via $der(t)$ with $NAC_{der(t)} = D_{g_c}(NAC_{p_c})$ and match k_0 given by pushouts (3) and (4) with $h, k_n \in \mathcal{M}'$.

- There are initial pushouts (5) and (6) over $h \in \mathcal{M}'$ and $k_n \in \mathcal{M}'$, respectively, with the same boundary-context morphism $B \rightarrow C$.

$$G_0 \xleftarrow{d_0} D_n \xrightarrow{d_n} G_n \qquad B \xrightarrow{b} D_n \qquad B \xrightarrow{d_n \circ b} G_n$$
$$\downarrow k_0 \quad (3) \quad \downarrow h \quad (4) \quad \downarrow k_n \qquad \downarrow \quad (5) \quad \downarrow h \qquad \downarrow \quad (6) \quad \downarrow k_n$$
$$G'_0 \leftarrow D'_n \rightarrow G'_n \qquad C \rightarrow D'_n \qquad C \rightarrow G'_n$$

Proof.
- See proof of item 1 in Theorem 6.16 in [29].

- We should prove that $k_0 \circ g_c$ with g_c the concurrent match induced by t satisfies NAC_{p_c} the concurrent NAC on the concurrent rule p_c induced by t. We prove this by induction over the number of direct transformation steps n.

  Basis. $n=1$. Consider the extension diagram over the direct transformation $t : G_0 \overset{p_0,g_0}{\Rightarrow} G_1$ (via match $g_0 : L_0 \rightarrow G_0$ and rule $p_0 : L_0 \leftarrow K_0 \rightarrow R_0$ with NAC_{p_0}) and extension morphism $k_0 : G_0 \rightarrow G'_0$. Because of Def. 3.7.4, $k_0 \circ g_0 \models NAC_{L_0}$, and therefore, k_0 is NAC consistent w.r.t. t.

  Induction Step. Consider the extension diagram over $t : G_0 \Rightarrow^n G_n \overset{p_n, m_n}{\Rightarrow} G_{n+1}$ (via the rules $p_0, p_1 \ldots, p_n$ with NACs) and the extension morphism $k_0 : G_0 \rightarrow G'_0$. Let $p'_c : L'_c \leftarrow K'_c \rightarrow R'_c$ (resp. $g'_c : L'_c \rightarrow G_0$, $h'_c : R'_c \rightarrow G_n$) be the concurrent rule with NACs (resp. concurrent match, comatch) induced by $G_0 \Rightarrow^n G_n$. The induction hypothesis says that k_0 is NAC consistent w.r.t. $t' : G_0 \Rightarrow^n G_n$. In particular, this means that $k_0 \circ g'_c$ satisfies $NAC_{p'_c}$. We should now prove that also $k_0 \circ g_c$ satisfies $NAC_{p_c} = DL_{p_c}(NAC_{L_n}) \cup D_{m_c}(NAC_{L'_c})$ the concurrent NAC on the concurrent rule p_c induced by t. Because of Lemma 3.3.13 and the induction hypothesis, we have that $k_0 \circ g_c \models D_{m_c}(NAC_{L'_c}) = D_{m_c}(NAC_{p'_c})$. Because of Def. 3.7.4 $k_n \circ g_n \models NAC_{L_n}$ and because of Lemma 3.3.13 and Lemma 3.3.7 therefore, $k_0 \circ g_c \models DL_{p_c}(NAC_{L_n})$.

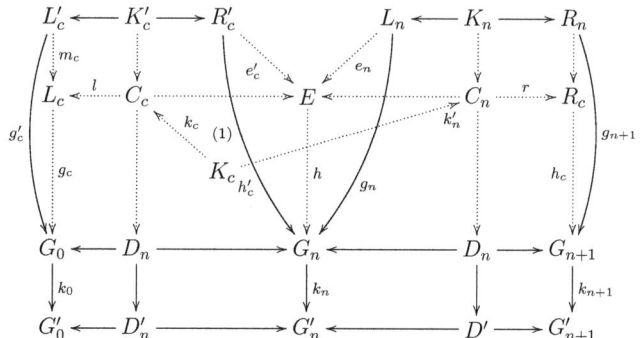

- In item 2 in Theorem 6.16 in [29] it is proven that there is a direct transformation $G'_0 \Rightarrow G'_n$ without NACs via $der(t)$ and k_0 given by the pushouts (3) and (4) with $h, k_n \in \mathcal{M}'$. So we still have to prove that $k_0 \models NAC_{der(t)} = D_{g_c}(NAC_{p_c})$. This follows because of Lemma 3.3.13 and the fact that $k_0 \circ g_c \models NAC_{p_c}$ as proven in the former item.

- See proof of item 3 in Theorem 6.16 in [29].

□

For the Critical Pair Lemma with NACs we need a stronger condition as in the case without NACs in order to obtain local confluence of the adhesive HLR system. In addition to strict confluence of the set of critical pairs we also need NAC confluence. If a critical pair is strictly confluent via some transformations t_1 and t_2, we call t_1 and t_2 a *strict solution* of the critical pair. NAC confluence of a critical pair expresses that the NAC consistency of an extension morphism w.r.t. a strict solution of the critical pair follows from the NAC consistency of the extension morphism w.r.t. the critical pair itself.

We reintroduce the definition of strict confluence first.

3.10.5 Definition (strict confluence of critical pairs). A critical pair $P_1 \overset{p_1,g_1}{\Longleftarrow} K \overset{p_2,g_2}{\Longrightarrow} P_2$ is called *strictly confluent* if we have the following:

Confluence The critical pair is confluent, i.e. there are transformations $P_1 \overset{*}{\Rightarrow} K'$, $P_2 \overset{*}{\Rightarrow} K'$ with derived spans $der(P_i \overset{*}{\Rightarrow} K') = (P_i \overset{v_{i+2}}{\Longleftarrow} N_{i+2} \overset{w_{i+2}}{\Longrightarrow} K')$ for $i = 1, 2$.

Strictness Let $der(K \overset{p_i,o_i}{\Longrightarrow} P_i) = (K \overset{v_i}{\Longleftarrow} N_i \overset{w_i}{\Longrightarrow} P_i)$ for $i = 1, 2$, and let N be the pullback object of the pullback (1). Then, there are morphisms z_3 and z_4 such that (2),(3), and (4) commute:

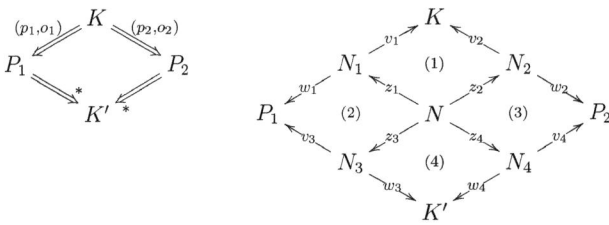

3.10.6 Definition (strictly NAC confluent). A critical pair $P_1 \overset{p_1,g_1}{\Longleftarrow} K \overset{p_2,g_2}{\Longrightarrow} P_2$ is *strictly NAC confluent* if and only if

- it is *strictly confluent* via some transformations $t_1 : K \overset{p_1,g_1}{\Longrightarrow} P_1 \Rightarrow^* X$ and $t_2 : K \overset{p_2,g_2}{\Longrightarrow} P_2 \Rightarrow^* X$

- and it is *NAC confluent for t_1 and t_2*, i.e. for every morphism $k_0 : K \to G \in \mathcal{M}'$ which is NAC consistent w.r.t. $K \overset{p_1,g_1}{\Longrightarrow} P_1$ and $K \overset{p_2,g_2}{\Longrightarrow} P_2$ it follows that k_0 is NAC consistent w.r.t.

t_1 and t_2.

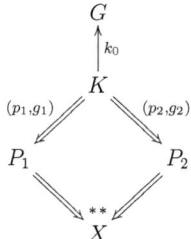

3.10.7 Fact (no critical pairs). *An adhesive HLR system with NACs is locally confluent if there are no critical pairs for this adhesive HLR system with NACs.*

Proof. Because of Fact 3.7.10, each pair of direct transformations $H_1 \Leftarrow G \Rightarrow H_2$ is parallel independent if there are no critical pairs for the system. Therefore, each pair is also locally confluent using Theorem 3.4.3. Consequently this adhesive HLR system with NACs is locally confluent. □

3.10.8 Theorem (local confluence theorem - critical pair lemma with NACs). *Given an adhesive HLR system with NACs, it is locally confluent if all its critical pairs are strictly NAC confluent.*

Proof. If a pair of direct transformations is parallel independent, then they are confluent because of the Local Church-Rosser Theorem. Suppose we have a pair of direct transformations $H_1 \Leftarrow G \Rightarrow H_2$ in conflict. Because of Theorem 3.7.6, a critical pair $P_1 \Leftarrow K \Rightarrow P_2$ exists that can be embedded into this pair of direct transformations. We know that each critical pair is strictly NAC confluent, and consequently locally confluent. This means that an object X exists as in the following picture. We still have to prove, however, that $H_1 \Longrightarrow^* H_3 \Longleftarrow^* H_2$.

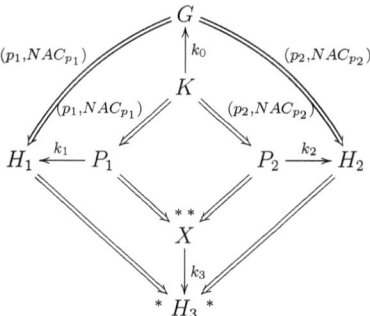

In the Critical Pair Lemma without NACs in [29] it is proven that the extension morphisms k_1 and k_2 are boundary consistent because of the fact that the critical pair $P_1 \Leftarrow K \Rightarrow P_2$ is not only locally confluent, but also strictly confluent. Therefore, extension diagrams without NACs over $t_1 : K \Rightarrow P_1 \Rightarrow^* X$ and $t_2 : K \Rightarrow P_2 \Rightarrow^* X$ can be constructed s.t. $G \Rightarrow H_1 \Rightarrow^* H_3$ and $G \Rightarrow H_2 \Rightarrow^* H_3$. The uniqueness of H_3 is proven in [29]. We should still prove that the extended matches in these extension diagrams satisfy the NACs of the rule sequences in t_1 and t_2. First we show that k_0 is boundary consistent w.r.t. $K \Rightarrow P_1$ (resp. $K \Rightarrow P_2$). This is

CHAPTER 3. RULE-BASED MODELING USING HIGH-LEVEL TRANSFORMATION

because we have an extension diagram over k_0 and $K \Rightarrow P_1$ (resp. $K \Rightarrow P_2$) and Theorem 3.10.4. Moreover, we have that $k_0 \circ g_1 \models NAC_{p_1}$ (resp. $k_0 \circ g_2 \models NAC_{p_2}$). This means that k_0 is also NAC consistent w.r.t. the direct transformation $K \Rightarrow P_1$ (resp. $K \Rightarrow P_2$). Since we have that the critical pair $P_1 \Leftarrow K \Rightarrow P_2$ is strictly NAC confluent via t_1 and t_2, it follows that k_0 is NAC consistent w.r.t t_1 and t_2. Since k_0 is NAC consistent, the Embedding Theorem for rules with NACs can be applied to k_0, t_1 and t_2 to conclude that the extended matches in the extension diagrams over k_0 and t_1 (resp. t_2) satisfy the NACs of the rule sequences in t_1 (resp. t_2). □

Given a critical pair and a strict solution for it, it is in general difficult to check for NAC confluence of this solution. It would be desirable to have a constructive method to check for NAC confluence. Therefore, the following theorem formulates a constructive sufficient condition (called implication condition) for a critical pair $P_1 \stackrel{p_1}{\Leftarrow} K \stackrel{p_2}{\Rightarrow} P_2$ that is strictly confluent via some transformations $t_1 : K \stackrel{p_1,g_1}{\Rightarrow} P_1 \Rightarrow^* X$ and $t_2 : K \stackrel{p_2,g_2}{\Rightarrow} P_2 \Rightarrow^* X$ to be also NAC confluent for t_1 and t_2. This means by definition that for every extension morphism $k_0 : K \to G$ in $\mathcal{M}'$ and NAC consistent w.r.t. $K \stackrel{p_1,g_1}{\Rightarrow} P_1$ and $K \stackrel{p_2,g_2}{\Rightarrow} P_2$, it follows that k_0 is also NAC consistent w.r.t. t_1 and t_2. In the following theorem, two different conditions on each single $NAC(n_{1,j})$ (resp. $NAC(n_{2,j})$) of the concurrent NAC induced by transformation t_1 (resp. t_2) are given leading to NAC confluence if one of them is satisfied. The first condition expresses that there exists a suitable NAC on p_1 (resp. p_2) evoking the satisfaction of $NAC(n_{1,j})$ (resp. $NAC(n_{2,j})$). The second condition first asks for a suitable morphism between the LHS's of the concurrent rules induced by both transformations t_1 and t_2. Moreover, it expresses that there exists a suitable NAC on p_2 (resp. p_1) evoking the satisfaction of $NAC(n_{1,j})$ (resp. $NAC(n_{2,j})$).

3.10.9 Theorem (implication condition for NAC confluence). *Consider a critical pair $P_1 \stackrel{p_1}{\Leftarrow} K \stackrel{p_2}{\Rightarrow} P_2$ that is strictly confluent via the transformations $t_1 : K \stackrel{p_1,g_1}{\Rightarrow} P_1 \Rightarrow^* X$ and $t_2 : K \stackrel{p_2,g_2}{\Rightarrow} P_2 \Rightarrow^* X$. Let $L_{c,1}$ (resp. $L_{c,2}$) be the left-hand side of the concurrent rule $p_{c,1}$ (resp. $p_{c,2}$) and $m_1 : L_1 \to L_{c,1}$ (resp. $m_2 : L_2 \to L_{c,2}$) the lhs-match induced by t_1 (resp. t_2). Then the critical pair $P_1 \stackrel{p_1}{\Leftarrow} K \stackrel{p_2}{\Rightarrow} P_2$ is also NAC confluent for t_1 and t_2, and thus, strictly NAC confluent if one of the following implication conditions holds for each $NAC(n_{1,j}) : L_{c,1} \to N_{1,j}$ (resp. $NAC(n_{2,j}) : L_{c,2} \to N_{2,j}$) of the concurrent $NAC_{p_{c,1}}$ induced by t_1 (resp. $NAC_{p_{c,2}}$ induced by t_2)*

- *there exists a $NAC(n'_{1,i}) : L_{c,1} \to N'_{1,i}$ (resp. $NAC(n'_{2,i}) : L_{c,2} \to N'_{2,i}$) in $D_{m_1}(NAC_{p_1})$ (resp. $D_{m_2}(NAC_{p_2})$) and a morphism $d_{ij} \in \mathcal{Q} : N'_{1,i} \to N_{1,j}$ (resp. $d_{ij} \in \mathcal{Q} : N'_{2,i} \to N_{2,j}$) such that (1) (resp. (1')) commutes.*

- *there exists a morphism $l_{21} : L_{c,2} \to L_{c,1}$ (resp. $l_{12} : L_{c,1} \to L_{c,2}$) s.t. (2) (resp. (2')) commutes, and in addition a $NAC(n'_{2,i}) : L_{c,2} \to N'_{2,i}$ (resp. $n'_{1,i} : L_{c,1} \to N'_{1,i}$) in $D_{m_2}(NAC_{p_2})$ (resp. $D_{m_1}(NAC_{p_1})$) with a morphism $m_{ij} : N'_{2,i} \to N_{1,j} \in \mathcal{Q}$ (resp. $m_{ij} :*

3.10. EMBEDDING AND CONFLUENCE

$N'_{1,i} \to N_{2,j} \in \mathcal{M}$) s.t. $n_{1,j} \circ l_{21} = m_{ij} \circ n'_{2,i}$ (resp. $n_{2,j} \circ l_{12} = m_{ij} \circ n'_{1,i}$).

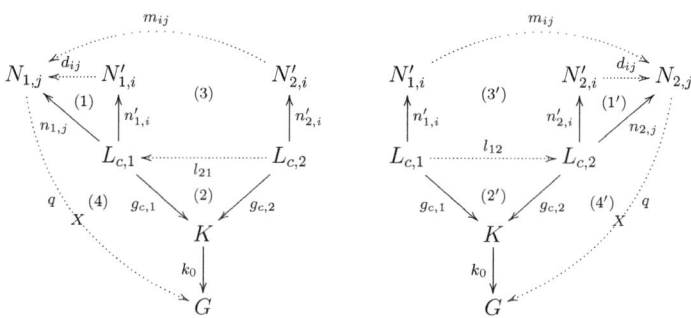

Proof. We shall prove that k_0 is NAC confluent for t_1 and t_2, i.e. each $k_0 : K \to G \in \mathcal{M}'$ that is NAC consistent w.r.t. $K \overset{p_1}{\Rightarrow} P_1$ and $K \overset{p_2}{\Rightarrow} P_2$ is also NAC consistent w.r.t. $t_1 : K \overset{p_1}{\Rightarrow} P_1 \Rightarrow^* X$ and $t_2 : K \overset{p_2}{\Rightarrow} P_2 \Rightarrow^* X$. Suppose that $k_0 \circ g_{c,1}$ does not satisfy the concurrent $NAC_{p_{c,1}}$ induced by t_1, i.e. k_0 is not NAC consistent w.r.t. t_1. Then we have a morphism $q \in \mathcal{Q}$ of a NAC object $N_{1,j}$ of the concurrent $NAC_{p_{c,1}}$ into G s.t. triangle (4) commutes, i.e. $k_0 \circ g_{c,1} = q \circ n_{1,j}$. Now one of the following two reasonings can be made:

- Because of the existence of a morphism d_{ij} such that (1) commutes, we have that $k_0 \circ g_{c,1} = q \circ d_{ij} \circ n'_{1,i}$. Moreover, $q \circ d_{ij}$ is a morphism in $\mathcal{Q}$ because $d_{ij}, q \in \mathcal{Q}$. This means that the extended match $k_0 \circ g_{c,1}$ does not satisfy $D_{m_1}(NAC_{p_1})$. Because of Lemma 3.3.13, now it follows that k_0 is not NAC consistent w.r.t. $K \overset{p_1}{\Rightarrow} P_1$, and this is a contradiction.

- Because of the existence of $l_{21} : L_{c,2} \to L_{c,1}$ s.t. (2) commutes and $m_{ij} : N_{2,i} \to N_{1,j}$ such that $n_{1,j} \circ l_{21} = m_{ij} \circ n'_{2,i}$, the following equations hold: $q \circ m_{ij} \circ n'_{2,i} = q \circ n_{1,j} \circ l_{21} = k_0 \circ g_{c,1} \circ l_{21} = k_0 \circ g_{c,2}$. Now $q \circ m_{ij} \in \mathcal{Q}$ because of the composition property, and thus, $k_0 \circ g_{c,2}$ does not satisfy $D_{m_2}(NAC_{p_2})$. Because of Lemma 3.3.13, now it follows that k_0 is not NAC consistent w.r.t. $K \overset{p_2}{\Rightarrow} P_2$. This is a contradiction.

Analogously, we can prove that each $k_0 : K \to G$ that is NAC consistent w.r.t. $K \Rightarrow P_1$ and $K \Rightarrow P_2$, is also NAC consistent w.r.t. t_2. □

The following corollary follows directly from this theorem.

3.10.10 Corollary (critical pair solution without NACs). *A critical pair $P_1 \overset{p_1}{\Leftarrow} K \overset{p_2}{\Rightarrow} P_2$ is strictly NAC confluent if*

- *it is strictly confluent via the transformations $t_1 : K \overset{p_1,g_1}{\Rightarrow} P_1 \Rightarrow^* X$ (resp. $t_2 : K \overset{p_2,g_2}{\Rightarrow} P_2 \Rightarrow^* X$) and both $P_1 \Rightarrow^* X$ and $P_2 \Rightarrow^* X$ are transformation sequences without NACs.*

Proof. In this case $NAC_{p_{c,1}} = D_{m_1}(NAC_{p_1})$, and therefore, $d_{ij} = id$ for each single NAC in $NAC_{p_{c,1}}$ such that the first condition of Theorem 3.10.9 always holds. Analogously, we can argue for the case $NAC_{p_{c,2}}$. □

In order to formulate not only a sufficient, but also a necessary and sufficient condition for local confluence of an adhesive HLR system with NACs we define the so-called set of extended critical pairs.

3.10.11 Definition (extended critical pair). For each critical pair $P_1 \Leftarrow K \Rightarrow P_2$ that is not strictly NAC confluent, an *extended critical pair* is a pair of direct transformations $H_1 \Leftarrow G \Rightarrow H_2$ as in the following figure, with $k_0 : K \to G \in \mathcal{M}'$ a NAC consistent and boundary-consistent morphism w.r.t. $K \Rightarrow P_1$ and $K \Rightarrow P_2$:

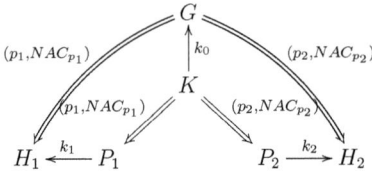

3.10.12 Remark. If we take $k_0 = id$, then each critical pair that is not strictly NAC confluent belongs to the set of its extended critical pairs.

3.10.13 Theorem (extended critical pair lemma). *An adhesive HLR system with NACs is locally confluent if and only if all its extended critical pairs are locally confluent.*

Proof.
- $\Rightarrow$ If one of the extended critical pairs is not locally confluent, then the system is not locally confluent, since an extended critical pair is nothing other than a pair of direct transformations.

- $\Leftarrow$ Let $H_1 \Leftarrow G \Rightarrow H_2$ be a pair of direct transformations. If they are parallel independent, then they are locally confluent, because of the local Church-Rosser property. If they are not, then because of Theorem 3.7.6, there exists a critical pair $P_1 \Leftarrow K \Rightarrow P_2$ that can be embedded into this pair of direct transformations. If this critical pair is strictly NAC confluent, then $H_1 \Leftarrow G \Rightarrow H_2$ is locally confluent as it is proven in Theorem 3.10.8. Suppose that the critical pair $P_1 \Leftarrow K \Rightarrow P_2$ is not strictly NAC confluent. Because of Theorem 3.10.4, we have that $k_0 \in \mathcal{M}'$ is boundary- and NAC consistent w.r.t. $K \Rightarrow P_1$ and $K \Rightarrow P_2$. Then $H_1 \Leftarrow G \Rightarrow H_2$ is an extended critical pair by definition, and all extended critical pairs are locally confluent by assumption. □

Since the set of extended critical pairs can become infinitely big, the necessary and sufficient condition based on extended critical pairs is difficult to check. Therefore, we still introduce a necessary condition for local confluence that can be checked statically. This condition might then demonstrate easily that a transformation system is not locally confluent.

3.10.14 Theorem (necessary condition for local confluence). *If an adhesive HLR system with NACs is locally confluent, then no critical pair $P_1 \Leftarrow K \Rightarrow P_2$ exists such that no rule of the adhesive HLR system is applicable to P_1 (resp. P_2), and thereby, P_1 and P_2 are not isomorphic.*

Proof. Since $P_1 \Leftarrow K \Rightarrow P_2$ is a pair of transformations that is not locally confluent, the corresponding adhesive HLR system with NACs is trivially not locally confluent either. □

3.11 Efficient Conflict and Causal Dependency Detection

The notion of critical pairs (resp. critical sequences) already allows a static conflict (resp. causal dependency) detection. Unfortunately, the standard construction is not very efficient. In Section 2.11 in Chapter 2, two alternative solutions are presented making the static conflict and causal dependency detection more efficient for the instantiation of typed graph transformation systems with NACs. The first solution presents a way to utilize *negative constraints*, holding for every system state, ruling out critical pairs (resp. sequences) not satisfying these constraints. The second solution introduces the concept of *essential critical pairs and sequences*, based on conflict resp. causal dependency reasons[2]. In both cases, efficiency is obtained because the set of critical pairs resp. sequences is reduced significantly without losing completeness with regard to detecting each conflict resp. dependency. Therefore, the set of representative conflicts (resp. causal dependencies) to be computed statically diminishes. Moreover, it is more efficient to analyze the reduced sets of critical pairs for strict confluence than it is for the larger set of critical pairs. Thus, not only conflict detection, but also conflict analysis becomes more efficient.

It is part of future work to generalize these more efficient constructions of critical pairs, and prove their correctness in the framework of adhesive HLR systems with NACs. It is expected to be straightforward to generalize the theory of critical pairs satisfying negative constraints from graph transformation to adhesive HLR systems with NACs. A more interesting question to be handled is which kind of nested constraints (see [46]) can reduce the set of critical pairs (resp. sequence) to consider with regard to critical pair (resp. critical sequence) detection.

It would as well be interesting to be able to generalize the theory of essential critical pairs, as presented in Section 2.11.2. for the instantiation of graph transformation to adhesive HLR systems with NACs. So far, it has not been possible to find out how this can be realized or, alternatively, to show that it is not possible at all.

---

[2] Note that, for now, by means of these essential critical pairs resp. sequences only conflicts and causal dependencies that are not caused by some NAC are detected.

Chapter 4
Certifying Rule-Based Models

4.1 Introduction

Having developed a rule-based model, it is desirable to test it for the satisfaction of certain properties. As long as this model does not fulfill these desired properties, it can be adapted until it conforms to the expectations. In this chapter, we introduce so-called certifications for rule-based models. Each *certification* corresponds to a specific *model property*. A certification may be added to the model if the corresponding property is fulfilled. The overall goal is to be able to add certifications to the model for each property expected to be true within the model.

Several kinds of model properties can be of interest depending on what is being modeled. For some rule-based models confluence might be a desired property, while for other models specific conflicting transformations might be desired. Moreover, often we are interested in analyzing specific aspects of a rule-based model. For example, we might be interested in a particular set of rules, some graph grammar, specific transformations, particular rule sequences, or also in certain control structures over rules.

How is it possible to add a certification for a specific property to a rule-based model? This is where *graph transformation theory* comes into play. It allows for analyzing a variety of properties. If the analysis is able to verify that a property is fulfilled, then the corresponding certification can be added to the rule-based model. Thereby, we are interested mainly in *static analysis techniques*. They run on components of the rule-based model without actually applying the rules (cf. compile time). In contrast, dynamic verification techniques might have to run through the whole state space generated by the rule-based model (cf. run time), which in many cases is infinitely large. However, static analysis techniques do not exist for every property one might want to investigate. In particular, some of the considered properties in this chapter, for example, confluence and termination [94, 96] are undecidable. If this is the case, then we follow the strategy that at least a sufficient condition of this property is searched for that can be checked statically. The satisfaction of this sufficient condition implies the satisfaction of the actual property under consideration. In general, static analysis techniques based on graph transformation theory are not only able to reveal that a property is satisfied, but also why it is satisfied. Summarizing, they allow to certify properties for rule-based models in a safe and very informative way. Moreover, static analysis techniques allow for refutation of a property in the case that they are able to verify the negation of the property under consideration. In this case, analogously, the static analysis techniques can clarify why the property does not hold in the rule-based model.

CHAPTER 4. CERTIFYING RULE-BASED MODELS

In Section 4.2, a *general road map* is presented *to certify properties* using graph transformation. For each kind of property, different analysis techniques based on graph transformation theory will be used to verify the property. Moreover, we briefly introduce the selection of properties, which will be handled in more detail in Section 4.3. Afterwards, in Section 4.2.3, we describe how certificates for more complex properties can be derived from certificates for more basic properties; a mechanism that we call certification bootstrapping. In Section 4.3, a *selection of properties* is presented together with their specific road to certification. This property catalog contains a representative set of properties that is of interest for the analysis of rule-based models. As soon as a road to certification for a specific property is available with tool support, also for non-expert users it becomes possible to certify this property on their rule-based models. In particular, by a non-expert user we mean someone who does not have to be capable of developing and implementing analysis techniques based on graph transformation theory. Each property is illustrated on our running example *Elevator*, and is provided with explanations on tool support in the tool environment AGG [114, 115, 13, 1]. It supports the algebraic approach to graph transformation as presented in this thesis, and consists of a graph transformation engine, analysis tools, and a graphical user interface for convenient user interaction. In Section 4.4, we describe typical *application areas* for certifying rule-based models using graph transformation, as presented in this thesis. Finally, in Section 4.5, we discuss *tool support* for certifying rule-based models. In particular, we present the state-of-the-art of tool support for the selection of properties, as presented in Section 4.3, in the tool environment AGG.

4.2 Road to Certification

In this section, we introduce a general road map for certifying properties, first. Afterwards, we introduce in an intuitive way a selection of properties that we will certify in particular in the next section. Thereby, these properties are illustrated on our running example *Elevator*.

4.2.1 General Road Map for Certifying Properties

In this section, we present a general road map for certifying properties of a rule-based model using graph transformation. In Fig. 4.1, it is possible to retrace the main steps on the road to certification.

Starting the road The road to certification starts with a *rule-based model*, describing the system to be validated. The part of the rule-based model that we are interested in can be of the following kinds: a graph transformation system, a graph grammar, graph transformation sequence(s), rule sequence(s) with or without start graph, a control structure over graph transformation rules, ... The corresponding rules and graphs may be typed and attributed. Having determined the part of the rule-based model to validate, it is necessary to accurately formulate the *property* to be certified. In this thesis, such properties are formulated in natural language. It is part of future work to investigate if a specific kind of logic can be used or developed that is appropriate to describe properties over rule-based models [1].

---

[1] This has been already investigated for other verification approaches for graph transformation such as, for example, in [5, 105].

4.2. ROAD TO CERTIFICATION

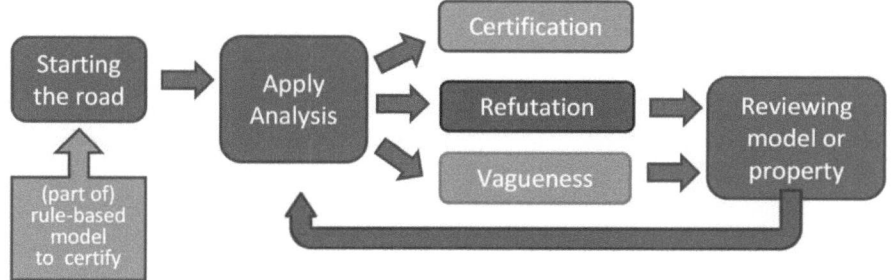

Figure 4.1: road to certification

Apply analysis Having determined a property to certify, we proceed with the road to certification as follows. Thereby, we need to distinguish two cases.

- In the first case, the property is characterized by a *necessary and sufficient condition* that can be *statically checked*. In this case, static analysis is able to definitely certify or refute the property for the given model. However, a necessary and sufficient condition, which can be statically checked does not exist for every property one might want to investigate. In particular, some of the considered properties in this chapter, for example, confluence and termination [94, 96], are undecidable. If this is the case, then we follow the strategy as explained in the next item.

- In the second case, the property holds only a *sufficient condition* or also *necessary condition* that can be *checked statically* (see Fig. 4.2). If the sufficient condition is identified to be true by static analysis, then the property can be certified. If the necessary condition is identified to be false by static analysis, then the property can be refuted. If the sufficient (resp. necessary) condition, however, appears to be false (resp. true), then both conditions are not powerful enough. If so, it is not clear whether the property is valid in the model or not. We call this situation vagueness about the validation of the property.

Certification, refutation or vagueness According to the last item, the result of analyzing a specific property for a given rule-based model can be of three different kinds. In the case that a sufficient condition for the property is fulfilled, it is possible to add the desired *certification* of the property to the model. Often, this certification provides not only the information that the property is fulfilled, but also information on why the property is fulfilled. Usually, this extra information is deduced from the statically checked corresponding sufficient condition. In Section 4.3, examples are given for specific certifications that come with such extra information, which we call the *reason for certification*. However, it is not always possible to award a model with the certification for a specific property. Sometimes, the undesired *refutation* of the property should be added to the model. This is the case if it is possible to verify that a corresponding necessary condition is false. Analogous to the certification case, the refutation usually comes with extra information on the reason for the property not to be fulfilled. In this case, this *refutation reason* is deduced from

CHAPTER 4. CERTIFYING RULE-BASED MODELS

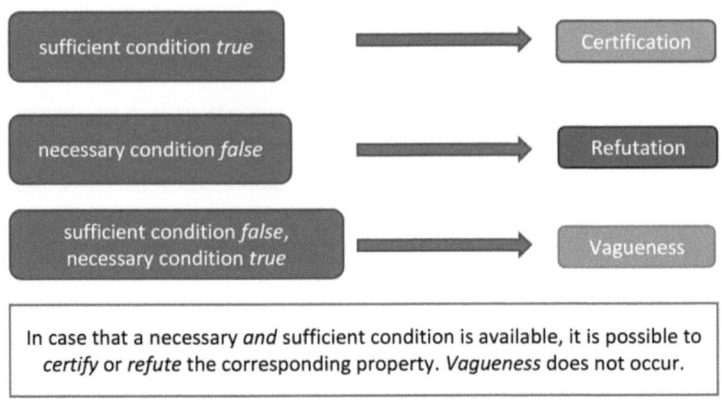

Figure 4.2: certification, refutation or vagueness

the non-satisfaction of the statically checked corresponding necessary condition. Finally, in some cases, after analyzing there is merely *vagueness* about the validation of the property in the model. Also, this information can be added to the model, together with the analysis technique that has been ineffective. It is explained in the next item why this may be important. In cases of refutation or vagueness, reviewing the model or property under consideration can be considered as described below.

Reviewing model or property Whenever it is not possible to add the certification of a specific property to the rule-based model, it might be adequate to review specific model parts or even review the property under consideration. Such kinds of reviews can be performed up until the desired certification is achieved for a corresponding model and property, which may be different to the model and property at the beginning of the road to certification. Thereby, it is important that the modeler is able to control these reviews in order to check if they still meet the corresponding system requirements.

reviewing model In cases of *refutation*, it is possible to review the model with regard to certification. This is an option, if according to the requirements, the property should definitely hold in the system being modeled. Usually, the reason for refutation indicates how the model can be reviewed. In practice, reviewing the model in cases of *vagueness* is an option as well. The model could be slightly changed such that its behavior still meets the requirements, and simultaneously allows for certification. However, *reviewing the model is not always an option* since it may not be allowed in some specific development phase. Then, the following considerations are important: in cases of vagueness, the property under consideration might not have been investigated extensively enough in the context of graph transformation theory. The model then serves as an example for theoreticians to possibly find a more adequate sufficient – this is weaker – condition or necessary – this is stronger – condition for the property under consideration. It is useful, therefore, that also the analysis technique leading to vagueness is recorded such that analysis can be rerun as soon as new analysis techniques for the property under consideration are available.

4.2. ROAD TO CERTIFICATION

As an alternative to static analysis techniques, it is possible to revert to dynamic and automatic analysis techniques such as, for example, model checking [24, 106] for graph transformation (see also related work in Section 5.1).

reviewing property As explained above, in cases of *refutation* of the property it is possible to review the model such that the property is fulfilled. On the other hand, sometimes this refutation clarifies that the property does not need to be fulfilled in the model. This is supported by the fact that the refutation of the property is often provided with a reason for the non-satisfaction of the property. If this reason was not noticed before, then a review of the property instead of the model could be appropriate. The reviewed property might then lead to certification for the unchanged model. Also, in cases of *vagueness*, it might be appropriate to review the property with regard to certification. It might be possible, for example, that a somewhat weaker version of this property is still significant enough, and moreover, can be certified.

consistent model evolution As time is evolving, a rule-based model will evolve as well because of changing requirements. At best, these requirements are expressed by properties that can be certified for the model. As soon as one property is added, or changed, it could be necessary to review the model in order to be able to certify this new property. It is important, however, to check that certificates for the properties that do not change are still valid for the reviewed model. If this is the case, then we call the corresponding model evolution consistent. In view of supporting such a consistent model evolution, it would be very desirable to be able to revert to a model version management system [110]. In this way, the model together with its certifications should be able to evolve without losing information on the history of the model and its certificates. Moreover, if only small changes are performed on the model, in many cases it will not be necessary to rerun the analysis for each certificate again. Such an incremental analysis will only be possible if model changes are recorded by the version management system, and passed to the analyzer. Part of future work is to describe how model reviews may influence already existing certificates, and in which cases a (partial) rerun of the static analysis becomes necessary. The topic of consistent model evolution based on incremental certification supported technically by model version management is not covered in this thesis, but is an interesting subject of future work.

4.2.2 A Selection of Properties to be Certified

In Section 4.3, the road to certification is outlined for a selection of properties. Here, we introduce these properties in an informal way. Moreover, we illustrate on our running example *Elevator* (as introduced in Example 2.2.1 in Chapter 2) the signification of each of the properties. Recall that the rules of *Elevator* are depicted in Fig. 2.6–2.19.

Conflicts As Expected In rule-based models the application of a certain rule can impede the application of another rule, although both rules are initially applicable to the same state. If this is the case, then we say that a rule causes a conflict with another rule. Now if the expectations on the occurrence of such conflicts between rules correspond to their actual occurrence in the rule-based model, then we say that Property *Conflicts As Expected* is fulfilled for the considered rules. Moreover, if for the rule-based model a set

CHAPTER 4. CERTIFYING RULE-BASED MODELS

of negative constraints (see Section 2.11.1) is available holding in every potential state of the rule-based model, then the analysis of this property becomes still more efficient.

Elevator Consider rules *process_call_down* and *process_stop_and_call* of *Elevator*. We expect these rules to be in conflict because they might both compete to process the same call request. We can certify the property *Conflicts As Expected* for these rules as explained in Example 4.3.4.

Causalities As Expected It is not only possible that, as described in the previous property, a rule impedes the application of another rule. Also, the following situation can occur: initially, two rules can be applied one after the other on a certain state. It is not possible, however, to switch the order in which they are applied. If this is the case, then we say that these rules are causally dependent. Now, if the expectations on the occurrence of such causalities correspond to their actual occurrence, then we say that Property *Causalities As Expected* is fulfilled for the considered rules. Moreover, if for the rule-based model a set of negative constraints (see Section 2.11.1) is available holding in every potential state of the rule-based model, then the analysis of this property becomes yet more efficient.

Elevator Consider rules *process_stop_up* and *move_up* of *Elevator*. We expect these rules to be causally dependent. This is because after a stop request on the elevator floor has been processed, the elevator should be able to move further upward in order to process other requests. We can certify the property *Causalities As Expected* for these rules as explained in Example 4.3.8.

Parallelism In many rule-based models, it is interesting to know which rules can be applied in parallel. This is the case if the order in which these rules are applied does not matter, independent of the context to which these rules are applied. If so, then we say that Property *Parallelism* is fulfilled for the corresponding rules.

Elevator Consider rule *call_request* and *stop_request* of *Elevator*. The order in which a call request and a stop request is made should not matter. They can be applied in any order with the same result. We can certify the property *Parallelism* for these rules as explained in Example 4.3.12.

Local Confluence Let two rules be applicable to the same state in a rule-based model. Then, it is important to know if no matter which rule I choose, it is possible to reach the same state again by applying other available rules of the rule-based model. If this is the case, then we say that the direct transformations via these two rules fulfill the Property *Local Confluence*.

Elevator Consider all rules of *Elevator* that may process requests if the elevator is in downward direction: *process_stop_down*, *process_call_down*, and *process_stop_and_call*. If two rules compete to process the same request in downward direction mode, then it should be possible to reach a common state afterwards anyway. In this case, this will be the state in which all requests on the elevator floor are processed. We can certify the property *Local Confluence* for these rules as explained in Example 4.3.18.

Termination For specific rule-based models it is important that when applying a set of rules non-deterministically and as long as possible, this application will finally terminate. This means that a state is reached to which none of the rules is applicable anymore. Note that the application of a set of rules is in general non-deterministic due to two reasons: given a state of the rule-based model to which one of the rules should be applied, then more than one rule could be applicable to that state. Therefore, there is freedom to choose which rule to apply. Secondly, once a rule to apply is chosen, it is possible that this rule is applicable to different fragments of this state. Therefore, there is also freedom to choose where to apply a rule.

Elevator Consider again all rules of *Elevator* that may process requests if the elevator is in downward direction mode: *process_stop_down*, *process_call_down*, and *process_stop_and_call*. The processing of requests on the elevator floor should terminate such that the elevator control is ready to serve new requests or existing requests on other floors. We can certify the property *Termination* for these rules as explained in Example 4.3.24.

Functional Behavior For specific rule-based models it is not only important to know that rule application is terminating. It can be also relevant to verify that when applying a set of rules non-deterministically and as long as possible to a certain state, the application will always terminate in the same state. If this is the case, then we say that this set of rules fulfills the Property *Functional Behavior*.

Elevator We continue with analyzing the rules of *Elevator* that may process requests if the elevator is in downward direction mode: *process_stop_down*, *process_call_down*, and *process_stop_and_call*. If these process rules are applied to an elevator in downward direction as long as possible, then this should always lead to the same terminal state. This means that the processing of requests in downward direction mode shows a functional behavior. We can certify the property *Functional Behavior* for these rules as explained in Example 4.3.29.

Applicability In order to ensure liveness of a rule-based model, it is important to know if specific rule sequences are applicable to a particular state. If this is the case for some rule sequence and state, then we say that they fulfill the Property *Applicability*. Note that the analysis of this property will allow for discovering also why a specific rule sequence is applicable to a certain state. This means that it can be indicated how rules are enabled by which predecessor rules.

Elevator In our running example *Elevator*, we consider a four-storey building in which the elevator is operating. Therefore, we expect that a rule sequence consisting of four call requests and four stop requests in any order is applicable to the initial state of *Elevator*. This state represents a four-storey building with the elevator car in upward mode on the ground floor without any request. We can certify the property *Applicability* for these rule sequences as explained in Example 4.3.35.

Non-Applicability For ensuring liveness, it is interesting to investigate applicability of rule sequences. On the contrary, for safety reasons one can investigate their non-applicability. We say that a rule sequence fulfills the Property *Non-Applicability* if it is not applicable to a specific state.

Elevator Consider an elevator in upward mode that is switched into downward mode. It is important that the elevator control does not get into an endless loop, changing the direction mode again into upward mode, and then in downward mode again and again. Therefore, we check that rule sequence *set_direction_down,set_direction_up* repeated arbitrary many times is not applicable. We can certify the property *Non-Applicability* for these rule sequences as explained in Example 4.3.40.

Constraint Preserved Because of safety reasons, it might be very important that rules preserve certain properties of the states to which they are applied. Therefore, we say that a rule fulfills the property *Constraint Preserved* if the following holds: whenever this rule is applied to some state fulfilling a given constraint, then the resulting state still fulfills this constraint as well.

Elevator Each request should be connected to one specific floor, and not to several. This safety constraint should be preserved by the rules modeling the elevator control. We can certify the property *Constraint Preserved* for this constraint and each of these rules as explained in Example 4.3.46.

Constraint Guaranteed Due to safety reasons, it might be interesting to check in what kind of state the application has arrived whenever a specific set of rules is no longer applicable to this state. Thus, after the rules have been applied as long as possible, the question arises as to whether it is guaranteed that the resulting state fulfills a specific constraint. If this is the case, then we say that the Property *Constraint Guaranteed* is fulfilled.

Elevator If the elevator control is in downward direction, and it cannot apply any of the rules *process_stop_down*, *process_call_down*, or *process_stop_and_call* anymore, then all requests on the elevator floor should have been processed. Thus, we formulate a constraint expressing that no requests are left on the elevator floor to be processed. Then, we can certify the property *Constraint Guaranteed* for this constraint and set of rules as explained in Example 4.3.52.

In the following table, the above properties are listed. In the second column of this table, it is recorded which kind of input is necessary in order to start the road to certification for the corresponding property. In the third column, it is recorded if the property can be certified (c), if it is possible to refute it (r), or if sometimes only vagueness (v) for the property may be determined. In Section 4.3, each property is formulated more precisely. Moreover, it is explained more in detail which analysis techniques may lead to certification, refutation, or also vagueness for each of the properties.

4.2. ROAD TO CERTIFICATION

property	input	output
conflicts as expected	sequence of two rules + expected conflicts (+ set of negative constraints)	(c) or (r)
causalities as expected	sequence of two rules + expected causalities (+ set of negative constraints)	(c) or (r)
parallelism	pair of rules	(c) or (r)
local confluence	pair of rules belonging to set of rules	(c), (r), or (v)
termination	set of rules	(c), (r), or (v)
functional behavior	pair of rules belonging to set of rules	(c), (r), or (v)
applicability	rule sequence + graph	(c), (r), or (v)
non-applicability	rule sequence + graph	(c), (r), or (v)
constraint preserved	constraint + rule	(c), (r), or (v)
constraint guaranteed	constraint + set of rules	(c), (r), or (v)

4.2.3 Bootstrapping Certificates

In this section, we outline briefly how it is possible to derive a certificate for a specific property from the certificate(s) of another property (resp. of other properties). For example, consider the case that the road to certification for a certain property P is specified, and at some point one is interested in the negation of property P. Then, the further road to certification for this negated property $\neg P$ can be derived automatically from the road to certification for the original property as follows: apply the same analysis as for property P, certify property $\neg P$ if property P is refuted, and refute property $\neg P$ if Property P is certified. Vagueness for Property $\neg P$ holds as usual whenever neither refutation nor certification is possible. Reviewing the model can be done in cases of refutation or vagueness of $\neg P$. This part has to be described afresh since now we want to review the model with regard to $\neg P$ instead of P. In Section 4.3, it is described how to derive the road to certification for the property *Non-Applicability* (see Property 4.3.36) from the one for the property *Applicability*.

In general, a road to certification can be derived for all first-order formulas of properties over rules for which the road to certification has been specified already. For example, it could be interesting to certify not only for one rule, but for a set of rules the property *Constraint Preserved*. Thus, it should be shown that the property *Constraint Preserved* holds for each rule in this set. It may also be the case that different types of certificates are combined. For example, the property *Functional Behavior* (see Property 4.3.25) for the rule set $\mathcal{P}$ as described in Section 4.3 can be specified as the following first-order formula over the property *Local Confluence* (see Property 4.3.13) and the property *Termination* (see Property 4.3.19): Property 4.3.13 holds for each rule pair in $\mathcal{P}$ and Property 4.3.19 holds for the rule set $\mathcal{P}$. The corresponding certificates, refutations, or also vagueness then follow the scheme of this first-order formula. Another example is the property *Parallelism* (see Property 4.3.9). Its certificate can be derived from the certificate of the property *CausalitiesAsExpected*. Property *Parallelism* holds for two rules p_1 and p_2 if and only if the Property *CausalitiesAsExpected* holds for the sequence of rules (p_1, p_2) as well as for (p_2, p_1), where the set of expected causalities is in both cases empty. It is part of future work to describe in a more elaborate way how to derive certificates for complex properties from certificates for more basic properties.

4.3 Certifying a Selection of Properties

For the selection of properties as introduced informally in Section 4.2.2, we outline in this section how the corresponding road to certification can be accomplished. Most of the theory needed to certify these properties has been presented in Chapter 2. Some of the properties, for example, termination [29] can be certified by means of already existing analysis techniques. The road to certification for each of the properties is explained on our running example *Elevator*, as introduced in Example 2.2.1. Moreover, it is shown to which extent AGG [114, 115, 13, 1] can automatically support the property analysis, and how it could be completed. AGG supports the algebraic approach to graph transformation as presented in this thesis, and consists of a graph transformation engine, analysis tools, and a graphical user interface for convenient user interaction.

4.3.1 Conflicts as Expected

Road to Certification:

starting the road A transformation causes a conflict with another transformation if the first one impedes the other one (see Def. 2.6.6). If such a conflict between transformations occurs, then we say that the rule from the first transformation causes a conflict with the rule from the other transformation (see Def. 2.8.11). Recall that different types of conflicts can occur between rules, and that they can occur in different contexts. With this certification, we want to find out the answer to the following question: Given a sequence of two rules, does the first rule actually cause each conflict with the second rule and no more conflicts than expected? The expected conflicts caused by the first rule with the second one can be given in several formats. It might be the case that it is just mentioned which type of conflicts are expected. Recall that either delete-use or also produce-forbid conflicts may occur. In this case, the set of expected conflicts consists of two boolean values *delete-use* and *produce-forbid*. They are true (resp. false) if conflicts of the corresponding type are expected (resp. not expected). If one of the boolean values is not set, then the analysis is not concerned with the corresponding type of conflict. It might be the case that the set of expected conflicts consists of concrete pairs of conflicting transformations. It might be the case that the set of expected conflicts is given more formally by a set of critical pairs, expressing the expected conflicts that the first rule can cause with the second one in a minimal context. Summarizing, the part of the model that we want to analyze is given by a sequence of two rules, for which we want to compare the actually caused conflicts, of the first with the second rule, with the set of expected conflicts. The above question can be answered positively if the following property is fulfilled for a sequence of two rules.

4.3.1 Property (Conflicts as Expected). Consider a sequence of two rules p_1, p_2, and a set of expected conflicts, called *expectedConflicts*, caused by p_1 with p_2 (and optionally a set of negative constraints holding for each potential state in the rule-based model). Rule p_1 actually causes every expected conflict with p_2, and no conflicts other than the expected ones are caused.

apply analysis In Chapter 2, it is shown that if a transformation causes a conflict with another transformation, then this conflict is represented by some critical pair (see Theorem

4.3. CERTIFYING A SELECTION OF PROPERTIES

2.7.8). Critical pairs are complete in this sense, and they represent each potential conflict in a minimal context. Therefore, Property 4.3.1 can be characterized by the following *necessary and sufficient condition* that can be checked statically: each expected conflict between rule applications is represented by a critical pair via these rules and, vice versa, each critical pair represents an expected conflict. For checking the above property, first we need to compute the set of critical pairs for a sequence of two rules. This means that we compute each potential conflict, which is caused by the first rule with the second rule, in a minimal context. Secondly, we check if this set of critical pairs corresponds to the set of expected conflicts.

compute critical pairs The computation of the set of critical pairs (see Def. 2.7.1) for two rules p_1 and p_2 is explained in Construction 2.7.10. Note that here we need to compute merely the critical pairs for a sequence of two rules p_1, p_2. This means that we restrict ourselves to critical pairs representing conflicts caused by the first rule p_1 with the second rule p_2, and rule out critical pairs representing conflicts caused by the second rule p_2 with the first rule p_1. The set of critical pairs can become quite large depending on the size of the rules and NACs for the rules. Therefore, two other types of critical pairs (critical pairs satisfying negative constraints[2] in Section 2.11.1 and essential critical pairs in Section 2.11.2) were introduced, which are smaller than the usual set of critical pairs, but still complete. Thus, in cases of many critical pairs, it is advisable to use these more efficient constructions.

correspondence of critical pairs with expected conflicts Checking the correspondence of the set of critical pairs with the expected conflicts is usually done manually. Thereby, for each entry in the automatically computed set of critical pairs, a check is made to determine whether it corresponds to an expected conflict in *expectedConflicts*, and, vice versa, a check is made to see if each expected conflict in *expectedConflicts* is represented by some critical pair.

certification or refutation It is possible to check for each sequence of two rules and corresponding set of expected conflicts if Property 4.3.1 is fulfilled or not by applying the analysis as explained above.

4.3.2 Certificate (Conflicts as Expected). If it is possible to verify Property 4.3.1 for a sequence of two rules p_1, p_2 and a set of expected conflicts *expectedConflicts*, then award p_1, p_2 and *expectedConflicts* this certificate. This certificate comes with a set of critical pairs, called *conflictsAsExpected*. Thereby, each expected conflict corresponds to a critical pair and each critical pair corresponds to an expected conflict.

4.3.3 Refutation (Conflicts as Expected). If it is possible to verify the negation of Property 4.3.1 for a sequence of two rules p_1, p_2 and a set of expected conflicts *expectedConflicts*, then add this refutation to p_1, p_2 and *expectedConflicts*. This refutation comes with three sets of critical pairs for p_1, p_2. The first set, called *conflictsAsExpected*, contains critical pairs corresponding to expected conflicts. The second set, called *notFound*, contains expected conflicts for which no critical pair was found. The third set, called *notExpected*, contains critical pairs corresponding to conflicts that were not expected.

---

[2] Note that this construction may be used only in the case that each potential state of the rule-based model always satisfies these negative constraints. They should be added in this case as input to Property 4.3.1.

reviewing model In cases of refutation, either some expected conflict does not actually occur, or some conflict occurs that was not expected. In the first case, no critical pair was found by the analysis for the expected conflict. Therefore, there will be an entry in the set *notFound* coming with refutation. For each of these entries it should be checked if the rules can be changed such that the expected conflict actually occurs. In the second case, some critical pair was found corresponding to a conflict that was not expected. Therefore, there will be an entry in the set *notExpected* coming with the refutation. For each of these entries, it should be checked if it is possible to change the corresponding rules such that the conflict does not occur anymore.

reviewing property In cases of refutation, either some expected conflict does not actually occur, or some conflict occurs that was not expected. Now it could be the case that some conflict was wrongly expected or the conflict that actually occurs was not expected. This can be discovered by investigating more closely the set *notFound* (resp. *notExpected*). After reviewing the expectations and rerunning the analysis, these sets should then become empty.

4.3.4 Example (Conflicts as Expected). Road to Certificate *Conflicts as Expected* for *Elevator*:

starting the road Consider rule sequence *process_call_down*, *process_stop_and_call* of *Elevator*. We expect that *process_call_down* causes a conflict with *process_stop_and_call* because *process_stop_and_call* might compete to process the same call request as *process_call_down*. Since both rules do not hold any NAC, we do not expect produce-forbid conflicts. We suppose that the set of *expectedConflicts* is given by the boolean values *delete-use* equal to true, and *produce-use* equal to false. Thus a *delete-use conflict* is expected caused by *process_call_down* with *process_stop_and_call*, and on the other hand no produce-forbid conflicts are expected. We can certify Property 4.3.1 (*Conflicts As Expected*) for rule sequence *process_call_down*, *process_stop_and_call*[3] as explained in the following procedure.

apply analysis: compute critical pairs AGG is able to compute the set of critical pairs $P_1 \overset{p_1}{\Leftarrow} K \overset{p_2}{\Rightarrow} P_2$ for a sequence of two rules. The debug option of the critical pair analysis module allows one to choose a sequence of two rules belonging to the active graph transformation system. Initially, an empty so-called conflict matrix is depicted containing as many rows and columns as rules in the graph transformation system. Entry (p_i, p_j) (row p_i, column p_j) of the matrix is filled with the number of critical pairs describing conflicts caused by rule p_i with p_j. In Fig. 4.3, the conflict matrix for *Elevator* is shown after computing the set of critical pairs for *process_call_down*, *process_stop_and_call*. The entry (*process_call_down*, *process_stop_and_call*) shows how many critical pairs have been computed. Clicking this number then shows the critical overlaps leading to this set of critical pairs as shown also in Fig. 4.3. In cases of a delete-use conflict, the overlap K of the left-hand sides of the rules p_1 and p_2 is shown. In AGG the conflict reason, consisting of the part in K that is deleted by p_1 and used by p_2, is depicted in green. In cases of a produce-forbid conflict, the overlap P_2 of a NAC of p_2 with the right-hand side of p_1 is shown. In AGG the

---

[3]Note that analogously, the other way round *process_stop_and_call* causes a delete-use conflict with *process_call_down*, but this is handled by the certificate *Conflicts as Expected* for rule sequence *process_stop_and_call*, *process_call_down*.

4.3. CERTIFYING A SELECTION OF PROPERTIES

conflict reason, consisting of the part in P_1 that is produced by p_1 and forbidden by p_2, is depicted in green. Moreover, for each of the overlaps it is shown which type of critical pair it leads to. In this case, we notice the case that 3 critical pairs of the type delete-use conflict have been computed. Analyzing these 3 critical pairs, we see that they all describe the same type of conflict since the reason for the conflict always consists of the call request that is deleted. In order to avoid this inefficiency as much as possible, two strategies can be followed. The first one is to set the CPA option *consistency*. Then, AGG merely computes the set of critical pairs with the constraints given for the active graph transformation system. In Section 2.11.1, it is shown that for so-called negative constraints this reduced set of critical pairs is still complete, provided that only states satisfying these constraints are valid in the rule-based model. The set of negative constraints for *Elevator*, expressing which kind of states are not allowed for *Elevator*, is depicted in Fig. 2.5. Moreover, for each maximal multiplicity in the type graph of *Elevator*, a corresponding negative constraint is added as well. They can all be used to reduce the set of critical pairs computed for *process_call_down, process_stop_and_call*. We notice that the set of critical pairs with negative constraints in our example consists of only one element. Overlaps 1 and 2 as depicted in Fig. 4.3 can be omitted since they do not correspond to the maximal multiplicities as given in the type graph of *Elevator* in Fig. 2.1. Alternatively, in order to obtain a more efficient critical pair detection, the option *essential* can be set. In this case, AGG computes only the essential critical pairs for *process_call_down, process_stop_and_call*. Note that this analysis is only valid up until now for rules without NACs. For more explanations, see Section 2.11.2. The set of essential critical pairs for *process_call_down, process_stop_and_call* consists of only one element as well. We continue working with the set of critical pairs, satisfying the negative constraints, consisting of one critical pair.

correspondence of critical pairs with expected conflicts AGG does not provide tool support for this part of the certification yet. Therefore, we now check manually if the computed set of critical pairs corresponds to the set *expectedConflicts*, given from the beginning for *process_call_down* and *process_stop_and_call*. The set *expectedConflicts* expresses by its boolean values that a delete-use conflict, but no produce-forbid conflict is expected. The computed set of critical pairs satisfying the negative constraints consists of one critical pair, describing a delete-use conflict. Thus, the set of computed critical pairs corresponds to the given set of *expectedConflicts*. Therefore, the set *conflictsAsExpected* corresponds to the set of computed critical pairs.

certification The previous analysis enables us to add Certificate *Conflicts as Expected* to the rule sequence *process_call_down, process_stop_and_call* with *expectedConflicts* as given above. It comes with the set *conflictsAsExpected*, containing the set of computed critical pairs for *process_call_down, process_stop_and_call*, and corresponding to the set of *expectedConflicts*.

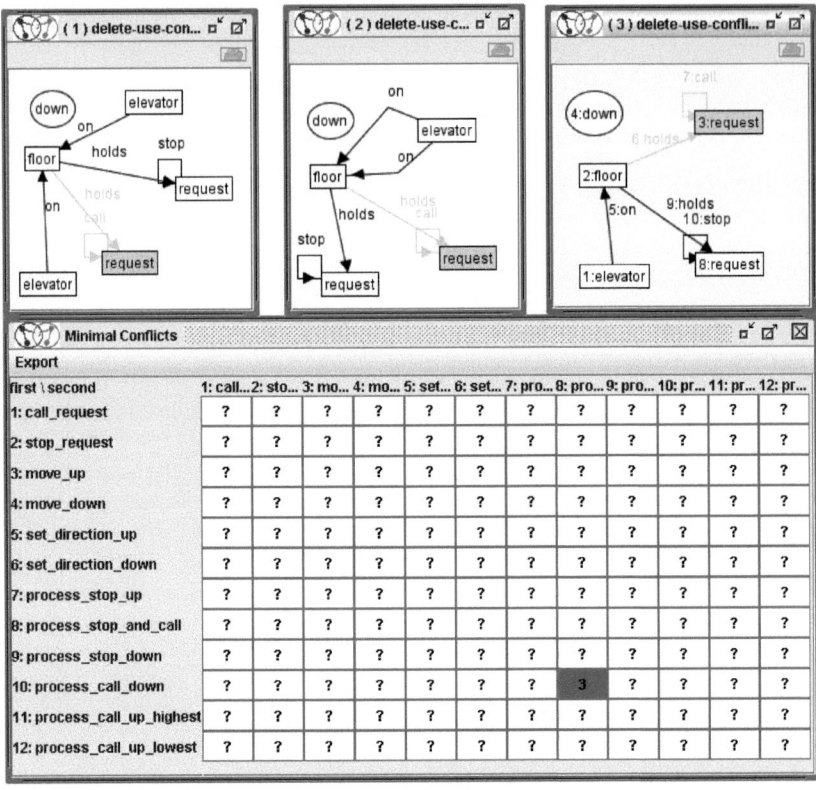

Figure 4.3: critical overlaps for (*process_call_down*, *process_stop_and_call*) in AGG

4.3.2 Causalities as Expected

starting the road Consider a sequence of two transformations, starting with T_1 via rule p_1, and afterwards T_2 via rule P_2. They are causally dependent, if T_2 is triggered by the other one or T_1 can no longer be made reversible after performing T_2 (see Theorem 2.6.7). If such a causal dependency occurs, then we say that rule sequence (p_1, p_2) is causally dependent (see Def. 2.8.8, 2.8.12, and 2.8.13). Recall that different types of dependencies can occur between rules, and that they can occur in different contexts. By means of this certification, we now want to find the answer to the following question: Does every expected causal dependency occur between T_1 and T_2, and no more dependencies as the expected ones occur? Note that the set of expected causal dependencies can be given in different formats analogous to the set of expected conflicts as introduced in Section 4.3.1. It might be the case that it is just mentioned which type of causal dependencies are expected. Recall that produce-use, delete-forbid, forbid-produce, or also deliver-delete dependencies can occur. In this case, the set of expected causalities consists of four boolean values *produce-use*, *delete-forbid*, *forbid-produce*, and *deliver-delete*. They are true (resp. false) if causal dependencies of the corresponding type are expected (resp. not

4.3. CERTIFYING A SELECTION OF PROPERTIES

expected). If one of the boolean values is not set, then the analysis is not concerned with the corresponding type of causal dependency. It might be the case that the set of expected causal dependencies consists of concrete sequences of causally depending transformations. It might be the case that the set of expected causalities is given more formally by a set of critical sequences expressing the expected causalities between the first and second rule in a minimal context. Summarizing, the part of the model that we want to analyze is given by a sequence of two rules for which we want to compare the expected causalities with the actually occurring causal dependencies. The above question can be answered positively if the following property is fulfilled for each sequence of two rules.

4.3.5 Property (Causalities as Expected). Consider a sequence of rules p_1, p_2 and a set of expected causal dependencies, called *expectedCausalities* (and optionally a set of negative constraints holding for each potential state in the rule-based model). Every expected causal dependency for p_1, p_2 actually occurs, and no other causal dependencies as the expected ones occur.

apply analysis We do not go into detail here since the analysis procedure is analogous to the one for Property 4.3.1. This is because analogous to conflict detection by critical pairs, we can detect causal dependencies by computing critical sequences (see Definition 2.7.3 and Construction 2.7.14). Afterwards, analogously, we compare these computed dependencies with the expected ones.

certification or refutation It is possible to check for each sequence of rules p_1, p_2 if Property 4.3.5 is fulfilled or not by applying the analysis as explained above.

4.3.6 Certificate (Causalities as Expected). If it is possible to verify Property 4.3.5 for a rule sequence of two rules and its expected dependencies *expectedCausalities*, then award them this certificate. This certificate comes with a set of critical sequences, called *causalitiesAsExpected*, for this rule sequence. Thereby, each expected causal dependency corresponds to a critical sequence and each critical sequence corresponds to an expected causal dependency.

4.3.7 Refutation (Causalities as Expected). If it is possible to verify the negation of Property 4.3.5 for a rule sequence of two rules and its expected dependencies *expectedCausalities*, then add this refutation. It comes with three sets of critical sequences for this rule sequence. The first set, called *causalitiesAsExpected*, contains critical sequences corresponding to expected causalities. The second set, called *notFound*, contains expected causal causalities for which no critical pair was found. The third set, called *notExpected*, contains critical sequences corresponding to causal dependencies that were not expected.

reviewing model or property Analogous to the reviewing of Property 4.3.1.

4.3.8 Example (Causalities as Expected). Road to Certificate *Causalities as Expected* for *Elevator*:

starting the road Consider rule sequence *process_stop_up*, *move_up* of *Elevator*. We expect that *move_up* is causally dependent on *process_stop_up*. This is because after a stop request on the elevator floor has been processed, the elevator should be able to move

CHAPTER 4. CERTIFYING RULE-BASED MODELS

further upward in order to process other requests, and therefore, a delete-forbid dependency should occur. Moreover, we expect a deliver-delete dependency since the elevator's position, which was delivered by *process_stop_up*, is changed by rule *move_up*. We do not expect a produce-use dependency since *process_stop_up* does not produce anything. Neither do we expect a forbid-produce dependency since *move_up* does not produce any call request forbidden by *process_stop_up*. Thus, we suppose that the set of *expectedCausalities* is given by the boolean values *produce-use* equal to false, *delete-forbid* equal to true, *deliver-delete* equal to true, and *forbid-produce* equal to false. We can certify Property 4.3.5 (*Causalities As Expected*) for rule sequence *process_stop_up, move_up* as described in the following procedure.

apply analysis: compute critical sequences AGG is able to compute the set of critical sequences for a sequence of two rules. This is analogous to the computation of critical pairs for a sequence of two rules. For more details, see the example for Property 4.3.1. Note that in order to compute all four kinds of causal dependencies the CPA (critical pair analysis) option *trigger and switch* should be set in AGG. The result of the computation in AGG of the set of critical sequences with negative constraints is shown in Fig. 4.4. We obtain two critical overlaps, expressing the expected delete-forbid and deliver-delete dependency.

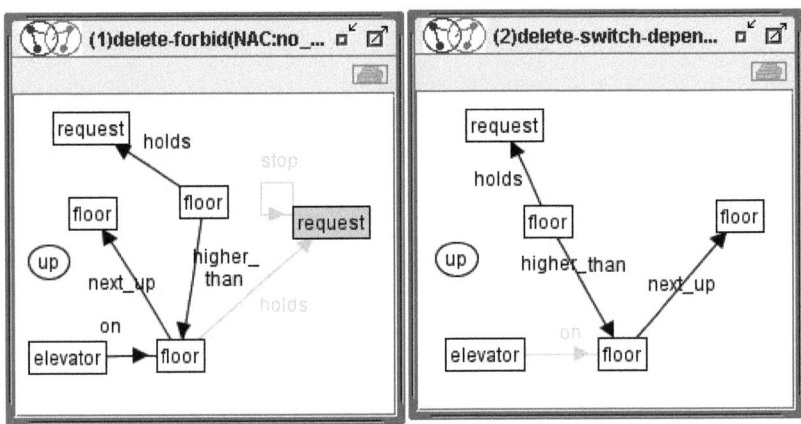

Figure 4.4: critical overlaps for (*process_stop_up, move_up*) in AGG

correspondence of critical sequences with expected causalities AGG does not provide tool support for this part of the certification yet. Therefore, we now check manually if the computed set of critical sequences corresponds to the expected causal dependencies for *process_stop_up, move_up*. We expected only delete-forbid and deliver-delete dependencies, and AGG computed exactly these kinds of critical sequences for *process_stop_up, move_up*. Thus, the set *causalitiesAsExpected* corresponds to the set of computed critical sequences.

certification The previous analysis enables us to add a Certificate *Causalities as Expected* to the rule sequence *process_stop_up, move_up* with *expectedCausalities* as given above. It comes with the set *causalitiesAsExpected*, containing the set of computed critical sequences for *process_stop_up, move_up*, corresponding to the set of *expectedCausalities*.

4.3.3 Parallelism

starting the road Sometimes, the order in which two graph transformations are performed does not matter. They can be applied in any order with the same result. It is possible to find out for two transformations if this is the case before performing them by analyzing the corresponding rules. Therefore, we are interested in certifying the following property:

4.3.9 Property (Parallelism). Consider two rules p_1 and p_2. If the sequence p_1, p_2 is applicable to some graph G, then also p_2, p_1 (and thus also the parallel rule $p_1 + p_2$) is applicable to G with the same result, and if the sequence p_2, p_1 is applicable to some graph G, then also p_1, p_2 (and thus also the parallel rule $p_1 + p_2$) is applicable to G. We say that p_1 and p_2 can always be applied in parallel.

apply analysis In Theorem 2.4.3 (Local Church-Rosser Theorem) it is stated that a sequence of direct transformations via p_1 and then p_2 on G can be applied in reversed order with the same result, if and only if the transformations in this sequence are sequentially independent. Moreover, in Theorem 2.4.6, it is stated that a sequence of sequentially independent transformations can be performed in parallel by applying the parallel rule $p_1 + p_2$. Each sequence of direct transformations via p_1 and then p_2 is sequentially independent if rule sequence p_1, p_2 is sequentially independent according to Def. 2.8.2. On the contrary, rule sequence p_1, p_2 is causally dependent if there exists at least one causally dependent sequence of direct transformations on some graph G (see to Def. 2.8.8). Therefore, Property 4.3.9 can be characterized for rules p_1 and p_2 by the following *necessary and sufficient condition*: rule sequence p_1, p_2 and rule sequence p_2, p_1 are sequentially independent. It is possible to check this condition statically as described in the following procedure.

no critical sequences Because of Characterization 2.8.4, a sequence of rules p_1, p_2 is sequentially independent if and only if there are no critical sequences $K \Rightarrow P_1 \Rightarrow P_2$ via p_1 and then p_2. Thus, we compute the set of critical sequences via p_1, p_2 (resp. p_2, p_1) and check that it is empty. How to compute this set of sequences is explained in Construction 2.7.14.

certification or refutation It is possible to check for each two rules if Property 4.3.9 is fulfilled or not by applying the analysis as explained above.

4.3.10 Certificate (Parallelism). If it is possible to verify Property 4.3.9 for a set of two rules, then award them this certificate.

4.3.11 Refutation (Parallelism). If it is possible to verify the negation of Property 4.3.9 for a set of two rules, then add this refutation. It comes with at least one critical sequence via (p_1, p_2) or (p_2, p_1). Such a sequence is called the *counterexampleCriticalSequence*. Optionally this refutation comes with a complete set of critical sequences via p_1, p_2 (called *criticalSequences*(p_1, p_2)) and a set of critical sequences via p_2, p_1 (analogously, called *criticalSequences*(p_2, p_1)).

CHAPTER 4. CERTIFYING RULE-BASED MODELS

reviewing model In cases of refutation, the model can be reviewed if the sets *criticalSequences*(p_1, p_2) and *criticalSequences*(p_2, p_1) are available. Each critical sequence has to be investigated, and the rules p_1 or p_2 should be modified such that afterwards no critical sequences occur anymore.

reviewing property In case of refutation, it is also possible that one has to admit that the property *Parallelism* for the rules p_1, p_2 cannot be fulfilled. If all entries in the sets *criticalSequences*(p_1, p_2) and *criticalSequences*(p_2, p_1) correspond to expected causal dependencies[4], the property *Parallelism* for the rules p_1, p_2 should be reviewed. It could be weakened, for example, such that rules p_1, p_2 are applicable in parallel in some specific context, instead of in any context. Then this new property should be formulated precisely in such a way that it can be analyzed with appropriate techniques as well.

4.3.12 Example (Parallelism). Road to Certificate *Parallelism* for *Elevator*:

starting the road Consider rules *call_request* and *stop_request* of *Elevator*. The order in which a call request and a stop request is made should not matter. It should be possible to apply these rules in any order with the same result no matter to which context they are applied. We can certify Property 4.3.9 (*Parallelism*) for these rules as described in the following procedure.

apply analysis: no critical sequences We need to check that neither critical sequences exist for *call_request, stop_request* nor *stop_request, call_request*. We use AGG to compute these sets of critical sequences as also explained for Property 4.3.5 (Causalities as Expected). Thereby, we notice that they are indeed both empty.

certification The previous analysis enables us to add a Certificate *Parallelism* to the rules *call_request* and *stop_request* of *Elevator*.

4.3.4 Local Confluence

starting the road Consider some state to which two rules can be applied. After applying both rules to this state, two new states are obtained. Is it possible to arrive at the same state again by a finite number of rule applications? In this case, the part of the rule-based model that we want to investigate consists of a pair of rules belonging to a set of rules, inducing potentially local confluence. Therefore, to find the answer to the above question we analyze the following property:

4.3.13 Property (Local Confluence). Given two rules p_1, p_2 and a set of rules $\mathcal{P}$ including p_1, p_2, then each pair of transformations via p_1 and p_2 is locally confluent via rules in $\mathcal{P}$.

apply analysis In the Local Confluence Theorem (see Theorem 2.10.9) in Chapter 2, it is shown that if each critical pair via p_1 and p_2 is strictly NAC confluent as given in Def. 2.10.7, then each pair of direct transformations via p_1 and p_2 is locally confluent. If the solution of the critical pair consists of rules belonging to $\mathcal{P}$, then each pair is locally confluent via rules in $\mathcal{P}$. Moreover, in Theorem 2.10.17, a necessary condition for local

---

[4]Note that this corresponds to validating Property 4.3.5 for p_1, p_2 (resp. p_2, p_1) as described in Section 4.3.2.

confluence is given. Therefore, the static analysis of Property 4.3.13 consists of the following parts:

compute critical pairs Compute the set of critical pairs via the rules p_1 and p_2 as explained in Construction 2.7.10. If this set is empty, then the Local Confluence property holds without further conditions. In this case, each pair of direct transformations via p_1 and p_2 is parallel independent. Theorem 2.4.3 states that for such transformations the same state can be reached again. This is because p_1 does not impede the application of p_2, and vice versa. If the set of critical pairs is not empty, then the following considerations should be regarded. Note that for efficiency reasons in the following cases, it is possible to compute only a subset of the set of critical pairs. If $\mathcal{P}$ is a set of rules without NACs, then because of Theorem 2.11.12 it is sufficient to compute the set of essential critical pairs. Note that based on Theorem 2.11.4, it will, alternatively, be possible to make the verification of local confluence more efficient for the case that a set of negative constraints is given, fulfilled by each potential state of the rule-based model. See Remark 4.3.17 for more details on this topic.

- **check for solution: solution length 0** For each critical pair $P_1 \Leftarrow K \Rightarrow P_2$ via p_1, p_2, a NAC confluent solution should be searched for using rules belonging to $\mathcal{P}$. As a first step of this search, one should check if P_1 and P_2 are isomorphic such that the isomorphism is compatible with the mutually preserved part of the critical pair (strictness). In cases of success, a solution of length 0 exists, and the next critical pair can be investigated.

- **non-isomorphic critical pair** In cases that no isomorphism between P_1 and P_2 exists and, moreover, each rule in $\mathcal{P}$ is neither applicable to P_1 nor to P_2, then the necessary condition of Theorem 4.3.1 is fulfilled. We call this critical pair a *nonResolvableCriticalPair*. Thus, in this case Property 4.3.13 is not fulfilled for p_1 and p_2 belonging to $\mathcal{P}$.

- **solution length > 0** If, on the other hand, it is possible to apply some rule of $\mathcal{P}$ to P_1 or P_2, then the following procedure can be followed: search stepwise for local confluent solutions of length > 0 via rules in $\mathcal{P}$ in a breadth-first manner. If a local confluent solution has been found, then first it is checked if this solution is also strict (see Def. 2.10.6). This is the case, intuitively speaking, if the mutual preserved part of the critical pair is also preserved by the solution. Afterwards, it is checked if the critical pair is also NAC confluent for this solution (see Def. 2.10.7). Checking if a critical pair is NAC confluent is more complex. However, there are sufficient conditions for this property that are easy to check: the easiest case is that the rules belonging to the strict solution of the critical pair do not hold NACs. Because of Corollary 2.10.11, the critical pair is automatically strictly NAC confluent then. In the second case, if the Implication Condition as given in Theorem 2.10.10 holds, then the critical pair is also strictly NAC confluent. Note that especially in the case of non-termination the search for solutions can be stopped after a predefined number of steps in order to avoid an infinite search. This predefined number (called *predefinedSolutionLength*) equals the maximal solution length, being the maximal transformation sequence length of the potential solution starting from P_1 (resp. P_2). The probability of finding an existing solution increases with the rate of this number, but the number of solution possibilities increases exponentially.

Note that if for some critical pair it is not possible to show strict NAC confluence, then in some cases one can argue by means of extended critical pairs that local confluence can be obtained anyway. This is not a generic static analysis technique anymore, but specific properties of the rules under consideration can be sufficient to conclude local confluence anyway.

certification, refutation or vagueness It is possible to certify that two rules p_1, p_2 belonging to a set of rules $\mathcal{P}$ fulfill (resp. do not fulfill) Property 4.3.13 if the above analysis procedure has been run through successfully. On the contrary, if the above explained necessary condition for local confluence is not fulfilled, then it is possible to refute it. In cases that neither the sufficient condition holds, nor is the necessary condition violated, vagueness should be added to p_1, p_2 with respect to Property 4.3.13.

4.3.14 Certificate (Local Confluence). If it is possible to verify Property 4.3.13 for two rules p_1, p_2 belonging to a set of rules $\mathcal{P}$, then award p_1, p_2, and $\mathcal{P}$ this certificate. This certificate comes with a list of solutions – one solution for each critical pair via p_1, p_2, making it strictly NAC confluent. This list is called *strictNacSolutionList*.

Having a pair of direct transformations $H_1 \Leftarrow G \Rightarrow H_2$ via p_1 and p_2 in conflict, then the solutions list coming with the certificate can be used as follows: find the critical pair in the list corresponding to the conflict under consideration. Now the solution of the critical pair outlines how the same state can be obtained also for the pair of direct transformations in a bigger context.

4.3.15 Refutation (Local Confluence). If it is possible to verify the negation of Property 4.3.13 for two rules p_1, p_2 belonging to a set of rules $\mathcal{P}$, then add this refutation to them. This refutation comes with at least one critical pair, called *nonResolvableCriticalPair*, which is not strictly confluent.

4.3.16 Vagueness (Local Confluence). If it is neither possible to award p_1, p_2 belonging to $\mathcal{P}$ Certificate 4.3.14 nor to add Refutation 4.3.15, then add vagueness to p_1, p_2 belonging to $\mathcal{P}$. Vagueness comes with four lists *noSolutionList*, *solutionList*, *strictSolutionList*, and *strictNacSolutionList*. Each entry in the first list holds a critical pair for which no solution has been found making it locally confluent. Each entry in the second (resp. third) list holds a solution for each critical pair that is locally confluent, but not strictly NAC confluent (resp. strictly confluent, but not strictly NAC confluent). The *strictNacSolutionList* holds solutions for each critical pair that is strictly NAC confluent[5]. Moreover, in cases that the analysis has been performed merely up until a predefined solution length, vagueness comes with the number *maximalSolutionLength*.

Vagueness means that for now Property 4.3.13 can neither be certified, nor refuted. If sufficient calculating capacity is still available though, then the *maximalSolutionLength*

---

[5]Note that in cases that each rule in $\mathcal{P}$ does not hold any NAC, the list *strictSolutionList* is always empty. This is because each critical pair that is strictly confluent, is automatically strictly NAC confluent (See Thm. 2.10.11).

4.3. CERTIFYING A SELECTION OF PROPERTIES

could be augmented in order to find potentially existing longer solutions. Maybe Property 4.3.13 can then be certified anyway in the end.

reviewing model In cases of vagueness and no more calculating capacity the following procedure can be followed reviewing p_1, p_2 and $\mathcal{P}$ with respect to local confluence. For each entry in the *noSolutionList*, check if some rules in $\mathcal{P}$ can be changed or should be added in order to obtain a solution. For each entry in the *solutionList*, check if the rules in the solution can be changed such that they preserve the mutually preserved part of the critical pair. For each entry in the *strictSolutionList*, check if some NACs can be strengthened or also added to the rules of the critical pair (resp. weakened or also deleted from the rules in the solution) such that it becomes NAC confluent. In cases of rule reviewing it should be checked if already existing solutions in *strictNacSolutionList* remain valid. In cases of refutation, check if some rules in $\mathcal{P}$ can be reviewed such that the *nonResolvableCriticalPair* becomes strictly NAC confluent. Again, in case of changing some of the rules, check if already existing solutions in *strictNacSolutionList* remain valid.

reviewing property In cases of refutation, a reviewing of Property 4.3.13 should be taken into consideration. Especially, if some *nonResolvableCriticalPair* was not expected before performing the analysis, but appears to be consistent for the system one is modeling. It might be appropriate, for example, to ask for local confluence of conflicts represented by some specific critical pair for p_1 and p_2.

4.3.17 Remark (rule-based models with constraints). Note that based on Theorem 2.11.4, it will be possible to make the verification of local confluence more efficient for the case that a set of negative constraints, fulfilled by each potential state of the rule-based model, is given. Also, for the case that not only a set of rules $\mathcal{P}$, but a grammar is given, the corresponding local confluence analysis may be adapted. Note that also for each graph generated by a graph grammar, it is possible to derive a set of constraints holding for this graph. It is part of future work to describe the road to certification for rule-based models with constraints in more detail.

4.3.18 Example (Local Confluence). Road to Certificate *Local Confluence* for *Elevator*:

starting the road Consider the subset of rules $\mathcal{P}$ of *Elevator* that may process requests if the elevator is in downward direction: *process_stop_down*, *process_call_down*, and *process_stop_and_call*. If two rules in $\mathcal{P}$ compete for processing the same request on the elevator floor in downward direction, then it should be possible to reach a common state afterwards anyway. We can certify the property *Local Confluence* for the rules *process_call_down* and *process_stop_and_call* belonging to $\mathcal{P}$ as described in the following procedure[6].

apply analysis: compute critical pairs As explained for Property 4.3.1 (Conflicts as Expected), it is possible with AGG to compute the set of critical pairs for a sequence of rules (p_1, p_2). Note that here we need to compute the set of critical pairs for two rules p_1 and p_2, consisting of the union of the sets of critical pairs for sequence (p_1, p_2) and (p_2, p_1). Thus, we compute the set of critical pairs for rule sequence (*process_call_down*, *process_stop_and_call*) and (*process_stop_and_call*, *process_call_down*).

---

[6] Note that the certification of *Local Confluence* of the other rule pairs belonging to $\mathcal{P}$ can be done analogously.

CHAPTER 4. CERTIFYING RULE-BASED MODELS

Note that because of Theorem 2.11.12 and the fact that *process_call_down* and *process_stop_and_call* are rules without NACs, it is sufficient to check for strict confluence of the corresponding essential critical pairs. We notice that both sets contain the same essential critical pair, expressing that *process_stop_and_call* causes a delete-use conflict with *process_call_down*, and the other way round[7]. Concluding, the set of essential critical pairs for rules *process_stop_and_call* and *process_call_down* consists of one element as depicted in Fig. 4.5, expressing this delete-use conflict. Note that the conflict reason is surrounded by a thick black dashed line. When embedding the essential critical pair into some context, both elevators need to be glued.

check for solution This part of the analysis is not supported in AGG. Therefore, we check manually for a solution for the above computed critical pair $P_1 \overset{process\_call\_down}{\Longleftarrow} K \overset{process\_stop\_and\_call}{\Longrightarrow} P_2$. After having applied *process_call_down* to graph K, containing two elevators on the elevator floor with a stop and a call request, in P_1 the elevators remain on the elevator floor with a stop request. On the other hand, in P_2, the elevators remain on the elevator floor with no request. At first, we can see that P_1 and P_2 are not isomorphic. Moreover, we see that rule *process_stop_down* can be applied to P_1 in order to obtain P_2. Since this solution does not delete anything that is preserved by the critical pair and the rules contain no NACs, we can conclude that we have a strict NAC confluent critical pair. This solution can be added to the *strictNacSolutionList*.

certification The previous analysis enables us to add a Certificate *Local Confluence* to the rules *process_call_down* and *process_stop_and_call* belonging to the subset $\mathcal{P}$ of *Elevator* consisting of *process_stop_down*, *process_call_down*, and *process_stop_and_call*. It comes with the *strictNacSolutionList* for the unique essential critical pair computed for *process_call_down* and *process_stop_and_call*.

4.3.5 Termination

starting the road Rule-based models may possess non-terminating traces. This is because specific sets of rules may lead to infinitely many rule applications if they are applied as long as possible in a non-deterministic way. In order to be able to eliminate these cases, the following property should be investigated:

4.3.19 Property (Termination). Given a set of rules $\mathcal{P}$, then their non-deterministic application as long as possible always terminates.

apply analysis In [29, 33], sufficient criteria are given for termination of a layered set of rules. In layered rule application, the rules of one layer are applied as long as possible before switching to the application of rules belonging to the next layer. Since here, first, we do not consider layers, the sufficient criteria as given in [29] should be checked for the case that there is only one layer. Moreover, in Corollary 2.9.40 a sufficient condition for non-termination of a graph grammar is given. This condition is fulfilled if a rule p exists

---

[7]Note that an implementation in AGG comparing the critical pairs arising from the computed critical overlaps for (p_1, p_2) and (p_2, p_1) would be useful. For now, it needs to be done manually in order to obtain the set of critical pairs for two rules p_1 and p_2.

4.3. CERTIFYING A SELECTION OF PROPERTIES

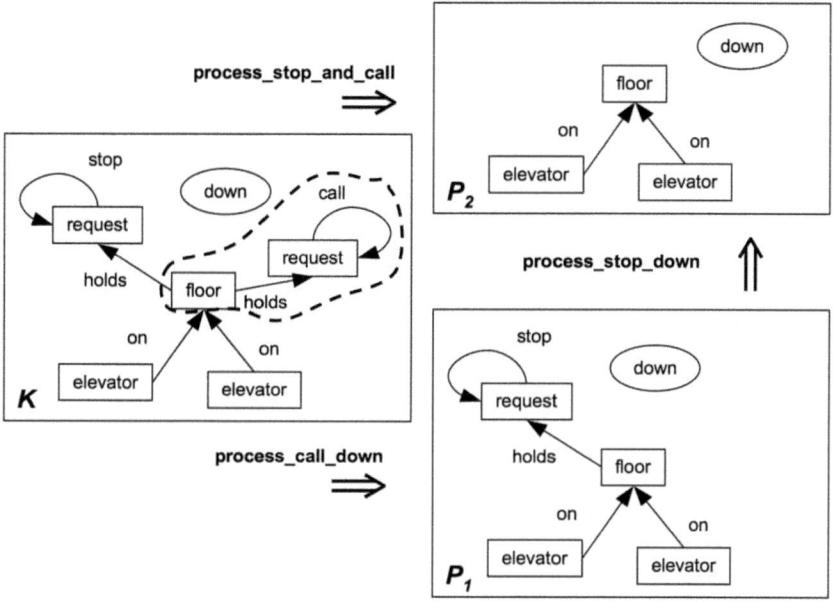

Figure 4.5: solution of essential critical pair for *process_call_down* and *process_stop_and_call*

such that no rule causes any conflict with p, and p is applicable to the start graph of the grammar. The negation of this condition is a necessary condition for termination of a graph grammar. Since here we consider termination of a set of rules, Property 4.3.19 for $\mathcal{P}$ can be refuted if a start graph S exists such that the grammar consisting of $\mathcal{P}$ and S does not fulfill the necessary condition.

check sufficient criteria For further explanations to this check we refer to the explanations in Section 12.3 in [29].

check necessary condition In Corollary 2.9.40, a sufficient condition for non-termination is given. Note that this corollary is only valid under the assumption that the gluing condition is fulfilled for each rule in $\mathcal{P}$ (see Assumption 2.9.1). Therefore, as described also for Property 4.3.30, it should be checked if this is the case for each p in $\mathcal{P}$. Now, in order to check the negation of the sufficient condition for non-termination in Corollary 2.9.40, we proceed as follows: compute successively for each rule p in $\mathcal{P}$ the set of critical pairs of the form $P_1 \overset{p_i}{\Leftarrow} K \overset{R}{\Rightarrow} P_2$, where p_i is a rule in $\mathcal{P}$ such that $K \overset{p_i}{\Rightarrow} P_1$ causes a conflict with $K \overset{R}{\Rightarrow} P_2$. If this set is empty, then check if a graph exists to which p can be applied. As soon as this is the case for some rule p, the necessary condition is not fulfilled, and therefore, Property 4.3.19 can be refuted. We call this rule p *always applicable*.

certification, refutation or vagueness It is possible to verify for a set of rules that transformations using these rules always terminate. This is the case if the above-described sufficient criteria hold.

CHAPTER 4. CERTIFYING RULE-BASED MODELS

4.3.20 Certificate (Termination). If it is possible to verify Property 4.3.19 for a set of rules $\mathcal{P}$, then award $\mathcal{P}$ this certificate.

It is possible to refute that a set of rules is terminating if the above-described necessary condition is not fulfilled.

4.3.21 Refutation (Termination). If it is possible to verify the negation of Property 4.3.19 for a set of rules $\mathcal{P}$, then add this refutation to $\mathcal{P}$. This refutation comes with at least one *always applicable* rule p.

If it is neither possible to add Certificate 4.3.20, nor Refutation 4.3.21, then we can only add *vagueness* about Property 4.3.19 to the rule set $\mathcal{P}$.

4.3.22 Vagueness (Termination). If neither Certificate 4.3.20 nor Refutation 4.3.21 can be added to $\mathcal{P}$, then add vagueness to $\mathcal{P}$.

reviewing model In cases of refutation, it should be investigated if it is adequate to change the *always applicable* rule p. At least one rule in $\mathcal{P}$ should cause a conflict with p. Take also the possibility into consideration of changing one of the other rules in $\mathcal{P}$ such that a conflict occurs. After such rule changes the sufficient criteria should be tested for satisfaction again.

reviewing property In cases of refutation and in cases that changing the model is not an option a review of Property 4.3.19 should be considered. Maybe it is possible to show termination if the *rules are divided into layers* as presented for the general case in [29]. Alternatively, it could be possible to add some other kind of control structure to the rules in $\mathcal{P}$.

4.3.23 Remark (rule-based models with constraints). Suppose that a set of constraints is fulfilled in each potential state of the rule-based model, then it will be possible to enhance the road to certification for termination. Also, for the case that not only a set of rules $\mathcal{P}$, but also a grammar is given, the corresponding termination analysis may be adapted. Note that also for each graph generated by a graph grammar, it is possible to derive a set of constraints holding for this graph. It is part of future work to describe the road to certification for rule-based models with constraints in more detail.

4.3.24 Example (Termination). Road to Certificate *Termination* for *Elevator*:

starting the road Consider again the subset of rules $\mathcal{P}$ of *Elevator* that may process requests if the elevator is in downward direction: *process_stop_down*, *process_call_down*, and *process_stop_and_call*. The processing of requests on the elevator floor should terminate such that the elevator control is ready to serve new requests or existing requests on other floors. We can certify the property *Termination* for the rules in $\mathcal{P}$ as explained in the following procedure.

apply analysis In AGG sufficient criteria leading to termination are implemented. For further explanations for this check, we refer to the explanations in Section 12.3 in [29]. Since each rule in $\mathcal{P}$ is deleting, it is clear that these criteria are fulfilled, and we can conclude for termination of $\mathcal{P}$.

certification The previous analysis enables us to add a Certificate *Termination* to the rules in $\mathcal{P}$: *process_call_down*, process_stop_and_call, and *process_stop_down*.

4.3.6 Functional Behavior

starting the road Rule-based models may exhibit functional behavior. A set of rules exhibits functional behavior if its rules can be applied non-deterministically as long as possible, and thereby, always yield the same result. In many rule-based models, such a functional behavior is a desired property at least for a subset of rules. Thus, in order to find out if a set of rules features such a behavior, the following property should be investigated:

4.3.25 Property (Functional Behavior). Given a set of rules $\mathcal{P}$, then their non-deterministic application as long as possible generates a unique result.

apply analysis By Lemma 6.25 in [29], a set of rules exhibits functional behavior if and only if it is locally confluent and terminating. A set of rules $\mathcal{P}$ is locally confluent if each pair of direct transformations on G via two rules in $\mathcal{P}$ is locally confluent. Therefore, Property 4.3.25 holds for a set of rules $\mathcal{P}$ if and only if Property 4.3.13 holds for each pair of rules in $\mathcal{P}$ and Property 4.3.19 holds for $\mathcal{P}$. Note that (as described more generally in Section 4.2.3) Property 4.3.25 can be understood as a first-order formula over the already known Properties 4.3.13 and 4.3.19. Consequently, the further road to certification of this Property can be derived from the certification procedure of these properties. The following two steps should be processed[8]:

check local confluence Apply the analysis as described in Section 4.3.4 for each pair of rules in $\mathcal{P}$. If Property 4.3.13 can be certified for each pair of rules, then $\mathcal{P}$ is locally confluent.

check termination Apply the analysis as described in Section 4.3.5 for $\mathcal{P}$. Check if Certificate *Termination* can be added to $\mathcal{P}$.

certification, refutation or vagueness The analysis procedure above enables us to draw the following conclusions. If each pair of rules in $\mathcal{P}$ can be awarded with Certificate 4.3.14 (Local Confluence) and $\mathcal{P}$ can be awarded with Certificate 4.3.20 (Termination), then Property 4.3.25 (Functional Behavior) is fulfilled. The analysis of Property 4.3.13 (Local Confluence) leads to certification, refutation, or vagueness. Because of this reason, also for Property 4.3.25 (Functional Behavior) refutation becomes possible, and vagueness can arise. Moreover, the analysis of Property 4.3.19 (Termination) can lead to certification, refutation or vagueness. Therefore, we have another potential reason for vagueness or refutation of Property 4.3.25 (Functional Behavior). The following certificate, refutation or vagueness come with analogous information for the success or failure of the analysis as the certificate, refutation, or vagueness of Property 4.3.13 (resp. Property 4.3.19).

4.3.26 Certificate (Functional Behavior). If it is possible to verify Property 4.3.25 for a set of rules $\mathcal{P}$, then award $\mathcal{P}$ this certificate. Thereby, the set of rules $\mathcal{P}$ holds Certificate 4.3.20. Each pair of rules in $\mathcal{P}$ holds Certificate 4.3.14, and comes with a *strictNacSolutionList* as introduced in Section 4.3.4.

4.3.27 Refutation (Functional Behavior). If it is possible to verify the negation of Property 4.3.6 for a set of rules $\mathcal{P}$, then add this refutation to $\mathcal{P}$. This refutation comes with two boolean variables *localConfluence* and *termination*[9]. The value of *localConfluence*

---

[8]Thereby, note that these steps are independent of each other and can be performed in parallel to obtain the analysis result in a faster way

[9]Note that at least one of these variables equals false.

CHAPTER 4. CERTIFYING RULE-BASED MODELS

is true if each pair in $\mathcal{P}$ holds Certificate 4.3.14; otherwise its value is false. The value of *termination* is true if $\mathcal{P}$ holds Certificate 4.3.20. In cases that *termination* equals false, it comes with an *always applicable* rule p as introduced in Section 4.3.5. In cases that *localConfluence* equals false it comes with at least one *nonResolvableCriticalPair* as introduced in Section 4.3.4.

4.3.28 Vagueness (Functional Behavior). If neither Certificate 4.3.26 nor Refutation 4.3.27 can be added to a set of rules $\mathcal{P}$, then add vagueness to $\mathcal{P}$. Vagueness comes with two boolean variables *localConfluence* and *termination*. The value of *localConfluence* is true if each pair in $\mathcal{P}$ holds Certificate 4.3.14; otherwise its value is false. The value of *termination* is true if $\mathcal{P}$ holds Certificate 4.3.20[10]. If *localConfluence* equals false, then each pair in $\mathcal{P}$ for which Vagueness 4.3.16 holds comes with the *noSolutionList*, *solutionList*, *strictSolutionList*, and *strictNacSolutionList* as introduced in Section 4.3.4.

reviewing model The reviewing of the model is analogous to the reviewing of the model in Section 4.3.4 and Section 4.3.5. The following circumstances determine the success of reviewing: in cases of refutation, $\mathcal{P}$ is non-terminating, and therefore, the reviewing as introduced in Section 4.3.5 can be followed. In cases of vagueness, and in cases that *localConfluence* equals false for each pair in $\mathcal{P}$ holding Vagueness 4.3.16, the reviewing as introduced in Section 4.3.4 can be followed.

reviewing property Analogous to Property 4.3.19 (resp. Property 4.3.13) in cases of refutation, and in cases that reviewing the model is not an option, a review of Property 4.3.25 should be taken into consideration. Maybe, functional behavior is a property that is too strong and, for example, merely termination (or local confluence) would be a strong enough requirement.

4.3.29 Example (Functional Behavior). Road to Certificate *Functional Behavior* for *Elevator*:

starting the road We continue with analyzing the subset $\mathcal{P}$ of rules of *Elevator* that may process requests if the elevator is in downward direction: *process_stop_down*, *process_call_down*, and *process_stop_and_call*. If these process rules are applied to an elevator in downward direction as long as possible, then this should lead always to the same terminal state. This means that the processing of requests in downward direction shows a functional behavior. We can certify the property *Functional Behavior* for these rules as described in the following procedure.

apply analysis: check local confluence As explained in the example of Property 4.3.13 (Local Confluence), it is possible to add to each pair of rules belonging to $\mathcal{P}$ the Certificate *Local Confluence*. Therefore, we know that $\mathcal{P}$ is locally confluent.

check termination As explained in the example of Property 4.3.19 (Termination) it is possible to add to $\mathcal{P}$ the Certificate *Termination*.

certificate The previous analysis enables us to add a Certificate *Functional Behavior* to the rules in $\mathcal{P}$: *process_call_down*, process_stop_and_call, and *process_stop_down*. It comes with a *strictNacSolutionList*, which can be constructed as explained in Section 4.3.4.

---

[10]Note that both values can not be true at the same time.

4.3.7 Applicability

starting the road Given some rule sequence and a specific state of a rule-based model, it can be useful to find out if this rule sequence will be applicable to this state, where the analysis is done in a static way – meaning that the rule sequence is not actually performed. Especially, if not only one initial state is given, but a collection of potential initial states, possibly defined by a set of properties fulfilled for this collection of states. In this case, it may become quite tedious to actually run the rule sequence on each of these potential initial states. This may become tedious also in cases that not only one single rule sequence should be tested for applicability, but a potentially infinite set of rule sequences (see Remark 4.3.34). Here, we consider first a single rule sequence, and ask us if it is applicable to a certain graph. The answer to this question depends on the satisfaction or non-satisfaction of the following property:

4.3.30 Property (Applicability). Given a rule sequence $p_0, p_1, \ldots, p_n$ and some start graph G_0, then this rule sequence is applicable to G_0.

apply analysis In Section 2.9.2, different variants of sufficient criteria for the applicability of a rule sequence to a graph are introduced. Moreover, in Section 2.9.3, a sufficient condition for non-applicability of a rule sequence to a graph is introduced. In consequence, its negation is a necessary condition for applicability. Finally, in Section 2.9.1, different types of reductions of rule sequences are presented, preserving the applicability or non-applicability of a rule sequence. Note that the sufficient criteria for applicability hold under the assumption that the rules belonging to the rule sequence under consideration always fulfill the gluing condition. Based on this theory, we can design the following analysis procedure:

check gluing condition Check if Assumption 2.9.1 is satisfied for all rules in the rule sequence $p_0, p_1, \ldots, p_n$. If not, then for the time being only vagueness can be diagnosed, but a review of the model is strongly advised. The result of this check is saved into the boolean variable *gluingCondition*, which is true (resp. false) if Assumption 2.9.1 is satisfied (resp. not satisfied). Note that each set of rules can be reviewed in such a way that they fulfill the gluing condition without changing their behavioral semantics significantly. For more explanations, see Assumption 2.9.1 and Example 2.9.2. More explanations for this reviewing can be found in the reviewing step.

check applicability criteria Check if each applicability criterion, as introduced in Definition 2.9.23, is fulfilled. If the *enabling predecessor criterion* is not fulfilled, then check if one of the alternative enabling predecessor criteria is fulfilled. They are presented in Definition 2.9.27, 2.9.31, and 2.9.35. If so, then together with the satisfaction of the gluing condition this leads to the fact that Property 4.3.30 is fulfilled, and can be certified. In cases of satisfaction, save the partial result of this check into the list, called *enablingPredecessorList*. Each item in this list describes for each rule in the sequence (except for the first one) the kind of enabling predecessor it possesses according to Definition 2.9.23, 2.9.27, 2.9.31, or 2.9.35, and as the case may be, which rule(s) are the enabling ones. In cases of failure, save the partial result of this check into the boolean variables *noImpedingPredecessor* and *enablingPredecessor*. The first one is true (resp. false) if the corresponding criterion in Definition

CHAPTER 4. CERTIFYING RULE-BASED MODELS

2.9.23 is fulfilled (resp. not fulfilled). In cases that *noImpedingPredecessor* is false, a pair of rules is saved into a variable, called *ruleWithImpedingPredecessor*, such that the first rule causes a conflict with the second one, and the first one is a predecessor of the second one. The variable *enablingPredecessor* is true (resp. false) if one of the *enabling predecessor criteria* is fulfilled (resp. any of them is fulfilled). If it is false, it comes with a rule number, called *ruleNo*, expressing that for p_{ruleNo} it was not possible to find an enabling predecessor.

check non-applicability criteria Check the non-applicability criteria as introduced in Definition 2.9.42. If one of them is true, then the rule sequence is non-applicable to graph G_0 and, therefore, Property 4.3.30 can be refuted. Therefore, the necessary condition for applicability expresses that both of the non-applicability criteria (*initialization error*, and *no enabling predecessor*) should be false. The result of this check is saved into the boolean variables *initializationError*, which is true (resp. false) if the *initialization error criterion* is true (resp. false), and *noEnablingPredecessor*, which is true (resp. false) if the *no enabling predecessor criterion* is true (resp. false). If *noEnablingPredecessor* is true, then the variable, called *ruleNo*, specifies an integer value such that $0 < \text{ruleNo} \leq n$, and p_{ruleNo} is a rule for which no enabling predecessor exists.

apply reductions If neither the applicability criteria nor non-applicability criteria are fulfilled for the considered rule sequence, then the reductions as presented in Section 2.9.1 can be applied. It is possible that after applying one or more of these reductions, the applicability criteria (resp. non-applicability criteria) for the reduced rule sequence are fulfilled. If this is the case, then applicability (resp. non-applicability) of the original rule sequence holds.

certification or refutation The above analysis procedure leads to certification if the steps *check gluing condition* and *check applicability criteria* are accomplished successfully for the original or reduced rule sequence. It leads to refutation if the necessary condition is not fulfilled. This means that one of the non-applicability criteria is true. In all other cases, only vagueness can be determined.

4.3.31 Certificate (Applicability). If it is possible to verify Property 4.3.30 for a rule sequence $s : p_0, p_1, \ldots, p_n$ and a graph G_0, then award s and G_0 this certificate. This certificate comes with a list, called *enablingPredecessorList* for s or a reduced sequence s^{red} of s as introduced in the analysis procedure above.

4.3.32 Refutation (Applicability). If it is possible to verify the negation of Property 4.3.30 for a rule sequence $s : p_0, p_1, \ldots, p_n$ and a graph G_0, then add this refutation to s and G_0. This refutation comes with the boolean variables *intializationError* and *noEnablingPredecessor*[11] for s or a reduced sequence s^{red} of s as introduced in the above analysis procedure. If *noEnablingPredecessor* is true, then, moreover, it comes with *ruleNo* as introduced in the above analysis procedure.

4.3.33 Vagueness (Applicability). If neither Certificate 4.3.31 nor Refutation 4.3.32 can be added to a rule sequence $p_0, p_1, \ldots, p_n$ and a graph G_0, then add vagueness to

---
[11]Note that either *initializationError* or *noEnablingPredecessor* should be true

4.3. CERTIFYING A SELECTION OF PROPERTIES

them. Vagueness comes with the tree boolean variables *gluingCondition*, *noImpedingPredecessor*, and *enablingPredecessor*[12] as introduced in the analysis procedure above. If *noImpedingPredecessor* (resp. *enablingPredecessor*) equals false, then, moreover, it comes with *ruleWithImpedingPredecessor* (resp. *ruleNo*).

reviewing model
- There can be two different reasons for refutation according to the non-applicability criteria (as presented in Def. 2.9.42). In cases that *initializationError* equals true, it should be investigated if either this rule p_0 or also G_0 can be changed such that p_0 becomes applicable. If *ruleNo* equals j, then this indicates that some rule p_j with $0 < j \leq n$ in the rule sequence $p_0, p_1, \ldots, p_n$ is not applicable to G_0 and is not causally dependent on some predecessor. Therefore, it should be investigated if either G_0 or p_j can be changed such that this rule becomes applicable, or some predecessor(s) rule of p_j can be changed such that p_j can be triggered by some predecessor(s).

- In cases of vagueness, the model can be reviewed as follows: if *gluingCondition* equals false, then it is possible for each rule-based model to review it such that it becomes true. If non-injective matching is allowed for the rules in rule sequence $p_0, p_1, \ldots, p_n$, then construct for each of the rules that can be applied in a non-injective way a set of equivalent rules as explained in [46]. The original rule is then applicable if and only if one of the equivalent rules is applicable with injective matching with the same result, and vice versa. This construction is illustrated in Example 2.9.2. In that way, rule sequence $p_0, p_1, \ldots, p_n$ can be changed into a rule sequence with rules that are matched in an injective way such that the identification condition is always fulfilled. If some rule p in $p_0, p_1, \ldots, p_n$ is deleting on nodes that may possess adjacent edges, then this rule can be reviewed as follows: insert for each node type that is deleted a container node in the type graph. Add this container node to the rule p such that it is not deleted by p. If rule p is not typed, then just add one container node that is not deleted to p. Add an edge to the left-hand side of p from the node to be deleted to the container node. Now instead of deleting the node, the edge to the container node is deleted. Thus, the deletion of nodes is simulated by decoupling the node from the container node. In that way, each rule becomes non-deleting on nodes. If *noImpedingPredecessor* equals false, then investigate if rule p with its potentially impeding predecessor p' as given in *ruleWithImpedingPredecessor* can be reviewed such that p' does not cause any conflict with p any more. If *enablingPredecessor* is false, then investigate if p_{ruleNo} or one of its predecessor can be changed such that one of the *enabling predecessor criteria* is fulfilled.

After reviewing the model, one should rerun the analysis in order to find out if *Applicability* can be certified for the reviewed model.

reviewing property In cases of refutation, and in cases that it is not adequate to change the rules or start graph such that the necessary condition is fulfilled, a review of Property 4.3.30 should be taken into consideration. For example, maybe it was overlooked that one of the rules (for example, p_{ruleNo}) in the sequence is not (or even should not be) triggered. In this case one should classify this sequence as one that should fulfill non-applicability.

---
[12]Note that at least one of these values equals false

4.3.34 Remark (set of rule sequences). Note that this property can be formulated not only for one rule sequence, but a (possibly infinite) set of rule sequences. Then, the reductions introduced in Section 2.9.1 play an even more important role. In the conclusion to this thesis, it is described briefly as outlook how rule-based models can be extended to rule-based models with some specific kind of control. This control can be of two types: it determines the order in which certain rules should be applied, or it determines completely or partially where to match a specific rule. As soon as the first kind of control is specified, sets of rule sequences can be generated expressing all the possible orders in which rules can be applied. Therefore, sets of rule sequences arise that can then be analyzed for applicability. Note that these sets can become infinitely large because of loops in the control structure, and, therefore, the reduction techniques as presented in Section 2.9.1 can be used to possibly reduce these infinite sets to finite ones.

4.3.35 Example (Applicability). Road to Certificate *Applicability* for *Elevator*:

starting the road In our running example *Elevator*, we consider a four-storey building in which the elevator is operating. Therefore, we expect that a rule sequence consisting of four call requests and four stop requests in any order is applicable to the initial state G_0 of *Elevator*, as depicted in Fig. 2.2. This state represents a four-storey building with the elevator car on the ground floor in upward mode without any request. Thus we consider a rule sequence $s : call\_request^4, stop\_request^4$, and certify property *Applicability* for this rule sequence and start graph G_0 as follows[13].

apply analysis: check gluing condition The rules *call_request* and *stop_request* fulfill the gluing condition for each potential match since they do not delete any node and we can assume injective matching. AGG supports in the following way the checking for a specific set of rules if the gluing condition is always fulfilled. It is possible in AGG to restrict to injective matching by choosing this option in the general option menu. Moreover, during the applicability check for a rule sequence it tests for a *restricted node deletion* criterion. This means that node-deletion is only allowed if nodes are deleted together with the maximal multiplicity adjacent edges. This ensures that when deleting the corresponding node, no edges are dangling.

check applicability criteria AGG supports the automatic checking of the applicability criteria (*initialization, no impeding predecessor*, and *enabling predecessor*) for a given rule sequence and graph. The *initialization criterion* for our example rule sequence $s : call\_request^4, stop\_request^4$ is fulfilled since *call_request* is applicable to the initial state G_0 of *Elevator*, as depicted in Fig. 2.2. The *no impeding predecessor criterion* is not fulfilled since *call_request* causes a conflict with itself[14]. This is because only one call request can be registered for the same floor. Therefore, we stop checking the applicability criteria and check if the non-applicability criteria are fulfilled. In the upper table of Fig. 4.6, it is shown that the applicability analysis for sequence s to G_0 delivers only vagueness. Therefore, in AGG sequence s is colored in orange.

---

[13]Note that by means of the shift-equivalent reduction (see Theorem 2.9.11) it is possible to certify *Applicability* in an analogous way for all rule sequences in which the four call requests (resp. stop requests) occur in any other order

[14]See Remark 2.9.24 for more explanations on improving the *no impeding predecessor* criterion such that not each potential conflict necessarily leads to the failure of this criterion.

4.3. CERTIFYING A SELECTION OF PROPERTIES

In the middle table of Fig. 4.6, the more detailed result of the applicability analysis for sequence s to G_0 is shown. Each row (resp. column) corresponds with a rule (resp. criterion)[15]. In AGG a table entry colored green (resp. orange) expresses that the corresponding applicability criterion for the corresponding rule is fulfilled (resp. not fulfilled). Moreover, in the *impeding predecessor* column, it is shown which rule may be an impeding one. In this case, *call_request* (resp. *stop_request*) may be impeding itself. Note also that only one of the criteria 4a-4d needs to be fulfilled for applicability. See [74] for more information to the implementation of this check in AGG.

check non-applicability criteria Since each rule in s : $call\_request^4, stop\_request^4$ is applicable to G_0, neither the *initialization error criterion* nor the *no enabling predecessor criterion* are fulfilled. The lower table of Fig. 4.6 shows the detailed result of the non-applicability analysis in AGG. In this case AGG colors each entry orange, meaning that none of the non-applicability criteria is fulfilled. If one of the entries was red, then one of the criteria would be fulfilled, and the sequence would be non-applicable.

apply reductions During checking the applicability criteria, we notice that the *no impeding predecessor criterion* is not fulfilled. Therefore, we try to apply the summary reduction (see Theorem 2.9.9) such that for the reduced sequence s^{red} this criterion is fulfilled. Note that applying these reductions is not supported yet in AGG. We can summarize the first four call requests into a concurrent rule *call_request_four*, generating a call request for four floors that do not hold any call request. Analogously, we can summarize $stop\_request^4$ into a concurrent rule *stop_request_four*, generating a stop request for four floors that do not hold any stop request. Now, we check if this reduced rule sequence s^{red} : *call_request_four, stop_request_four* is applicable to G_0.

check gluing condition The gluing condition of *call_request_four* and *stop_request_four* is fulfilled for each potential match since these rules do not delete any node and we can assume injective matching.

check applicability criteria The applicability criteria for the reduced rule sequence s^{red} : *call_request_four, stop_request_four* are fulfilled. This is because *call_request_four* is applicable to G_0 leading to the satisfaction of the *initialization criterion*. Moreover, rule *stop_request_four* is also applicable to G_0 leading to the satisfaction of the *enabling predecessor criterion (not needed)*. The *enablingPredecessorList* for s^{red} contains just one entry of the type not needed.

certification The previous analysis enables us to add a Certificate *Applicablity* to the rule sequence s : $call\_request^4, stop\_request^4$ and G_0 of *Elevator* as depicted in Fig. 2.2. It comes with the *enablingPredecessorList* for the reduced rule sequence s^{red} : *call_request_four, stop_request_four* as described above.

---

[15]Note that AGG checks for each rule if it is non-deleting on nodes such that, when injective matching is assumed, the corresponding rule always fulfills the gluing condition.

CHAPTER 4. CERTIFYING RULE-BASED MODELS

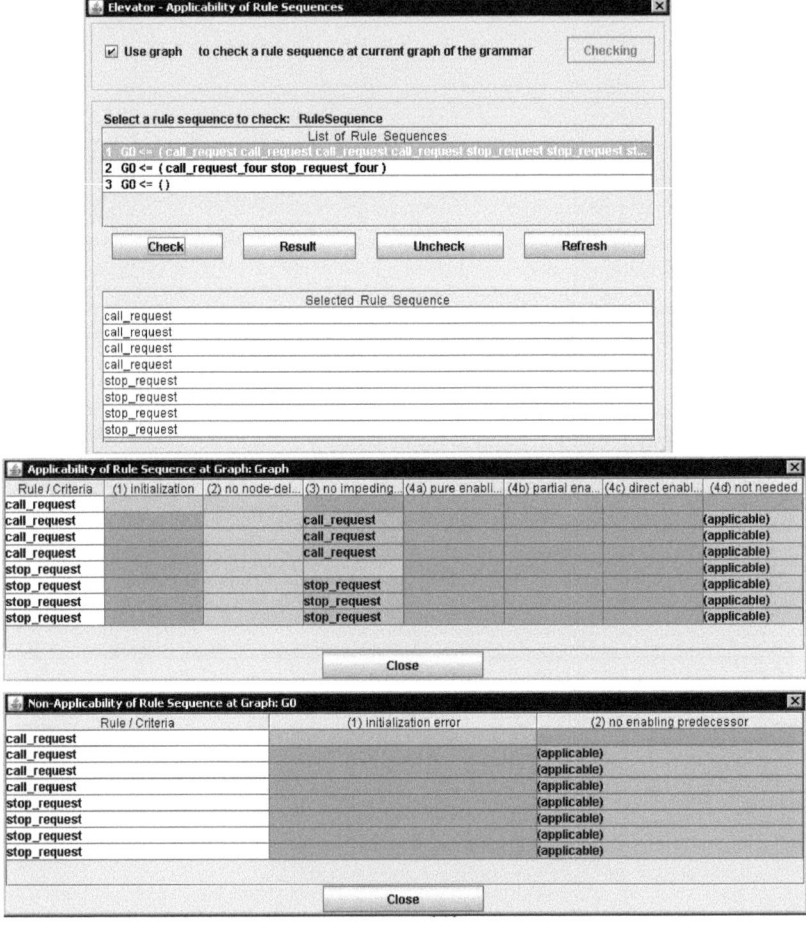

Figure 4.6: applicability analysis result for s in AGG

4.3.8 Non-Applicability

starting the road Sometimes one would like to investigate if for some (part of a) rule-based model the negation of a property, for which the road to certification is specified already, holds. Here, we present such a case. For safety reasons, it may be useful to know about certain rule sequences that they are not applicable to a specific state. To this end, one checks if a specific rule sequence cannot become applicable to a certain graph G_0, expressing this state, under any circumstance. This situation is expressed by the following property, which is a negation of Property 4.3.30. Therefore, the road to certification can be derived from the one specified for Property 4.3.30, as described in Section 4.3.7, as mentioned already in the more general context of certification bootstrapping in Section 4.2.3,

4.3.36 Property (Non-Applicability). Given a rule sequence $p_0, p_1, \ldots, p_n$ and some start graph G_0, then this rule sequence is not applicable to G_0.

apply analysis The same analysis procedure as for Property 4.3.30 can be applied. However, note that it is sensible to switch the order of the corresponding analysis steps *check gluing condition, check applicability criteria, check non-applicability criteria* into *check non-applicability criteria, check gluing condition, check applicability criteria*. This is because it is expected that the non-applicability criteria are fulfilled leading, possibly, to a faster certification. The analysis result that led to refutation (resp. certification) of Property 4.3.30 leads now to certification (resp. refutation). If vagueness was obtained in the above analysis procedure, then only vagueness can be diagnosed here as well.

certification, refutation or vagueness The analysis procedure described for Property 4.3.30 leads for Property 4.3.36 to certification if one of the non-applicability criteria is true for the original sequence or a reduced sequence. It leads to refutation if the steps *check gluing condition* and *check applicability criteria* are accomplished successfully for the original rule sequence or a reduced sequence. In all other cases, only vagueness can be determined.

4.3.37 Certificate (Non-Applicability). If it is possible to verify Property 4.3.36 for a rule sequence $s : p_0, p_1, \ldots, p_n$ and a graph G_0, then award s and G_0 this certificate. This certificate comes with the boolean variables *intializationError* and *noEnablingPredecessor*[16] for s or a reduced sequence s^{red} of s as introduced in the analysis procedure for Property 4.3.30. In the case that *noEnablingPredecessor* equals true, then it comes with *ruleNo* as introduced in the analysis procedure for Property 4.3.30.

4.3.38 Refutation (Non-Applicability). If it is possible to verify the negation of Property 4.3.36 for a rule sequence $s : p_0, p_1, \ldots, p_n$ and a graph G_0, then add this refutation to s and G_0. This refutation comes with a list, called *enablingPredecessorList*, for s or a reduced sequence s^{red} of s as introduced in the analysis procedure for Property 4.3.30.

4.3.39 Vagueness (Non-Applicability). If neither Certificate 4.3.36 nor Refutation 4.3.36 can be added to a rule sequence $s : p_0, p_1, \ldots, p_n$ and a graph G_0, then add vagueness to them. Vagueness comes with the boolean variables *gluingCondition*,

---
[16]Note that either *initializationError* or *noEnablingPredecessor* should be true

CHAPTER 4. CERTIFYING RULE-BASED MODELS

noImpedingPredecessor, and *enablingPredecessor*[17] as introduced in the analysis procedure above. If *noImpedingPredecessor* (resp. *enablingPredecessor*) equals false, then moreover, it comes with *ruleWithImpedingPredecessor* (resp. *ruleNo*).

reviewing model In cases of refutation, we need to review the model such that the rule sequence becomes non-applicable to G_0. Therefore, we can try to change the rules or G_0 such that the first rule is not applicable anymore. Alternatively, we can change them such that one of the rules in the rule sequence is neither applicable on G_0 nor triggered by some predecessor rule. Thereby, the *enablingPredecessorList* can be helpful. In cases of vagueness, the following reviewing could be taken into account. If *gluingCondition* equals false, then review the model as described for Property 4.3.30 such that it becomes true. If *enablingPredecessor* equals false, then one could try and change the rules in $p_0, p_1, \ldots, p_n$ such that p_{ruleNo} is neither applicable to G_0 nor triggered in any means by a predecessor rule. After reviewing the model, the analysis should be rerun in order to find out if it can be certified now.

reviewing property In cases of refutation, it might be the case that after analyzing the rule sequence, it becomes clear that the sequence should indeed be applicable instead of non-applicable to G_0.

4.3.40 Example (Non-Applicability). Road to Certificate *Non-Applicability* for *Elevator*:

starting the road Consider an elevator in upward mode, which is switched into downward mode because no higher requests are available anymore, and a lower request is registered. It is important that the elevator control does not get into an endless loop changing the direction mode again into upward mode, and then in downward mode, ... Therefore, we check that rule sequence *set_direction_down, set_direction_up* repeated arbitrarily many times is not applicable to the graph G_0 as depicted in Fig. 4.7. We can certify the property *Non-Applicability* for the rule sequence s : *set_direction_down, set_direction_up* repeated three times and graph G_0 as follows[18].

apply analysis: check non-applicability criteria AGG supports the automatic checking of the non-applicability criteria (*initialization error*, and *no enabling predecessor*) for a given rule sequence and graph. The *initialization error criterion* for our example rule sequence s is not fulfilled since *set_direction_down* is applicable to the start graph G_0, as shown in Fig. 4.7. On the contrary, the *no enabling predecessor criterion* is fulfilled for the second rule in the sequence: *set_direction_up*. This is because *set_direction_up* is neither applicable to G_0 nor triggered by *set_direction_down*.

certification The previous analysis enables us to add a Certificate *Non-Applicability* to the rule sequence s : *set_direction_down, set_direction_up* repeated three times and the start graph G_0 as depicted in Fig. 4.7. It comes with the boolean variables *initializationError* equal to false, *noEnablingPredecessor* equal to true, and *ruleNo* equal to 2. This means, in particular, that the second rule, being *set_direction_up*, is not triggered making the whole sequence non-applicable. In fact, all subsequent rules in the sequence will also fulfill the *no enabling predecessor* criterion.

---

[17]Note that at least one of these values equals false

[18]Note that analogously, it is possible to certify each rule sequence with *set_direction_down, set_direction_up* repeated arbitrarily many times

4.3. CERTIFYING A SELECTION OF PROPERTIES

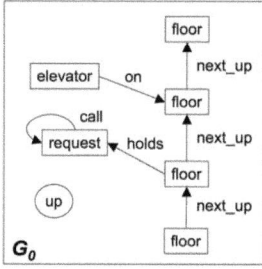

Figure 4.7: start graph G_0 – elevator in upward mode with lower request

4.3.9 Constraint Preserved

starting the road In order to ensure safety in a rule-based model, the preservation of specific properties by certain rules is essential. The following property specifies that this is the case:

4.3.41 Property (Constraint Preserved). Given a rule p and a constraint C, then p preserves the satisfaction of constraint C. This means that for each rule application $G \overset{R}{\Rightarrow} H$ via p it holds that H satisfies C if G satisfies C.

Note that C is a graph constraint as given in Definition 2.2.13. The certification of this property can be generalized to nested constraints as presented in [46], but this is not within the scope of this thesis.

apply analysis Consider a rule application $G \overset{R}{\Rightarrow} H$ via p such that G satisfies C. Property 4.3.41 expresses that in this case also H must satisfy C.

$$\begin{array}{ccccc} L & \leftarrow & K & \rightarrow & R \\ {\scriptstyle m}\downarrow & & \downarrow & & \downarrow{\scriptstyle m'} \\ G & \leftarrow & D & \rightarrow & H \end{array}$$

In [29], it is presented how to translate a constraint C into an equivalent right application condition $AC_{p,R}^{C,after}$ for rule p.[19] Moreover, in [29], it is shown how to translate $AC_{p,R}^{C,after}$ into an equivalent left application condition $AC_{p,L}^{C,after}$ for rule p. Summarizing, $AC_{p,L}^{C,after}$ is fulfilled by match $m : L \to G$ if and only if graph H satisfies C. Note that we can translate C also into an equivalent left application condition $AC_{p,L}^{C,before}$ such that $m : L \to G$ fulfills $AC_{p,L}^{C,before}$ if and only if G satisfies C. Based on this knowledge, we can perform the analysis of Property 4.3.41 into two steps:

compute left application conditions Compute for p and the constraint C the left application conditions $AC_{p,L}^{C,after}$ and $AC_{p,L}^{C,before}$ as described in [29], and sketched above.

---

[19]Note that our notion of constraints (see Def. 2.2.13) is more general than the notion of application conditions arising from these constraints after the translation. In this thesis, we consider only NACs, but in general also positive application conditions arise. They express that in addition to the LHS (or RHS) some extra graph part should be present that is not changed by the rule application.

check implication Check for p if for each valid direct transformation via p the already existing NAC_p together with $AC_{p,L}^{C,before}$ imply $AC_{p,L}^{C,after}$. This means that if NAC_p and $AC_{p,L}^{C,before}$ are satisfied for some match m satisfying the gluing condition for p, then m satisfies also $AC_{p,L}^{C,after}$. It is part of future work to come up with a general procedure to verify the implication of application conditions. For the special case of negative application conditions, the following simple implication rule holds: $NAC(n_1) : L \to N_1$ implies $NAC(n_2) : L \to N_2$ if there exists an injective graph morphism $i : N_1 \to N_2$ such that $i \circ n_1 = n_2$. It expresses that if N_1 cannot be found in an instance graph G via match m, then neither can the bigger N_2 be found. Note that in [90], how to check that one constraint implicates another one is described more in detail. Since application conditions can be seen as a special kind of nested constraint over the empty graph, it should be possible to relate both problems.

Note that the difference between this approach and constraint preservation as presented in [50, 29, 46] is that rules are not changed by adding application conditions. Only if it is not possible to verify the above presented implication of application conditions, then rules may be changed during reviewing. Moreover, note that in [46], it is shown that the implication and tautology problem for nested graph conditions is undecidable. In [93], it is described how theorem proving can be used to approach this problem. In [92], it is shown that for a suitable subclass of nested graph conditions these problems are decidable.

certification, refutation or vagueness By the above analysis procedure, it is possible to certify Property 4.3.41 if it can be verified that the implication from NAC_p and $AC_{p,L}^{C,before}$ to $AC_{p,L}^{C,after}$ holds. It may be possible, on the other hand, to refute Property 4.3.41. In cases of failure of the above-described techniques, only vagueness can be determined.

4.3.42 Certificate (Constraint Preserved). If it is possible to verify Property 4.3.41 for p and some constraint C, then award p and C this certificate. This certificate comes with $AC_{p,L}^{C,before}$ and $AC_{p,L}^{C,after}$ for p as introduced in the analysis procedure above.

4.3.43 Refutation (Constraint Preserved). If it is possible to verify the negation of Property 4.3.41 for a rule p and constraint C, then add this refutation to p and C. This refutation comes with $AC_{p,L}^{C,before}$ and $AC_{p,L}^{C,after}$ for p as introduced in the analysis procedure above.

4.3.44 Vagueness (Constraint Preserved). If neither Certificate 4.3.42, nor Refutation 4.3.43 can be added to the rule p and constraint C, then add vagueness to them. Vagueness comes with $AC_{p,L}^{C,before}$ and $AC_{p,L}^{C,after}$ for p as introduced in the analysis procedure above.

reviewing model In cases of vagueness, the implication check for p was not successful. Check in this case if $AC_{p,L}^{C,after}$ for p can just be added to p permanently. If so, then the implication check is trivially successful and, therefore, the model review concerning Property 4.3.41 as well.

reviewing property In cases of vagueness, and in cases that it is impossible to review the model as described above, one could take into consideration weakening the constraint C such that the implication check becomes successful. In case of refutation, it might be

4.3. CERTIFYING A SELECTION OF PROPERTIES

the case that it becomes clear that p should indeed not preserve C. Maybe a weaker constraint C can be taken into consideration.

4.3.45 Remark (rule-based model with constraints). Note that it might be the case that some constraints are available that hold in the rule-based model (at any time or at least) before applying rule p. These constraints could be used in order to make the precondition of the above-described implication stronger. Note that also for each graph generated by a graph grammar, it is possible to derive a set of constraints holding for this graph. It is part of future work to describe this topic in more detail.

4.3.46 Example (Constraint Preserved). Road to Certificate *Constraint Preserved* for *Elevator*:

starting the road Each request should be connected to one specific floor, and not several. This safety constraint should be preserved by the rules modeling the elevator control. Note that this negative constraint $NC(floors\_no\_same\_req)$ is depicted on the upper right in Fig. 4.8. We can certify the property *Constraint Preserved* for this constraint and each of the rules in $GTS_{Elevator}$ as introduced in Example 2.3.16. We explain it here exemplarily for the rule *stop_request* (see Fig. 2.6) as follows:

apply analysis: compute left application conditions Computing at first the application condition $AC_{p,L}^{C,before}$, corresponding to the construction in [29], we notice that it consists of two negative application conditions. Note that this computation is not supported yet by AGG. Basically, all injective overlaps of *floors_no_same_req* with the left-hand side of *stop_request* are computed and interpreted as a NAC. The first NAC expresses that no two other floors pointing to the same request may exist. The second one expresses that the floor for which the request should be produced is not already pointing to some request to which another floor is pointing as well (see also Fig. 4.8). Computing then also $AC_{p,L}^{C,after}$, corresponding to the construction in [29], we notice that it consists of exactly the same set of two negative application conditions. This computation is partly supported by AGG , since it can compute the equivalent right application condition for a rule and a given constraint. The translation of this constraint to the left-hand side of the rule is not supported yet. Basically, all injective overlaps of *floors_no_same_req* with the right-hand side of *stop_request* are constructed and interpreted as NACs obtaining $AC_{p,R}^{C,after}$. Afterwards, if it is possible, the inverse rule of *stop_request* is applied to each of these NACs, obtaining $AC_{p,L}^{C,after}$.

check implication We conclude that $AC_{p,L}^{C,before}$ implicates $AC_{p,L}^{C,after}$ since they are equal. An implication check of application conditions is not supported yet in AGG either.

certification The previous analysis enables us to add a Certificate *Constraint Preserved* to the rule *stop_request* and negative constraint $NC(floors\_no\_same\_req)$. It comes with the application conditions $AC_{p,L}^{C,before}$ and $AC_{p,L}^{C,after}$, both consisting of the same two negative application conditions as depicted in Fig. 2.6.

CHAPTER 4. CERTIFYING RULE-BASED MODELS

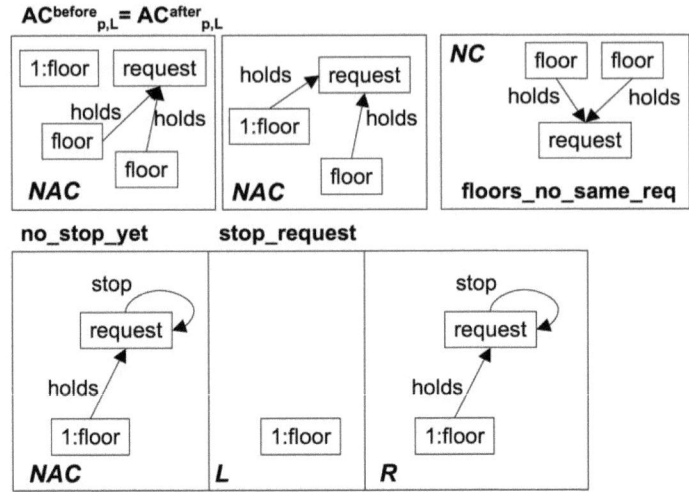

Figure 4.8: AC^{before} equals AC^{after} for *stop_request* and $NC(floors\_no\_same\_req)$

4.3.10 Constraint Guaranteed

starting the road The following question arises when applying a specific set of rules in a rule-based model non-deterministically and as long as possible: If the application terminates, does the terminal state fulfill certain properties? In order to answer this question, one can investigate if a certain constraint C holds after having applied a specific set of rules $\mathcal{P}$ as long as possible and non-deterministically by analyzing the following property:

4.3.47 Property (Constraint Guaranteed)**.** Given a set of rules $\mathcal{P}$ and some constraint C, then C is satisfied by any graph G to which no rule in $\mathcal{P}$ is applicable.

Note that C is a graph constraint as given in Definition 2.2.13. The certification of this property can be generalized to nested graph constraints as presented in [46], but this is not within the scope of this thesis.

apply analysis In Section 2.9 (see Corollary 2.9.5), a constraint is presented that is satisfied by a graph G if and only if rule p is not applicable to G. Note that Corollary 2.9.5 holds only under the condition that the gluing condition is fulfilled for each rule and potential match. Therefore, we can outline the analysis of Property 4.3.47 by the following two steps:

check gluing condition Check if Assumption 2.9.1 is satisfied for all rules in $\mathcal{P}$. If not, then for the time being only vagueness can be diagnosed, but a review of the model is strongly advised in this case. The result of this check is saved into the boolean variable *gluingCondition*, which is true (resp. false) if Assumption 2.9.1 is satisfied (resp. not satisfied). Each set of rules can be reviewed in such a way that they fulfill the gluing condition. This is obtained by simulating node deletion by means

4.3. CERTIFYING A SELECTION OF PROPERTIES

of deleting special edges to a container for this node. More explanations can be found in the reviewing step of the road to certification for Property 4.3.30.

compute non-applicability constraints Compute the constraint, called $C_{applNot}(\mathcal{P})$, consisting of the conjunction of $C_{applNot}(p)$ for each rule p in $\mathcal{P}$. $C_{applNot}(p)$ is introduced in Corollary 2.9.5, and expresses the non-applicability of rule p. Note that $C_{applNot}(p)$ can be computed according to Corollary 2.9.5 only for rules without NACs or rules with a single NAC. It is part of future work to generalize this corollary to rules with more NACs, or even nested application conditions as presented in [46].

check implication Check that $C_{applNot}(\mathcal{P})$ implies the given constraint C. This means that each graph G satisfying $C_{applNot}(\mathcal{P})$, then also satisfies C. Thus, we need to check that $\neg C_{applNot}(\mathcal{P}) \vee C$ holds for each graph G. If this is successful, then Property 4.3.30 holds. In [90], how to check that one constraint implicates another one is described more in detail.

Note that there is a difference between this approach and constraint guarantee as presented in [29, 46]. In these approaches, specific application conditions are added to a rule such that a constraint is guaranteed after rule application. On the other hand, in this approach, rules are not changed by adding application conditions. Only if the above introduced implication is not verifiable, then rules may be changed by adding specific application conditions during reviewing. Another difference is that, in this thesis, it is investigated if a constraint is guaranteed after applying as long as possible a set of rule applications, instead of requiring constraint guarantee after one rule application. Note that [91] shows a refutation procedure for a more general class of graph conditions with attributes. Moreover, in [46], it is shown that the implication and tautology problem for nested graph conditions is undecidable. In [93], it is described how theorem proving can be used to approach this problem. In [92], it is shown that for a suitable subclass of nested graph conditions these problems are decidable.

certification, refutation or vagueness By the above analysis procedure, it is possible to certify Property 4.3.47 if it can be verified that the implication between $C_{applNot}(\mathcal{P})$ and C holds. On the other hand, it may be possible to refute Property 4.3.47. In cases of failure of the above techniques, only vagueness can be determined.

4.3.48 Certificate (Constraint Guaranteed). If it is possible to verify Property 4.3.47 for a set of rules $\mathcal{P}$ and some constraint C, then award $\mathcal{P}$ and C this certificate. This certificate comes with $C_{applNot}(\mathcal{P})$ as introduced in the analysis procedure above.

4.3.49 Refutation (Constraint Guaranteed). If it is possible to verify the negation of Property 4.3.47 for a set of rules $\mathcal{P}$ and constraint C, then add this refutation to $\mathcal{P}$ and C. This refutation comes with $C_{applNot}(\mathcal{P})$ as introduced in the analysis procedure above.

4.3.50 Vagueness (Constraint Guaranteed). If neither Certificate 4.3.48 nor Refutation 4.3.49 can be added to $\mathcal{P}$ and some constraint C, then add vagueness to $\mathcal{P}$ and C. Vagueness comes with the boolean variable *gluingCondition* and $C_{applNot}(\mathcal{P})$ as introduced in the analysis procedure above.

reviewing model If *gluingCondition* equals false, then it is strongly advised to review the rules as explained also for Property 4.3.30. If there is no implication between $C_{applNot}(\mathcal{P})$

CHAPTER 4. CERTIFYING RULE-BASED MODELS

and C, then one could try to review the model such that $C_{applNot}(\mathcal{P})$ becomes stronger. One might review some of the rules in $\mathcal{P}$ by adding (or scaling down) some NAC or enlarging their left-hand side. In this way the probability that the rule is not applicable becomes higher and, therefore, $C_{applNot}(\mathcal{P})$ becomes stronger.

reviewing property In cases of refutation or vagueness without the possibility of reviewing the model, proceed as follows: check if it is possible to weaken constraint C such that it is implicated by $C_{applNot}(\mathcal{P})$ (resp. $C_{applNot}(\mathcal{P})$ and $C_{pres}(\mathcal{P})$). Often, a slightly weaker version of C is still expressive enough to meet the requirements, and therefore, in this case a property review can be appropriate.

4.3.51 Remark (rule-based model with constraints). Note that for the set of rules in $\mathcal{P}$ a constraint, called $C_{pres}(\mathcal{P})$, might be available that is fulfilled in each potential state (or at least each terminal state) of the rule-based model. It could be an imposed constraint, but also the following case can occur. Suppose that the as-long-as-possible rule application of rules in $\mathcal{P}$ starts with a graph G_0 satisfying $C_{pres}(\mathcal{P})$ such that each rule in $\mathcal{P}$ preserves $C_{pres}(\mathcal{P})$. Then, we know that also the resulting graph G still satisfies $C_{pres}(\mathcal{P})$. In such a case, the above-described implication obtains a stronger precondition since also the satisfaction of $C_{pres}(\mathcal{P})$ can be taken into consideration. The implication check then consists of showing that the conjunction of $C_{applNot}(\mathcal{P})$ and $C_{pres}(\mathcal{P})$ implies the given constraint C.

4.3.52 Example (Constraint Guaranteed). Road to Certificate *Constraint Guaranteed* for *Elevator*:

starting the road Suppose that the elevator control is in downward direction and it can no longer apply any process rule in downward direction. This means that no rule belonging to $\mathcal{P}$, consisting of *process_stop_down*, *process_call_down*, and *process_stop_and_call* is applicable anymore. Then, all requests on the elevator floor should have been processed. We can formulate a constraint $NC(req\_on\_el\_floor\_down)$, expressing that no requests are left on the elevator floor to be processed for an elevator in downward direction. We can certify the property *Constraint Guaranteed* for this constraint and set of rules $\mathcal{P}$ as follows.

apply analysis: check gluing condition The rules *process_stop_down*, *process_call_down*, and *process_stop_and_call* fulfill the gluing condition for each potential match, since they delete only request nodes together with the *call* or *stop* loop attached to it, and we can assume injective matching. AGG supports in the following way the checking for a specific set of rules if the gluing condition is always fulfilled. It is possible in AGG to restrict to injective matching by choosing this option in the general option menu. It is not possible yet to check, in general, if a rule will always fulfill the dangling edge condition. More explanations to the satisfaction of the gluing condition for *Elevator* can be found in Example 2.9.2.

compute non-applicability constraints The rules *process_stop_down*, *process_call_down*, and *process_stop_and_call* do not hold NACs. We compute the constraint, called $C_{applNot}(\mathcal{P})$, consisting of the conjunction of $C_{applNot}(p)$ for each rule p in $\mathcal{P}$. According to Corollary 2.9.5 we then obtain the conjunction of the following constraints: $NC(stop\_on\_el\_floor\_down)$, $NC(call\_on\_el\_floor\_down)$,

4.3. CERTIFYING A SELECTION OF PROPERTIES

and $NC(stop\_and\_call\_on\_el\_floor)$. See also Fig. 4.9 in which these constraints are depicted in more detail. Note that none of these computations is supported yet by AGG.

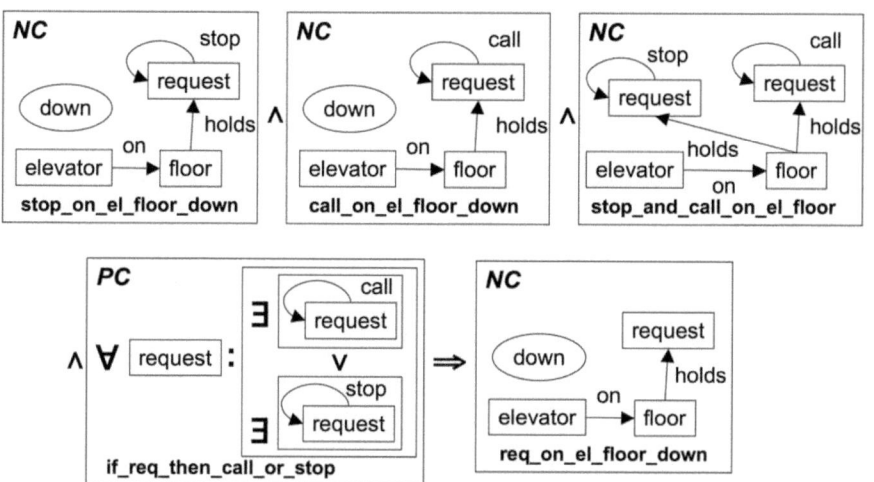

Figure 4.9: Constraint $NC(req\_on\_el\_floor\_down)$ guaranteed

check implication Now we sketch that this conjunction of constraints implicates $NC(req\_on\_el\_floor\_down)$, expressing that no request at all is left on the elevator floor for an elevator in downward direction. In order to show this implication, we see that we still need another constraint $C_{pres}(\mathcal{P}) = PC(if\_req\_then\_call\_or\_stop)$ (see Remark 4.3.51), expressing that each request holds either a stop loop or a call loop, meaning that each request is of type call or type stop. Note that this type of constraint does not correspond to Def. 2.2.13 of constraints in this thesis, but this is a nested constraint as described in [46]. By means of certificate *Constraint Preserved* (see Section 4.3.9) it is possible to attest that this constraint always holds for *Elevator*. Then, it is relatively straightforward to see that the conjunction of $NC(stop\_on\_el\_floor\_down)$, $NC(call\_on\_el\_floor\_down)$, and $NC(stop\_and\_call\_on\_el\_floor)$ together with $PC(if\_req\_then\_call\_or\_stop)$ implicates indeed $NC(req\_on\_el\_floor\_down)$. The reason for this is as follows. Suppose that a request on the elevator floor for an elevator in downward direction exists. Then, this request is either a call request or a stop request, but exactly these kinds of requests are not allowed. This is a contradiction and, therefore, the implication holds. Note that this implication check is not supported yet by AGG either.

certification The previous analysis enables us to add a Certificate *Constraint Guaranteed* to the rules *process_stop_down*, *process_call_down*, and *process_stop_and_call* and negative constraint $NC(req\_on\_el\_floor\_down)$ provided that $C_{pres}(\mathcal{P}) = PC(if\_req\_then\_call\_or\_stop)$ holds in each terminal state G as well (see Remark 4.3.51). It comes with the constraint $C_{applNot}(\mathcal{P}) = PC(if\_req\_then\_call\_or\_stop)$,

211

consisting of the conjunction of $NC(stop\_on\_el\_floor\_down)$, $NC(call\_on\_el\_floor\_down)$, and $NC(stop\_and\_call\_on\_el\_floor)$.

4.4 Application Areas

As pointed out in the introduction of this thesis, rules occurring in a rule-based model can be characterized according to the type of modification they are describing. Roughly speaking, we can distinguish three kinds of modifications: *syntactical, operational,* or *transformational*. In the first case, rules define how to generate – and afterwards edit – the *syntactical structure of a system*. Thereby, these rules are applied to graphs, modeling some state of the system structure. In the second case, rules define the *operational semantics of a system*. Thereby, these rules are applied to graphs, modeling some operational state of the system. In the third case, rules define some *model transformation*. Thereby, these rules are applied to graphs, modeling some state of the model transformation. Such model transformations can have as an objective to structurally improve the model of the system one is modeling. Moreover, model transformations may lead to refined models, describing the system one is modeling in a more detailed way. Model transformations may also lead to adapted models, describing the system one is modeling fulfilling some revised requirements.

In this section, first we give a survey on different application areas of rule-based modeling. Afterwards, we outline which kind of properties, as considered in this thesis, may be interesting to certify for the above-mentioned kinds of rule-based modifications.

4.4.1 Applying Rule-Based Modeling

In this thesis, as an application to rule-based modeling, we modeled the *control of an elevator system*. We developed rules describing the *generation* of the elevator system, and rules describing its *operational semantics* (see Example 2.3.16). For elaborated examples of *model transformation* rules, we refer to, for example, [29], where a simple version of UML statecharts [89] is transformed to Petri nets [103] using graph transformation. Thereby, the syntax of the Statechart visual language was defined by a generating graph grammar first. Roughly speaking, rule-based modeling using graph transformation can be applied to the following application areas: visual modeling and specification, model transformation, modeling concurrency and distribution, and software development – as stated more generally in the introduction of [29]. Moreover, in Chapter 5 of this thesis, we briefly refer to several other examples fitting into these application areas. Note that the theory of graph transformation dates back to the 1970s, and a state-of-the-art report for applications of rule-based modeling using graph transformation developed in the first 30 years is given in [30, 108].

We continue with an overview of several kinds of rule-based models using graph transformation that have been elaborated for different application areas in previous work by different teams including the author. In [99, 98], it is shown how to apply rule-based modeling to *model refactoring*, where the rules, in particular, *transform* finite automata into more well-arranged counterparts by eliminating unreachable states. Moreover, in the following work, the *operational semantics* of different kinds of systems has been modeled using graph transformation. In [13], for example, a *conference scheduling system* is being modeled and analyzed by means of tool support in AGG [115, 114, 1] and EMF TIGER [39]. In [74, 75], it is illustrated how to apply applicability (resp. non-applicability) analysis for verifying safety and liveness properties of a simple *mutual exclusion algorithm* modeled by graph transformation. In [78, 77] (resp. [54, 76]), live sequence charts (LSCs) [48] (resp. UML-activity diagrams [89]) are integrated with graph transformation, leading to controlled rule-based modeling, as explained in more detail in the future-work section in Chapter 5. These integrated models are used to describe and analyze, for example, *adaptable service-based applications* [78, 77]. It is shown, in particular, how to model a *personal mobility manager* [80] using graph transformation. On the other hand in [54, 76], it is shown how requirements analysis can be performed for an *online pizza service*, modeled using graph transformation. A more expressive kind of integrated models is presented in [55, 56] by adding object flow to activity diagrams integrated with graph transformation. This is illustrated, in particular, by the model-driven development of a *service-based web university calendar*. In [102], an *airport control system* (AirCS) that organizes the take-off and landing runways of an airport is modeled and analyzed using reconfigurable place/transition systems. Note that in this example, it is not graphs that are modified by rules, but *place/transition nets*. In particular, in [102], it is demonstrated that the rule-based modification of place/transition systems with NACs fits into the framework of adhesive HLR systems with NACs. Moreover, note that in many of the above-described papers [13, 77, 54, 55], not only typed graphs, as used in Chapter 2, but typed attributed graphs – as presented in [29] – are used for modeling. In Fact 3.2.16 of Chapter 3, it is demonstrated that the category of *typed attributed graphs* is NAC-adhesive HLR, and therefore the theory presented in this thesis applies to the rule-based modification of typed attributed graphs as well.

4.4.2 Certifying Rule-Based Models

In Section 4.3, it is described in detail how to certify several properties for the rules, modeling the *operational semantics* of our running example, *Elevator*. Here, we describe which kind of certifications, as presented in this thesis, may be interesting to investigate with regard to rules, describing not only operational, but also syntactical, or transformational kinds of modifications. Thereby, we illustrate the certification of properties with regard to syntactical and operational kind of rules on our running example, *Elevator*. For the transformational kind of rules, we refer to the following examples: in [29], a model transformation is presented of a simplified version of UML statecharts [89] into Petri nets [103] and in [84, 85], object-oriented refactorings are modeled using graph transformation. Moreover, note that in Chapter 5, we refer briefly to other applications for which analogous properties – or also different ones as presented in this thesis – are verified.

For the *syntactical kind of modifications*, it may be interesting to certify the following properties, as presented in Section 4.3, of the corresponding rules in the rule-based model. By means of the property *Conflicts as Expected*, it can be investigated how generating or editing steps, defined by specific rules, can conflict with each other. Moreover, the property *Causalities as Expected* investigates how generating or editing steps is causally dependent on each other. By means of *Applicability* (resp. *Non-Applicability*) analysis it may be investigated if a specific kind of generating (or editing) rule sequence can (resp. may not) be performed. For many systems, it is important that during generation or editing, specific system properties are preserved. Therefore, it may be interesting to investigate the property *Constraint Preserved* for specific rules, describing this kind of syntactical modifications. Moreover, it may be interesting to investigate if the property *Constraint Guaranteed* is fulfilled after applying as long as possible in a non-deterministic way a set of generating rules.

CHAPTER 4. CERTIFYING RULE-BASED MODELS

Consider, for example, the rules add_floor, rule initial_higher, and rule transitive_higher as presented in Example 2.3.16, generating the structure of our elevator system. We expect that the application of rule add_floor triggers the applicability of rule initial_higher, and this rule in turn triggers the rule transitive_higher since by the addition of a floor the need emerges to complete the transitive closure, expressing which floors are higher than other floors (Causalities as Expected). Moreover, we expect that the rule add_floor is in conflict with itself since it may not be applied twice at the same place. This ensures that no branching structure of floors arises in the model building (Conflicts as Expected). We could also investigate, for example, if the rule transitive_higher truly computes the transitive closure of higher_than edges by certifying the corresponding property Constraint Guaranteed. For each of the generating rules, it would be interesting to check that the multiplicity constraints as given in the type graph in Fig. 2.1 are preserved (Constraint Preserved). This avoids checking these constraints for each rule application. Analogously, the preservation of the negative constraints as presented in Fig. 2.5 could be certified. Finally, note that in Example 2.9.19 applicability analysis is illustrated for rules extending the elevator system by modeling the persons being present in the elevator building.

For the *operational kind of modifications*, it may be interesting to certify the property *Conflicts as Expected* for specific rules, investigating how the operations that they define are conflicting with each other. Moreover, also the property *Causalities as Expected* may be interesting to investigate, expressing which system operations that they define are causally depending on each other. Depending on the operational semantics of the system, one may expect specific rule sets in the corresponding model to be locally confluent, terminating, or deterministic. Therefore, it may be interesting to certify the properties *Local Confluence*, *Termination*, or *Functional Behavior*. In order to ensure safety properties of the operational semantics of a system, it may be interesting to investigate that specific operations always preserve some specific constraints. Therefore, the property *Constraint Preserved* may be certified for the rules, defining these operations. Moreover, in a terminal state of the operational semantics, it may be expected that some specific constraint is guaranteed. Therefore, the property *Constraint Guaranteed* may be certified for the rules, defining this semantics. Finally, for ensuring liveness and safety properties in the operational semantics of the system one is modeling, it may be interesting to certify the properties *Applicability*, resp. *Non-Applicability* for specific rule sequences.

In Section 4.3, it is described in detail how to certify each of these properties for rules, modeling the operational semantics *of our running example,* Elevator *(as introduced in Example 2.3.16).* One could consider certifying analogous properties of this kind as, for example, the following: if the elevator car is in a terminal state – after having applied as long as possible each operating rule except for the request rules – then are there no requests pending in the elevator building (Constraint Guaranteed)? Does each operational rule preserve the multiplicity constraints as given in the type graph in Fig. 2.1 (Constraint Preserved)? Analogously, do they preserve the negative constraints as presented in Fig. 2.5? Considering, all operational rules except for the request rules, do they terminate or even show functional behavior? Note that it would be quite tedious to certify these properties in this thesis with explanatory details, but the same principle can be followed as for the corresponding smaller examples as presented in Section 4.3.

Finally, for the *transformational kind of modifications*, the following properties may be interesting to certify. If the model transformation is defined by a set of rules without any additional control structure, it may be interesting to investigate if their non-deterministic as long as possible application leads to a functional behavior of the corresponding transformation. Therefore, it may be interesting to certify property *Functional Behavior* for the rules defining the transformation. Moreover, it may be expected that the model transformation must preserve (resp. guarantee in some resulting terminal state) a specific constraint. Therefore, it might be interesting to investigate the property *Constraint Preserved* (resp. *Constraint Guaranteed*) for the corresponding rules. Finally, if the model transformation is, for example, performed by distributed teams, it might be interesting to certify properties like *Conflicts as Expected* and *Causalities as Expected* in order to find out how single model transformation steps may exclude each other, resp. depend on each other.

In [84, 85], it is analyzed how expected conflicts and causalities of refactoring steps can drive the application of refactorings possibly performed by different developers. Moreover, by means of analyzing the property *Constraint Preserved*, it could be verified that refactoring steps preserve specific constraints needing to hold at any time in object-oriented models. For the model transformation of UML statecharts [89] into Petri nets [103] as described in [29], it is verified that it shows functional behavior, by showing local confluence and termination for the corresponding rules. Note that in [29], the theoretical foundation for showing local confluence of rules with NACs was not given yet, but is presented in this thesis. Finally, the property *Constraint Guaranteed* could be investigated, for example, with regard to verifying that after transforming some statechart, specific constraints in the resulting Petri net are fulfilled.

Finally, note that it is part of future work to continually extend the catalog of certifiable properties using graph transformation as presented in Section 4.3. For example, as mentioned in the introduction of Corollary 2.9.3 in Section 2.9, deadlock-freeness might be another worthwhile property to certify.

4.5 Tool Support

Tool support relying on static analysis techniques for certain properties is present in only few graph transformation tools (see, for example, [61, 2, 12]). Some other tools support verification on the basis of model-checking techniques (see, for example, [24, 106]). In the following, we concentrate on the static analysis possibilities in AGG [115, 114, 1, 13]. It supports the algebraic approach to graph transformation as presented in this thesis. AGG is a tool environment consisting of a graph transformation engine, analysis tools and a graphical user interface for convenient user interaction. For each certificate presented in the following section, it is explained how AGG can support the automatic verification of the property to be certified. Moreover, it is discussed how tool support can be enhanced or extended in future. For example, AGG is able to perform a significant part of the analysis procedure for many kinds of properties already, but does not yet support the explicit adding of certificates, refutations or vagueness to a (part of the) rule-based model. Also, the possibility of reviewing the model or property under consideration with regard to consistent model evolution (as explained at the end of Section 4.2.1) is still to be developed. Moreover, note that the interchange of models based on graph transformation is supported by common exchange formats [113, 66]. Their use should enable the interchange of analyzed models in AGG with other rule-based tools that may not feature analysis modules or that feature other kinds of analysis modules. As remarked in [66], it is, moreover, important to support as much as possible the translation of different graph

CHAPTER 4. CERTIFYING RULE-BASED MODELS

transformation approaches (for example, described in [17, 52]) into each other, allowing for exchange also between tools using different approaches. Summarizing, the further development of tool support in this regard is indispensable for certification based on static analysis.

Tool Support for Selection of Properties in AGG We give a brief overview of the extent to which AGG is able to support the road to certification by automatic analysis of the selection of properties as introduced in Section 4.2.2, and dealt with in more detail in Section 4.3.

Conflicts As Expected In AGG it is possible to compute the set of potential conflicts occurring between two rules in a minimal context represented by the so-called critical pairs. The comparison of these conflicts with the expected ones is not supported yet.

Causalities As Expected In AGG it is possible to compute the set of potential causalities occurring between two rules in a minimal context represented by the so-called critical sequences. The comparison of these causalities with the expected ones is not supported yet.

Parallelism In order to find out if rules can be applied in parallel under any circumstance, it is sufficient to check that they are causally independent of each other. As mentioned already for the previous property, AGG can compute the set of critical sequences for these rules, and check if it is empty. Therefore, AGG is able to support the automatic verification of this property.

Local Confluence A set of rules is locally confluent if all conflicts in a minimal context via these rules can be resolved in a specific way. AGG can support this check by computing the set of all critical pairs. Currently, AGG does not support the check if each critical pair can be resolved in a suitable way.

Termination AGG has implemented the checking of sufficient criteria leading to termination of a set of rules. Moreover, AGG is also able to compute for each rule if it is conflicting with other rules. Since rules that are not conflicting with any other rule may lead to non-termination, AGG also supports the potential refutation of termination.

Functional Behavior Functional behavior of a set of rules is given if this set is confluent. Confluence means that given two (not necessarily direct) transformations of the same state, it is possible to reach the same state again. A set of rules is confluent if and only if local confluence holds for each pair belonging to this set and, moreover, termination holds. We have already described to which extent AGG delivers tool support for verifying local confluence and termination.

Applicability In AGG , it is possible to check for single rule sequences if they are applicable to a specific start graph. This automatic check relies on sufficient criteria, which in cases of satisfaction, imply applicability. Analogously, in AGG , the checking of a sufficient condition for non-applicability of a rule sequence to a specific start graph is implemented. Therefore, AGG supports also the refutation of applicability.

Non-Applicability As described above, AGG has implemented the checking of a sufficient condition for non-applicability as well as applicability of a rule sequence to a specific start graph. Therefore, AGG supports the certification as well as refutation of this property.

Constraint Preserved In AGG , it is possible to compute for a given constraint and a rule a corresponding right application condition. A sufficient condition for the constraint to be preserved consists of checking if this application condition computed by AGG is implicated by the application conditions, holding before applying the given rule. However AGG does not support to check this implication.

Constraint Guaranteed AGG merely supports the testing if a given constraint holds after having applied a set of rules for as long as possible. The computation of a constraint that definitely holds in a terminal state after applying a specific set of rules could be implemented relatively easily. Checking afterwards that this constraint implies the given constraint is still open.

Chapter 5

Comparing, Concluding, and Continuing

This chapter starts with describing work related to this thesis. Thereby, we compare this work to other approaches verifying rule-based models using graph transformation. In the second section of this chapter, we summarize again the most important topics presented in this thesis and outline the relationship to own work published already. Finally, we conclude this thesis with an outline of future work.

5.1 Related Work

The theory of graph transformation dates back to the 1970s, and a state-of-the-art report for the first 30 years is given in the three handbooks of graph transformation [109, 30, 108]. The main topic presented in this thesis comprises the development of a new theory to support *static analysis techniques for graph transformation*. A significant part of this new theory is concerned with generalizing the theory as presented in [29] to transformations with *negative application conditions* (NACs) [44]. Thereby, theory is developed for algebraic graph transformation in the double-pushout approach [23, 29] as well as the more abstract framework of adhesive high-level replacement (HLR) [37]. This framework allows for applying the corresponding theory to other instantiations, for example, attributed graph transformation [29], or Petri net transformation [102]. The development of adhesive high-level replacement (HLR) categories was inspired by the notion of HLR-systems [36] and the notion of adhesive categories as introduced in [65].

We continue with giving an overview of static as well as dynamic techniques verifying models based on graph transformation. Thereby, please note that we try to address the main different kinds of approaches by selecting and presenting, exemplarily, some representative publications, and that it is not intended to give a complete overview of related work.

An important part of the newly developed theory in this thesis is concerned with *static conflict and dependency detection, and confluence analysis* for transformations with NACs. Theory related to the static analysis of confluence has been developed for the case of hyper graph transformation in [95, 94]. In [65] (resp. [16]), parallel and sequential independence have been described for adhesive rewrite systems (resp. borrowed contexts). In [22], it is described how to characterize conflicts and dependencies for subobject transformation systems. [118] describes how to use matrix graph grammars for conflict and dependency recognition.

CHAPTER 5. COMPARING, CONCLUDING, AND CONTINUING

To the best of our knowledge these analysis approaches do not consider application conditions yet. Note that conflict and dependency detection has been applied successfully, for example, in [83, 84, 49, 63, 21]. In [88], confluence is investigated for domain-independent product line transformations seeming similar to graph transformations. The problem of verifying model transformations performed by graph transformation [26] is related to confluence analysis as well. [38] describes, for example, how to analyze confluence for model transformations based on triple graph rules [111], which are a special kind of rules fitting particularly well for specifying model transformations. However, with regard to analyzing model transformations not only confluence, but also termination – as investigated by means of static analysis, for example, in [33] – is a desired property. The satisfaction of both properties leads to a functional behavior of the corresponding model transformation. Another important research topic is concerned with checking if a model transformation is *semantic-preserving*. In [86], a technique is proposed to check in a static way for a particular input and output model of the transformation if they behave similarly with respect to a specific property. Moreover, a static analysis technique verifying semantic preservation applied to refactoring has been proposed for the borrowed context approach in [99]. Finally, for example, in [35], semantical correctness and completeness of model transformations is investigated.

In this thesis, a notion of *graphical constraints* in the sense of [29] is considered. Note that more general application conditions and constraints are described, for example, in [46, 104]. In Chapter 2, it is shown how to relate rule applicability (resp. non-applicability) to the notion of constraints provided that the gluing condition is always fulfilled. This theory leads to a general technique, as proposed in Chapter 4, verifying that a specific constraint is guaranteed in a terminal state. Moreover, a general technique is proposed in Chapter 4, verifying the preservation of constraints. Both properties and corresponding analysis techniques can be lifted to more general application conditions and constraints [46] relatively straightforwardly, but this is part of future work. The verification of constraint preservation and guarantee is reduced to the problem of constraint implication, investigated extensively in [90, 91, 92, 93]. Further research efforts in this direction should enable a successful certification of the above-described properties. Note that in [12], a specific analysis technique is proposed to check for symbolic invariants in graph transformation systems. This is related to the verification of constraint preservation as presented in this thesis. However, the advantage of the approach in this thesis is that the problem of constraint preservation is reduced to the problem of constraint implication, and this reduction mechanism can be generalized to nested constraints [46] and all kinds of transformation systems fitting into the framework of adhesive HLR systems.

As an alternative to static analysis techniques, it is possible to revert to *dynamic techniques like model checking* [82] for graph transformation as described, for example, in [24, 106, 57]. These techniques have the advantage that it is possible to analyze (see, for example, [40]) more straightforwardly any property which can be expressed in a specific kind of temporal logic. In many cases though, the *state space* of rule-based models using graph transformation becomes very large or even infinite, and then, model-checking techniques have their limitations. Note that static analysis techniques do not have this drawback. Moreover, model-checking techniques require the existence of initial states in order to construct the state space of the graph-transformation-based model. However, their existence is not necessarily required for applying static analysis techniques. Another advantage of using static graph transformation analysis techniques instead of dynamic ones is the following. Whenever it is possible to certify a specific property, in most cases, the corresponding analysis also delivers a clarifying and compact

5.1. RELATED WORK

reason for this certification. For example, in the case of local confluence analysis, possible solutions for conflicting transformations are pointed out in a minimal context. Analogously, the applicability analysis for rule sequences clarifies why some sequence is applicable by highlighting enabling predecessors for each rule in the sequence. Analogously, if the investigated property is refuted because some necessary condition is violated, then in most cases it comes with a clarifying and compact reason for the refutation. For example, consider some rules that are expected to be conflict-free (see Property 4.3.1 (Conflicts as Expected)), and instead after analysis they appear to be conflicting. Then, the refutation comes with the reason for the rules being in conflict, that is, each kind of potential conflict between those rules is shown in a minimal context. Note that checking if a necessary condition is violated using static analysis techniques can be compared with the notion of finding a counterexample in the case of model checking. However, although in the latter case a counterexample is given, in the first case a possibly more clarifying and compact reason (cf. conflicting rules) might be given for the property not to be fulfilled. Thereby, note that if a sufficient and necessary condition is available for the property that can be statically checked, it is possible to output the refutation reason in such a complete way that the corresponding model can be reviewed successfully. For example, in the case of checking for conflict-free rules, the reason for refutation might come with each potential conflict occurring in a minimal context such that the rules can be adapted accordingly.

In this regard, it is interesting to discuss how to *combine the advantages of static and dynamic approaches* into powerful analysis strategies for graph transformation. In particular, static analysis techniques may lead to property-preserving abstractions of rule-based models with infinite state space such that model checking can be applied to the model abstraction successfully. This idea has been described, for example, in [25, 79]. Abstraction techniques have been developed for graph transformation as presented, for example, in [9, 6, 60, 4]. Note that for example, the reductions of rule sequences as presented in Section 2.9 can be interpreted as property-preserving abstractions with regard to the applicability of rule sequences. Accordingly, model-checking techniques, instead of static analysis, could be used to check for applicability of the reduced sequences. It is part of future work to study the interplay of static and dynamic techniques in more detail.

Another approach for the verification of graph transformation is the following one: it is possible to *translate* a graph-transformation-based model *into another modeling language* for which possibly more convenient analysis techniques are available (see, for example, [27]). Note that, for example, Petri nets [103] are a kind of models for which static analysis techniques have been developed successfully in order to verify liveness and safety properties. In [117], for example, it is shown that termination for graph transformation can be analyzed in the Petri net domain. [4] follow a similar approach, translating graph-transformation grammars into so-called Petri graphs on which properties, for example, the absence of deadlocks can be verified. In [3], the unfolding grammar approach is developed for the abstract setting of rewriting over adhesive categories. Finally, another example of this approach is described in [18], translating graph transformation into the domain of term rewriting. Note that static *analysis techniques developed directly for graph transformation* have the following advantage making it worthwhile investigating and improving them further: a translation of the graph-transformation-based model – with potential over-approximation or over-abstraction – is not necessary. An analogous problem has been addressed in [106] for the case of applying model checking, as a dynamic verification technique, either directly to graph-transformation-based models [107, 57] or to a translation of these models, suitable as input for existing model checkers [24].

As mentioned in Chapter 4 [93, 46], automated *theorem proving* can support the verification of properties of rule-based models using graph transformation. It is part of future work to investigate how theorem provers such as, for example, Isabelle/HOL [87] can be applied to support property certification of rule-based models. For example, in [42], it is investigated how theorem proving can support the verification of semantic equivalence between the model specification and the generated code, where the corresponding transformation is described by graph transformation. Theorem provers have the advantage that they support also proof reasoning for models with infinite state space. In particular, the process of finding the road to certification for some new property, or finding property-preserving model abstractions as mentioned above could be supported by interactive theorem proving in the future. In this context, it should be analyzed how to combine the advantage of concise tool support based on approved theorem provers with the user-friendliness of special-purpose analysis tools for graph transformation. [112] proposes some first ideas in this respect.

Summarizing, the use of the certification approach for rule-based models using graph transformation, as presented in this thesis, has the following advantages compared to other verification approaches: a catalog of properties is presented – and can be extended continually – for which tool support can be developed allowing for *automatic certification*. Moreover, usually, each certificate comes with a compact and clarifying *reason* for the successful verification of the corresponding property. In cases of refutation or vagueness – neither sufficient condition fulfilled nor necessary condition violated – automatic proposals can be made enabling the *successful reviewing* of the model with regard to certification. The analysis techniques, presented in this thesis, are applied directly to the graph transformation-based model, allowing for verification *without the necessity to translate* the model into some other specification language. Moreover, since we consider merely static analysis techniques, it is possible to verify rule-based models with very large or *infinite state space*.

5.2 Summary

The main results of this thesis are, on the one hand, of a theoretical and, on the other hand, of a conceptual kind.

Concerning theory, the following new results have been achieved: already existing *graph transformation theory* has been *extended* to the more expressive variant of graph transformation with *negative application conditions* (NACs). Thereby, the main results are the generalization of notions like parallel and sequential independence, local Church-Rosser, conflict and causal dependency, critical pairs and their completeness, local confluence theory based on the critical pair lemma, concurrency, embedding, and extension of graph transformations. New theory has been introduced allowing for applicability (resp. non-applicability) analysis of rule sequences together with some new reduction techniques. A characterization of conflicts and causal dependencies on the transformation as well as the rule level has been introduced, allowing for a more elaborate conflict and causal dependency detection. Moreover, a more efficient kind of conflict and causal dependency detection is proposed based on critical pairs (resp. sequences) satisfying negative constraints (resp. essential critical pairs).

The main part of this new theory has not only been introduced for typed graph transformation systems with NACs, but is formulated also in the categorical framework of *adhesive*

HLR systems. Therefore, it can be instantiated as well for other visual modeling techniques, for example, for Petri net transformation or for graph transformation with attribution. The theoretical part of this thesis paves the ground for the verification of such *rule-based models*.

In the second, more conceptual part of the thesis, it is explained how to apply graph transformation theory with regard to verifying successfully, and thus being able to certify, specific properties for rule-based models. This *road to certification* is based on applying static analysis techniques rooted in graph transformation theory. Thereby, note that these techniques operate independently of the size of the state space, which might become very large or even infinite for rule-based models. Nevertheless, some of the considered properties are undecidable, and therefore, it is proposed to revert to sufficient (resp. necessary) conditions which can be statically checked. They then lead in cases of satisfaction to certification (resp. refutation) of the corresponding property. In some cases, merely vagueness about the property can be determined. If so, it might be sensible to review parts of the model in order to be able to cope with it. The road to certification is developed for a selection of properties that are very significant for rule-based models. This catalog of properties can serve as a consultation document in view of the use (or further extension) of analysis techniques for certifying rule-based models, and to develop (or extend current) corresponding tool support.

Finally, note that several results, in particular in the theoretical part of this thesis, have already been published by different teams including the author in technical reports, conference proceedings, and journals. In the following, we give a *short overview* of how this kind of *"own work"* has been used as a *basis for this thesis*: in [68], an efficient method for the computation of critical pairs is proposed, leading in [71, 70], to a subset of critical pairs – so-called essential critical pairs – being still complete with regard to conflict detection. In this thesis, we were still able to slightly reduce the set of essential critical pairs. Moreover, we added another improved notion of critical pairs using negative constraints, holding in the corresponding rule-based model. In [69], conflict characterization and detection by means of critical pairs for graph transformation with NACs is presented. In this thesis, in addition, we formulated the corresponding theory for the framework of adhesive HLR systems with NACs. Moreover, we described the characterization and detection of causal dependencies, closely related to conflicts, as well.

In [78], the need for applicability analysis of rule sequences emerged. This kind of consistency analysis is addressed with more formal details in different applications [77, 54], based on the formulation of sufficient criteria for applicability in [74, 75]. Moreover, in [77, 54, 76], first reduction mechanisms for rule sequences with regard to applicability (resp. non-applicability) are presented. In this thesis, the applicability (resp. non-applicability) criteria and reductions are presented with more formal details and partly optimized. Moreover, the corresponding theory is lifted to the framework of adhesive HLR systems with NACs. The further improvement of the criteria and reductions is part of future work, and it will be based on the notion of partial rule dependencies as introduced in [55, 56]. Note that in [78, 77], some first proposals are made with regard to reviewing models in cases that inconsistencies are diagnosed. In Chapter 4 of this thesis, this idea is picked up with regard to reviewing in cases of refutation or vagueness.

In [67], adhesive HLR systems with NACs are introduced, and the notions of parallelism and concurrency [72] are described for transformations with NACs. In this thesis, we improved the corresponding Parallelism Theorem with NACs, and added a characterization of parallelism via concurrency. Moreover, we explicitly described the corresponding theory for the instantiation of typed graph transformation with NACs. In [31], parallelism and concurrency are described already for the more general case of rules with nested application conditions. In [99, 98], the concurrency theorem is applied to come up with a method for statically verifying behavior preservation of refactorings. Often, it is not possible to verify that a single refactoring rule is behavior-preserving, but this verification is possible for a concurrent rule, also considering subsequent refactoring steps. Embedding and confluence of graph transformation with NACs is described in [73]. Analogous to other results, this theory is extended to adhesive HLR transformation with NACs. Moreover, in the *Elevator* case study it is illustrated that the critical pairs for locally confluent transformations are not necessarily locally confluent. It is shown in this example how extended critical pairs can support the verification of local confluence anyway. In [102], it is demonstrated that NACs can be added to reconfigurable place/transition systems such that they fit into the framework of adhesive HLR systems. In this thesis, however, we restrict ourselves to describing the instantiation of typed graph transformation with NACs. In [97], it is described how to construct adhesive HLR categories, satisfying some additional properties, from already existing ones. It is part of future work to generalize these results to the set of extra properties fulfilled in NAC-adhesive HLR categories.

Finally, with regard to tool support and applications, the following work can be mentioned: in [66], a new version of GTXL [113], a common exchange format for graph transformation was proposed. In [13], a report of current tool support of the modeling and analysis possibilities in AGG [115, 114, 1] and EMF TIGER [39] is given, which is presented in the case study of modeling a conference scheduling system. Moreover, note that in the already mentioned work, concerned mainly with introducing new theory, systems from different application fields have been modeled and analyzed as well. In [74, 75], it is illustrated how to apply applicability (resp. non-applicability) analysis for verifying safety and liveness properties of a simple mutual exclusion algorithm. In [78, 77] (resp. [54, 76]), live sequence charts (LSCs) [48] (resp. UML-activity diagrams [89]) are integrated with graph transformation, leading to controlled rule-based modeling, as explained in more detail in the future work section. These integrated models are used to describe and analyze, for example, adaptable service-based applications [78, 77]. It is shown, in particular, how to develop a personal mobility manager [80] in an iterative way. On the other hand, in [54, 76], it is shown how requirements analysis can be performed for an online pizza service. A more expressive kind of integrated models is presented in [55, 56] by adding object flow to activity diagrams integrated with graph transformation. This is illustrated, in particular, by the model-driven development of a service-based web university calendar. In [102], an airport control system (AirCS) that organizes the starting and landing runways of an airport is modeled and analyzed using reconfigurable place/transition systems. Finally, in [99, 98], it is shown how to apply rule-based modeling to model refactoring. In particular, it is shown how to eliminate unreachable states from finite automata.

5.3 Future Work

We can consider the following important lines of future work arising from this thesis.

It would be interesting to investigate *which kind of other properties* could be added to the catalog of properties that can be *certified* by means of analysis techniques based on graph transformation theory as presented in this thesis. In this context, it should also be studied which is the most appropriate way to express these properties, as investigated for other approaches already, for example, in [5, 105]. Other than verifying, for example, by means of model-checking techniques, it is not possible to analyze straightforwardly any property that can, for example, be expressed in some specific kind of temporal logic. However, once the road to certification using graph transformation for specific properties is known, it is possible to automatize it with corresponding tool support. Moreover, the road to certification for more complex properties based on properties that are already certifiable can be derived straightforwardly. This is related to *certification bootstrapping*, as mentioned earlier in this thesis, which is a concept to be handled in a more elaborate way in the future as well.

As soon as models evolve over time, the concept of *consistent model evolution* becomes very important. In this thesis, first proposals are made how to ensure and enable it also technically. It is part of future work to develop a more elaborate concept with regard to consistent model evolution. In particular, it should be investigated extensively how to transfer certificates from one model to an adapted one.

As already mentioned in Section 5.1, it is part of future work to *compare more extensively* the approach in this thesis with other verification techniques like model checking and theorem proving. In this regard, it is also part of future work to study the interplay of static and dynamic techniques in more detail. Moreover, it is part of future work to investigate how theorem provers such as, for example, Isabelle/HOL [87] can be applied to support property certification of rule-based models. In this context, it should be analyzed how to combine the advantage of concise tool support based on approved theorem provers with the user-friendliness of special-purpose analysis tools for graph transformation.

Finally, it is not sufficient to generalize graph transformation theory to the more expressive variant of graph transformation with NACs. As the use of graph transformation to model rule-based behavior of systems grows, the need to make this modeling technique *more expressive* becomes more urgent as well. The *generalization of graph transformation theory* to nested constraints [46, 31], for example, is one of the next main steps to tackle. Moreover, the fact that specific constraints might hold at any time in the rule-based model should be regarded in order to make already available analysis techniques (see Remarks 4.3.17, 4.3.45, and 4.3.51) more powerful. However, the development of analysis techniques should not be restricted to extensions like application conditions or constraints. With regard to broadening the scope of applying graph transformation techniques to model-driven software development, concepts like, for example, more elaborate kinds of typing [58, 7, 14] and amalgamation [15] will deserve our further attention.

Another kind of extension is the powerful concept of *controlled graph transformation*. Analysis techniques (see, for example, [45]) should be adapted to this kind of graph transformation, in which rule application is controlled by structures like, for example, sequential and parallel composition, loops, or branching (see, for example, [47, 41, 62, 43]). In addition, it is possible to add more control to the matching process by defining, for example, partial rule dependencies as introduced in [55]. Moreover, in [78, 77, 54], different kind of control mechanisms (live sequence charts (LSCs) [48] or UML-activity diagrams [89]) are integrated with graph transformation rules. These controlled rule-based models are then analyzed for consistency [77, 54]. This kind of work should be continued in order to support the certification of a variety of properties for controlled rule-based modeling as well.

Bibliography

[1] AGG. AGG Homepage. http://tfs.cs.tu-berlin.de/agg.

[2] Karl Azab, Annegret Habel, Karl-Heinz Pennemann, and Christian Zuckschwerdt. ENFORCe: A System for Ensuring Formal Correctness of High-level Programs. In *Proc. 3rd International Workshop on Graph Based Tools (GraBaTs'06)*, volume 1, pages 82–93. Electronic Communications of EASST, 2007.

[3] P. Baldan, A. Corradini, T. Heindel, B. König, and P. Sobocinski. Unfolding Grammars in Adhesive Categories. In *Calco '09*, Lecture Notes in Computer Science. Springer, 2009.

[4] Paolo Baldan, Andrea Corradini, and Barbara König. A Static Analysis Technique for Graph Transformation Systems. In *CONCUR '01: Proceedings of the 12th International Conference on Concurrency Theory*, pages 381–395, London, UK, 2001. Springer-Verlag.

[5] Paolo Baldan, Andrea Corradini, Barbara König, and Alberto Lluch Lafuente. A Temporal Graph Logic for Verification of Graph Transformation Systems. In *Proc. of WADT '06 (Workshop on Algebraic Development Techniques)*, Lecture Notes in Computer Science, pages 1–20. Springer, 2007.

[6] Paolo Baldan, Barbara König, and Arend Rensink. Graph Grammar Verification through Abstraction. In *Abstracts Collection – Graph Transformations and Process Algebras for Modeling Distributed and Mobile Systems*, Dagstuhl Seminar Proceedings 04241, 2005.

[7] R. Bardohl, C. Ermel, and I. Weinhold. AGG and GENGED: Graph Transformation-Based Specification and Analysis Techniques for Visual Languages. In T. Mens, A. Schürr, and G. Taentzer, editors, *Proc. Graph Transformation-Based Tools (GraBaTs'02), Satellite Event of ICGT'02*, Electronic Notes in Theoretical Computer Science, pages 14–24. Elsevier Science, October 2002.

[8] Luciano Baresi and Reiko Heckel. Tutorial Introduction to Graph Transformation: A Software Engineering Perspective. In *ICGT '02: Proceedings of the First International Conference on Graph Transformation*, pages 402–429, London, UK, 2002. Springer-Verlag.

[9] J. Bauer, I. B. Boneva, M. E. Kurban, and A. Rensink. A Modal-Logic Based Graph Abstraction. In H. Ehrig, R. Heckel, G. Rozenberg, and G. Taentzer, editors, *International Conference on Graph Transformations (ICGT), Leicester, UK*, volume 5214 of *Lecture Notes in Computer Science*, pages 321–335, Berlin, 2008. Springer Verlag.

[10] BAUNETZ WISSEN. Aufzüge und Fahrtreppen: Brandfallsteuerung. http://www.baunetzwissen.de/standardartikel/Aufzuege-und-Fahrtreppen_Brandfallsteuerung-im-Landkreis-Muenchen_149170.html. in German.

BIBLIOGRAPHY

[11] BAUNETZ WISSEN. Aufzüge und Fahrtreppen: Einknopf-Sammelsteuerung. http://www.baunetzwissen.de/standardartikel/Aufzuege-und-Fahrtreppen_Einknopf-Sammelsteuerung_149062.html. in German.

[12] Basil Becker, Dirk Beyer, Holger Giese, Florian Klein, and Daniela Schilling. Symbolic Invariant Verification for Systems with Dynamic Structural Adaptation. In *ICSE '06: Proceedings of the 28th international conference on Software engineering*, pages 72–81, New York, NY, USA, 2006. ACM.

[13] E. Biermann, C. Ermel, L. Lambers, U. Prange, and G. Taentzer. Introduction to AGG and EMF Tiger by Modeling a Conference Scheduling System. *Software Tools for Technology Transfer*, 2009. To appear.

[14] E. Biermann, C. Ermel, and G. Taentzer. Precise Semantics of EMF Model Transformations by Graph Transformation. In K. Czarnecki, editor, *Proc. ACM/IEEE 11th International Conference on Model Driven Engineering Languages and Systems (MoDELS'08)*, volume 5301 of *Lecture Notes in Computer Science*, pages 53–67. Springer, 2008.

[15] Paul Boehm, Harald-Reto Fonio, and Annegret Habel. Amalgamation of Graph Transformations with Applications to Synchronization. In *CAAP '85: Proceedings of the International Joint Conference on Theory and Practice of Software Development (TAPSOFT), Volume 1*, pages 267–283, London, UK, 1985. Springer-Verlag.

[16] Filippo Bonchi, Fabio Gadducci, and Tobias Heindel. Parallel and Sequential Independence for Borrowed Contexts. In *ICGT '08: Proceedings of the 4th international conference on Graph Transformations*, pages 226–241, Berlin, Heidelberg, 2008. Springer-Verlag.

[17] I. B. Boneva, F. Hermann, H. Kastenberg, and A. Rensink. Simulating Multigraph Transformations Using Simple Graphs. In *Proceedings of the Sixth International Workshop on Graph Transformation and Visual Modeling Techniques, Braga, Portugal*, volume 6 of *Electronic Communications of the EASST*, page 42. EASST, 2007.

[18] Artur Boronat, Reiko Heckel, and José Meseguer. Rewriting Logic Semantics and Verification of Model Transformations. In *FASE '09: Proceedings of the 12th International Conference on Fundamental Approaches to Software Engineering*, pages 18–33, Berlin, Heidelberg, 2009. Springer-Verlag.

[19] P. Bottoni, A. Schürr, and G. Taentzer. Efficient Parsing of Visual Languages based on Critical Pair Analysis and Contextual Layered Graph Transformation. In *VL '00: Proceedings of the 2000 IEEE International Symposium on Visual Languages (VL'00)*, pages 59–60, Washington, DC, USA, 2000. IEEE Computer Society.

[20] Ronald Brown and George Janelidze. Van Kampen Theorems for Categories of Covering Morphisms in Lextensive Categories. *Journal of Pure and Applied Algebra*, 119:255–263, 1997.

[21] A. Bucchiarone, P. Pelliccione, C. Vattani, and O. Runge. Self-Repairing Systems Modeling and Verification using AGG. In *Joint Working IEEE/IFIP Conference on Software Architecture 2009 & European Conference on Software Architecture (WICSA'09)*, 2009.

[22] A. Corradini, F. Hermann, and P. Sobociński. Subobject Transformation Systems. *Applied Categorical Structures*, 16(3):389–419, 2008.

[23] A. Corradini, U. Montanari, F. Rossi, H. Ehrig, R. Heckel, and M. Löwe. Algebraic Approaches to Graph Transformation I: Basic Concepts and Double Pushout Approach. In G. Rozenberg, editor, *Handbook of Graph Grammars and Computing by Graph Transformation, Volume 1: Foundations*, chapter 3, pages 163–245. World Scientific, 1997.

[24] György Csertán, Gábor Huszerl, István Majzik, Zsigmond Pap, András Pataricza, and Dániel Varró. VIATRA — Visual Automated Transformations for Formal Verification and Validation of UML Models. In *ASE '02: Proceedings of the 17th IEEE international conference on Automated software engineering*, page 267, Washington, DC, USA, 2002. IEEE Computer Society.

[25] D. Dams. *Abstract Interpretation and Partition Refinement for Model Checking*. PhD thesis, Eindhoven University of Technology (Netherlands), 1996.

[26] Juan de Lara and Gabriele Taentzer. Automated Model Transformation and Its Validation Using AToM 3 and AGG. In *Diagrams*, Lecture Notes in Computer Science, pages 182–198. Springer, 2004.

[27] Juan de Lara and Hans Vangheluwe. Translating Model Simulators to Analysis Models. In José Luiz Fiadeiro and Paola Inverardi, editors, *FASE*, volume 4961 of *Lecture Notes in Computer Science*, pages 77–92. Springer, 2008.

[28] H. Ehrig. Introduction to the Algebraic Theory of Graph Grammars (A Survey). In *Graph Grammars and their Application to Computer Science and Biology*, volume 73 of *Lecture Notes in Computer Science*, pages 1–69. Springer, 1979.

[29] H. Ehrig, K. Ehrig, U. Prange, and G. Taentzer. *Fundamentals of Algebraic Graph Transformation*. EATCS Monographs in Theoretical Computer Science. Springer, 2006.

[30] H. Ehrig, G. Engels, H.-J. Kreowski, and G. Rozenberg, editors. *Handbook of Graph Grammars and Computing by Graph Transformation, Vol. 2: Applications, Languages, and Tools*. World Scientific Publishing Co., Inc., River Edge, NJ, USA, 1999.

[31] H. Ehrig, A. Habel, and L. Lambers. Parallelism and Concurrency Theorems for Rules with Nested Application Conditions. In *Festschrift dedicated to Hans-Jörg Kreowski at the Occasion of his 60th Birthday*. EC-EASST, 2010.

[32] H. Ehrig, M. Pfender, and H.J. Schneider. Graph Grammars: an Algebraic Approach. In *Proceedings of FOCS 1973*, pages 167–180. IEEE, 1973.

[33] Hartmut Ehrig, Karsten Ehrig, Juan de Lara, Gabriele Taentzer, Dániel Varró, and Szilvia Varró-Gyapay. Termination Criteria for Model Transformation. In Maura Cerioli, editor, *Fundamental Approaches to Software Engineering: 8th International Conference, FASE 2005*, volume 3442 of *Lecture Notes in Computer Science*, pages 49–63. Springer, 2005.

[34] Hartmut Ehrig, Karsten Ehrig, Annegret Habel, and Karl-Heinz Pennemann. Theory of Constraints and Application Conditions: From Graphs to High-Level Structures. *Fundamenta Informaticae*, 74:135–166, 2006.

BIBLIOGRAPHY

[35] Hartmut Ehrig and Claudia Ermel. Semantical Correctness and Completeness of Model Transformations Using Graph and Rule Transformation. In *ICGT '08: Proceedings of the 4th international conference on Graph Transformations*, pages 194–210, Berlin, Heidelberg, 2008. Springer-Verlag.

[36] Hartmut Ehrig, Annegret Habel, Hans-Jörg Kreowski, and Francesco Parisi-Presicce. From Graph Grammars to High Level Replacement Systems. In *Proceedings of the 4th International Workshop on Graph-Grammars and Their Application to Computer Science*, pages 269–291, London, UK, 1991. Springer-Verlag.

[37] Hartmut Ehrig and Ulrike Prange. Weak Adhesive High-Level Replacement Categories and Systems: A Unifying Framework for Graph and Petri Net Transformations. In *Algebra, Meaning and Computation*, volume 4060/2006 of *Lecture Notes in Computer Science*, pages 235–251, Berlin, Heidelberg, June 2006. Springer.

[38] Hartmut Ehrig and Ulrike Prange. Formal Analysis of Model Transformations Based on Triple Graph Rules with Kernels. In *ICGT '08: Proceedings of the 4th international conference on Graph Transformations*, pages 178–193, Berlin, Heidelberg, 2008. Springer-Verlag.

[39] EMF Tiger. EMF Tiger Homepage. http://tfs.cs.tu-berlin.de/emftrans.

[40] Gregor Engels, Christian Soltenborn, and Heike Wehrheim. Analysis of UML Activities Using Dynamic Meta Modeling. In *FMOODS*, pages 76–90, 2007.

[41] Thorsten Fischer, Jörg Niere, Lars Torunski, and Albert Zündorf. Story Diagrams: A New Graph Rewrite Language Based on the Unified Modeling Language and Java. In *TAGT*, pages 296–309, 1998.

[42] Holger Giese, Sabine Glesner, Johannes Leitner, Wilhelm Schäfer, and Robert Wagner. Towards Verified Model Transformations. In *Proc. of the 3rd International Workshop on Model Development, Validation and Verification (MoDeV2a), Genova, Italy*, pages 78–93. Le Commissariat Ĺ l'Energie Atomique - CEA, 2006.

[43] Martin Große-Rhode, Francesco Parisi-Presicce, and Marta Simeoni. Refinements of Graph Transformation Systems via Rule Expressions. In *TAGT'98: Selected papers from the 6th International Workshop on Theory and Application of Graph Transformations*, pages 368–382, London, UK, 2000. Springer-Verlag.

[44] A. Habel, R. Heckel, and G. Taentzer. Graph Grammars with Negative Application Conditions. *Fundamenta Informaticae*, 26(3-4):287–313, 1996.

[45] A. Habel, K.-H. Pennemann, and A. Rensink. Weakest Preconditions for High-Level Programs. In A. Corradini, H. Ehrig, U. Montanari, L. Ribeiro, and G. Rozenberg, editors, *Graph Transformations (ICGT)*, volume 4178 of *Lecture Notes in Computer Science*, pages 445–460, Berlin, September 2006. Springer Verlag.

[46] Annegret Habel and Karl-Heinz Pennemann. Correctness of High-Level Transformation Systems relative to Nested Conditions. *Mathematical Structures in Computer Science*, 19:1–52, 2009.

BIBLIOGRAPHY

[47] Annegret Habel and Detlef Plump. Computational Completeness of Programming Languages Based on Graph Transformation. In *FoSSaCS '01: Proceedings of the 4th International Conference on Foundations of Software Science and Computation Structures*, pages 230–245, London, UK, 2001. Springer-Verlag.

[48] D. Harel and R. Marelly. *Come, Let's Play - Scenario-Based Programming Using LSCs and the Play-Engine*. Springer, 2003.

[49] J.H. Hausmann, R. Heckel, and G. Taentzer. Detection of Conflicting Functional Requirements in a Use Case-Driven Approach. In *Proc. of Int. Conference on Software Engineering 2002*, pages 105–115, Orlando, USA, 2002. IEEE Computer Society.

[50] Reiko Heckel and Annika Wagner. Ensuring Consistency of Conditional Graph Rewriting - a Constructive Approach. *Electronic Notes in Theoretical Computer Science*, 2, 1995.

[51] Frank Hermann. Permutation Equivalence of DPO Derivations with Negative Application Conditions based on Subobject Transformation Systems. *Electronic Communications of the EASST*, 16, 2009.

[52] Frank Hermann, Harmen Kastenberg, and Tony Modica. Towards Translating Graph Transformation Approaches by Model Transformations. *ECEASST*, 4, 2006.

[53] Gérard Huet. Confluent Reductions: Abstract Properties and Applications to Term Rewriting Systems. *Journal of the ACM*, 27(4):797–821, 1980.

[54] S. Jurack, L. Lambers, K. Mehner, and G. Taentzer. Sufficient Criteria for Consistent Behavior Modeling with Refined Activity Diagrams. In *Proc. 11th Int. Conf. on Model Driven Engineering Languages and System MoDELS08*, volume 5301 of *Lecture Notes in Computer Science*, pages 341–355. Springer, October 2008.

[55] S. Jurack, L. Lambers, K. Mehner, G. Taentzer, and G. Wierse. Object Flow Definition for Refined Activity Diagrams. In M. Chechik and M. Wirsing, editors, *Proc. Fundamental Approaches to Software Engineering (FASE'09)*, volume 5503 of *Lecture Notes in Computer Science*, pages 49 – 63. Springer, 2009.

[56] S. Jurack, L. Lambers, K. Mehner, G. Taentzer, and G. Wierse. Object Flow Definition for Refined Activity Diagrams: Long Version. Technical Report 2009-1, Technische Universität Berlin, 2009.

[57] H. Kastenberg and A. Rensink. Model Checking Dynamic States in GROOVE. In A. Valmari, editor, *Model Checking Software (SPIN), Vienna, Austria*, volume 3925 of *Lecture Notes in Computer Science*, pages 299–305, Berlin, 2006. Springer-Verlag.

[58] A.G. Kleppe and A. Rensink. On a Graph-Based Semantics for UML Class and Object Diagrams. In C. Ermel, J. De Lara, and R. Heckel, editors, *Graph Transformation and Visual Modelling Techniques*, volume 10 of *Electronic Communications of the EASST*. EASST, 2008.

[59] Manuel Koch, L. V. Mancini, and Francesco Parisi-Presicce. Graph-Based Specification of Access Control Policies. *Journal of Computer and System Science*, 71(1):1–33, 2005.

BIBLIOGRAPHY

[60] Barbara König and Vitali Kozioura. Counterexample-guided Abstraction Refinement for the Analysis of Graph Transformation Systems. In *Proc. of TACAS '06*, Lecture Notes in Computer Science, pages 197–211. Springer, 2006.

[61] Barbara König and Vitaly Kozyura. Case Study: Verification of a Leader Election Protocol using Augur, 2009. Solution for the GraBaTs '09 tool contest.

[62] Hans-Jörg Kreowski and Sabine Kuske. Graph Transformation Units with Interleaving Semantics. In *Formal Aspects of Computing*, pages 690–723. Springer-Verlag, 1999.

[63] Jochen Küster, Christian Gerth, and Gregor Engels. Dependent and Conflicting Change Operations of Process Models. In *Proceedings of the 5th European Conference on Model-Driven Architecture Foundations and Applications (ECMDA-FA'09)*, pages 158–173, Berlin/Heidelberg, 2009. Springer.

[64] S. Lack and P. Sobociński. Adhesive Categories. In *Foundations of Software Science and Computation Structures, FoSSaCS '04*, volume 2987 of *Lecture Notes in Computer Science*, pages 273–288. Springer, 2004.

[65] S. Lack and P. Sobociński. Adhesive and Quasiadhesive Categories. *RAIRO - Theoretical Informatics and Applications*, 39(2):522–546, 2005.

[66] L. Lambers. A New Version of GTXL: An Exchange Format for Graph Transformation Systems. In T. Mens, A. Schürr, and G. Taentzer, editors, *Proc. Workshop on Graph-Based Tools (GraBaTs'04), Satellite Event of ICGT'04*, volume 127 of *Electronic Notes in Theoretical Computer Science*, pages 51–63. Elsevier Science, 2004.

[67] L. Lambers. Adhesive High-Level Replacement Systems with Negative Application Conditions. Technical Report 2007-14, Technische Universität Berlin, 2007.

[68] L. Lambers, H. Ehrig, and F. Orejas. Efficient Detection of Conflicts in Graph-Based Model Transformation. In *Proc. International Workshop on Graph and Model Transformation (GraMoT'05)*, volume 152 of *Electronic Notes in Theoretical Computer Science*, pages 97–109. Elsevier Science, September 2005.

[69] L. Lambers, H. Ehrig, and F. Orejas. Conflict Detection for Graph Transformation with Negative Application Conditions. In *Proc. Third International Conference on Graph Transformation (ICGT'06)*, volume 4178 of *Lecture Notes in Computer Science*, pages 61–76. Springer, September 2006.

[70] L. Lambers, H. Ehrig, and F. Orejas. Efficient Conflict Detection in Graph Transformation Systems by Essential Critical Pairs. Technical Report 2006-07, Technische Universität Berlin, 2006.

[71] L. Lambers, H. Ehrig, and F. Orejas. Efficient Conflict Detection in Graph Transformation Systems by Essential Critical Pairs. In *Proc. International Workshop on Graph Transformation and Visual Modeling Techniques (GTVMT'06)*, volume 211 of *Electronic Notes in Theoretical Computer Science*, pages 17–26. Elsevier Science, April 2008.

[72] L. Lambers, H. Ehrig, F. Orejas, and U. Prange. Parallelism and Concurrency in Adhesive High-Level Replacement Systems with Negative Application Conditions. In H. Ehrig, J. Pfalzgraf, and U. Prange, editors, *Proceedings of the ACCAT workshop at ETAPS 2007*, volume 203 / 6 of *Electronic Notes in Theoretical Computer Science*, pages 43–66. Elsevier, 2008.

[73] L. Lambers, H. Ehrig, U. Prange, and F. Orejas. Embedding and Confluence of Graph Transformations with Negative Application Conditions. In H. Ehrig, R. Heckel, G. Rozenberg, and G. Taentzer, editors, *Proc. International Conference on Graph Transformation (ICGT'08)*, volume 5214 of *Lecture Notes in Computer Science*, pages 162–177, Heidelberg, 2008. Springer.

[74] L. Lambers, H. Ehrig, and G. Taentzer. Sufficient Criteria for Applicability and Non-Applicability of Rule Sequences. In J. de Lara C. Ermel and R. Heckel, editors, *Proc. Workshop on Graph Transformation and Visual Modeling Techniques (GT-VMT'08)*, volume 10. Electronic Communications of the EASST, 2008.

[75] L. Lambers, H. Ehrig, and G. Taentzer. Sufficient Criteria for Applicability and Non-Applicability of Rule Sequences. Technical Report 2008-2, Technische Universität Berlin, 2008.

[76] L. Lambers, S. Jurack, K. Mehner, O. Runge, and G. Taentzer. Sufficient Criteria for Consistent Behavior Modeling with Refined Activity Diagrams. Technical Report 2008-11, Technische Universität Berlin, 2008.

[77] L. Lambers, L. Mariani, H. Ehrig, and M. Pezze. A Formal Framework for Developing Adaptable Service-Based Applications. In J.L. Fiadeiro and P. Inverardi, editors, *Proc. Fundamental Approaches to Software Engineering (FASE'08)*, volume 4961 of *Lecture Notes in Computer Science*, pages 392–406. Springer, 2008.

[78] L. Lambers, L. Mariani, M. Pezze, and H. Ehrig. Iterative Model-driven Development of Adaptable Service-Based Applications. In *Proceedings of the twenty-second IEEE/ACM international conference on Automated software engineering ASE 07*, pages 453–456. ACM, 2007.

[79] Claire Loiseaux, Susanne Graf, Joseph Sifakis, Ahmed Bouajjani, and Saddek Bensalem. Property Preserving Abstractions for the Verification of Concurrent Systems. *Formal Methods in System Design*, 6(1):11–44, 1995.

[80] Davide Lorenzoli, Stefano Mussino, Mauro Pezzè, Daniela Schilling, Andrea Sichel, and Davide Tosi. A SOA-based Self-Adaptive Personal Mobility Manager. In *IEEE Conference on Service Computing*, pages 479–486, 2006.

[81] M. Löwe. *Extended Algebraic Graph Transformations*. PhD thesis, TU Berlin, 1990.

[82] Kenneth L. McMillan. *Symbolic Model Checking*. Kluwer Academic Publishers, Norwell, MA, USA, 1993.

[83] K. Mehner, M. Monga, and G. Taentzer. Interaction Analysis in Aspect-Oriented Models. In *Proc. 14th IEEE International Requirements Engineering Conference (RE'06)*, pages 66–75, Minneapolis, Minnesota, USA, September 2006. IEEE Computer Society.

BIBLIOGRAPHY

[84] T. Mens, G. Taentzer, and O. Runge. Detecting Structural Refactoring Conflicts using Critical Pair Analysis. In *Proc. Workshop on Software Evolution through Transformations: Model-based vs. Implementation-level Solutions (SETra'04), Satellite Event of ICGT'04*, volume 127 of *Electronic Notes in Theoretical Computer Science*, pages 113–128, Rome, Italy, 2004. Elsevier Science.

[85] Tom Mens, Gabriele Taentzer, and Olga Runge. Analysing Refactoring Dependencies using Graph Transformation. *Software and Systems Modeling*, 6(3):269–285, 2007.

[86] Anantha Narayanan and Gabor Karsai. Towards Verifying Model Transformations. *Electronic Notes in Theoretical Computer Science*, 211:191–200, 2008.

[87] Tobias Nipkow, Lawrence C. Paulson, and Markus Wenzel. *Isabelle/HOL — A Proof Assistant for Higher-Order Logic*, volume 2283 of *Lecture Notes in Computer Science*. Springer, 2002.

[88] Jon Oldevik, Oystein Haugen, and Birger Moller-Pedersen. Confluence in Domain-Independent Product Line Transformations. In *FASE '09: Proceedings of the 12th International Conference on Fundamental Approaches to Software Engineering*, pages 34–48, Berlin, Heidelberg, 2009. Springer-Verlag.

[89] OMG. UML Resource Page of the Object Management Group. http://www.uml.org/.

[90] F. Orejas, H. Ehrig, and U. Prange. A Logic of Graph Constraints. In J.L. Fiadeiro and P. Inverardi, editors, *Proc. Fundamental Approaches to Software Engineering (FASE'08)*, volume 4961 of *Lecture Notes in Computer Science*, pages 179–198. Springer-Verlag, 2008.

[91] Fernando Orejas. Attributed Graph Constraints. In *Graph Transformations (ICGT'08)*, volume 5214 of *Lecture Notes in Computer Science*, pages 274–288. Springer-Verlag, 2008.

[92] Karl-Heinz Pennemann. An Algorithm for Approximating the Satisfiability Problem of High-level Conditions. In *Proc. Graph Transformation for Verification and Concurrency (GT-VC'07)*, volume 213 of *Electronic Notes in Theoretical Computer Science*, pages 75–94. Elsevier Science Publishers B. V., 2008.

[93] Karl-Heinz Pennemann. Resolution-Like Theorem Proving for High-Level Conditions. In *Graph Transformations (ICGT'08)*, volume 5214 of *Lecture Notes in Computer Science*, pages 289–304. Springer-Verlag, 2008.

[94] D. Plump. Confluence of Graph Transformation Revisited. In A. Middeldorp, V. van Oostrom, F. van Raamsdonk, and R. de Vrijer, editors, *Processes, Terms and Cycles : Steps on the Road to Infinity*, volume 3838 of *Lecture Notes in Computer Science*, pages 280–308. Springer, 2005.

[95] Detlef Plump. Hypergraph Rewriting: Critical Pairs and Undecidability of Confluence. In M.R. Sleep, M.J. Plasmeijer, and M.C. van Eekelen, editors, *Term Graph Rewriting: Theory and Practice*, pages 201–213. John Wiley and Sons Ltd., Chichester, UK, 1993.

[96] Detlef Plump. Termination of Graph Tewriting is Undecidable. *Fundam. Inf.*, 33(2):201–209, 1998.

[97] U. Prange, H. Ehrig, and L. Lambers. Construction and Properties of Adhesive and Weak Adhesive High-Level Replacement Categories. *Applied Categorical Structures*, 16(3):365–388, 2008.

[98] G. Rangel, L. Lambers, B. Koenig, H. Ehrig, and Baldan P. Behavior Preservation in Model Refactoring using DPO Transformations with Borrowed Contexts. Technical Report 2008-12, Technische Universität Berlin, 2008.

[99] G. Rangel, L. Lambers, B. König, H. Ehrig, and P. Baldan. Behavior Preservation in Model Refactoring using DPO Transformations with Borrowed Contexts. In *Proc. International Conference on Graph Transformation (ICGT'08)*, volume 5214 of *Lecture Notes in Computer Science*, pages 242–256, Heidelberg, 2008. Springer.

[100] J. C. Raoult. On Graph Rewriting. *Theoretical Computer Science*, 32:1–24, 1984.

[101] A. Rein. Negative Application Conditions for Reconfigurable Algebraic High-Level Systems. In P. Baldan and B. König, editors, *Proc. Third International Workshop on Petri Nets and Graph Transformations*. Electronic Communications of the EASST, 2008.

[102] A. Rein, U. Prange, L. Lambers, K. Hoffmann, and J. Padberg. Negative Application Conditions for Reconfigurable Place/Transition Systems. In Claudia Ermel, Juan de Lara, and Reiko Heckel, editors, *Proc. Workshop on Graph Transformation and Visual Modeling Techniques (GT-VMT'08)*, volume 10. Electronic Communications of the EASST, 2008.

[103] Wolfgang Reisig. *Petri Nets: An Introduction*, volume 4 of *Monographs in Theoretical Computer Science. An EATCS Series*. Springer, 1985.

[104] A. Rensink. Representing First-Order Logic Using Graphs. In H. Ehrig, G. Engels, F. Parisi-Presicce, and G. Rozenberg, editors, *International Conference on Graph Transformations (ICGT)*, volume 3256 of *Lecture Notes in Computer Science*, pages 319–335, Berlin, 2004. Springer Verlag.

[105] A. Rensink. Model Checking Quantified Computation Tree Logic. In C. Baier and H. Hermanns, editors, *Concurrency Theory (CONCUR), Bonn, Germany*, volume 4137 of *Lecture Notes in Computer Science*, pages 110–125, Berlin, 2006. Springer-Verlag.

[106] A. Rensink, Á. Schmidt, and D. Varró. Model Checking Graph Transformations: A Comparison of Two Approaches. In H. Ehrig, G. Engels, F. Parise-Presicce, and G. Rozenberg, editors, *International Conference on Graph Transformations (ICGT)*, volume 3256 of *Lecture Notes in Computer Science*, pages 226–241, Berlin, 2004. Springer Verlag.

[107] Arend Rensink. The GROOVE Simulator: A Tool for State Space Generation. In John L. Pfaltz, Manfred Nagl, and Boris Böhlen, editors, *AGTIVE*, volume 3062 of *Lecture Notes in Computer Science*, pages 479–485. Springer, 2004.

[108] G. Rozenberg, U. Montanari, H. Ehrig, and H.-J. Kreowski, editors. *Handbook of Graph Grammars and Computing by Graph Transformation, Volume 3: Concurrency, Parallelism, and Distribution*. World Scientific Publishing Co., Inc., River Edge, NJ, USA, 1999.

BIBLIOGRAPHY

[109] Grzegorz Rozenberg, editor. *Handbook of Graph Grammars and Computing by Graph Transformation, Vol. 1: Foundations*. World Scientific Publishing Co., Inc., River Edge, NJ, USA, 1997.

[110] Rutle, Adrian and Rossini, Alessandro and Lamo, Yngve and Wolter, Uwe. A Category-Theoretical Approach to the Formalisation of Version Control in MDE. In *FASE '09: Proceedings of the 12th International Conference on Fundamental Approaches to Software Engineering*, pages 64–78, Berlin, Heidelberg, 2009. Springer-Verlag.

[111] Andy Schürr and Felix Klar. 15 Years of Triple Graph Grammars. In *ICGT '08: Proceedings of the 4th international conference on Graph Transformations*, pages 411–425, Berlin, Heidelberg, 2008. Springer-Verlag.

[112] Martin Strecker. Modeling and Verifying Graph Transformations in Proof Assistants. *Electronic Notes in Theoretical Computer Science*, 203(1):135–148, 2008.

[113] G. Taentzer. Towards Common Exchange Formats for Graphs and Graph Transformation Systems. In *UNIGRA 2001, Uniform Approaches to Graphical Process Specification Techniques (a Satellite Event of ETAPS 2001)*, volume 44 of *Electronic Notes in Theoretical Computer Science*, pages 28–40. Elsevier Science, 2001.

[114] G. Taentzer. AGG: A Graph Transformation Environment for Modeling and Validation of Software. In J. Pfaltz, M. Nagl, and B. Boehlen, editors, *Application of Graph Transformations with Industrial Relevance (AGTIVE'03)*, volume 3062 of *Lecture Notes in Computer Science*, pages 446 – 456. Springer, 2004.

[115] G. Taentzer, C. Ermel, and M. Rudolf. The AGG-Approach: Language and Tool Environment. In H. Ehrig, G. Engels, H.-J. Kreowski, and G. Rozenberg, editors, *Handbook of Graph Grammars and Computing by Graph Transformation, volume 2: Applications, Languages and Tools*, pages 551–603. World Scientific, 1999.

[116] Gabriele Taentzer, Karsten Ehrig, Esther Guerra, Juan de Lara, László Lengyel, Tihamér Levendovszky, Ulrike Prange, Dániel Varró, , and Szilvia Varró-Gyapay. Model Transformation by Graph Transformation: A Comparative Study. In *ACM/IEEE 8th International Conference on Model Driven Engineering Languages and Systems*, Montego Bay, Jamaica, October 2005.

[117] D. Varró, S. Varró-Gyapay, H. Ehrig, U. Prange, and G. Taentzer. Termination Analysis of Model Transformations by Petri Nets . In A. Corradini, H. Ehrig, U. Montanari, L. Ribeiro, and G. Rozenberg, editors, *Proc. Third International Conference on Graph Transformation (ICGT'06)*, volume 4178 of *Lecture Notes in Computer Science*, pages 260–274, Natal, Brazil, September 2006. Springer.

[118] Pedro Pablo Pérez Velasco and Juan de Lara. Using Matrix Graph Grammars for the Analysis of Behavioural Specifications: Sequential and Parallel Independence. In *Proceedings of the Seventh Spanish Conference on Programming and Computer Languages (PROLE 2007)*, volume 206, pages 133–152, Amsterdam, The Netherlands, 2008. Elsevier Science Publishers B. V.

Die VDM Verlagsservicegesellschaft sucht für wissenschaftliche Verlage abgeschlossene und herausragende

Dissertationen, Habilitationen, Diplomarbeiten, Master Theses, Magisterarbeiten usw.

für die kostenlose Publikation als Fachbuch.

Sie verfügen über eine Arbeit, die hohen inhaltlichen und formalen Ansprüchen genügt, und haben Interesse an einer honorarvergüteten Publikation?

Dann senden Sie bitte erste Informationen über sich und Ihre Arbeit per Email an *info@vdm-vsg.de*.

Sie erhalten kurzfristig unser Feedback!

VDM Verlagsservicegesellschaft mbH
Dudweiler Landstr. 99
D - 66123 Saarbrücken

Telefon +49 681 3720 174
Fax +49 681 3720 1749

www.vdm-vsg.de

Die VDM Verlagsservicegesellschaft mbH vertritt

Printed by Books on Demand GmbH, Norderstedt / Germany